Jefferson's Freeholders and the Politics of Ownership in the Old Dominion

Jefferson's Freeholders and the Politics of Ownership in the Old Dominion explores the historical processes by which Virginia was transformed from a British colony into a Southern slave state. It focuses on changing conceptualizations of ownership and emphasizes the persistent influence of the English common law on Virginia's postcolonial political culture. The book explains how the traditional characteristics of land tenure became subverted by the dynamic contractual relations of a commercial economy, and assesses the political consequences of the law reforms that were necessitated by these developments. Nineteenth-century reforms seeking to reconcile the common law with modern commercial practices embraced new democratic expressions about the economic and political power of labor, and thereby encouraged the idea that slavery was an essential element in sustaining republican government in Virginia. By the 1850s, the ownership of human property had replaced the ownership of land as the distinguishing basis for political power, with tragic consequences for the Old Dominion.

Christopher Michael Curtis is Associate Professor of History at Claflin University, where he is Chair of the Department of History and Sociology. He previously held appointments at Iowa State University and at the State University of West Georgia. His work has appeared in the *Journal of Southern History*, the *Virginia Magazine of History and Biography*, and *Legal History*.

"Christopher Curtis's book is a remarkable and welcome hybrid, its research meticulous and exhaustive. Curtis's judgments about the evidence are judicious and balanced. His arguments and conclusions are important and portable, for he demonstrates how the cultural and legal effects of commercial developments remapped Virginians' understanding of the justification of popular political participation, and even of political legitimacy. The concluding chapter on a 'new jurisprudence' is a tour de force. This is a book for many seasons."

– Gerard V. Bradley, Unviersity of Notre Dame Law School

"This book is impressive from various perspectives. Chris Curtis has written an engaging historical treatise on Virginian property relations and law from colonial days to the antebellum era. He adroitly demonstrates how local legal history provides a window into law and legal change regionally, nationally, and internationally in the common law world. Moreover, by tapping political, economic, and social records he has produced a rich narrative of the changing imperatives of political thought and action and economic realities that influenced the development of local law in this slaveholding jurisdiction, and explained its inner contradictions. This book merits a broad readership."

– John McLaren, Emeritus Professor of Law, University of Victoria

Cambridge Studies on the American South

Series Editors

Interdisciplinary in its scope and intent, this series builds on and extends Cambridge University Press's long-standing commitment to studies on the American South. The series not only will offer the best new work on the South's distinctive institutional, social, economic, and cultural history, but also will feature works in national, comparative, and transnational perspectives.

Titles in the Series

Robert E. Bonner, *Southern Slaveholders and the Crisis of American Nationhood*
Peter McCandless, *Slavery, Disease, and Suffering in the Southern Lowcountry*
Christopher Michael Curtis, *Jefferson's Freeholders and the Politics of Ownership in the Old Dominion*

To Gloria,

With love

Ch

Jefferson's Freeholders and the Politics of Ownership in the Old Dominion

CHRISTOPHER MICHAEL CURTIS
Claflin University

CAMBRIDGE
UNIVERSITY PRESS

CAMBRIDGE UNIVERSITY PRESS
Cambridge, New York, Melbourne, Madrid, Cape Town,
Singapore, São Paulo, Delhi, Mexico City

Cambridge University Press
32 Avenue of the Americas, New York, NY 10013-2473, USA

www.cambridge.org
Information on this title: www.cambridge.org/9781107017405

First published 2012

Printed in the United States of America

A catalog record for this publication is available from the British Library.

Library of Congress Cataloging in Publication data
Curtis, Christopher Michael.
Jefferson's freeholders and the politics of ownership in the Old Dominion /
Christopher Michael Curtis.
p. cm. – (Cambridge studies on the American South)
Includes bibliographical references and index.
ISBN 978-1-107-01740-5 (hardback)
1. Virginia – Politics and government – 1775–1865. 2. Slavery – Political aspects – Virginia – History – 19th century. 3. Slaveholders – Political activity – Virginia – History – 19th century. 4. Land tenure – Political aspects – Virginia – History – 19th century. 5. Common law – Virginia – History – 19th century. 6. Virginia – Economic conditions – 19th century. I. Title.
F230.C87 2012
975.5′03–dc23 2011048129

ISBN 978-1-107-01740-5 Hardback

For Betsey, in memoriam

Gratias tibi ago

Contents

Acknowledgments

Sir Thomas More, ever the saint, felt compelled to apologize to his publisher because he delivered his manuscript for *Utopia* after a year's delay instead of in a month and a half as expected. This book has taken a bit longer. And although any apologies undoubtedly would fall on insensitive ears, a few words of gratitude and appreciation remain in order.

Generous fellowships from the Virginia Historical Society, the Earhart Foundation, the Brown Southern Studies Award at Emory University, and Iowa State University enabled me to complete the necessary archival research for this study. My participation in summer workshops hosted by the Institute for Constitutional Studies and the Jack Miller Center have allowed me to articulate and refine my findings in intellectually rich, interdisciplinary forums. The Institute for Southern Studies at the University of South Carolina graciously provided me with library and parking privileges during a sabbatical semester, which allowed me to spend that time with my family. Since coming to Claflin University, Dean Peggy Stevenson Ratliff has been particularly generous in allowing me some time away from the perpetual duties of a department chair to complete this project.

Some of my preliminary conclusions have been published previously as journal articles. An early and abridged version of Chapter 3 appeared in the *Journal of Southern History* (2008) under the title "Reconsidering Suffrage Reform in the 1829–1830 Virginia Constitutional Convention," and parts of Chapters 5 and 6 provided context for my article, "Codification in Virginia: Conway Robinson, John Mercer Patton, and the Politics of Law Reform," in the *Virginia Magazine of History and Biography* (2009). I am grateful to the editors for the opportunity to publish in these journals of long-standing excellence and for their permission to use the material here.

A number of excellent scholars, whom I have the privilege to count as friends, have read and commented on the manuscript in its various incarnations. Andrew Buck, Lou Ferleger, Gene Genovese, and Peggy Hargis all read early drafts and offered excellent critiques. A distinguished group of scholars at Iowa State that included Mike Bailey, Patrick Barr-Melej, Kat Charron,

Sara Gregg, Paul Griffiths, David Hollander, Laura Mielke, John Monroe, and Leonard Sadowsky, collectively known as the BPPG, also read portions of it, usually over wine or beer, and probably helped in some way. David Moltke-Hansen merits special praise, however, for the multiple readings (including one in Norway) and brilliant editorial comments that have helped me think about what needed to be said and honed my focus. The book is dedicated, however, to Elizabeth Fox-Genovese. Words cannot adequately express my gratitude for the opportunity to learn the craft from her. She was enthusiastic about the project from its awkward beginnings, and it is my sincere hope that she would have been proud of its fruits.

Lastly, I need to say thank you to my family. At some point, while I was enmeshed in the splendid intricacies of Virginia property law, my children, Lara, Thomas, and William, all grew up and turned into interesting and capable adults. They remain my greatest blessing. Acknowledgments rarely mention grandchildren, but omission of Michael seems absurd. He did not really help with the book, but he certainly has made me a better person. My parents, William and Susan Curtis, have been a source of constant support and encouragement. And Karen, who thought she knew what her life would be like when she married a young Marine Second Lieutenant, has adapted well to the sea change of being married to a historian – rooms full of books and all. Indeed, she has been through everything with me.

It is customary after recognizing such debts and favors for a writer to take full responsibility for any errors or omissions remaining in text. So I will embrace this custom, although, as the prophet reminds us, this too is vanity.

Abbreviations

AH	*Agricultural History*
EPLP	*Papers of Edmund Pendleton*
GMP	*Papers of George Mason*
GWP	*Papers of George Washington*
JSH	*Journal of Southern History*
LHR	*Law and History Review*
LOV	Library of Virginia
PDVSC	*Proceedings and Debates of the Virginia State Convention of 1829–1830*
RV	*Revolutionary Virginia: A Documentary History*
SAL	Hening, *Statutes-At-Large*
SLM	*Southern Literary Messenger*
TB	*Tucker's Blackstone*
TJP	*Papers of Thomas Jefferson*
UVA	Alderman Library, University of Virginia
VHS	Virginia Historical Society
VMHB	*Virginia Magazine of History and Biography*
WMQ	*William & Mary Quarterly*

Introduction

The Tragedy of Ownership

Addressing an audience of local citizens, James Philemon Holcombe warned that all the harbingers "of a great popular revolution" were in evidence. He explained that "recent events" had conspired to convince even "the most unbelieving amongst us" of the danger to "our constitutional rights" in the Union. His warning undoubtedly resonated with the crowd coming, as it did, a mere month after John Brown had been hung for attempting to spark a slave insurrection at Harper's Ferry. Nevertheless, they may have been surprised to hear this jeremiad being delivered not by some aspiring demagogue but by an aloof, bespectacled law professor who was best known for mastering the obscure principles of equity jurisprudence. Perhaps even more perplexing to the crowd, however, was Holcombe's explanation as to the source of this imminent revolution. He acknowledged the legitimate anxiety caused by Brown's raid but assured his listeners that it had been easily suppressed and that peace had been lawfully restored. More daunting than this abolitionist design to ferment slave rebellion, he insisted, was the foreboding "spectacle" of the free-soil-inspired Republican Party grasping "possession of the Government" with its declared intention of using its power "to promote their interests at the expense of ours."[1]

The interests to which Professor Holcombe referred were the private ownership rights to property – especially the right to own slaves. For him, the upstart Republicans represented a "purely Northern party" committed to undermining the integrity of the relationship between master and slave – the fundamental relationship on which Virginia's social order and democratic government were grounded. He comfortably asserted to the sympathetic crowd that the paternalist virtues found in the master-slave relation sustained the cherished principles

[1] James Philemon Holcombe, *The Election of a Black Republican President an Overt Act of Aggression on the Right of Property in Slaves: The South Urged to Adopt Concerted Action for Future Safety: A Speech before the People of Albemarle on the 2d Day of January, 1860* (Richmond: 1860), 1–3. E. Lee Shepherd, "James Philemon Holcombe" in *Legal Education in Virginia: A Biographical Approach*, edited by W. Hamilton Bryson (Charlottesville: University Press of Virginia, 1982): 291–295.

of "property, liberty, honor, and [even] civilization itself." He believed that Republicans actively sought to destroy these principles in order to replace them with the individualistic dogmas of contract and self-ownership that defined modern commercial society. Accordingly, he urged the crowd to consider separating from the Union unless they received specific constitutional guarantees to protect their private property rights in slaves.[2]

Holcombe's comments hardly surprise those scholars who have studied the movement for Southern Independence. Indeed, they were quite mundane. For the past half-century, most historians have identified the preservation of slavery as the ideological cornerstone of the Southern Confederacy and the principal explanatory cause of the American Civil War.[3] When, a year later, Virginia's statesmen followed Holcombe's advice and seceded from the Union, they did so knowing full well that they were going to war to preserve slavery. Their decision reflected the culmination of a decades-long struggle to defend slavery from the pressures of a commercial *mentalite* that increasingly found all forms of "unfree" labor intolerable. Like Holcombe, they understood that slavery stood at the foundation of their political and social institutions and that the core values of the Republican Party were inherently hostile to their way of life.[4]

Yet Professor Holcombe's commitment to slavery as the foundation of liberty and self-government would have sounded odd – and perhaps even foolish – to an earlier generation of Virginians who also had decided to break the bonds of union in order to preserve their way of life. Unlike Holcombe and his contemporaries, the Virginian forbearers who chose to separate themselves from the British Empire believed that land tenure provided the only solid foundation for liberty and self-government. When given the historical opportunity to define anew both their form of government and their understanding

[2] Holcombe, *Election of a Black Republican President*, 5–6.

[3] See especially, Eugene Genovese, *The Political Economy of Slavery: Studies in the Economy and Society of the Slave South* (New York: Pantheon Press, 1965); Kenneth Stampp, *The Peculiar Institution: Slavery in the Ante-Bellum South* (New York: Vintage Books, 1956); Drew Gilpin Faust, *The Creation of Confederate Nationalism: Ideology and Identity in the Civil War South* (Baton Rouge: Louisiana State University Press, 1988); and William Freehling, *The Road to Disunion: Secessionists at Bay, 1776–1854* (New York: Oxford University Press, 1990). The consequences of this historiographical revolution have been tremendous; the centrality of slavery and the corresponding issues of race have come to serve as the principal explanation for southern distinctiveness within the grand sweep of the American historical narrative – from Jamestown to the Reagan Revolution. Indeed, even those who have disagreed with Genovese's Marxist interpretation of the Old South have tended to side with him on the issue of causation and have contributed to refuting the preceding generation of revisionists who generally attributed the cause of disunion to the inability of politicians to transcend prevalent institutional flaws.

[4] Eric Foner, *Free Soil, Free Labor, Free Men: The Ideology of the Republican Party before the Civil War* (New York: Oxford University Press, 1995); William Gienapp, *The Origins of the Republican Party, 1852–1856* (New York: Oxford University Press, 1988); Robert J. Steinfeld, *The Invention of Free Labor: The Employment Relation in English & American Culture, 1350–1870* (Chapel Hill: University of North Carolina Press, 1991); and Amy Dru Stanley, *From Bondage to Contract: Wage Labor, Marriage, and the Market in the Age of Slave Emancipation* (Cambridge: Cambridge University Press, 1998).

of individual liberty during the American Revolution, Virginians specifically chose the ownership of land as their organizing principle in each instance. In establishing a republican form of government, political privileges and offices were awarded exclusively to those individuals who owned land. Land, not slaves, served as the cornerstone of the republican ideal that informed the creation of the Commonwealth.

It warrants mentioning at the outset that to suggest the primacy of land tenure in the republican ideology of Virginia's revolutionaries does not necessarily infer that these men were opposed to slavery. Much confusion has been caused already by those who have sought to transpose a rigid categorical dichotomy between slavery and freedom on the ambience of eighteenth-century social relations. Virginians of the period never considered the political and ideological privileges conferred on land tenure as antithetical to slavery. On the contrary, the acreage required by law to qualify a piece of land as a freehold often encouraged the acquisition of enslaved laborers in order to make the land productive. Slavery, as a preferred form of labor in the eighteenth century, was an important component of Virginia's republic.

Slavery was not, however, fundamental to the principles of republican government. Virginia's postcolonial lawmakers refused to blur the historical distinction between two separate categories of property in the English common law. The laws of personal property applied to cases dealing with moveable property such as chattels or goods, whereas a different set of laws dealt with issues involving real property in land. These categories were governed by different forms of actions and consequently existed as "distinct systems of jurisprudence" within the common law.[5] Eighteenth-century Virginians were well schooled in this legal distinction and consciously chose the advantages of establishing real property as the basis for political rights and participation. They preferred real property over other forms, such as slaves or money, because the immobility of the land vested its owner with a permanent interest in the tangible community in which it was situated. Furthermore, these legislators never forgot that the law recognized slaves as persons as well as property. This recognition imbued the jurisprudence of slavery with an ambiguity that, in the minds of the Commonwealth's founders, made chattel property an unsuitable base on which to ground a republican polity.[6] Virginians did not initially

[5] John Taylor Lomax, *A Digest of the Laws Respecting Real Property Generally Adopted and in Use in the United States; Embracing more Especially the Law of Real Property in Virginia* (Philadelphia: 1839).

[6] On the complexity of slave law and the persistent efforts of southern courts to balance the considerations of humanity and interest, see: Thomas D. Morris, *Southern Slavery and the Law, 1619–1860* (Chapel Hill: University of North Carolina Press, 1996); Mark Tushnet, *The American Law of Slavery, 1810–1860: Considerations of Humanity and Interest* (Princeton, NJ: Princeton University Press, 1981); Ariela Gross, *Double Character: Slavery and Mastery in the Antebellum Southern Courtroom* (Princeton, NJ: Princeton University Press, 2000); William E. Wiethoff, *A Peculiar Humanism: The Judicial Advocacy of Slavery in the High Courts of the Old South, 1820–1850* (Athens: University of Georgia Press, 1996).

create a slaveholding republic. Only after the proprietary characteristics of land ownership had been eroded, and land itself had adopted the commercial qualities of mobile property, did they specifically emphasize slave ownership as a foundational source of republican government.

This study examines the historical processes by which Virginia was transformed from a British colony into a southern slave state. It approaches the problem from a jurisprudential perspective and emphasizes the persistent hegemony of English common-law concepts and institutions on Virginia's postcolonial political culture. It focuses particularly on the legal construction of ownership and its changing political significance amid debates over economic development, the democratization of law and government, and slavery. Accordingly, the study begins by exploring the foundations of colonial land tenure – the traditional source of franchise – and investigates the revolutionary consequences wrought by imposing a concept of private land ownership on a common-law framework to make land tenure an adequate basis for republican citizenship. It details how the principles of ownership corrupted the customary offices of landed status and generated efforts to reform real property law to reconcile it with the dynamic contractual relations of a capitalist economy. These reforms embraced new democratic expressions of economic and political power, most notably the belief that the ownership of productive labor power should replace the freehold and other archaic forms of property qualifications as the principle source for conferring political right. In the northern states, as in England, this formula fostered the construction of workingmen's democracies.[7] In the South, however, the process was complicated by slavery because the ownership of labor power was not concentrated in the individual laborer. As democracy developed in Virginia, it encouraged the idea that slavery was an essential element in sustaining republican government and thus expanded the power of the slave-owning class. By 1850, the ownership of human property replaced the ownership of land as the distinguishing basis for political power in Virginia.

My findings thus suggest that the political reformation responsible for ushering in a slave-owning democracy in the Old Dominion was intrinsically linked to reforms made to the common law. Indeed, it is a principal argument of this study that it is nigh impossible to comprehend the truly revolutionary significance of republican citizenship without understanding the legal language in which it was articulated. Although it is not necessarily incorrect to generalize by using terms such as "white-male elites," or even "property owners," to describe the powerful in early America, such terms are far from

[7] Sean Wilentz, *Chants Democratic: New York City & the Rise of the American Working Class, 1788–1850* (New York: Oxford University Press, 1984); Ronald P. Formisano, *The Transformation of Political Culture: Massachusetts Parties, 1790s-1840s* (New York: Oxford University Press, 1884); Harry L. Watson, *Liberty and Power: The Politics of Jacksonian America* (New York: Oxford University Press, 1990); and E. P. Thompson, *The Making of the English Working Class* (New York: Vintage Books, 1963).

accurate. Indeed, such generalizations tend to obscure the actual mechanisms of power and, in this particular instance, serve to marginalize the novelty of a regime established by the rule of law. Additionally, because the common law was rooted in local custom, it proved particularly malleable to the varieties of governance in both colonial and postcolonial America. The history of the common law in Virginia is distinct from its history in South Carolina and Massachusetts, for example, and this distinctiveness helps explain the local nature of American political development. Understanding the nuanced complexities of the common law in each of its particular American contexts is thus essential, not only to decipher the language of Anglo-American republicanism, but also to understand the subsequent creative process that conceptualized liberal democratic citizenship.[8]

Admittedly, much has been written already about the political languages that informed the American Revolution. Indeed, linguistic studies have defined a generation of scholarship on the subject. An array of interpretations have demonstrated the significant influence of civic humanist, radical Whig, country ideology, natural rights, evangelical Christian, and liberal discourses on the formation of republican political thought in the intellectual cauldron of the eighteenth century.[9] This study does not presume to repudiate any of these particular contributions. It posits that the eclectic nature of eighteenth-century British politics encouraged a judicious blending of ideas and languages, which have sometimes come to be considered as distinct or even rival discourses. Nevertheless, this study follows a path trodden by other legal scholars who

[8] See John Phillip Reid, *Rule of Law: The Jurisprudence of Liberty in the Seventeenth and Eighteenth Centuries* (DeKalb: Northern Illinois University Press, 2004) on the historical development of the "Rule of Law" as a principle of governance. For a similar but more elaborate statement concerning the preeminence of legal discourse in the postcolonial period, see Christopher L. Tomlins, *Law, Labor, and Ideology in the Early American Republic* (Cambridge: Cambridge University Press, 1993), especially 21–34. Richard R. Beeman, *The Varieties of Political Experience in Eighteenth-Century America* (Philadelphia: University of Pennsylvania Press, 2004) provides an excellent synthesis of the multiple social and political structures in colonial America as well as explaining the ramifications of these original structures on the sporadic and particularistic development of democracy in America.

[9] Bernard Bailyn, *The Ideological Origins of the American Revolution* (Cambridge, MA: Harvard University Press, 1967); Caroline Robbins, *The Eighteenth-Century Commonwealthman* (Cambridge, MA: Harvard University Press, 1959); Louis Hartz, *The Liberal Tradition in America* (New York: Harcourt Brace Jovanovich, 1955); Trevor Colburn, *The Lamp of Experience: Whig History and the Intellectual Origins of the American Revolution* (Indianapolis, IN: Liberty Fund, reprint edition, 1998); J. G. A. Pocock, *The Machiavellian Moment: Florentine Political Thought and the Atlantic Republican Tradition* (Princeton, NJ: Princeton University Press, 1975); Gordon Wood, *The Creation of the American Republic, 1776–1787* (Chapel Hill: University of North Carolina, 1969); Michael P. Zuckert, *The Natural Rights Republic: Studies in the Foundation of the American Political Tradition* (Notre Dame, IN: University of Notre Dame Press, 1996); and Mark Noll, *America's God: From Jonathan Edwards to Abraham Lincoln* (New York: Oxford University Press, 2002) remain essential treatments among a very abundant field of scholarship about the ideas and languages informing the American Revolution.

have noted the prominent influence of common lawyers on the revolutionary experience and who have suggested that their early education as lawyers contributed much to their interpretation of political texts. If natural rights, civic humanism, or any other discourse offered Virginia's revolutionaries a language in which to articulate republican ideas, it did so acting as a second language, and as such was habitually translated into the vulgate of the common law.[10]

As prime example, the political privilege accorded to land tenure in postcolonial Virginia reflected a confluence of political discourses that situated land distribution and access at the fulcrum of government. In republican form, the possession of land was equated with an individual's ability to achieve the economic self-sufficiency required for the exercise of self-government. This agrarian ideal, however, was embodied in the Virginia Commonwealth by the very specific common-law concept of the freehold. Although, as this study indicates, both the legal definition and social construction of the freehold experienced substantial change during the eighteenth and nineteenth centuries, it was understood consistently as a specific form of tenure that signified the status of a freeman. Nominally defined at the time of the American Revolution as an estate for life of twenty-five acres of improved, or one hundred acres of unimproved, land, a freehold estate actually represented much more. Possession of a freehold had long conferred a franchise on an individual, replete with both the rights and responsibilities of political participation. In addition to the well-known freehold qualification for suffrage, freeholders served in various official capacities such as magistrates, sheriffs, and grand jurors. Through the exercise of the traditional duties of these offices, freeholders carried out the essential administration of local governance.[11]

Eighteenth-century Virginians embraced the common-law tradition as their own. They considered themselves as heirs of this tradition and readily imbibed the belief that it served as the historical basis for English liberties.[12] With the

[10] John Phillip Reid, *The Concept of Liberty in the Age of the American Revolution* (Chicago: University of Chicago Press, 1988). Reid has dedicated much of his scholarship to understanding the legal and constitutional contexts of the American Revolution, and his general thesis articulated here is readily explained in his four-volume *Constitutional History of the American Revolution* (Madison: University of Wisconsin Press) and most recently in *The Ancient Constitution and the Origins of Anglo-American Liberty* (DeKalb: Northern Illinois University Press, 2005).

[11] Charles Sydnor, *Gentlemen Freeholders: Political Practices in Washington's Virginia* (Chapel Hill: University of North Carolina Press, 1952), and Rhys Isaacs, *The Transformation of Virginia, 1740–1790* (Chapel Hill: University of North Carolina Press, 1982).

[12] Warren M. Billings, "The Transfer of English law to Virginia, 1606–50," in K. R. Andrews, N. P. Canny, and P. E. H. Hair, eds., *The Westward Enterprise: English activities in Ireland, the Atlantic, and America 1480–1650* (Detroit, MI: Wayne State University Press, 1979), 215–244; A. G. Roeber, *Faithful Magistrates and Republican Lawyers: Creators of Virginia Legal Culture* (Chapel Hill: University of North Carolina Press, 1981); W. Hamilton Bryson, "English Common Law in Virginia," *Journal of Legal History* 6 (1985): 249–256; Frank Dewey, *Thomas Jefferson: Lawyer* (Charlottesville: University Press of Virginia, 1986); and Charles Warren, *A History of the American Bar* (Boston: Little, Brown and Company 1911), 39–48. On the larger

outbreak of the Revolution, they even justified their rebellion as an effort to purify what they perceived to be a corrupted legal inheritance. In the process of constructing a republic, however, they transformed their inherited concept of the freehold. They abolished its traditional association as a feudal tenure, which had long defined freeholders as tenants and subjects and had served as the basis for defining status and rights. In the place of the doctrine of tenure, they vested freeholders with an absolute right of ownership in their lands.

Within the common law, such a theory of ownership was ambiguous at best. Several scholars have noted that, in many instances, the common law proved antagonistic to the idea of absolute ownership – especially in regard to real property. Robert Gordon has examined the paradoxical claims to ownership in the common law as it was understood in the eighteenth-century law and concluded that it actually contained "very few plausible instances of absolute dominion rights" and indeed even included a multiplicity of "property relations that actually seemed to traduce the ideal of absolute individual rights." From another perspective, E. P. Thompson's classic study of customary rights has documented the persistence of such practices as lamas-lands and gleaning in England through the last years of the century offering clear evidence of limitations on private property rights. In British North America, Elizabeth Mensch has detailed how contradictory social and economic tendencies in colonial New York fostered profound incoherence in conceptualizing property rights in any modern sense. In one such instance, William Nelson's notable study of Massachusetts has emphasized the significance of the act of seisin – the public investiture of land rights – in maintaining communal order and authority. Similarly, Holly Brewer's study of entail has demonstrated how the persistence of this practice limited the transferability of land in colonial Virginia and thus created the perception of a land shortage and aristocratic consolidation. These studies challenge a persistent scholarly consensus that suggests that liberal property relations were the de facto norm in the colonial wilderness. Scholars advancing this mainstream interpretation have pointed to the ubiquity of fee simple estates, frequent remission in paying quitrents, and the easy transferability of colonial lands. In so doing, they have tended to confuse the daily autonomy of colonial landholders with the vested security and authority inherent in liberal ownership. As this study argues, a profound insecurity over land tenure propelled colonial Virginians toward independence and facilitated the

process of transmitting the common law into the colonial settlements, see Peter Karsten, *Between Law and Custom: "High" and "Low" Legal Cultures in the Lands of the British Diaspora – The United States, Canada, Australia, and New Zealand, 1600–1900* (Cambridge: Cambridge University Press, 2002); David Konig, "Community Custom and the Common Law: Social Change and the Development of Land Law in Seventeenth-Century Massachusetts," *American Journal of Legal History*, 18 (1974): 137–177; and William E. Nelson, *The Common Law in Colonial America: Volume I, The Chesapeake and New England, 1607–1660* (New York: Oxford University Press, 2008). More recently, Mary Sue Bilder, *The Transatlantic Constitution: Colonial Legal Culture and the Empire* (Cambridge, MA: Harvard University Press, 2004) has portrayed the reciprocal nature of the transatlantic legal culture.

truly revolutionary revisions to land law in the new republic. Much more scholarship is needed on the subject of colonial property rights, but the picture increasingly looks far more complicated and, arguably, less liberal than has been typically assumed.[13]

That said, professions of absolute ownership rapidly gained currency in the commercially oriented world of the eighteenth-century British Empire. The redefinition of the freehold in Virginia reflected this trend and represented an effort to impose a liberal theory of land ownership on the framework of the common law. Virginians referred to this form of ownership as allodial[14] and associated it with the customary practices of the mythic Saxon constitution. They reified this allodial vision of the freehold by sanctifying it as the sole source of political rights and responsibilities in the Commonwealth. Grounding republican citizenship in the allodial freehold expressed a belief that the absolute ownership of a tangible piece of property would reconcile the indulgent characteristics of economic individualism with a vested social attachment to a particular local community and, accordingly, foster civic virtue through self-interest. In this manner, Virginians believed that they could preserve their republic from the historic pitfalls of corruption.

This agrarian republican vision has most often been ascribed to the political thought of Thomas Jefferson. In a well-known passage from his *Notes on the State of Virginia*, Jefferson articulated a preference for a republican polity composed entirely of citizen-farmers – whom he famously proclaimed the "chosen people of God."[15] Lewis Simpson has referred to this particular passage as

[13] Robert W. Gordon, "Paradoxical Property," in John Brewer and Susan Staves, eds., *Early Modern Conceptions of Property* (London and New York: Routledge, 1995): 95–110; E. P. Thompson, *Customs in Common: Studies in Traditional Popular Culture* (New York: The New Press, 1993); Elizabeth V. Mensch, "The Colonial Origins of Liberal Property Rights," *Buffalo Law Review*, 31 (1982): 635–735; William E. Nelson, *Americanization of the Common Law: The Impact of Legal Change on Massachusetts Society, 1760–1830* (Cambridge, MA: Harvard University Press, 1975), esp. 48–49; Holly Brewer, "Entailing Aristocracy in Colonial Virginia: 'Ancient Feudal Restraints' and Revolutionary Reform," *WMQ*, 3rd series (1997): 307–346; and James W. Ely, Jr., ed. *Property Rights in the Colonial Era and Early Republic* (New York: Garland Publishing, 1997). *cf.* Lawrence M. Friedman, *A History of American Law*, Second Edition (New York: Simon & Schuster, 1985), 58–65, and Kermit L. Hall, *The Magic Mirror: Law in American History* (New York: Oxford University Press, 1989), 42–45 for summary statements of the historiographical consensus. Stuart Banner, *American Property: A History of How, Why, and What We Own* (Cambridge, MA: Harvard University Press, 2011) was published as this manuscript was in the final days of completion, and its arguments, which perpetuate the consensus about colonial rights but emphasize the transformative consequences of the American Revolution, have not been fully incorporated into the discussion here.

[14] For the sake of consistency, I have chosen to use the eighteenth-century spelling of "allodial" throughout the text. Medieval historians tend to spell the word "alodial," reflecting its derivation from the term "alod," signifying a particular form of allotment. See Susan Reynolds, *Fiefs and Vassals: The Medieval Evidence Reinterpreted* (New York: Oxford University Press, 1994) for a thorough explanation of the concept.

[15] Thomas Jefferson, *Notes on the State of Virginia*, edited by William Peden (Chapel Hill: University of North Carolina Press, 1954), 164–165.

"the supreme text of the American pastoral" and it stands as the touchstone for Jefferson's political thought.[16] His comments remain particularly significant because they have become the standard evidence of a Jeffersonian agrarian vision that has exerted tremendous influence over American history and its historiography. In popular manifestations, Jefferson's yeoman farmers have been invoked by Americans of various political persuasions as the model of individual freedom and, by extension, have served as a foundational ideal for America's liberal democracy. For historians, the agrarian vision has served equally as an effective interpretative concept to explain America's persistent commitment to a liberal-individualist ethic, while simultaneously, by setting the ideal against the reality, it has been used to offer a devastating criticism of that very same ethic. To paraphrase Richard Hofstadter: For a nation that was born in the country but moved to the city, the Jeffersonian vision has provided both an ideological repository for the memories of a world that has been lost, as well as an inspirational fountainhead for professions of a democratic future.

Yet despite substantial commentary on Jefferson's agrarian political vision, previous scholars have considered it almost exclusively from a national perspective.[17] Traditionally, Jeffersonian agrarianism has been contrasted with and measured against Hamilton's commercial platform for national development. From this nationalist lens, the Louisiana Purchase represents the consummate effort to implement this agrarian philosophy and spread the seeds of democracy across an empire of liberty. Tellingly in this respect, Charles Beard began his classic study on the origins of Jeffersonian democracy by examining the debates over the Federal Constitution. And Beard was hardly alone among his contemporaries; Edward Channing's study of "the Jeffersonian system" confined itself to the period of Jefferson's presidency. Even Douglass Adair's notable refutation of Beard's interpretation grounded the roots of a national agrarian program in the collaboration between Jefferson and Madison in 1792 leading to the formation of the republican political party. More recent scholarship has offered a relatively broader perspective, but the bias of national history persists. Contemporary scholars of Jefferson's agrarianism have asked such question as "what is still American" in his political thought, and their studies include such revealing subtitles as: "the American Sphinx" and "the Language of American Nationhood."[18]

[16] Lewis P. Simpson, *The Dispossessed Garden: Pastoral and History in Southern Literature* (Baton Rouge: Louisiana State University Press, 1983), 24–33. For classic elaborations on this theme, see Henry Nash Smith, *Virgin Land: The American West as Symbol and Myth* (Cambridge, MA: Harvard University Press, 1950), and William R. Taylor, *Cavalier & Yankee: The Old South and the American National Character* (Cambridge, MA: Harvard University Press, 1979).

[17] David M. Potter, "The Historian's Use of Nationalism and Vice Versa" in David M. Potter, ed., *The South and the Sectional Conflict* (Baton Rouge: Louisiana State University Press, 1968) discussed the propensity to write national histories and the limitations it has imposed on our historical understanding.

[18] Charles Beard, *The Economic Origins of Jeffersonian Democracy* (New York: The Free Press, 1915), and Edward Channing, *The Jeffersonian System, 1801–1811* (New York: Harper, 1906).

The preponderance of Jefferson's agrarian writings, however, concerned the creation of Virginia's republic, not an American empire of liberty. He explicated the core tenets of his republican vision while drafting a proposed constitution for Virginia and again during the process of revising the colonial laws for the new Commonwealth. Jefferson's political vision was, foremost, a vision for Virginia. There, his ideal of allodial land ownership was formed in the specific context of the problems of colonial land grants and the settlement of the western lands. There, he advocated his agrarian republican ideas, not against an alternative commercial republicanism, but in opposition to a more orthodox, Christian-inspired vision of republicanism. There, his ideals initially triumphed and were legislated into practice. And there, he first recognized the limits of his freeholders' republic and sought to replace it instead with a ward system of local governance styled after the New England Township.

It is, however, deeply misleading even to speak of a Jeffersonian vision. Writings trumpeting the benefits of an agrarian-based citizenry had a long history and often were attributed to the classical political philosophy of Aristotle. This classical doctrine experienced an ideological resurgence in the face of the proliferating influence of merchant capital in early modern Europe, and it was adopted and transposed onto the English constitutional struggles by a number of political writers during the seventeenth century. J. C. A. Pocock, within his considerable body of scholarship, has devoted significant attention to the resurgence of these classical ideas and their corresponding influence on the development of modern republican political thought. Pocock situated the writings of James Harrington as pivotal in incorporating the language of civic humanism into the discourses on English republicanism during the seventeenth century, and at the core of the "country ideology" employed in opposition to the patronage power of the court during the eighteenth century. John Murrin and Lance Banning, among others, have traced the transmission, limitations, and adaption of these ideas to the soil of eighteenth-century North America. Banning, however, despite the general excellence of his study, has contributed significantly to fostering the reductive perception that agrarian ideology was simply a "Jeffersonian persuasion."[19]

Even Douglass Adair's strong refutation of Beard concentrated on identifying the roots of the national agrarian program in the Constitutional debates. Adair's unpublished 1943 manuscript has since been published as *The Intellectual Origins of Jeffersonian Democracy: Republicanism, the Class Struggle, and the Virtuous Farmer*, edited by Mark E. Yellin (Lanham, MD: Lexington Books, 2000). Recent work by Peter S. Onuf, *Jefferson's Empire: The Language of American Nationhood* (Charlottesville: University Press of Virginia, 2000) and Roger G. Kennedy, *Mr. Jefferson's Lost Cause: Land, Farmers, Slavery, and the Louisiana Purchase* (New York: Oxford University Press, 2003) continue to emphasize the national implications of Jefferson's agrarian policies. Both of these authors recognize, however, the significant influence that the problem in settling the Western Lands –especially Kentucky – had on Jefferson's subsequent political theories.

[19] Pocock, *Machiavellian Moment* and his edited volume of James Harrington, *The Commonwealth of Oceana and a System of Politics* (Cambridge: Cambridge University Press, 1992) are the writings directed most particularly at examining Harrington's influence. John

Furthermore, the agrarian ideal was espoused as a commonplace by many of Jefferson's contemporaries as well. Although some scholars have attributed the popularity of the pastoral theme to the "land rich environment" of North America, the agrarian theme flourished in the political thought of eighteenth-century Europe and its colonial diaspora. Perhaps most recognizably in this respect stood the doctrine of Physiocracy developed by French *Economistes* Francois Quesnay and the marquis de Mirabeau. Quesnay and Mirabeau, writing during the waning phase of the *ancien regime*, founded the first modern school of economics on the consideration that land represented the source of all national wealth. They advocated for the private ownership of land, a free market in grain, and government by legal despotism. More immediately, issues of land use – access to it and control over it – defined both sides of the pitched debates in Great Britain over Parliamentary Enclosure. Those advocating enclosure, especially, sought to increase agricultural productivity by encouraging individual responsibility over real property. Meanwhile, half a world away, land tenure was proposed as the key element in effecting colonial control by both William Hastings and his political adversary, Philip Francis, whose agrarian ideas subsequently informed the legislation enacting the Permanent Settlement in Bengal. Quesnay, Jefferson, Francis, Hastings, Arthur Young, and Thomas Spence were all drawing water from the same well. And with good reason; answering the land question was considered a necessary precondition to reconcile the social order with the new forces of merchant capitalism. Indeed, Eric Hobsbawm, in his comprehensive survey of the *Age of Revolution*, identified the question of agrarian social relations as the fundamental problem characterizing the late-eighteenth-century Occidental world.[20]

M. Murrin, "The Great Inversion, or Court versus Country: A Comparison of the Revolution Settlements in England (1688–1721) and America (1776–1816)," in J. C. A. Pocock, ed., *Three British Revolutions: 1641, 1688, 1776* (Princeton, NJ: Princeton University Press, 1980), 368–455. Lance Banning, *The Jeffersonian Persuasion: Evolution of a Party Ideology* (Ithaca, NY: Cornell University Press, 1978).

20 See Chester E. Eisinger, "The Freehold Concept in Eighteenth-Century American Letters," *WMQ*, 3rd series, 4 (1947), 42–59 for the association of the pastoral with the "land rich environment" of the American colonies. The seminal statement is, of course, Frederick Jackson Turner, "The Significance of the Frontier in American History," a paper read at the meeting of the American Historical Association in 1893. Comparative contemporary agrarian expressions can be found in Elizabeth Fox-Genovese, *The Origins of Physiocracy: Economic Revolution and Social Order in Eighteenth-Century France* (Ithaca, NY: Cornell University Press, 1976); Ranajit Guha, *A Rule of Property for Bengal: An Essay on the Idea of Permanent Settlement* (Durham, NC: Duke University Press, 1996); J. M. Neeson, *Commoners: Common Right, Enclosure and Social Change in England, 1700–1820* (Cambridge: Cambridge University Press, 1993); and Phillip Girard, "Land Law, Liberalism, and the Agrarian Ideal: British North America, 1750–1920," in John McLaren, A. R. Buck, and Nancy Wright, eds., *Despotic Dominion: Property Rights in British Settler Societies* (Vancouver: UBC Press, 2005): 120–143. Historian Eric Hobsbawm has supported this viewpoint as well by asserting that the question of "agrarian property relations" posed the most pressing social problem for the West at the end of the eighteenth century. See Hobsbawm, *Age of Revolution* (New York: Vintage Books, 1962), 13. A more recent analysis that provides a provocative synthesis on the relation between

Such ubiquity suggests that Jefferson's republican vision needs to be considered in the context of the much larger reconciliation between landed property and the capitalist agricultural enterprise. Certainly, the preponderance of these agrarian expressions reflected a reactionary response to the encroachment of capitalist social norms on traditional communal relations. As Lewis Simpson has noted, agrarian expressions were perpetually infused with nostalgia whenever and wherever they appeared.[21] Such was the case in postcolonial Virginia where Jefferson offered his agrarian vision as an effort to restore integrity to the inherited rights of British subjects from the corruption he attributed to the growing power of merchant capitalists within the Empire. In this sense, by employing Joanna Innes's very useful linguistic analysis of contemporary British social discourse, Jefferson's agrarian program can be contemplated as an effort at renovation, not one of innovation or even reform. He and his fellow Virginia Whigs essentially understood their revolution against the British Crown as a conservative one.[22]

Still, eighteenth-century agrarian expressions were more than just a mere longing for the world that had been lost. Rather, they represented an effort to renovate the relevance of landed status in an emerging commercial world. In this respect, the agrarian vision proved to be more Janus-faced than simply backward-looking. Abolishing the vestiges of feudal law and creating absolute property rights in land stood at the core of this renovation project. Absolute land rights were created in different guises; Jefferson, like the French Physiocrats, called for its private ownership, whereas in Great Britain, those who advocated enclosure balked at embracing private land ownership but still sought to establish individual responsibility and authority for the productive use of land. Jefferson's success in constructing and imposing a regime of private land ownership in Virginia thus represents a notable episode in the modern development of allodial property relations.

A full assessment of just how significant an episode it was remains outside the immediate boundaries of this study. The path tracing the history of allodial land ownership in America is particularly uneven, and, in some cases, elusive. Maryland and North Carolina both followed Virginia (and, by accident,

property rights and the development of global food production in settler societies is found in John C. Weaver, *The Great Land Rush and the Making of the Modern World, 1650–1900* (Montreal: McGill-Queen's University Press, 2003).

21 Simpson, *The Dispossessed Garden*, 1–33. An interesting comparison revealing similar tendencies can be found in Jennie Purnell's study of the Mexican Revolution, *Popular Movements and State Formation in Revolutionary Mexico: The Agraristas and Cristeros in Michoacan* (Durham, NC: Duke University Press, 1999).

22 Joanna Innes, "'Reform' in English Public Life: The Fortunes of a Word," in Arthur Burns and Joanna Innes, eds., *Rethinking the Age of Reform: Britain, 1780–1850* (Cambridge: Cambridge University Press, 2003), 71–97. Innes identifies the pre-Christian, classical origins of the word *renovatio*, signifying "the renewal of something that had been lost or become corrupted." It had a positive connotation in contrast to the term *innovation*, which ultimately, following the French Revolution, came be juxtaposed with the word "reformation."

Kentucky) in adopting allodial land ownership in the wake of independence. New York passed a statute in 1787 stipulating that all lands granted from the state would be allodial, but considerable confusion surrounded the law, particularly relative to reservations for rights and duties arising from for grants made before the statute. It certainly did not upset the feudalistic claims of the manorial estates along the Hudson and Mohawk Rivers (at least not immediately). New Jersey passed a similar statute in 1795. In Missouri, following the Louisiana Purchase, legislators and judges embarked on a decades-long project to bring all real property rights under the paradigm of private ownership, but they rejected allodial ownership in favor of more traditional common-law categories, despite the fact that allodial property was a recognized concept in the civil law that had governed the land as a French and Spanish colony. Law reformers in New York returned to the issue, in 1829, to clarify the initial ambiguity and specifically incorporated a provision into the new state code explicitly abolishing all feudal tenures and their incidences in a manner similar to Virginia's original statute. Yet, New York's statute was passed in very different circumstances and resulted in far different consequences, most notably the fostering of anti-rent protests and class violence. Nevertheless, despite this popular resistance and democratic reforms, including the incorporation of allodial property into the 1846 state constitution, the New York Court of Appeals, in 1859, upheld the authority of Van Rensselaer descendants to collect traditional rents from their manorial tenants. Georgia waited until after it seceded from the Union in 1861 to declare its lands allodial, while, two years later, in 1863, the Pennsylvania Supreme Court was still openly discerning the question of whether or not land was privately owned or was held as tenure.[23]

This study aims to unravel some of the myths surrounding the history of private ownership by providing an extended account of its creation and subsequent mutation in postcolonial Virginia. Although the agrarian ideal had widespread appeal during the eighteenth century, the creation of both the allodial freehold and the Virginia Commonwealth represented a specific response to the problems of British imperial policy. How colonial Virginians initially perceived these problems, particularly regarding the status of their land tenures, and the correspondent imperial responses, facilitated the development of a

[23] William R. Vance, "The Quest for Tenure in the United States," *The Yale Law Journal* (1924): 248–271; Marshall Dees Harris, *Origins of the Land Tenure System in the United States* (Ames: Iowa State University Press, 1953). In some instances, the question was adjudicated in the courts in the absence of clear legislation; see Matthews v. Ward, 10 Gill & J (Maryland) 443; Mills v. McAllister (North Carolina) 1796; and Wallace v. Harmstad, 44 Penn. 492 (1863). On the legal issues of ownership in Missouri, see Stuart Banner, *Legal Systems in Conflict: Property and Sovereignty in Missouri, 1750–1860* (Norman: University of Oklahoma Press, 2000). For New York, see Charles W. McCurdy, *The Anti-Rent Era in New York Law and Politics, 1839–1865* (Chapel Hill: University of North Carolina Press, 2001) and Reeve Huston, *Land and Freedom: Rural Society, Popular Protest, and Party Politics in Antebellum New York* (New York: Oxford University Press, 2000).

commitment to allodial land ownership. Thomas Jefferson figured prominently in this process, but he did not act alone. He was, however, principally responsible for carrying the allodial revolution forward and, of equal importance, for ensuring that land remained a distinct form of property – one distinguished by its political attributes.

In the end, however, Virginia's agrarian republican ideal proved elusive. The freehold as the repository of both virtue and self-interest proved unsuitable once applied to the actual conditions of the Commonwealth. Allodial ownership, which was intended to unify and balance the political and economic characteristics of land ownership, proved unable to restrain individual owners from the lure of the marketplace, where chance and avarice were prized. Indeed, the very allodial nature of land, with its inherent right to dispose and enjoy as one saw fit, encouraged the commercial practices of land transfer, speculation, and absentee ownership. This consideration that land was primarily a commodity provided the seedbed for the undoing of the agrarian ideal. Far from attaching an individual to a particular community, absentee land owning and speculation fostered a transient interest in the land and perpetuated the existence of a tenant class. Rent-paying tenants, who possessed and used the land but were not freeholders, were alienated from political participation despite the fact that they too cultivated Jefferson's "germ of virtue." External factors, such as the disruption of Atlantic trade caused by the Napoleonic wars, forced Virginians to reconsider many of the assumptions that underlay their ideal of an agrarian political economy as well. To be sure, this reconsideration did not result in a complete abandonment of either the agrarianism or the commitment to free trade, but by 1816, even Jefferson acknowledged that "we must now place the manufacturer by the side of the agriculturalist."[24]

In response, Virginia's legal and political leaders embarked on a persistent attempt at reform in order to reconcile the Commonwealth's republican vision with an increasingly hegemonic conception of land as a mere form of capital. The proper role of property in a modern self-governing polity figured at the perpetual center of these debates and raised corresponding questions about the changing social values of property ownership and what privileges should thus be accorded its various forms. Similar to the contemporary process in other states, modern democratic ideals of rights vested in personhood in lieu of status gained political currency. Political reform came to be seen under the guise of democratic reform. Of equal importance were the corresponding legal reforms that sought to conform common-law precedents and categories to the emerging dynamic of capitalist social relations. Virginia's lawyers

[24] Jefferson to Benjamin Austin, January 9, 1816, in Merrill D. Peterson, ed., *The Portable Thomas Jefferson* (New York: Penguin Books, 1975): 547–550. For commentary on some of the material factors working against agrarian republicanism, see Allan Kulikoff, *The Agrarian Origins of American Capitalism* (Charlottesville: University Press of Virginia, 1992), and Drew McCoy, *The Elusive Republic: Political Economy in Jeffersonian America* (Chapel Hill: University of North Carolina Press, 1980).

engaged in a contemporary dialogue of legal reform that characterized similar efforts wherever the common law had taken root across the British Empire.[25] In Virginia, however, this process of legal reform was colored distinctively by the presence of slavery. The experience there thus departed significantly from law reforms in Great Britain, Australia, Canada, and even New York.

The Virginia debates of the 1830s stand as a watershed in this reformation process. During these pivotal constitutional and legislative debates, Virginians rejected the original political value assigned to land ownership and created an alternative republican vision premised on the idealized principle of stewardship incumbent in the ownership of slaves. Similar to the democratic trajectory in other states, the productive power of labor was afforded a privileged position in defining citizenship at the expense of landed status. Of course, the master-slave relation was by no means equivalent to the wage labor-contract relation emerging rapidly in the northern states, and so the democratic reformation took a divergent turn in the different regions of the Union. The embrace of democracy exacerbated sectional differences and focused tensions on the issue of labor relations.

In Virginia, the recognized failure of allodial land ownership infected discussions surrounding the appropriate legal basis for slavery. Slave ownership, like land ownership, was grounded in an allodial conception of property. By the middle decades of the nineteenth century, Virginians recognized that the pressures of the marketplace, particularly the potential reduction of slaves to the cash nexus through hiring practices and the domestic slave trade, threatened their new vision of a modern slaveholding republic as well. Accordingly, although they embraced legal reforms designed to facilitate a commercial conception of property ownership in all other areas, they increasingly isolated their property in slaves and afforded them specific legal protections to preserve the social relation between master and slave as the foundation for republican self-government. A second state constitutional convention in 1850–1851 constructed a bureaucratic framework for an administrative state government that was designed to foster the individualistic tendencies of commercial property and democratic politics and, simultaneously, to restrain those tendencies in the defense of slavery as needed. By the 1850s, Virginia's legal culture largely had embraced the core elements of a proslavery argument that positioned slavery, not land, as the cornerstone of the southern political vision. Indeed, conservatives such as George Fitzhugh went so far as to reject the

[25] Charles M. Cook, *The American Codification Movement: A Study of Antebellum Legal Reform* (Westport, CT: Greenwood Press, 1981); Gregory Alexander, *Commodity and Propriety: Competing Visions of Property in American Legal Thought, 1776–1970* (Chicago: University of Chicago Press, 1997); Perry Miller, *The Life of the Mind in America from the Revolution to the Civil War* (New York: Harcourt, Brace & World, 1965), 99–265; and Michael Lobban, "'Old Wine in New Bottles': The Concept and Practice of Law Reform c. 1780–1830," in Arthur Burns and Joanna Innes, eds., *Rethinking the Age of Reform: Britain, 1780–1850* (Cambridge: Cambridge University Press, 2003): 114–135.

idea of private ownership outright and called for the reinstitutionalization of archaic common-law forms of real property law. The fate of law reform in Virginia was thus a tragic one. The choices made as a consequence of the failure of allodial ownership had profound repercussions for subsequent political decisions over the questions of slavery, property rights, and, ultimately, for the fate of the American Union.

PART I

RENOVATIO

What has been, that will be; what has been done, will be done. Nothing is new under the sun. Even the thing of which we say, "See, this new!" has already existed in the ages that preceded us.

Ecclesiastes 1: 9–10

1

Taking Notice of an Error

Writing on the eve of revolution, a rather precocious Virginia lawyer made what seemed to be an unusual suggestion to his fellow insurgents. He proposed that an opportune moment had arrived to "take notice of an error" in the colony's land laws. This error, he explained, had corrupted colonial jurisprudence from its earliest decades and concerned the wrongful application of the English common-law doctrine of tenures to landholdings in Virginia. Significantly, this particular doctrine rejected the notion that any one person could individually own a piece of land. Rather, it maintained that landholding was defined by a complex system of legal arrangements between those who granted lands and those who received them in exchange for undertaking specific obligations and services. Under this system, every landholder was a tenant. Although each tenant possessed their own individual relation to the land – an estate – with its distinct rights and privileges, these rights were not exclusive. Other tenants too, of both superior and inferior status, might possess their own rights to the same parcel of land. This idea that people of different status shared interests in a common piece of land was reflected most clearly in the popular understanding that all British lands were held ultimately by the king.

Since time immemorial, this system of tenures had served as the foundational principle of English land law. Yet the brash, young lawyer rejected this common sense and insisted that this feudal doctrine had been introduced illegitimately by the Norman Conquest. Prior to that time, he maintained, feudal tenures were few, if not "altogether unknown" to the common law. He contended instead that "our Saxon ancestors held their lands" in the same manner as they held their personal property – "in absolute dominion," not bound to any superior lords or demands of service. In so doing, he suggested that private land ownership represented the true custom of the British people and the original basis of the English common law.[1]

[1] Thomas Jefferson, "Draft of Instructions to the Virginia Delegates in the Continental Congress," in *The Papers of Thomas Jefferson, Volume 1: 1760–1776*, edited by Julian P. Boyd (Princeton, NJ: Princeton University Press, 1950), 121–137, and Appendix 1: 670–676 (Hereafter cited as

The lawyer was Thomas Jefferson. And he crafted this provocative argument during the volatile summer of 1774 as a means of edifying his fellow colonial legislators. Despite recently being prorogued by the governor, these insurgent lawmakers were determined to convene anyway to choose delegates to send to the First Continental Congress. Jefferson had intended to participate in this rump assembly too, but a bout of dysentery prevented him from making the four-day, one-hundred-mile trip from his home in Monticello to the colonial capital in Williamsburg. Instead, he took pen in hand and composed an essay designed to inform a protest resolution being drafted by the assembly and addressed to the king. Jefferson's narrative on land tenures served as part of his larger examination of colonial rights within the British Empire. In it, he denied the legislative authority of Parliament over the colonies and questioned the legitimacy of the king's dominion over colonial lands. Upon receiving these provocative instructions, this intrepid group of legislators, who were audacious enough to assemble illegally at the Raleigh Tavern, found Jefferson's arguments far too radical to discuss, let alone endorse. A few sympathetic associates, however, decided to publish his essay and it appeared later that summer in both London and North America as a pamphlet entitled *A Summary View of the Rights of British America*.[2]

Despite the initial dubious response that Jefferson's argument about land tenure received among his peers, the course of the American Revolution brought his historical interpretation of English land law to prominence as a matter of fact. A mere five years later, the Virginia legislature rejected the colonial orthodoxy that considered all land rights as emanating from the reciprocity of tenure. In enacting a series of laws designed to organize and administer land in the newly created Commonwealth, they explicitly decreed that "the proprietors of lands" would no longer be subject "to any servile, feudal, or precarious tenure." Furthermore, they declared the traditional prerogatives of the sovereign "null and void" and stipulated that, henceforth, all lands already granted or appropriated in the future would be considered the absolute, unconditional property of the individual owner. They referred to this form of private ownership as

TJP). Thomas Jefferson, *Summary View of Rights in British North America* reprinted in *The Portable Thomas Jefferson*, edited by Merrill Peterson (New York: Penguin Books, 1975), 3–21. On Jefferson's use of history for political ends see H. Trevor Colburn, "Thomas Jefferson's Use of the Past" *WMQ*, 3rd ser., 15 (1958), 56–70.

[2] Anthony M. Lewis, "Jefferson's *Summary View* as a Chart of Political Union," *WMQ* 3d ser., 5 (1948): 34–51; Dumas Malone, *Jefferson and His Time, Volume One: Jefferson the Virginian* (Boston: Little, Brown and Company, 1948), 180–191; Gilbert Chinard, *Thomas Jefferson: The Apostle of Americanism* (Boston: Little, Brown, and Company, 1929), 47–49; Noble E. Cunningham, *In Pursuit of Reason: The Life of Thomas Jefferson* (Baton Rouge: Louisiana State University Press, 1987), 23–35; Merrill Peterson, *Thomas Jefferson and the New Nation* (New York: Oxford University Press, 1970); Peter Onuf, *Jefferson's Empire: The Language of American Nationhood* (Charlottesville: University Press of Virginia, 2000), 61–62; David N. Mayer, *The Constitutional Thought of Thomas Jefferson* (Charlottesville: University Press of Virginia, 1994); and Garrett Ward Sheldon, *The Political Philosophy of Thomas Jefferson* (Baltimore: Johns Hopkins University Press, 1991), 19–39.

allodial property, which they understood as a contradictory system of property rights to the doctrine of feudal tenures. Freeholders were no longer characterized as tenants and subjects. Instead, through their ownership of the land, they were perceived to embody the vital characteristics of economic independence and communal attachment required of virtuous republican citizens.[3]

For all intents and purposes, it appeared as if the English common law – the historical basis for the rights and privileges of British freemen – was being rapidly dismantled by the revolutionary process. Certainly, the logic of republican revolution against the British Crown supported this opinion as well. Yet, closer scrutiny reveals that far from trying to discard the common law, Virginia's lawmakers generally believed that they were trying to preserve it. The abolition of feudal tenures reflected a desire to purify what they perceived to be a corrupted legal inheritance. This desire manifested itself most clearly in their effort to replicate the ancient Saxon laws of possession – specifically embodied in the custom of gavelkind – as the historical basis for a republican land law in the new Commonwealth. Jefferson's tirade against the Norman Conquest, particularly his emphasis on the dialectical tensions between feudal and allodial elements of the common law thus became an ideological touchstone for constructing a republican form of citizenship. It served as the principal historical source used to reconcile a theory of private land ownership with the common-law tradition and, by extension, offered a historical justification for establishing allodial property rights as the foundation of Virginia's republic.[4]

"AMERICA WAS NOT CONQUERED BY WILLIAM THE NORMAN"

Jefferson's indictment of William the Conqueror as the source of tyrannical corruption was by no means original. The familiar concept of the Norman Yoke was a controversial but persistent historical trope used to debate the origins of England's ancient constitution during the political crises of the seventeenth century. Christopher Hill, in his extended essay surveying the trope, outlined its main themes and identified at least four different manifestations of the narrative that developed during the English Revolution, each corresponding to the competing political agendas of parliamentarians, monarchists, Levellers, and Diggers. Although significant distinctions were made between these interpretations, reflecting the various political aims of the respective narrators, two fundamental elements of the trope were present in almost all of its manifestations.

[3] William Waller Hening, *The Statutes at Large; Being a Collection of all the Laws of Virginia, 1619–1792* (Richmond: 1823), 10: 50–65, esp. 64 (hereafter, *SAL*). On the origins of allodial property, see Susan Reynolds, *Fiefs and Vassals: The Medieval Evidence Reinterpreted* (Oxford: Oxford University Press, 1994).

[4] Gregory Alexander, *Commodity and Propriety: Competing Visions of Property in American Legal Thought, 1776–1970* (Chicago: University of Chicago Press, 1997), 51–55. Alexander has noted that this dialectic between feudal and allodial forms of property provided a central theme in the political and legal discourses of the Revolution and thus proved instrumental in enabling American revolutionaries to define and characterize their Revolution.

First, the story was grounded on the belief that prior to the Norman Conquest, "the Anglo-Saxon inhabitants" of England had "lived as free and equal citizens" and had governed themselves through "representative institutions." The Conquest represented the enthronement of an alien king, along with his noble landlords, who deprived the Saxons of their natural liberty and their historical forms of law and government. Second, and of equal importance, was the corresponding belief that the Saxons had never forgotten that these ancient rights had been usurped. Indeed, they had "fought continuously to recover them," across the centuries with varying degrees of failure and success. Under the auspices of the Norman Yoke theory, then, English history became a tale of a perpetual popular struggle against the encroachments of an illegitimate and tyrannical monarchy in order to restore the constitutional rights of a primitive golden age.[5]

Hill attributed the literary origins of this Saxon mythology to a thirteenth-century antimonarchical treatise, *The Mirror of Justice*, but he credited the development of the Norman Yoke narrative to a select group of lawyers affiliated with the parliamentary opposition in the crises leading up to the English Civil War. Edward Coke, John Selden, Henry Spelman, and even the poet John Milton all invoked the Norman Yoke to legitimate parliamentary resistance against the absolutist tendencies of the Stuart Monarchy. During the Interregnum, however, more radical variants of the trope became popular among Levellers, who used it to justify their calls for law reform on the basis of natural rights, and Diggers, who sought to impose social equality through agrarian redistribution. Accordingly, variations on the theme were employed frequently at cross-purposes even among those united in opposition against the monarchy. As Hill astutely pointed out, however, the true significance of the Norman Yoke theory lay in its ability to provide a historical (or mythological) counter-authority for opposition discourses to evaluate and critique the actions of the government. He suggested that these interpretative conflicts diminished and, eventually, were settled along with the constitutional conflicts by the Glorious Revolution. Thereafter, he maintained, the trope entered a period of dormancy as political rhetoric until it emerged again as a component of the workers' reform movements of the late eighteenth century.[6]

Throughout the eighteenth century, however, the myth of the Norman Yoke remained a mainstay of English constitutional thought and appeared

[5] Christopher Hill, "The Norman Yoke" in *Puritanism and Revolution: Studies in Interpretation of the English Revolution of the 17th Century* (New York: Schocken Books, 1958), 57, 50–122; See J. G. A. Pocock, *The Ancient Constitution and the Feudal Law: A Study of English Historical Thought in the Seventeenth Century: A Reissue with a Retrospect* (Cambridge: Cambridge University Press, 1987), and Alan Cromartie, "The Constitutionalist Revolution: The Transformation of Political Culture in Early Stuart England," in *Past and Present* 163, 76–120 as well. The transmission of these ideas in American is comprehensively discussed in Trevor Colburn, *The Lamp of Experience: Whig History and the Intellectual Origins of the American Revolution* (Indianapolis, IN: Liberty Fund, reprint edition, 1998).

[6] Hill, "The Norman Yoke," 81–82.

frequently in the histories written during the period. In this literature, two rival interpretations of the Conquest persisted: a Whig version and a Tory version. Whig writers continued to champion the legacy of popular resistance stretching back to Magna Charta and considered the Glorious Revolution as a millennial episode marking the restoration of all ancient liberties. The Tory narrative, on the other hand, advanced the belief that the Saxons ultimately had consented to the circumstances of the Conquest. Tory writers suggested that, as had been the case in France, allodial lands in England had been surrendered to the king and subsequently regranted as feuds. Unlike the interpretations advanced during the seventeenth century, however, both Whig and Tory versions appeared more as a means to praise the mixed and balanced features of the English constitution rather than to offer a basis for criticism.[7]

Thomas Jefferson embraced this partisan categorization of eighteenth-century historical interpretations. Writing late in life, he praised John Cartwright's book on the English constitution for presenting the Whig interpretation. Jefferson maintained that the fundamental "difference between the Whig and the Tory of England" could be derived by determining their opinion of the Norman Conquest. He believed that Whigs deduced their "rights from the Anglo-Saxon source," whereas the Tories identified theirs "from the Norman." Cartwright's work was praised because he had correctly identified the Saxon roots of the constitution. David Hume's six-volume history of England, on the other hand, was dismissed repeatedly by Jefferson because it reflected a Tory orientation.[8]

Jefferson's fascination with the Saxon constitution spanned his public life. He had imbibed the Whig perspective as a young law student under the tutelage of George Wythe, and most notably from his assigned readings of Edward Coke's *Institutes of the Laws of England*. In the months preceding the publication of *A Summary View*, however, Jefferson embarked on an earnest personal study on the origins of English feudalism that significantly informed his understanding of land law and shaped the development of his agrarian political philosophy. He recorded the key components of this study in his legal commonplace book. These records reveal the progress of Jefferson's learning on the subject and demonstrate that, by the summer of 1774, his understanding of allodial property had been informed chiefly from the historical treatises of John Dalrymple, Henry Spelman, and William Somner. Many of these accounts had been summarized in William Blackstone's four-volume *Commentaries on the Laws of England*, a work with which Jefferson was also familiar, but his detailed study afforded him a more sophisticated view of the issue than had been presented by Blackstone.[9]

7 For example, see John Cairns, "Blackstone, The Ancient Constitution and the Feudal Law," *The Historical Journal* 28 (1985): 711–717.

8 Thomas Jefferson to Major John Cartwright, June 5, 1824, in Peterson, *Portable Jefferson*, 578.

9 Gilbert Chinard, ed., *The Commonplace Book of Thomas Jefferson: A Repertory of his Ideas on Government* (Baltimore: Johns Hopkins University Press, 1926.) I have followed Chinard's approximation of the chronology of Jefferson's entries.

The fruits of this study became evident in the *Summary View*. In it, Jefferson echoed the traditional tenets of the Norman Yoke pertaining to monarchical usurpation and popular resistance, but he went beyond these orthodox criticisms and offered some nuanced variations on the theme as well. He asserted that following William's victory at the Battle of Hastings, much of the land in England actually remained "in the hands of his Saxon subjects," who continued to resist Norman rule. Because these Saxon lands had never been "surrendered to the king," Jefferson posited that they were not "derived from his grant" and thus "not subject to feudal conditions." He admitted that, eventually, "Norman lawyers" managed to saddle the entire English landholding system with feudal burdens and advanced the proposition that "all lands in England were held...of the crown." Although this claim pertained only to those lands that had been conquered, he contended that it had been indiscriminately applied to other forms of holdings simply "for the purposes of illustration." Consequently, all lands in England came to be considered feudal tenures. According to Jefferson's reading of history, however, English land law actually consisted of multiple forms of both landholding and land ownership – with Norman feudal tenures existing as mere exceptions to the customary Saxon laws of possession.[10]

He acknowledged the controversial nature of his interpretation. He contended, however, that in many respects, its veracity was irrelevant to the issue at hand. Beyond the historical question of the origin of English feudalism, he asserted that feudal tenures could not exist in Virginia because America had never been "conquered by William the Norman." Following a line of reasoning previously laid down by fellow colonial lawyer Richard Bland, Jefferson suggested instead that "America was conquered, and her settlements made...at the expense of individuals." These individuals had expended their own blood and their own fortunes to acquire lands for their own settlement, not for the sovereign or "the British public." He thus challenged the idea that the colony's land grants had martial origins, which were the recognized foundation of the feudal tenures. Rather, he explained, the original settlers had fought and conquered "for themselves" and "for themselves alone they have the right to hold." He admitted that in Virginia, as in England, the Norman fiction claiming that "all lands originally belong[ed] to the King" had infiltrated the landscape. Still, he excused the early settlers for their lapse in vigilance because they "were farmers, [and] not lawyers." Now, however, on the eve of revolution, he proposed that it was a suitable time "to lay this matter before his majesty, and to declare that he [had] no right to grant lands for himself."[11]

[10] *TJP*, 1: 132–133. James R. Stoner, "Sound Whigs or Honeyed Tories: Jefferson and the Common Law Tradition," in *Reason and Republicanism: Thomas Jefferson's Legacy of Liberty*, edited by Gary L. McDowell and Sharon L Noble (Lanham, MD: Rowman and Littlefield, 1997): 103–117.

[11] *TJP*, 1: 133, 122. Jefferson changed "Farmers" to "laborers" in the final draft. See Boyd's note 35, page 137; and Appendix I, 669–676. For a previous exposition of this argument, see Colonel Richard Bland, *An Inquiry into the Rights of the British Colonies* (Williamsburg: Alexander Purdie, 1766) republished in *Revolutionary Virginia: The Road to Independence*, Volume I,

Jefferson's challenge to the sovereign's authority to grant lands represented something much more than a mere rhetorical swipe at the king. It was a manifesto for republican revolution couched in conservative terms. It summarily dismissed the centuries-old orthodoxy of tenures, which had served as the bulwark of English land law, and replaced it with a new historical narrative that repudiated all feudal elements of the law as products of usurpation. His references to the ancient Saxon practices sought to legitimize individual land ownership within the common law. Furthermore, by situating the constitutional authority of allodial property in the time before memory, he attempted to reconcile the common law with the liberal theory of a natural right to property. Significantly in this regard, in tandem with his study of English feudalism, Jefferson had immersed himself in the *Historical Law Tracts* of the Scottish natural-rights philosopher, Lord Kames. Kames's writings exemplified the backward-looking gaze of Enlightenment thought, which esteemed the practices of antiquity because they preceded the corruption ascribed to medieval churchmen and nobles. Jefferson fully embraced this idealized perspective and considered the ancient Saxon practices as more closely reflecting the conceptual state of nature, which served as the creation myth for liberal theory. Allodial property was preferred because it fostered natural equality.[12]

Jefferson's desire to abolish tenures thus implied making a revolutionary conceptual change to the basis of legal rights as well. Traditionally, tenure determined the relative status between litigants and served to define the expected rights and duties of the parties. In the absence of tenure, litigants would be compelled to articulate their legal standing through a new language of rights grounded in nature, not in status. Increasingly, Jefferson came to understand natural rights as a more conducive formula for facilitating republican equality. Although many of his contemporaries believed that the common law, grounded in the customs of the people, reflected a coherent expression of the law of nature, he himself balked at the idea. He did not think such coherence had been realized as yet because the common law had been corrupted by the inequalities of feudal law. Only by correcting the grave error of land tenure would the common law achieve its pure state as a law of natural freedom. Significantly then,

compiled by William J. Van Schreeven, edited by Robert L. Scribner (Charlottesville: University Press of Virginia, 1973), 27–44 (hereafter *RV*); K. R. Constantine Gutzman, "Jefferson's Draft Declaration of Independence, Richard Bland, and the Revolutionary Legacy: Giving Credit Where Credit is Due," *The Journal of the Historical Society* I: 2–3 (2000), 137–154. For a similar discussion of the centrality of the question of conquest in colonial land tenures, see James Muldoon, "Discovery, Grant, Charter, Conquest, or Purchase: John Adams on the Legal Basis for English Possession of North America," in *The Many Legalities of Early America*, edited by Christopher Tomlins and Bruce Mann (Chapel Hill: University of North Carolina Press, 2001), 25–46.

12 Chinard, *Commonplace Book*. Chinard discusses Jefferson's persistent spelling of Lord Kames as "Kaims." In so doing, Jefferson followed the usage of Dalrymple. On the backward-looking tendency of Enlightenment thought, see Peter Gay, *The Enlightenment: The Rise of Modern Paganism* (New York: W. W. Norton, 1966) and Henry F. May, *The Enlightenment in America* (New York: Oxford University Press, 1976).

Jefferson's critique of feudal tenures served as a catalyst for the development of the natural-rights philosophy for which he is best identified. His proposal to abolish tenures inferred an egalitarian legal order and embraced the core tenets of what is often referred to as liberal jurisprudence.[13]

"REFINED AND OPPRESSIVE CONSEQUENCES"

Much of Jefferson's agenda might reasonably be considered as part and parcel of a social transition from feudalism to liberalism. Traditionally, historians have rejected the notion that feudalism existed in the American colonies, and certainly the absence of a hereditary aristocracy gives immediate credence to this view. Feudalism as a social order never developed in British North America. Nonetheless, Virginia's colonial lawyers were members of an eighteenth-century British legal culture in which it was considered axiomatic that the common law had developed within the context of feudal society and reflected feudal principles. Far removed from the political rhetoric of the revolutionary period, and nearly three decades after the publication of Jefferson's *Summary View*, William & Mary law professor St. George Tucker could still write with confidence that, because many of the "rules respecting landed property, to be found in the common law, are derived from the feudal system," it would be valuable for the American law student to peruse the subject, even though "it was expected that that every trace of that system would have been abolished...when the republic was established." Accordingly, knowledge of feudal law was considered imperative to understanding the origins, concepts, and complexities of the English common law and, by association, of the development of colonial land law as well.[14]

[13] Michael Zuckert, *The Natural Rights Republic: Studies in the Foundation of the American Political Tradition* (South Bend: University of Notre Dame Press, 1996).

[14] St. George Tucker, *Blackstone's Commentaries: with Notes of Reference to the Constitution and Laws of the Federal Government of the United States; and of the Commonwealth of Virginia*, in Five Volumes (Philadelphia: 1803; reprinted by The Lawbook Exchange, Ltd., 1996), 3: 44 (hereafter *TB*). The classic statement on the absence of feudalism in American history is Louis Hartz, *The Liberal Tradition in America* (New York: Harcourt, Brace and World, 1955) and, more explicitly, in *The Founding of New Societies: Studies in the History of the United States, Latin America, South Africa, Canada, and Australia* (New York: Harcourt Brace Jovanovich, 1964). But see Rowland Berthoff and John M. Murrin, "Feudalism, Communalism, and the Yeoman Freeholder: The American Revolution Considered as a Social Accident," in Stephen G. Kurtz and James H. Hutson, eds., *Essays on the American Revolution* (Chapel Hill: University of North Carolina Press, 1973), 256–288 for a strong argument about a potential feudal revival. On the controversy surrounding the concept of feudalism in general see, Elizabeth A. R. Brown, "The Tyranny of a Construct: Feudalism and Historians of Medieval Europe," *AHR* 79 (1974), 1063–88; and Susan Reynolds, *Fiefs and Vassals: The Medieval Evidence Reinterpreted* (New York: Oxford University Press, 1994) 1–16. The social structure of late colonial Virginia has attracted considerable scholarly attention. See: Bernard Bailyn, "Politics and Social Structure in Virginia," in James Morton Smith, ed., *Seventeenth-Century America: Essays in Colonial History* (Chapel Hill: University of North Carolina Press, 1968); Thad W. Tate, "The Coming of the Revolution in Virginia: Britain's Challenge to Virginia's

Eighteenth-century students of the common law, on both sides of the Atlantic, learned that contemporary forms of tenure had originated from the doctrine of feuds. Feuds represented a system of military assurances and alliances that were derived from the customary practices of the Germanic tribes who migrated into the lands of the Roman Empire. Land served as the basis for this arrangement and, to that end, the conquering lord allotted large parcels of land, called feuds, to his leading officers on the condition that, in return, they would serve him faithfully for life. The grant was one of pure donation, and the lord paramount who issued it retained the ultimate dominion over the feud. Receivers of these grants, known as vassals, were deeded the possession and use of the feud in return for a specified condition of service.[15]

The condition of service determined the form of tenure. Tenures were established by a public ceremony known as corporal investiture. The ceremony began with the act of *homagium* (literally translated as manhood) whereby the vassal paid homage by kneeling and professing his allegiance to the lord from that day forth. The lord then stipulated the condition of service by which the vassal held his land, signifying his newly achieved status as a tenant within the community. Given that the initial conditions of service were military in nature, the prescribed duties were directed toward the preservation of the peace. Typically, vassals were required to be officers of the lord's court and to serve in his army during times of conflict. Performance of these services directly assisted the lord in the execution of his responsibilities as legislator, judge, and protector over the entire dominion. If a vassal failed to uphold any conditions

Ruling Class, 1763–1776," in *WMQ*, 3rd series, 19 (1962): 323–343; Emory G. Evans, "Planter Indebtedness and the Coming of the Revolution in Virginia," *WMQ*, 3rd series, 19 (1962): 511–533; Gordon Wood "Rhetoric and Reality in the American Revolution," *WMQ*, 3rd series, 23 (1966), 3–32; and Clarence Ray Keim, "Primogeniture and Entail in Colonial Virginia," *WMQ* 3rd ser, 25 (1968): 545–586. More recently, however, Holly Brewer, "Entailing Aristocracy in Colonial Virginia: 'Ancient Feudal Restraints' and Revolutionary Reform," *WMQ* 3rd series, 54 (1997), 307–346 has challenged most of Keim's findings. Brewer demonstrated how methodological flaws in Keim's study led to a gross underestimation of the percentage of land actually entailed in Virginia on the eve of the revolution. She has suggested that nearly 40% of Virginia's granted land was "docked in entail" in the years prior to the revolution, in effect fostering a land shortage in the colony.

15 Giles Jacob, *The General Laws of Estates: or, Freeholder's Companion: containing the laws, statutes, and customs relating to the freehold and other estates, in which is comprised the whole law of tenures of lands* (London: 1740). Historical analysis on tenure and estates are found in A. W. B. Simpson, *A History of the Land Law*, 2nd edition (Oxford: Clarendon Press, 1986) and Marshall Harris, *Origin of the Land Tenure in the United States* (Ames: Iowa State University Press, 1953). J. C. A Pocock, in *Ancient Constitution*, 70–123, has detailed the important debate over whether the feudal system was of Roman or Germanic origin. For other resources available to law students in the Virginia colony, see William Hamilton Bryson, *Census of Law Books in Colonial Virginia* (Charlottesville: University Press of Virginia, 1978); and "Subscribers in Virginia to Blackstone's Commentaries on the Laws of England, Philadelphia, 1771–1772," *WMQ*, 2d ser., 1 (1921): 183–185. Examples of Jefferson's legal education abound in Chinard, *Commonplace Book*, and are described in Frank L. Dewey, *Thomas Jefferson: Lawyer* (Charlottesville: University Press of Virginia, 1986).

of his service, the lands reverted back to the grantor. Because of the essential military nature of these original feuds, vassals could neither alienate nor dispose of their feuds by sale or mortgage, nor even devise them by will, without the explicit consent of the lord. Vassals did, however, through a process called sub-infeudation, further divide the original feud into smaller parcels for inferior officers and soldiers on similar conditions of service. Accordingly, a ladder of tenurial relations was established between men and the land in which various men possessed distinct relationships, or *status*, in relation to a particular piece of real property.[16]

The original feuds were precarious because they were held solely by the will of the lord. Over time, however, tenures became more permanent but also more complex. Once the simplicity of the original feuds had broken down, the system took on a life of its own. Feuds descended to the heirs of a vassal and were even purchased. Conditions of tenure were altered and, in many cases, services were divorced from the martial characteristics of the originals. Payments to the grantor in the forms of relief, aids, and fines developed in conjunction with the increasing transfers of feuds. Henceforth, tenures were distinguished between proper (military) and improper feuds. Significantly, however, they still were not classified by the quantity or quality of acreage but by the condition of service. Services were characterized as either free or base services, depending on the nature of the prescribed task. Free services included activities that befitted the nobility, such as serving his lord in wartime, providing counsel, judging disputes, or paying a monetary stipend. Base services, on the other hand, consisted of private labors "fit only for peasants, or persons of servile rank" and tended to include ploughing the lord's land, trimming his hedges, or "carrying out his dung."[17]

Services were also distinguished by the length of time for which they were required. Accordingly, they were further classified as either certain or uncertain. Certain services were prescribed for a set time, whereas uncertain services were dependent on contingency. The most notable uncertain service was military service, but uncertain service could also be formulated as a base service by simply instructing a tenant "to do whatever the lord should command." From the various combinations of these services a matrix of tenures could be devised. Students of the common law learned early on that the fundamental distinction between free and base tenure was manifested in the two legal forms of landholding: the freehold and villenage. Freeholds defined by uncertain services were referred to as knight-service, which initially represented the more esteemed form of tenure. Freeholds based on certain services were known as socage tenures.[18]

But landholding in England, and indeed the land law itself, was complicated further by the presence of such things as church lands, customary tenures, the

[16] Simpson, 1–24.

[17] *TB*, 3: 60–61.

[18] *TB*, 3: 60–61, Simpson, 6–7.

development of copyholds from base tenures, and the doctrine of estates. The doctrine of estates was devised toward the end of the thirteenth century to address an array of issues surrounding those who had a limited or future interest in a particular plot of land. The term "estate" derived from the Latin root *status* and connoted the legal relationship to which a person held the land. Because land was held for time, people of different status might have rights at different times. For example, a freeholder possessed the land, but his wife simultaneously held an estate in dower, and his children held in either remainder or reversion. The doctrine of estates protected the interests of each of these parties. Three fundamental forms of estate emerged: the fee simple, the fee tail, and the life estate. Fee simple represented the most privileged estate because it allowed for the status (not the land) to be alienated by sale, gift, or devise. Fee tail was more limited; it allowed a person to use the estate for a specified time, but its future descent remained under the control of the grantor. The recognition of the future interest in an entailed estate inhibited its ability to be sold or gifted. A life estate conveyed only possession with no other rights of alienation. Eventually, tenants with a life estate were classified as either tenants at will or tenants for years, depending on the circumstances of the estate.[19]

By the end of the fifteenth century, Sir Thomas Littleton, in his influential treatise that defined all subsequent discussions of English land law, readily identified at least seven different forms of tenure with multiple types of service and status associated with each one. Over the next 300 years, legal treatise writers were prone to decry the fact that the original feuds had been corrupted by an expanding process of aids, fees, and additional obligations attached to the natural transfer of property. They especially lamented the devaluation of knight-service, which had once been considered the most noble of tenures, embodying, as it did, the Christian virtues of stewardship, obligation, and chivalry. Writing from a eulogistic perspective in the eighteenth century, Blackstone echoed the contention that "the most refined and oppressive consequences" had resulted from this original plan of "simplicity and liberty," and he eloquently proclaimed that "a slavery so complicated, and so extensive as this, called aloud for a remedy in a nation that boasted of its freedom."[20]

For young Jefferson and his fellow students of the common law, such a remedy had appeared in the guise of the substantial land reforms that had occurred during the English Revolution. In 1660, as part of the settlement legislation of the Restoration, all military tenures were abolished by the Military Tenures Abolition Act. The statute brought about an end to knight-service and all the fines, aids, and rituals of homage associated with it. It declared that all tenures, except for those lands that still belonged to the church, were to be classified simply as either a freehold or a copyhold. Henceforth, all freeholds were

[19] Simpson, 81–102. A succinct and clear explanation of the doctrine of estates is provided in Mary Sue Bilder, *The Transatlantic Constitution: Colonial Legal Culture and the Empire* (Cambridge, MA: Harvard University Press, 2004), xii.

[20] *TB*, 3: 75; Simpson, 7–15.

deemed to be held in free and common socage. For common lawyers, these land reforms marked an end to absolutist tyranny because they apparently destroyed the most notorious mechanisms of royal abuse. Blackstone, invoking his own version of the Norman Yoke, characterized this historic legislation as marking "the complete restitution of English liberty," and he boldly proclaimed that it represented "a greater acquisition to the civil property of this kingdom than even the *magna carta* itself."[21]

Virginia's colonial lawyers embraced this history of land tenure as their own but also understood that their experience had been exceptional in some significant ways. Most notably, the headright system distinguished colonial tenures from common practices in England. Headrights were land patents of fifty acres issued to any settler who paid for the passage of an immigrant laborer into the colony. Initially devised during the first decades of settlement to solve the labor shortage problem for the Virginia Company, headrights were largely responsible for the development of the indentured servant system. Settlers paid for the passage of a laborer who would customarily serve a seven-year indenture and then be freed to petition for his own land patent. In return, the settlers received a headright for which they were required to pay an annual quitrent of one shilling. In addition to providing a stable labor force for the production of tobacco, the system allowed for the relatively easy acquisition of land and thereby encouraged the consolidation of estates by the colonial landed elite.[22]

The headright system emerged in the heady, speculative days of the colony's first decades but, like the tobacco crop that it supported, it quickly took root as a colonial institution. In 1634, it survived Governor John Harvey's challenge to its legal authority when the Lords Commissioners of Foreign Plantations – headed by Archbishop William Laud – resolved a local dispute between the governor and his council by endorsing the headright system as a legitimate form of grant. Harvey's subsequent ouster by the colonial landholders on the council inaugurated a period that historian Anthony Parent has accurately styled as a "land grab." In the four decades following Harvey's expulsion, more than 2 million acres of Virginia land was patented by filing approximately 2,000 headright claims a year. The crisis of Bacon's Rebellion in 1676 – an agrarian uprising against the colonial government by a group of landless settlers – brought an end to these permissive practices and ushered in a transformation in the colony's land and labor policies.[23]

[21] *TB*, 5: 439 and 3: 76–77. Donald Veall, *The Popular Movement for Law Reform 1640–1660* (Oxford: Clarendon Press, 1970); Christopher Hill, "Feudal Tenures" in *Intellectual Origins of the English Revolution Revisited* (Oxford: Clarendon Press, 1997), 318–326; Robert Willman, "Blackstone and the 'Theoretical Perfection' of English Law in the Reign of Charles II," *Historical Journal*, 26 (1983), 39–70.

[22] Philip Alexander Bruce, *Economic History of Virginia in the Seventeenth Century* (New York: Macmillan & Co., 1896) 1: 487–571.

[23] There are several fine works on this period in Virginia history, the most recent being Anthony Parent, Jr., *Foul Means: The Formation of a Slave Society in Virginia, 1660–1740* (Chapel Hill: University of North Carolina Press for the Omhundro Institute for Early American

Historians of seventeenth-century Virginia have longed recognized Bacon's Rebellion as a watershed moment in the colony's history but, generally, have treated it as a local phenomenon. Yet, it might be considered within the contemporary context of revising the borough charters and thus as part of the larger restructuring of the English polity that occurred immediately following the Restoration. Virginia's charter was rewritten in the wake of Bacon's Rebellion in correspondence with the revision of the borough charters. During this process, the king affirmed the legality of the headrights but did so by explicitly classifying them as a form of socage tenure. The 1676 Charter accordingly brought Virginia's colonial tenures into correspondence with the historic land reforms of the Restoration. Thereafter, many of the exceptional qualities associated with headrights disappeared. Virginians understood these grants simply as a form of free and common socage. By the middle decades of the eighteenth century, Landon Carter readily explained that the purchase of land grants in Virginia occurred just as they did in all the other "British Plantations," where lands were held by the king and granted to "every lawful Adventurer" in fee upon the payment of one Crown Sterling for every fifty acres he intended to enter.[24]

In addition to headright grants, freehold estates in the colony could be acquired through inheritance or by conveyance. Traditionally, a freehold so acquired was created by a livery of seisin – a public act replicating the ancient ceremony of corporal investiture. As late as the 1740s, livery-of-seisin ceremonies continued to be commemorated in Virginia with the symbolic exchange of "twig and turf." Increasingly, however, they were supplanted by modern forms of conveyances – most notably the transfer of property through written deeds. Unclaimed lands could be claimed by first obtaining a warrant of entry, an authorization enabling one to conduct a survey of a specified tract. Tracts of land larger than 400 acres required a grant from the Executive Council. Once the survey was completed, a plat was filed along with a petition to the House of Burgesses to request a patent from the Crown, which legally established a freehold in socage tenure. As a rule, actual possession of the land was required upon reception of the patent, because the idea of improvement served as the principal ends of colonial grants. Possession was not confined to the individual freeholder, however, and he could establish a tenant on the estate and still meet the terms of the requirement. In practice, however, this requirement was never rigorously enforced in the colony, because land was so abundant. By the

History and Culture, 2003). The classic interpretations on the changing colonial policies remain Allan Kulikoff, *Tobacco and Slaves: The Development of Southern Cultures in the Chesapeake, 1680–1800* (Chapel Hill: University of North Carolina Press, 1986); and Edmund Morgan, *American Slavery, American Freedom: The Ordeal of Colonial Virginia* (New York: W. W. Norton, 1975).

[24] Landon Carter, *A Letter from A Gentleman in Virginia*, 7. See the commentary by St. George Tucker as well, *TB*, 3: 77 (footnote). On the constitutional reforms of the Restoration, see Paul Halliday, *Dismembering the Body Politic: Partisan Politics in England's Towns, 1650–1730* (Cambridge: Cambridge University Press, 1998).

middle of the eighteenth century, it was openly ignored in favor of the practice of making provisional claims, which granted lands in anticipation of future settlement. This shift in policy opened the door to the creation of land companies and the subsequent rampant land speculation in the colony.[25]

The normal service prescribed for holding colonial lands in socage tenure took the form of a pledge of fealty and an annual payment of a quitrent. Quitrents had developed over the centuries to replace the terms of the original feudal arrangements. They were not the same as a rent, which was a payment for the use of land. Nor were they a tax, which – in theory, at least – was the privilege of someone not immediately beholden to the lord. Instead, quitrents were understood as a payment that commuted the original service prescribed to the tenure – hence their name. Quitrents perpetually confirmed the granting authority of the lord over the land, as did the oath of fealty. They also provided the grantor with an annual revenue from the lands possessed by his tenants. In Virginia, quitrents were paid directly to the Crown through the treasurer, except for those tenants in the Northern Neck – the land between the Potomac and Rappahannock rivers that comprised the Fairfax grant. There, tenants paid quitrents to the Fairfax estate (administered throughout much of the eighteenth century by Robert "King" Carter) because, through the process of sub-infeudation, they were held "mediately" of the Crown through Lord Fairfax. After 1685, the Crown administered the revenue from the colonial quitrents more closely and used them to supplement the ordinary functions of colonial government, most notably by paying the salaries of Crown officials. In theory then, the practice afforded the appointed royal officeholders a degree of financial autonomy independent of the colonial legislature.[26]

Throughout the colonial period, it was a widely accepted belief that because Virginians held their lands under the generous terms of socage tenure, they had always been exempted from the oppressive vestiges of the feudal system. They noted that neither military tenures (with their corresponding aids and fines) nor copyholds had ever existed in the colony. By the eve of the American Revolution, socage tenure represented the esteemed landholding status throughout the Empire and signified the essence of British liberty. The ubiquity of socage freeholds in Virginia fostered this belief, and any colonist reading Blackstone only found further confirmation. In his etymological discussion of the word "socage," he contended that the word derived from the Saxon word *soc*, signifying liberty or privilege, and dismissed previous interpretations that suggested that the word emanated from the Latin *soca*, meaning

[25] Turk McClesky, "Shadow Land: Provisional Real Estate Claims and Anglo-American Settlement in Southwestern Virginia," in *The Southern Colonial Backcountry* (Knoxville: University of Tennessee Press, 1998), 56–68. On the persistence of "twig and turf" ceremonies, see Rhys Isaac, *The Transformation of Virginia, 1740–1790* (Chapel Hill: University of North Carolina Press, 1982), 19–22.

[26] Beverley W. Bond, Jr., *The Quit-Rent System in the American Colonies* (New Haven, CT: Yale University Press, 1919).

plough. Edmund Pendleton, one of the colonies' most learned jurists, and the man who would become the most outspoken critic of Jefferson's allodial scheme, echoed the orthodox Whig view that attributed "the slavish nature of the Feuds" to specific historical corruptions of aids and fees, which had made them "oppressive to the tenant and inconsistent with Freedom." The argument advanced by Jefferson in his *Summary View* claiming that the tenurial system represented a burden and signified a badge of oppression thus ran contrary to long-established convention. His initial appeal to abolish the doctrine of tenures was deemed repugnant by the Williamsburg Assembly, not because he suggested that colonial landholdings were feudal in design, but instead because he claimed that they were essentially oppressive.[27]

CRISIS OVER LAND TENURE, 1752–1774

Yet, despite the positive perception of socage tenure in the colony, Jefferson's arguments against the tenurial system quickly gained traction among his peers. To be sure, his concerns about the source of colonial land tenures represented only one part of his larger argument pertaining to the constitutional rights of British Virginians, but it was an important part. The freehold was the source of the franchise. All political and legal rights emanated from landed status. Accordingly, his assertions about land tenure were by no means tangential to his analysis of the constitutional relation between Great Britain and the colony. Any change to the form of landholdings correspondingly conveyed a change in political rights, and vice versa. By invoking the Norman Yoke, he appealed to a generation of Virginians who understood the relationship between their rights as British subjects and the English common law, but who also perceived a growing uncertainty about the legal basis of their land tenure, and, by extension, their status within the Empire.

At the time Jefferson penned his resolutions, uncertainty about the source of Virginia's land tenures had been a persistent concern in the colony for more than two decades. Although perennial conflicts had occurred between the gentry and colonial administrators over issues of land grants and the collection of quitrents, a more complicated struggle emerged during the latter half of the eighteenth century. It began rather inadvertently, in 1752, with a parochial controversy stemming from a new lieutenant governor's attempt to impose an additional fee on land patents. It subsequently developed, however, to include an effort to establish a new form of military tenures, a Royal Proclamation prohibiting the settlement of lands west of the Appalachian Mountains, and public rivalries between transatlantic corporate interests over the right to organize these very same western lands (lands to which Virginia claimed charter rights). The crisis culminated in the spring of 1774 with a governmental

[27] *TB* 3: 77; Letter from Pendleton to Jefferson, August 26, 1776, in the *Letters and Papers of Edmund Pendleton*, edited by David May, 1: 200–201(hereafter *LPEP*). For discussion, see Cairns, "Blackstone, The Ancient Constitution, and the Feudal law."

plan to auction off Virginia's land claims south of the Ohio River and the corresponding transfer of lands north of the river to the recently acquired province of Quebec by parliamentary fiat. These efforts by the British government aimed at resolving the question of colonial land tenure ultimately led to what historian St. George Sioussat has characterized as "the breakdown of the Royal management of lands" that occurred in advent of the Revolution. By that time, Virginia's gentry were well poised to refute these innovations because they had been dealing with the issue for two decades. Indeed, they responded to the initial uncertainty by crafting a historical narrative of colonial land tenures that, in turn, became the seedbed for the constitutional ideas advanced in Jefferson's *Summary View*.[28]

The crisis over colonial land tenure was not unique to Virginia. Similar questions were being raised contemporaneously throughout the British dominions and reflected the changing nature of empire. In many respects, issues that arose during the decade of the 1750s served as a crucible for forging the ideological premises of what P. J. Marshall has styled the "new empire" that emerged from the Seven Years' War. In 1757, for example, the question of lands acquired by the East India Company was submitted to the Privy Council to resolve the ambiguity of tenure. At issue in India, as elsewhere, was the fundamental question of whether or not a private company could obtain indigenous lands through purchase or cession by treaty, and, if so, what was the relation of such lands to the British realm. The question of land tenure, and the corresponding question of the transmission of the common law, thus stood at the core of a nascent dialogue on an Imperial Constitution. In responding to the East India Company's petition, Attorney General Lord Camden and Solicitor General Charles Yorke framed an opinion for the Privy Council that distinguished between the lands of India conquered by the Crown and those lands privately acquired by the Company. Their opinion was intended to be confined solely to the question of India, but it provoked distinctions between private acquisitions and royal conquest. Significantly, too, it legitimized the private purchase

[28] St. George L. Sioussat, "The Breakdown of the Royal Management of Lands in the Southern Provinces, 1773–1775," *AH*, 3 (1929): 67–98. The following paragraphs provide a summary of the major events of this crisis from the perspective of the development of land law in Virginia, but by no means do they intend to present a comprehensive narrative to the issues and complexities surrounding the development of an imperial land policy for the North American colonies. For more detailed accounts, the reader should refer to Thomas Perkins Abernathy, *Western Lands and The American Revolution* (New York: Russell & Russell, 1959); Patrick Griffin, *American Leviathan: Empire, Nation, and Revolutionary Frontier* (New York: Hill and Wang, 2007); Eric Hinderaker, *Elusive Empires: Constructing Colonialism in the Ohio Valley, 1673–1800* (Cambridge: Cambridge University Press, 1997); Michael McConnell, *A Country Between: The Upper Ohio Valley and its Peoples, 1724–1774* (Lincoln: University of Nebraska Press, 1992); Jack M. Sosin, *Whitehall and the Wilderness: The Middle West in British Colonial Policy, 1760–1775* (Lincoln: University of Nebraska Press, 1961); and the classic study by Clarence Walworth Alvord, *The Mississippi Valley in British Politics: A Study of the Trade, Land Speculation, and Experiments in Imperialism Culminating in the American Revolution*, 2 vols. (Cleveland: The Arthur H. Clark Co., 1917).

of lands from indigenous peoples by recognizing their preemption rights as the "natural owners" of the land. Accordingly, although the opinion was limited in initial application, its manifestations resonated across the "extended polities of the British Empire."[29]

In British North America, the Crown's desire to establish a uniform policy of granting and settling lands was generated principally by the colonial gentry's aggressive desire to open lands west of the Appalachian Mountains on a speculative basis. Land speculation was certainly nothing new to Virginia (or to any of the North American colonies, for that matter) but during the late 1740s, many of the colony's leading landholders began forming corporations designed to purchase, survey, and settle vast tracts of western lands. These land companies were transatlantic in nature, combining interests from across the British dominions and generally composed of planters and merchants from the Tidewater as well as merchant capitalists in London, Plymouth, and Liverpool. From such alliances arose the great enterprises in land speculation carried on by the likes of the Greenbrier Company, the Loyal Company, the Ohio Company, and the Dismal Swamp Company. Although these corporations were nominally private ventures, most of the Virginians involved also served as members in the House of Burgesses or on the Executive Council and held important administrative posts in the colony. Speaker of the House John Robinson and Secretary Thomas Nelson were the chief architects of the Greenbrier and Loyal Companies. Northern Neck landholders George Mason, Arthur, Richard Henry, and Thomas Ludwell Lee, and Lawrence and George Washington shared interests in the Ohio Company. Even Thomas Jefferson, despite his subsequent aversion to purchasing lands, involved himself with the Lees, the Washingtons, and Patrick Henry, in the ill-fated Mississippi Company.

In such a context, issues of personal interest and colonial policy often became conflated. Indeed, since 1701, these corporate land grants were justified to better strengthen the frontiers against potential threats from indigenous or French incursions. The principal motivation, however, was profit – and much was to be made in the sale of Virginia's abundant land in the Ohio and Kentucky

[29] P. J. Marshall, *The Making and Unmaking of Empires: Britain, India, and America, c. 1750–1783* (London: Oxford University Press, 2005); Fred Anderson, *Crucible of War: The Seven Years' War and the Fate of Empire in British North America, 1754–1766* (New York: Alfred A. Knopf, 2000); and Jack P. Greene, *Peripheries and Center: Constitutional Development in the Extended Polities of the British Empire and the United States, 1607–1788* (New York: W. W. Norton, 1990). Discussion of the Camden-Yorke opinion is found in Sosin, *Whitehall in the Wilderness*, 229–231, and later in the chapter. Although not developed here, uncertainty over colonial land titles was exacerbated further by contemporary discussions within the imperial legal culture over whether or not the common law had been transplanted to the colonies. Ironically, the most influential legal commentator in Virginia, William Blackstone, did not believe that English common-law jurisdiction extended to the colony. Blackstone explained that the "American plantations" had been obtained either by conquest or treaty; accordingly, they were not part "of the mother country" but distinct (albeit dependent) dominions, and the common law had no "authority there." *TB* I: 108. Virginians naturally disagreed. They considered themselves very much a part of the British Empire and the inheritors of the common law.

River Valleys. Over the long term, such preeminent considerations of land as a commodity proved the tragic undoing for the idea of a self-governing polity of individual land owners. More immediately, however, this commodity conceptualization of land created friction within the framework of colonial government and, accordingly, forced the development of imperial land policies.[30]

In Virginia, the crisis over land tenures began as a local affair within the context of an emerging rivalry between the Ohio Company and the Loyal Company. In 1747, Thomas Ludwell Lee organized the Ohio Company to engage in trade with the Indians and land speculation in the Upper Ohio River Valley. The company was comprised predominantly of landholders from the Northern Neck, and reflecting the particular status of the Fairfax manor within Virginia, its members sent a petition directly to the king and Privy Council for a grant of 200,000 acres near the Forks of the Ohio. The grant was approved much to the ire of the colonial government, which had been left out of the loop. Most notably, the Ohio Company grant was awarded without the customary approval of the powerful John Robinson, who served simultaneously as Speaker of the House and Colonial Treasurer and who had his own designs on speculating in the western lands. Robinson and other members of the colonial administration reacted to the Ohio grant by organizing the Loyal Company and successfully petitioning for a grant of 800,000 acres along the colony's southern frontier. The rival grants, although sufficiently ambiguous, both lay within Virginia's recognized charter rights and did not necessarily conflict with one another. And certainly, over time, the rivalry between the companies diminished as their interests and members became integrated. In 1750, however, their relationship was adversarial. Both companies sought to survey their grants, but the College of William & Mary, which certified all surveyors in the colony, approved the certification of Dr. Thomas Walker of the Loyal Company but refused the credentials of Christopher Gist of the Ohio Company. The Ohio Company responded by challenging the Loyal Company grant as being in conflict with its own and thus preventing the necessary surveys and settlement.[31]

Into the midst of this factional divide, newly appointed Lieutenant Governor Robert Dinwiddie arrived from New York. Dinwiddie, who was not immune

[30] Abernathy, *Western Lands*, 1–13; McClesky, "Shadow Lands," 56–68. See as well Charles Royster, *The Fabulous History of the Dismal Swamp Company: A Story of George Washington's Times* (New York: Alfred A. Knopf, 1999); Warren R. Hofstra, "Land Policy and Settlement in the Northern Shenandoah Valley," in Robert D. Mitchell, ed., *Appalachian Frontiers: Settlement, Society, & Development in the Preindustrial Era* (Lexington: University Press of Kentucky, 1991), 105–126, and more fully in Hofstra, *The Planting of New Virginia: Settlement and Landscape in the Shenandoah Valley* (Baltimore and London: The Johns Hopkins University Press, 2004).

[31] Abernathy, *Western Lands*, 7–13. In 1751, Joshua Fry and Peter Jefferson set out on an expedition to map the inhabited areas of Virginia. They published a map based on their observations four years later. An interactive version of the map can be seen as part of the American Memory collection of the Library of Congress at: http://memory.loc.gov/cgi-bin/query/r?ammem/gmd:@filreq(@field(NUMBER+@band(g3880+ct000370))+@field(COLLID+armap))

to the desire for profit himself, was recruited immediately to be a member of the Ohio Company, setting himself at odds with most of the colonial leadership in the House of Burgesses. He had loftier ambitions as well, however, and quickly sought to get control of all the land transactions in the colony. In April 1752, he attempted to impose an additional fee on land transfers to be paid in exchange for his signature. The fee designated was a pistole, a Spanish coin worth somewhere around $3.60 at that time. Not surprisingly, the fee met with overt resistance from the House of Burgesses.

The strong reaction from the Burgesses evinced the powerful influence of the land companies but reflected serious constitutional concerns as well. They knew that, heretofore, colonial governors had been considered as administrative entities – representatives of the Crown – but persons who did not hold their office by virtue of any form of tenurial status. Indeed, in Virginia, the office had long been a sinecure. For more than half a century, the appointed governors had remained in England and never set foot in the colony. From the perspective of the Burgesses, Dinwiddie represented just another in a line of proxy lieutenant governors. Accordingly, they considered his effort to impose the pistole fee as an attempt to prescribe a new condition of service and, in effect, to interpose himself into the ladder of tenure relations between landholders and king. Within the context of the English common law, it appeared that Dinwiddie was suggesting that he, as an individual, possessed all the unchartered lands in the Virginia colony. A protracted showdown between the lieutenant governor and the legislature ensued. Over the objections of the Lieutenant Governor, the House of Burgesses dispatched Attorney General Peyton Randolph to London to serve as an emissary and to argue their case before the Board of Trade. Randolph's mission, although couched in the particulars of the pistole fee affair, was, in effect, to resolve whether or not the traditional tenurial system of granting land applied in the colony.[32]

In support of Randolph's mission, two Virginia planters, Landon Carter and Richard Bland, both well schooled in the common law, penned essays in opposition to the fee that were to be published in England correspondent with Randolph's testimony. Both essayists questioned the legality of such expansive gubernatorial authority within the parameters of the common law. Landon Carter concluded that, under the logic of the tenurial relationship, only the king himself possessed the authority to issue such a fee. For Richard Bland, however, even that much was in doubt. In his *Fragment on the Pistole Fee*, he noted that, in 1609, James I had already granted "all the Lands in Virginia" to the Virginia Company and gave them the power to establish the laws and government necessary to govern the colony. Bland's recourse to the colonial charter marked his initial foray into an extensive historical investigation into the exact nature

[32] On the controversy, see Glenn Curtis Smith, "The Affair of the Pistole Fee, Virginia, 1752–1755," *VMHB*, 48 (1940), 209–221; and Jack P. Greene, "The Case of the Pistole Fee: The Report of a Hearing on the Pistole Fee Dispute Before the Privy Council, June 18, 1754," *VMHB*, 66 (1958), 399–422.

of colonial landholding as it had been expressed in the original charters. He published the fruits of this research more than a decade later in an essay entitled *An Inquiry*, which was composed to counter the argument that the colonies were virtually represented in Parliament. In this essay, he returned to the theme of the Crown's original grant to the colony as a constitutional moment. He substantiated his previous claim by noting the circumstances and conditions of Queen Elizabeth's original grant to Sir Walter Raleigh, which Bland characterized as the most remarkable "the Crown could grant, or had ever granted before to any Person or Persons." It was remarkable because it conferred on Raleigh the power to legislate and to establish a civil government. For Bland, the original charters represented the "sacred Band of Union between England and her Colonies," and they could not be infringed on "without Injustice." He admitted that this original agreement had gone awry and been subverted by the Stuarts, but nonetheless, he reminded his readers, the America had never been "part of the Kingdom of England." Rather, he maintained, it was an "independent Country" that had been settled not by fugitives seeking civil and religious liberty, but by Englishmen, "who came over voluntarily, at their own Expense, and under Charters from the Crown." This assertion, which originally arose in response to his challenge of the pistole fee, thus became the basis for Jefferson's constitutional narrative subsequently expressed in *A Summary View*.[33]

The Board of Trade resolved the immediate crisis over the pistole fee by announcing a compromise that, on the surface at least, was considered more amenable to the position of the Burgesses than to Dinwiddie. The fee was allowed to stand but it would not apply to grants of less than one hundred acres, those already awaiting patent, or those lands west of the Appalachians. Yet the resolution proved a pyrrhic victory at best for Virginia's speculators. The outbreak of hostilities initiating the French and Indian War stymied any speculative ventures into the western lands and caused the permission to survey the lands immediately in question to lapse. Furthermore, the controversy also signaled the end of any era of salutary neglect pertaining to colonial land patents. In permitting the fee to stand, even in its restricted form, the Board of Trade determined that the laws and practices governing colonial land tenures were to be distinct from those in England. Colonial tenures were now explicitly considered something exceptional. The circumstances of the war, especially the disruptions and dislocations on the frontier, only exacerbated this orientation and encouraged the British government to devise a centralized policy for granting lands in the North American colonies. Most significantly, the course of the

[33] Richard Bland, "A Fragment on the Pistole Fee, claimed by the Governor of Virginia, 1753," edited by Worthington Chauncey Ford (Brooklyn: 1891); and Landon Carter, *A Letter from a Gentleman in Virginia to the Merchants of Great Britain* (London: 1754). For Carter's authorship of the essay, see Jack P. Greene, "Landon Carter and the Pistole Fee Dispute" *WMQ*, 3rd Ser, 14 (1957), 66–69. Also note his comments on the ambiguous publication history of Bland's *Fragment* in his footnote on page 69. For further development of this argument see, Richard Bland, *An Inquiry by Colonel Richard Bland* republished in *RV* I: 27–44.

war revealed that a coherent imperial land policy was needed as a measure of controlling foreign diplomacy with the Cherokee and Iroquois.[34]

In 1755, Edmund Atkin, a Charleston merchant and former member of the South Carolina executive council, submitted a report to the Board of Trade criticizing colonial management of Indian relations. He endorsed a proposal to divide the frontier into northern and southern districts, which would be superintended by Crown-appointed officers. The Board approved the findings of Atkin's report and appointed him Superintendent of Indian Affairs for the southern district the following year. William Johnson, a notable New York trader and agent for the Iroquois, was appointed to administer the northern district. Initially, both Johnson and Atkin spent the preponderance of their time shoring up Indian alliances and preventing defections to the French. Upon Atkin's death in 1761, his post was filled by the Scottish-born colonial official, John Stuart. Thereafter, both Johnson and Stuart figured prominently in the British government's attempts to devise a successful policy for control and settlement of the western lands. Most of these policies inherently conflicted with what Virginians understood as their charter rights to those lands.[35]

Controversy revolving around the authority to grant lands often set the diverse interests of different colonies, competing land companies, squatters, British policy, and rival Indian nations against one other. In London, the problem initially was perceived of as one of how to best protect the westernmost colonial settlements from recurrent Indian raids, but by the end of the French and Indian War, it was more accurately considered as a problem of how to protect the various Indian nations from the aggressively encroaching settlers and speculators. The colonial secretaries charged with oversight, Lord Hillsborough until 1772 and Lord Dartmouth thereafter, struggled to find an effective land policy that would protect settlers, ameliorate the various indigenous groups of the trans-Appalachian west, and clarify competing claims to the lands of the Ohio and Kentucky River Valleys. Ideally, it was hoped that a coordinated granting system would generate revenue to defer the necessary expense of military protection for the western settlements as well. Imperial policy proved to be neither consistent nor necessarily effective during the period, but it did undermine the traditional local autonomy of the colonial gentry. Furthermore, it increasingly put the British administration at odds with the members of the land companies. It also allowed for some innovative ideas in making land grants as long as one was not particular about following the precepts of the common law.[36]

One of the earliest of these innovations was no innovation at all; it was the resurrection of granting lands as military tenures – a policy that had been legally abolished a century earlier as part of the Restoration land reforms.

[34] Sosin, *Whitehall*, 3–51.

[35] Wilbur R. Jacobs, ed., *The Appalachian Frontier: The Edmond Atkin Report and Plan of 1755* (Lincoln: University of Nebraska Press, 1967).

[36] Sosin, *Whitehall*, 52–164; Sioussat, "Breakdown of Royal Management."

Admittedly, the idea originated in Virginia, not in London, but it was embraced by Hillsborough as effective policy. In 1754, with hostilities against the French seemingly eminent in the Ohio River Valley, Governor Dinwiddie and the executive council called for volunteers from the militia to march to the forks of the Ohio, and construct a fort there "for the Security & protection of his Majestys Subjects in this Colony." To support this fort, Dinwiddie promised the men 200,000 acres of land (equivalent to the former Ohio Company claim), at least half of which was to be contiguous to the fort and the other half on or near the Ohio River. Dinwiddie's proclamation was not the first time that the colonial government had sought to settle the frontier for reasons of military security. As early as 1701, the Burgesses had passed a statute authorizing the granting of lands in the Shenandoah Valley for the "better strengthening of the frontiers." Several similar efforts followed. What made Dinwiddie's plan novel were the terms of the tenure. He promised the volunteers who faithfully discharged their service that the land would be divided up in proportions based on "their respective merit" as it would be conveyed to him by the officers, for them to hold and enjoy "without paying any Rights & also free from the payment of quitrents for the term of fifteen years." Although Dinwiddie did not specify these tenures as expressly military, the waiver of the quitrent suggest that they be considered as something other than socage tenure. George Washington, who eventually acted as the chief advocate for awarding these grants, left little doubt in his correspondence that future military service was an expected condition of these estates. Dinwiddie's successors also continued to pursue these grants so as to settle the territory in a more defensible pattern. One of them, Francis Fauquier, sought assurances to give precedence to these military grants over rival claims in order to implement what he considered a necessary public policy.[37]

Any actual settlement of these Ohio River lands was stymied by the outbreak of hostilities and the French occupation of the area. Indeed, between 1754 and 1758, many British settlers in the western regions abandoned their homes in the face of raids from the French-allied Ohio Indians. The retreat of the French garrison at Fort Duquesne in November 1758 and the subsequent establishment of a British trading post at Fort Pitt, however, revived the issue of settlement. The French had abandoned the region following the defection of several Shawnee and Delaware allies who had made a separate treaty with the Pennsylvania governor. In this treaty, the Treaty of Easton, they agreed to ally themselves with the British in return for a guarantee that the colonist would not settle the lands west of the Appalachians. Colonel Henry Bouquet, commanding at Fort Pitt, honored the terms of the treaty. He prohibited both the

[37] Copy of the Order of the Virginia Council 18 February 1754, *Papers of George Washington* (Charlottesville: University Press of Virginia, 1993), Colonial Series, 8: 390 (hereafter *GWP*); George Washington letter to Botetourt, *GWP*, Colonial Series, 8: 391–392; *SAL* 3: 204–209; George Reese, ed., *The Official Papers of Francis Fauquier, Lieutenant Governor of Virginia 1758–1768* (Charlottesville: University Press of Virginia, 1981) I: 165–166, 331–332, 352–353, 375–376.

settlement and the resettlement of the region, not just by the Pennsylvanians, but by settlers from Maryland and Virginia as well. Virginia had not been a party to the Treaty of Easton, and speculators comprising the remnants of the Ohio Company were outraged with Bouquet's refusal to acknowledge their prior claims. In 1759, George Washington and other members of the Ohio Company petitioned Fauquier to secure permission to settle the Ohio lands based on these prior claims, especially the military bounty lands. Fauquier responded by writing to the Board of Trade to seek permission. The Board of Trade recognized that settlement would break the recently established peace in the region, and, given the pertinent fact that the war with France still continued in other parts of the world at the time, they easily refused Fauquier's request.[38]

The decision by the Board of Trade reflected the beginnings of an official policy of containment that sought to prevent western settlement in order to ensure peace with the various indigenous tribes. This containment policy exponentially exacerbated the growing sense of uncertainty about western land claims in Virginia. Patents originally filed fifteen years earlier by the Loyal, Greenbrier, and Ohio companies had technically expired because no one has been able to survey the lands. First the pistole fee controversy and then the war had interrupted these surveys. Suddenly, Virginians were prohibited from settling lands that had long been considered within the colony's explicit charter rights because a rival colony had agreed to a separate peace with a common belligerent. As hostilities on the frontier waned, Virginians found that their charter lands had been organized into a capriciously established district controlled by the Board of Trade in London. Upon conclusion of the war, the British government codified the containment policy by issuing the Proclamation of 1763 forbidding the issue of patents to any titles to lands beyond the crest of the Appalachians. In conjunction with the Proclamation, the Earl of Shelbourne was directed to inquire into the possibilities of increasing revenue from the colonies by pursuing a more immediate policy of royal administration of the western lands.

The Proclamation itself has received considerable attention from scholars who have examined both its intended and unintended consequences. Commonly, it is acknowledged to have troubled speculators far more than individual settlers, who proved ready to take their chances settling without the authority of legal title. Indeed, by denying the claims of land companies, the Proclamation protected squatters from the threat of potential ejectment and in this manner may have actually encouraged western settlement. Furthermore, a number of settlers who had settled legitimately beyond the mountains before the Proclamation now stopped paying their quitrents because they technically resided beyond the limits of colonial control. Both speculators and legislators were annoyed by these actions and by the rapidity with which squatters were occupying the lands. Most interested parties, however, understood the Proclamation as did George Washington – as a "temporary expedient" designed to "quiet the Minds

[38] Sosin, *Whitehall*, 39–51; Anderson, *Crucible of War*, 267–285, 560–571.

of the Indians." They believed that it was intended to remain in effect only until London could resolve the various adversarial claims and establish an effective settlement policy. In this manner, the Proclamation actually fueled the speculative frenzy over western lands. The various land companies dispatched emissaries to London to lobby on their behalf, recruit influential members, and engage in other forms of social jostling to ensure an advantageous position in anticipation of the forthcoming colonial land policy.[39]

Cessions made by the Six Nations to the Ohio Valley lands in the Treaty of Fort Stanwix in 1768, and the Cherokee cession of Kentucky lands the following year, only exacerbated this frenzy. Speculative designs began in earnest, but the landscape had changed dramatically. Former rivalries between Virginia's speculators were marginalized in the face of powerful mercantile interests from outside the colony seeking to establish their own claims in the lands of the Ohio watershed. In 1769, a group dominated by London and Philadelphia merchants proposed establishing an interior colony, named Vandalia, in the lands formerly claimed by both the Ohio and Loyal companies. These lands had long been considered to be conferred to Virginia by charter rights, and Virginians reacted to the proposed new colony by petitioning for their own claims against those of the Vandalia project. In 1771, Lord Dunmore, the new governor of Virginia, started processing the long-standing military bounty claims in the Ohio Valley. George Mason officially reorganized the Ohio Company the next year, and the Loyal Company followed suit and revived its claims as well. For three years, however, the chief impediment to the Vandalia scheme proved to be the colonial secretary, Lord Hillsborough. As time went on, Hillsborough increasingly came to view western expansion as a bad idea, and in this spirit he frustrated the Vandalia plan until the powerful lobbyists of the company forced his resignation. Hillsborough was replaced by Lord Dartmouth, who was perceived to be more favorable to the Vandalia scheme, but by 1773, the project had fallen out of favor with key members of the Privy Council and remained stalled.[40]

British colonial policy took a new direction under the ministry of Dartmouth. In April 1773, exasperated by the lobbying of rival land companies and facing increasing colonial resistance in the form of nonimportation, the Privy Council instructed the Board of Trade to reconsider the policy of colonial land grants and to propose any recommended alterations. Simultaneously, they ordered all appropriate officials to cease granting lands, authorizing surveys, or sanctioning the private purchase of lands from Indians. Within a few months, a sketch of a plan for granting lands had been drawn up by Dartmouth. The initial

[39] Letter from George Washington to William Crawford, September 17, 1767, in *GWP*, Colonial Series 8: 28. Eugene Del Papa, "The Royal Proclamation of 1763: Its Effect on the Virginia Land Companies," *VMHB*, 83 (1975): 406–411; Woody Holton, *Forced Founders: Indians, Debtors, and Slaves and the Making of the American Revolution in Virginia* (Chapel Hill: University of North Carolina Press, 1999); Griffin, *American Leviathan*, 19–45.

[40] Abernathy, *Western Lands*, 59–78; Sosin, *Whitehall*, 181–210.

proposal underwent a series of revisions, and in February 1774, the Privy Council adopted what thereafter was referred to as the Dartmouth Plan. It marked a significant departure in that it removed private land companies from the process of grant and settlement and instead vested all authority and administration in the colonial governments. Dartmouth's plan called for surveys to be conducted in order to identify the actual lands of the colonies that were not already granted. From these surveys, a comprehensive map was to be compiled, which numerically would identify the vacant lands in a particular district. One copy of the survey map was to be installed in the office of each colonial secretary, while duplicates were to be kept on file by Board of Trade in London. Once the entire survey was completed, and after a four-month notice was given, authorized colonial officials would be permitted to sell the vacant lands at auction. Lots were required to be at least 100 acres but limited to not more than 1,000 acres. The price of the lots was to be fixed based on their quality, with six pence per acre established as the minimum price. The Crown stipulated a quitrent of one half-penny sterling per acre and reserved its traditional rights to any gold, silver, or precious stones. Dartmouth's plan concluded with the stipulation that colonial governors were prohibited from granting lands on any other terms without the special authority of the king, the only exception being the military bounty lands granted to the officers and soldiers of the French and Indian war (although whether or not this exemption applied to militia remained ambiguous). The plan was to be grandfathered in; those who had claims already underway were to complete their title under the existing system, but this allowance applied only to those claiming lands that lay east of the Proclamation line.[41]

After two decades of conflict, Virginia's crisis over colonial land tenures climaxed when word of the Dartmouth Plan reached the colony. Irrespective of the merits of the auction system, the plan represented a clear departure from the traditional forms of granting lands and thus fueled colonial suspicions that a new form of imperial citizenship – a new constitution – was being devised for them in London. The timing of the announcement naturally informed the reception. All new polices were considered in light of ongoing events in Boston, where the port had been closed down in response to the Boston Tea Party. Although the Dartmouth Plan was never formally considered one of the Coercive Acts, the fact that it was announced in the midst of the debates over those acts certainly did not help. By the spring of 1774, many in Virginia believed (with some legitimacy) that Lord North's administration had shifted from a policy of colonial control to one of colonial suppression. Adding fuel to the fire, on the heels of the Dartmouth Plan, Parliament also announced the controversial Quebec Act that ceded all the lands northwest of the Ohio River

[41] Sioussat, "Breakdown in Royal Management," 68–71; Alvord, *Mississippi Valley*, 2: 214–216. On the colonial reception and subsequent perception of Dartmouth, see Pauline Maier, *From Resistance to Revolution: Colonial Radicals and the Development of American Opposition to Britain, 1765–1776*, 2nd edition (New York: W. W. Norton, 1992), 229–234.

to the recently conquered province. The Quebec Act reflected the conviction that the best way to resolve colonial intransigence over rival western land claims was by denying every colonial claim to these prized lands. It was a heavy-handed approach designed to abate further resistance to imperial policies and to assert the royal prerogative of sovereign dominion.

THE REFUTATION OF SOVEREIGN DOMINION

Jefferson's denunciation of the doctrine of tenures in the *Summary View* was written in the immediate context of the Dartmouth Plan and the Quebec Act. The historic error of tacitly accepting the doctrine as fundamental to colonial land law enabled the Crown to alter or amend the landholding system on a discretionary basis. The authority to do so emanated from the king's tenurial claim of sovereign dominion over all the lands of the realm. The Dartmouth Plan and the Quebec Act expressly manifested the historical danger to the rights of freeholders imbedded in the doctrine of tenures. Any perceived autonomy that colonial landholders might have thought they had over their free, common socage lands represented an exercise in self-deception. Accordingly, Jefferson believed that this perennial threat necessitated the repudiation of the entire system – not just the plans themselves. As long as the legal fiction of sovereign dominion persisted, all tenures were ultimately precarious and colonial landholders would remain subject to persistent uncertainty.

Despite the fact that Jefferson's argument was dismissed by many of his peers, he did not stand alone in being unsettled by the constitutional ramifications of recent imperial policies. During that volatile summer, Thomas Mason, John Randolph, Arthur Lee, and Robert Carter Nicholas all published separate commentaries on the constitutional crisis as well. Their essays reflected a range of political opinions and, although none took as radical a stance as did Jefferson, each protested against the overt policies of usurpation being issued from London. Lee, writing under the pseudonym "Tribunus," drafted a preface to the London edition of the *Summary View*, which he addressed to the king. Lee endorsed the essay as a cautionary tale for the king and his ministers, which aptly demonstrated the potential consequences of the continued unconstitutional use of the royal prerogative.[42]

Nor was Jefferson alone in drafting resolutions that summer. During the months of June and July, the "Freeholders and Inhabitants" of more than thirty Virginia counties met and drafted "resolves" protesting the recent constitutional violations by the British Crown toward the North American colonies, and especially the town of Boston. Of these resolves, the Fairfax Resolve has attracted

[42] "Observations on Conditions and Some Tractarians and Others in the Virginia Colonial Twilight, June–August 1774: An Editorial Note," in *RV*: 105–108. Each of the commentaries, along with Jefferson's *Summary View*, is published in that volume: Mason's, *Letters of the British American* (168–203), Randolph's, *A Plea for Moderation* (204–218), and Nicholas's response to Randolph, *Strictures on the Attorney General's Plea* (257–285).

significant historical attention, in part because George Washington and George Mason are considered its writers, but also because it elegantly and succinctly outlined the colonial constitutional argument. Approved on July 18, it was one of the earliest resolves that summer and quickly came to be considered one of the more moderate as well. Yet it began with the rather dramatic statement that "this Colony and Dominion of Virginia, cannot be considered as a Conquered Country; and, if it was...the present Inhabitants are the descendants, not of the Conquered, but of the Conquerors." Its authors reiterated Richard Bland's argument that the colony had been settled at private expense, but they deviated from Jefferson's interpretation by suggesting that by "Solemn Compact" the settlers had accepted the "auspices and protection of the British Crown" and henceforth consider themselves as subjects to the king. They repeated the conviction "that our Ancestors, when they...Settled in America, brought with them...the Civil Constitution and form of Government," from England – even if the relation was not specified in the original charters. Accordingly, they maintained that they were entitled to all the "privileges, immunities and advantages" of the British constitution, "to be as fully enjoyed," as if they still lived "within the Realm of England." Later, in the ninth resolution, the authors concluded that there had been "a premeditated design and System, formed and pursued by the British Ministry, to Introduce an Arbitrary Government into his Majesty's American Dominions." This assertion, certainly informed by the controversy over the western lands, was not cast as a radical argument. Rather, it followed the political orthodoxy of loyal opposition by indicting the policies of Dartmouth, Shelbourne, and Parliament while simultaneously professing perpetual loyalty to the Crown and Constitution. In this respect, the petition diverges substantially from the more radical assertions made by Jefferson a few weeks later. Nevertheless, with its initial emphases on the terms of settlement and charter rights, the Fairfax Resolve situated the question of colonial land rights at the fore of the constitutional crisis too.[43]

George Mason offered a more overt challenge to the Dartmouth Plan as well. In May 1774, he sought to test the bounds of the new land policy by petitioning for headrights to lands in the western Fincastle County – a huge district encompassing much of modern-day southwestern Virginia and Kentucky. Significantly, Mason justified his petition on the basis of established custom. As in the Fairfax Resolve, he echoed Bland's justification by referring to the explicit authority to grant lands as it was conferred by James I to the Virginia Company in the 1609 Charter. He then recounted the long history of subsequent agreements between the Crown and the colony culminating with the sanction of acquiring land by treasury-rights in 1710. Mason considered headright claims

[43] "The Petition from Freeholders & Inhabitants of Fairfax County [Fairfax Resolves], July 18, 1774," *RV*, I: 127–133. For the drafting by George Washington, Robert Harrison, and, perhaps, George Mason, see the editorial commentary on 109–111. The oppositional politics of British Empire are detailed in Bernard Bailyn, *The Ideological Origins of the American Revolution*, Enlarged edition (Cambridge, MA: Harvard University Press, 1992).

as a fundamental part of the "Ancient Rights to Lands" that had existed under the "Royal Charter" since the earliest days of settlement. He directly challenged the Dartmouth Plan by supposing that any "Late Regulations, respecting the ungranted Lands in the Colony," certainly were never meant to subvert the traditional grants of lands in headrights. With tongue firmly in cheek, Mason observed that there must be some kind of mistake – that "our present gracious" sovereign king, "ever observant of the Laws, and attentive to the just Rights of his People," would never renege on his commitment to the ancient rights and customs of his people. Mason's provocative petition failed to reap any immediate results, however, because the Executive Council refused to forward it to London. [44]

Ironically, however, in their effort to subvert the newly proposed land policies, Jefferson, Mason, and their fellow insurgents found their most significant support in the activities of the colonial governor, Lord Dunmore. By the spring of 1774, John Murray, the fourth Lord Dunmore, had served as governor of Virginia for three years already. He represented the new generation of colonial administers who had emerged in the second half of the century, whose focus was bureaucratic and who considered colonial officialdom as a career. Dunmore had already served as governor of New York prior to being assigned to Virginia. He was, however, unusually well connected even for a colonial administrator in that his daughter was engaged to the king's son. He earnestly embraced his assignments in America as an opportunity for his ambition and fortune. Not surprisingly then, he did not shy away from the mantle of power, and, like most of his predecessors, had a strong personal appetite for western land grants. From the outset of his term in Virginia, Dunmore attempted to appease the colonial gentry by pursuing an aggressive policy toward securing their western land claims. He vehemently opposed the Vandalia project and engaged in a series of activities designed to thwart it. In response to repeated urgings from George Washington, Dunmore clashed with Dartmouth over the issue of the long-promised Ohio land grants to members of the Virginia militia. Although Dunmore was instructed to suspend issuing grants to provincial officers, he ignored the order a continued to authorize surveys to be conducted on the lands south of the Ohio River.

Upon receiving the new land policy from Dartmouth in April 1774, however, Dunmore found himself caught in an untenable balancing act between the interest of the gentry and his duties as a colonial official. It would all end poorly for the governor, but not for want of effort. Recognizing the controversial elements of the auction plan, he sent a reply to Dartmouth warning him that the plan would be considered repugnant in Virginia. The colonial secretary dismissed the advice and censured the governor for his lackluster support of the ministry's position. But Dunmore knew the temper of the Virginians.

[44] "Petition of George Mason for Warrants for Lands in Fincastle County," *TJP*, I: 112–116 (with commentary). "Inventory of Mason's Headright Certificates," *Papers of George Mason*, II: 532.

Fortunately, in this respect, he was able to dissolve the House of Burgesses in response to their resolutions decrying the closure of the Boston Harbor before he announced the terms of the Dartmouth Plan. With the convenience of a prorogued legislature, he delayed announcing the plan for nearly ten months. In the interim, he hoped to secure Virginia's charter right claims to all the lands south of the Ohio, from the Forks at Pittsburgh to the Mississippi River – charter claims that corresponded to the long-standing claims of the Ohio and Loyal companies.[45]

Even before Dunmore learned of Dartmouth's plan, he had been engaged in an effort to bring the area around Forks of the Ohio securely under the control of the Virginia government. This area had long been subject to rival claims between settlers from Virginia and Pennsylvania. Since 1758, it had been under the actual control of the British forces stationed at Fort Pitt. In 1772, however, when the garrison was evacuated because of the expense of maintaining the western outposts, the dispute between the two colonies reemerged. The Vandalia group now staked a claim to the region as well. In August 1773, Dunmore traveled to Pittsburgh to assess the situation and to cultivate allegiance from the approximately 10,000 settlers in the area. Six months later, he dispatched an expedition under the command of John Connolly to seize the vacated fort and establish institutions of local government. The county of West Augusta was created, which overlapped the Pennsylvania county of Westmoreland. Violence erupted between the Pennsylvanian and Virginian factions, but by May, Connolly had gained the upper hand and asserted Virginia's claim over the area. Dartmouth, faced with this fait accompli, recognized the legitimacy of the Virginia's local government over the area of the Forks of the Ohio.[46]

Dunmore undoubtedly understood that a significant element of the Dartmouth plan was that it allowed colonies to award any vacant lands within their respective territory. Accordingly, he sought to gain effective control of all the lands claimed by Virginia. With the Forks of the Ohio secured, he turned his attention downstream toward the lands around the mouths of the Kanawha and Kentucky Rivers. These lands had been ceded to Virginia by the Cherokee already, but they were also used as hunting grounds by the Ohio tribes, most notably the Shawnee, Mingo, and Delaware. The spate of frontier violence wrought by the increasing number of British settlers moving into these western lands afforded Dunmore an excuse to go to war against the Ohio Indians. Fear reigned that summer as western settlers built forts to defend their families in anticipation of an impending Indian war arising from a series of killings and reprisal murders in the spring. By September, Dunmore had assembled an

45 Dunmore to Dartmouth, May 16, 1774 in K. G. Davies, ed., *Documents of the American Revolution, 1770–1783*, Colonial Office Series (Shannon: Irish University Press, 1972), 8: 65–66.

46 Griffin, *American Leviathan*, 102–114; Sioussat, "Breakdown of Royal Management," 81, 90–91; Abernathy, *Western Lands*, 56; Sosin, *Whitehall in the Wilderness*, 227–229.

expedition of volunteers and launched a two-pronged attack into the Ohio valley against the Shawnee and their allies. After a skirmish at Point Pleasant, where the Kanawha River meets the Ohio, the Virginia expedition received the surrender of the Shawnee. Dunmore negotiated the Treaty of Camp Charlotte with them, which included a purchase deed ceding all Indian rights to the lands south of the Ohio River. When the Mingo refused to comply with the terms of the treaty, Dunmore dispatched a raiding party to burn a nearby Mingo town and take hostages. He also ordered the expedition to continue to garrison Point Pleasant until the legislature (which, of course, was prorogued) could authorize a more permanent fortification. [47]

In less than a year, Dunmore had gained effective control over all the lands claimed as part of the colony's charter rights. He did so contrary to the wishes of the British government and in this manner challenged the sovereign dominion to these western lands. He certainly did not act in his capacity as royal governor in his efforts to secure the Pittsburgh area, and for all practical purposes, the expedition against the Shawnee had been conducted as a private adventure. Dunmore apparently considered his actions in this light as well. According to Patrick Henry, Dunmore had justified Virginia's claims to the lands acquired by the Treaty of Camp Charlotte by invoking the 1757 Camden-Yorke opinion. The opinion concerned the status of lands in Bengal acquired by the East India Company and distinguished between colonial lands administered by the Company, under the cognizance of its charter rights, from those lands conquered by the Crown. According to the testimony of Patrick Henry (whose interests may or may not have aligned with the governor), Dunmore had attained possession of the abridged version and cited it before launching his Ohio expedition.[48]

By 1775, British authority over the western land policy had evaporated. In March, Dunmore formally announced Dartmouth's plan for auctioning lands but, by that time, it came as a surprise to no one. A week later, the Virginia legislature, once again prorogued and sitting as a rump assembly, passed a resolution protesting that the Dartmouth Plan represented "an innovation on

[47] Jack M. Sosin, "The British Indian Department and Dunmore's War," *VMHB*, 74 (1966): 34–50; Griffin, *American Leviathan*, 97–123. McConnell, *A Country in Between* depicts Kentucky as a proverbial no-man's land. Used as a hunting area for Iroquois, Shawnee and Mingo, and the Cherokee, it was the source of conflict between these peoples for a century before European colonization. The presence of the British and French only exacerbated the historical conflicts over the region.

[48] Sosin, *Whitehall in the Wilderness*, 228–234 and esp. 259–267. Although the opinion pertained only to the situation in India, Sosin traced how an amended version of the opinion came to be transplanted to North America during the latter stages of the land tenure crisis. Members of the Illinois Company and the Vandalia Company – of which Lord Camden was himself a member – circulated the opinion during the spring of 1773, and by the following year, it seems to have been ubiquitous along the frontier. Ironically, the Transylvania Company used the opinion to claim the same Kentucky lands that Dunmore claimed for Virginia. Virginia's complicated negotiations with the Transylvania Company are detailed in Abernathy, *Western Lands*, 123–135; and Sioussat, "Breakdown," 92–93, 97.

the established usage of granting lands." They appointed a special committee tasked "to enquire whether his majesty may of right advance the terms of granting lands in this colony." Thomas Jefferson, Richard Bland, Patrick Henry, Robert Carter Nicholas, and Edmund Pendleton were assigned to the committee and charged with reporting their findings at the next meeting of the assembly. Jefferson immediately began to assemble sources, mostly garnered from Bland's previous historical inquiry into the early colonial charters, in an effort to present an accurate portrait of the colony's system of land tenure. When the Convention reassembled in August, it did so as the governing authority of the colony since Governor Dunmore had fled Williamsburg. Robert Carter Nicholas informed the delegates, however, that the committee was not prepared to make a full report at that time. Accordingly, the Convention resolved to suspend all land grants and all surveys until the committee could accomplish its task.[49]

The outbreak of hostilities and the consequent events of the Revolution forestalled the committee from delivering their formal report for another three years. Still, Jefferson did not abandon the issue. In January, he took issue with an October speech by the king in which he reminded the British nation that they had "planted…nursed…and defended" the colonies with "much expense and treasure." Jefferson responded to this royal assertion by cataloguing a detailed history of the incidents of settlement resulting from the initial grants awarded to Sir Humphrey Gilbert and Sir Walter Raleigh. The essay was compiled from information found in Richard Hakluyt's *Voyages*, William Stith's *History of Virginia*, and from Richard Bland's previous research on the charters. He titled the essay a "Refutation of the Argument that the Colonies were Established at the Expense of the British Nation," and although he never published it as separate piece, most of the content eventually was summarized in his *Notes on the State of Virginia*. As he had done in the *Summary View*, Jefferson once again contested the king's claim to dominion over the colonial lands. He did not, however, emphasize the allodial nature of Saxon lands but, instead, narrated an account of how a private venture, when conducted within the context of feudal land laws, became corrupted by the customary prerogatives of the sovereign. He acknowledged the pervasive influence of feudal tenures from the earliest days of the colony in describing the replication of an investiture ceremony whereby "Okisko, king of the Weopomeiocs," proclaimed homage to Sir Walter Raleigh and the queen. Yet Jefferson maintained that the colony had been settled by private adventurers – at a cost of "a hundred thousand pounds" – and that the Crown did not possess a claim of dominion. He suggested that corruption of the original constitution occurred under the Stuarts when, in 1624, the Virginia Company's charter was suspended by royal proclamation. The usurpation was completed two years later when Charles I "took the government of the country into his own hands." He noted that rumors circulated suggesting that a

[49] "Resolution of Land Grants," March 27, 1775, *TJP*, I: 162–163; Letters from George Wythe, April 5 and 6, 1775, *TJP*, I; 163–164.

"quo warranto" had been issued against the company, but he believed that this had been done to cloak these "arbitrary proceedings" under "the veil of legal form" – and he doubted that a judgment had ever been obtained.[50]

Despite remaining unpublished, Jefferson's "Refutation" represents a remarkable historical document. Written in the months leading up to the Declaration of Independence, his narrative justified the call for revolution against king and Parliament on the basis that the doctrine of tenures, with its premise of sovereign dominion, encouraged corruption, usurpation, and despotism. Significantly, his call to revolution was directed not only to those of British North America, but to all Britons everywhere. In January 1776, Jefferson hoped that the American insurgency would inspire revolution in England and throughout the Empire and advance the liberties stymied by the settlement of the Glorious Revolution. This revolution, however, would require land reforms abolishing all forms of tenure, not merely the military ones. Otherwise, as long as the tenurial system remained at the heart of the common law, Britons would remain subject to the inevitable tyranny gestating in the principle of sovereign dominion. Chillingly, he closed his "Refutation" by returning to the theme of taking notice of an error. Now, however, he charged the king with propagating a falsehood, not simply an error. An error, Jefferson explained, represented "a weakness of human nature," something to be "pitied and pardoned." On the other hand, "the vice of solemnizing falsehoods was not pardonable," and he warned that the king who did so "justifies the revolution of fortune which reduces him to a private station."[51]

At the close of the American Revolution, Jefferson again took pen in hand and drafted a historical account of Virginia's place in English legal history. Now, however, his purpose was not to inspire revolution but to justify it. In his *Notes on the State of Virginia*, he returned to the evidence presented in his "Refutation" and emphasized a history of colonial land tenures that was characterized by ambiguity, frequent misunderstandings, encroachments, and usurpations. Corruption provided the thread of continuity as long as the colony remained bound to the doctrine of tenures. Other writers echoed Jefferson's interpretation. In the wake of independence, Edmund Randolph, St. George Tucker, John Daly Burke, and John Marshall joined Jefferson in writing histories of Virginia. These histories included explorations into the legal arguments for colonial land grants, noted the absence of actual conquest by the English crown, challenged the legitimacy of feudal doctrines, championed the reception of the common law, and proclaimed the integrity of Virginia's charter rights.[52]

[50] *TJP*, 1: 277–285. See Boyd's discussion of the context on 284.

[51] *TJP*, 1: 283.

[52] Jefferson, *Notes on the State of Virginia*, Query XIII, edited by William Peden (Chapel Hill: University of North Carolina Press, 1954), 110, 111–117; Edmund Randolph, *History of Virginia* (Charlottesville: University Press of Virginia, 1970); John Marshall, *A History of the Colonies Planted by the English on the Continent of North America from their Settlement, to the Commencement of that war which Terminated in their Independence* (Originally the introductory part of the *Life of Washington*); John Daly Burke, *History of Virginia*, 4 vols.

Of all these new republican histories, the narrative composed by the College of William & Mary law professor St. George Tucker arguably exerted the most pervasive and lasting influence. Tucker's history was appended to his 1803 American edition of Blackstone's *Commentaries* and represents the culmination of the extensive historical investigations that had been conducted, first by Bland and then by Jefferson, on the subject of land tenures. Like them, Tucker understood Virginia's law to be the product of the historical development of the English common law. He diverged from their histories, however, in concerning himself less with the earliest colonial charters and emphasizing instead the 1676 Charter issued by Charles II. Tucker shared with Blackstone the belief that the Restoration law reforms, which abolished military tenures in favor of socage tenures, represented a defining moment in the development of a modern system of tenures, and he considered the 1676 Charter an integral part of these reforms. He also understood that Charter to represent a historical fulcrum delineating between a process of institutionalizing colonial law and the juridical ambiguity that had characterized the earliest decades of settlement. Accordingly, Tucker emphasized that the 1676 Charter had defined the nature of colonial landholdings until the eve of the Revolution. He allowed, however, that in many respects it confirmed the rights that Jefferson and Bland claimed had been assigned by the colony's earlier charters.[53]

Tucker explained that the 1676 Charter specifically detailed the process of granting fifty-acre headrights to encourage colonial settlement and clearly stipulated that such grants were to be held in the same manner that had been "allowed since the first plantation." He emphasized that according to these charter rights, colonial landholdings were specified to conform to the "manor of East Greenwich within our county of Kent in *free and common socage*." Tucker's inference suggested that the colonial arguments for the integrity of Virginia's charter rights represented something more than a mere territorial claim. They also conveyed the nature of the landholdings, which were to conform to the customs of Kent. Well schooled in the language of the common law, Tucker explained that gavelkind had never existed in colonial Virginia because it was founded on immemorial custom and dependent "upon local and accidental circumstances."[54] His

(Richmond: 1804–1816). St. George Tucker, "Concerning the Tenure of Lands in Virginia, and the Mode of Acquiring them under the Former, and Present Government" published in volume 3 of his annotated edition of Blackstone's *Commentaries*. *TB*, III: Appendix A, 1–10. In addition to an intellectual contribution, Jefferson provided both Randolph, Burke, and Tucker with many of their primary-source materials from his personal collection. Jefferson had inherited many of these from Bland and arguably had the most extensive collection of documents pertaining to Virginia's colonial history extant at that time. For discussion, see Arthur H. Schaffer, "Introduction" to Randolph, *History of Virginia*, i–xxxvi; Dewey, *Thomas Jefferson: Lawyer*; and Jack Greene, "The Intellectual Reconstruction of Virginia," in Peter S. Onuf, ed., *Jeffersonian Legacies* (Charlottesville: University Press of Virginia, 1993): 225–253.

53 *TB*, III: Appendix A.

54 *TB*, III: 77, note 2; Appendix A, 4. Tucker cited Jefferson's *Notes on the State of Virginia* as his authority and suggested that identical words were to be found in the charter of James I and

historical narrative, however, appended to a pedagogical manual for aspiring lawyers, provided a comprehensive justification for understanding Virginia's Revolution as the casting-off of the Norman Yoke and the restoration of ancient integrity to the common law. The heroic actions of the Virginia revolutionaries simply emulated the historic resistance of the liberty-loving men of Kent – their historical and ideological ancestors. The Saxon custom of allodial ownership had survived across the centuries because of this resistance, and now it provided the essential foundation for republican government.

perhaps even the original charter from Elizabeth I to Sir Walter Raleigh. Tucker reminded his readers that the legal definition of immemorial custom meant from before the reign of Richard I, and that any custom "may be destroyed by the evidence of its non-existence in any part of that period from that time to the present." Accordingly, time immemorial could not legally exist in Virginia because the reign of Richard preceded the settlement of Virginia by 400 years.

2

The Chosen People of God

Virginians made allodial land ownership the cornerstone of their republic. In June 1779, in the midst of the struggle for independence, the legislature passed two statutes designed to construct a land policy for the new Commonwealth. These land acts established a land office, provided for the appointment of land commissioners in each district, detailed a procedure for settling claims on unpatented lands, and stipulated that only the government could purchase lands from Indians. Most significantly, however, they abolished all forms of feudal tenures and declared that all lands in Virginia were henceforth to be held as the "absolute and unconditional property" of the individual freeholder. The laws relieved the sovereign of all the "prerogatives of income," which traditionally had come from quitrents, mines, or any other conditions attached to the grant of land. These traditional rights of the sovereign – be it king or commonwealth – were deemed "null and void," and the diverse estates of landholding were concentrated in the ownership rights of the individual freeholder. Freeholders were no longer defined as tenants, but as private owners who possessed an exclusive right that allowed them to develop, transfer, or sell their land as they saw fit. These land acts thus marked the end of the centuries-old doctrine of tenure in Virginia and its replacement by Jefferson's allodial theory of private land ownership.[1]

Yet despite this radical redefinition of the freehold, Virginia's republicans also passed a reception statute that confirmed the English common law as the foundational source of their laws. The statute ensured continuity with colonial legal practices and thus preserved the fundamental ideas, elements, and institutions of the common law.[2] Consequently, many of the particular attributes long associated with the freehold persisted despite its consideration as an allodial form of property. Postcolonial Virginians continued to distinguish

[1] *SAL*, 10: 50–65, esp. 64.

[2] Proceedings of the Forty-Ninth Day of Session, Fifth Virginia Convention, July 2, 1776 in *RV*, 7: 679–683, see fn. 4; *SAL*, 9: 127. William H. Bryson, "English Common Law in Virginia," *Journal of Legal History* 6 (1985): 249–256.

freehold estates from lesser estates by determining the "quantity of interest" of the estate as it was derived from the "duration and extent" of the grant. Freeholds remained a quantity of interest that lasted for an indeterminate duration instead of being specified for a fixed period of time.[3] Furthermore, at least initially, the colonial statute qualifying a freehold in terms of acreage was also maintained. It specified that a freehold consisted "of one hundred acres of uncultivated land without a house, or twenty-five acres of improved land with a house on it." Also, a house on a lot in an incorporated town was considered to be a freehold.[4]

Most significantly, however, the freehold retained its traditional political characteristics as the sole source of franchise and office. Freeholds continued to provide the determining qualification for suffrage, representation, and, most importantly, the influential local offices of police and justice – magistrates, sheriffs, coroners, jurors, and grand jurors – that formed the juridical structure of the county courts. Nevertheless, these political attributes experienced some ideological modification as well. The franchise had been attached to the freehold because it represented the permanence of the estates within the realm and reflected the reciprocity inherent in the condition of tenure. Now, allodial freeholders, through their absolute ownership of land, were also considered to possess the economic self-sufficiency and physical independence needed to exercise the individual liberty essential to republican government. Simultaneously, because land ownership was tangible and immovable (unlike other forms of property), it vested individual freeholders in a specific community with common interests and concerns. This common attachment, known as vicinage, would encourage the necessary performance of the duties of citizenship in order to administer and preserve a republic – or so it was believed. Nowhere were these duties more evident than in the county and corporation courts, which served as the institutional nexus of justice, administration, taxation, and local governance in the new regime. Virginia's republic was thus grounded in the hope that the absolute ownership of a tangible piece of property would reconcile the indulgent characteristics of economic individualism with a vested social attachment to a particular local community. Civic virtue was to be fostered through self-interest. In this manner, Virginians believed that they could best preserve their

[3] Tucker, *TB*, 3: Appendix B, 12. John Tayloe Lomax, *A Digest of Laws Respecting Real Property Generally Adopted and in Use in the United States; Embracing, More Especially the Law of Real Property in Virginia* (Philadelphia, 1839), 3–4. On the doctrine of estates, see Simpson, *Land Law*, 81–102. Lomax explained the principle to his law students by noting that "if lands are conveyed to a man and his heirs, or for his life, or for the life of another, or until he is married, or goes to Rome; he has an estate of freehold: but if lands are limited to a man for 500 years, or for 99 years, if he shall so long live, he has not an estate of freehold."

[4] *SAL*, 4: 475–476; 12: 102–121. The colonial statute also clarified the right of suffrage in cases of joint tenancy or tenants in common. Julian A. C. Chandler, *The History of Suffrage in Virginia* (Baltimore: Johns Hopkins Press, 1901), 9–15. Chandler refers to Governor Spotswood's comments about "worthless representatives" in the 1712 Assembly.

republic from the historic pitfalls of corruption that had ruined previous experiments in self-government.[5]

Thomas Jefferson echoed these sentiments in his famous passage in *Notes on the State of Virginia* when he anointed "those who labour in the earth" as the "chosen people of God." In so doing, Jefferson contrasted his agrarian design against the impending alternative of a market-oriented system of capitalist social relations. He proclaimed farmers blessed with a "substantial and genuine virtue" that inoculated them from the corrupting vices that inflicted merchants and tradesmen – those occupations whose very subsistence depended on the "caprice of customers." Such dependency, Jefferson contended, necessarily encouraged the lamentable trait of personal "ambition" and suffocated "the germ of virtue" in the merchant and manufacturing classes. Indeed, in reiterating his opinion two years later, Jefferson derided the commercial classes as "panders of vice" who historically acted as agents "by which the liberties of a country" were vanquished. Accordingly, he contended that merchants and manufacturers were particularly unsuited for the demands of self-government. Conversely, he maintained that the "corruption of morals" in the agricultural class was a phenomenon that "no age nor nation" had furnished an example.[6]

Of equal significance, however, Jefferson also recognized that farmers were "tied to their country and wedded to its interests by the most lasting bands" – the land. Merchant capital, with its wealth in the form of currency and stocks, was easily moveable; the land was not. In a system of government that derived its authority from the consent of the governed, grounding political rights in immovable property prevented citizens from opting out when policies contrary to an individual's self-interest were implemented. In a moment of clairvoyance, Jefferson understood that profit would prove transcendent to patriotism in the mind of the capitalist. Consequently, Jefferson believed it better politics for republican Virginia to dedicated itself to an agrarian economy that would grow and supply the necessary raw materials for the workshops of Europe than for merchants and craftsmen to bring their sordid "manners and principles" to the Commonwealth. Characterizing the proletarian and business classes as "sores" on the body politic, he prayed that as long as Virginia had "land to labour" he hoped never to see its citizens "occupied at a work bench."[7]

[5] On the centrality of agrarian thought in revolutionary ideology, see Drew McCoy, *The Elusive Republic: Political Economy in Jeffersonian America* (Chapel Hill: University of North Carolina Press, 1980); T. H. Breen, *Tobacco Culture: The Mentality of the Great Tidewater Planters on the Eve of the Revolution* (Princeton, NJ: Princeton University Press, 1985); Allan Kulikoff, *The Agrarian Origins of American Capitalism* (Charlottesville: University Press of Virginia, 1992); and Bruce Ragsdale, *A Planter's Republic: The Search for Economic Independence in Revolutionary Virginia* (Madison, WI: Madison House, 1996).

[6] Thomas Jefferson, *Notes on the State of Virginia*, edited by William Peden (Chapel Hill: University of North Carolina Press, 1982), 164–165. All subsequent citations are from this edition. Jefferson to John Jay, August 23, 1785, *TJP*, 8: 426–428. There is considerable irony and contradiction, of course, in Jefferson the slave owner championing the virtue of those who "labour in the earth."

[7] Jefferson, *Notes*, 165.

Jefferson's peers generally embraced the agrarian political vision as well, despite serious disagreements over the particular form that republican government should take. They considered an agrarian economy preferable to the menacing prospect of mercantile and manufacturing interests corrupting the essential attitudes of constitutional government. Even Edmund Pendleton, Jefferson's principal adversary in constituting Virginia's republic, embraced the agrarian bias. In a letter written to James Madison, Pendleton confirmed that "all experience" demonstrated that manufacturing was disadvantageous "in any Countrey [sic] which hath land for husbandry and a market for their Crops." Pendleton believed that any efforts to develop manufacturing would prove "ruinous" to the experiment in self-government. The republic of freeholders was intended to inhibit the nefarious traits of ambition, greed, and influence peddling that many Virginians believed had corrupted Great Britain. In this sense, its ideological motivations represented a collective reaction against the rampant influence of merchant capital and its corresponding vices of avarice and luxury.[8]

Tragically for Virginia's experiment in self-government, however, Jefferson's agrarian vision demanded a standard of virtue that seemingly exceeded even God's own expectations. In the end, his chosen people were tempted by fruits of capitalism as well. They proved to be just as subject to the sins of avarice and the designs of ambition as any group of merchants or manufacturers. When freeholders were given the exclusive rights of sole ownership over the land, they squandered it. They exhausted the soil, contracted extravagant debts, and mortgaged their estates for immediate material gain. Some of the chosen people preyed on the misfortune of others and managed to accumulate large estates by buying land that had to be sold to stave off hunger or as payment for debt. All of these transactions fostered the idea that land itself was merely a commodity and undermined any sense of communal attachment. Ironically then, Jefferson's agrarian vision, which was designed as a brace against the pressures of merchant capitalism, actually facilitated the advent of capitalist social relations by enhancing the transferability of land and encouraging its economic conceptualization as a mere commodity. In the end, this economic conceptualization of the land eroded the republican political values attached to the freehold. Within the life span of a generation, Archibald Stuart, one of Jefferson's peers at the bar, wrote dismayingly that "experience has taught us how even free holders" could readily find themselves "in a State of Dependence" and easily tempted "to commit foolish acts."[9]

[8] Pendleton to James Madison, December 19, 1786 in *LPEP*, 2: 493; on the problems of avarice and luxury in eighteenth-century thought, see J. E. Crowley, *This Sheba, Self: The Conceptualization of Economic Life in Eighteenth-Century America* (Baltimore: Johns Hopkins University Press, 1974); Lewis Simpson, *The Dispossessed Garden: Pastoral and History in Southern Literature* (Baton Rouge: Louisiana State University Press, 1983), xi; and Drew McCoy, *Elusive Republic*.

[9] Archibald Stuart to William Wirt, August 25, 1816, *WMQ*, 6 (1926): 340–343.

A PECULIARLY REMARKABLE TENURE

The vision of a republic composed of independent farmers has long been synonymous with the political thought of Thomas Jefferson. It is misleading, however, to portray him as the sole architect of Virginia's agrarian republic or as the creator of private ownership. The substance and form of Virginia's postcolonial republic resulted from a series of political negotiations, compromises, and decisions made in response to specific problems facing the new regime. Edmund Pendleton and George Mason also played significant roles in the legislative process of state formation. Outside the halls of power, the military adventures of George Rogers Clark and the host of illegal settlers who flooded into the lands of Kentucky in his wake determined the immediate context in which agrarian republican ideals would be discussed. That said, Jefferson was ubiquitous in the creation of Virginia's republic. Although his initial ideological contributions designed to craft Virginia's original constitution were largely shunned, he managed to impose his theory of allodial property by assuming leadership over the committee to reform Virginia's laws. Under the guise of the committee, he abolished primogeniture and entail and redesigned the laws of inheritance to resemble gavelkind. In alliance with George Mason, he composed the land laws that achieved his desired goal of abolishing tenure and shepherded them through a prolonged and contentious legislative process. Ultimately, he drafted the original bill for religious freedom that marked the culmination of the allodial revolution by making religion itself a matter of conscience; in other words, something else that was now also individually owned.

Jefferson articulated the theory of allodial ownership as an alternative to the doctrine of tenures. During his ambitious investigation into the historical writings of the British feudalists, he paid particular attention to their commentaries on allodial property. The essays of John Dalrymple and Henry Spelman provided Jefferson with general accounts of how allodial property was distinguished from feuds. The most comprehensive exposition of allodial property in Jefferson's legal commonplace book, however, was copied from William Robertson's *History of the Reign of the Emperor Charles V.* Robertson explained that the etymology of the word *allodium* came from the German and meant "land assigned by lot." He suggested that allodial property had emerged as a phase in the development of land rights among the Germanic people who migrated into lands of the Roman Empire. Conquered lands were divided among the soldiers based on the valor they displayed in battle. These lands were not, however, military tenures. Robertson maintained that a soldier "took possession" of the parcel "as a freeman in full property"; he could "dispose of it at pleasure, or transmit it as an inheritance to his children." Allodial owners "held of no sovereign or superior lord," although they were bound by conscience "to take arms in defence of the community." Robertson's *History* suggested that allodial property was the dominant method of landholding in Europe during the fifth and sixth centuries and that it had persisted in Italy into the eleventh century.[10]

Although Robertson's continental history significantly informed Jefferson's own writings on allodial property, his focus remained on the customs of the Saxons. Not only did the ancient Saxon practices permit the suggestion of historical continuity for Jefferson, but they seemed to replicate the social patterns of Virginia as well. In reading John Dalrymple, Jefferson discovered that "the Saxons like the other northern nations, had their princes and chieftains…[and] likewise their slaves, who were labourers of land." Dalrymple explained that the Saxons had been a migrating people who fought "not for glory or dominion, but for habitations." Furthermore, although their lands were distributed widely, they were not distributed equally. Specific allotments were designated as "reserved for the prince," whereas the rest were parceled out to the chieftains who allocated divisions to "their followers of an inferior degree, and their slaves" in a manner similar to feuds. The Saxons allowed, however, for anyone who was not affiliated with a particular chieftain to take possession of any vacant lands and hold them without a grant. Dalrymple maintained that these lands were allodial and by custom had been termed bocland, or folkland, in contrast to lands granted as feuds, which he suggested were referred to as "Thane-land." Dalrymple's account generally confirmed the earlier scholarship of Henry Spelman, a seventeenth-century historian of English feudalism, who also considered allodial lands as outside of the law of feuds. Much to Jefferson's chagrin, however, both of these scholars maintained that the allodial holdings of the Saxons had been extinguished by the Norman Conquest.[11]

Jefferson found a more sympathetic interpretation in William Somner's *A Treatise on Gavelkind*. In 1676, Somner published the results of his detailed etymological and legal investigation into the qualities of the customary form of landholding known as gavelkind. He described gavelkind as a property of "eminent singularity," which characterized the particular customary possessions of the men of the county of Kent. Bringing to bear his extraordinary knowledge of the Saxon and Old English language, Somner conducted a detailed etymological review of the word and concluded that gavelkind signified a partition of land that descended through inheritance in equal shares. Much of his treatise is an engagement with what others had written about gavelkind and, on most occasions, he went to great lengths to discount their interpretations. The strength of the treatise, however, lay in Somner's recognition that the custom itself had changed over time. Accordingly, he could assert from the vantage point of the seventeenth century that gavelkind represented a contemporary form of tenure, albeit one that had emerged from ancient custom. It possessed four distinguishing features: dower of the moiety – meaning that a widow's life estate would consist of half of the estate instead of a third; an exemption from

[10] Chinard, *Commonplace Book*, 229–233.
[11] Chinard, *Commonplace Book*, 129–130.

primogeniture that allowed for the estate to descend to all sons equally; the ability to alien gavelkind estates by deed from the age of fifteen; and protection from escheat in cases of attainder or felony execution.[12]

Judging from the entries made in the commonplace book, Jefferson seems to have read Somner and Spelman concurrently and in dialogue with Dalrymple's history of feudal property. He believed Somner to be the better Saxon scholar, no doubt in part because of his mastery of the language but probably too because his research identified the persistence of allodial lands after the Conquest. Somner identified the charters delivered to St. Lawrence Hospital and Christchurch in 1137 as clear evidence that the owners of these lands "were responsible to none." He also noted that the same language was found in the Pinenden Plea, when the sheriff of Kent restored the lands of the Archbishop of Canterbury. Indeed, Somner contended that the "Canterbury houses and grounds" still did not pay any quitrent in his own time. Jefferson thus found in Somner's treatise explicit confirmation for the persistence of allodial property after the Conquest. On the other hand, however, certain aspects of Somner's history poorly suited Jefferson's agenda. In particular, Somner devoted considerable effort to debunking the myth that gavelkind had persisted because of the forcible resistance of the "Kentish allodiarii" to William the Conqueror. He attributed the myth to the work of a cleric named Spot, whose writings he dismissed as a "monkish fabrication." Somner suggested that any precise reason for the persistence of gavelkind in the area of Kent remained elusive, but the existing evidence suggested a connection between it and the lands of the Abbott of Canterbury. Jefferson undoubtedly chafed at this explanation, dedicated as he was to purging any element of Christianity from the common law. Less surprisingly, then, his commonplace book entries dismissed or minimized those arguments made by Somner, which he found inconvenient.[13]

In the end, Jefferson seems to have decided not to push the investigation too far and preferred the brief synthesis of gavelkind found in Blackstone's *Commentaries*. Drawing from most of the same sources, Blackstone described gavelkind as a "peculiarly remarkable" species of socage tenure. He identified its four distinctive features but also suggested that holders in gavelkind had been permitted the custom of devising their lands through wills long before the practice was allowed to the realm in general. Furthermore, he

[12] William Somner, *A Treatise of Gavelkind, Both Name and Thing*, Second Edition (London, 1676); Chinard, *Commonplace Book*, 189–191; D. Bonney, "Early Boundaries and Estates in Southern England," in P. Sawyer, ed., *Medieval Settlement, Continuity and Change* (London: Edward Arnold, 1976), 72–81. Simpson, *Land Law*, 21; W. S. Holdsworth, *Historical Introduction to the Land Law* (Oxford, 1927). Kent had a special relationship with Virginia. David Hackett Fischer, in his extensive study of cultural migration to the colonies, has called Kent the "cradle of Virginia," and with due reason; he estimated that more than two-thirds of Virginia's elite families had emigrated from Kent and the surrounding region. David Hackett Fischer, *Albion's Seed: Four British Folkways in America* (New York: Oxford University Press, 1989), 240–246.

[13] Chinard, *Commonplace Book*, 189–190.

contended that prior to the Norman Conquest, gavelkind was the "general custom" of the entire realm. Disagreeing with Somner, Blackstone maintained that it had persisted from the "universally known" struggles of the men of Kent "to preserve their ancient liberties" in the face of the usurpations and "innovations of the Norman conqueror." He provided evidence of its persistence in citing some examples of "disgavelling" allodial lands by converting them into feudal tenures.[14]

Because of these contradictory historical interpretations, Jefferson could not present a definitive account of the ancient Saxon landholding patterns. They did allow him, however, an adequate enough description to argue for the presence of allodial ownership in English law and to portray it in tension with the feudal doctrine of tenures. This dialectical tension between feudal and allodial property, which was incumbent in his assertion of an error in the colony's landholdings, served not only as reason for revolution, but also provided the Revolution with a narrative imbued with historical context and meaning.[15]

Jefferson initially tried to ingrain allodial land ownership into Virginia's constitution. Educated as a common lawyer of the eighteenth century, he did not dissociate land law from the fundamental elements of constitutional law. Land was inherently political. Accordingly, he considered his advocacy for an allodial land system inseparable from the fundamental process of republican constitutional construction. Early in 1776, when he began considering the necessary components of a written constitution for a republican government in Virginia, he determined that land tenure should be represented as a fundamental article of such a constitution. In May, when the Williamsburg Convention declared independence from Great Britain and established a committee to constitute a republican form of government, Jefferson had only just arrived in Philadelphia to serve as a delegate to the Continental Congress. In the midst of assuming his duties there – and despite his subsequent assertions that the Williamsburg Convention did not possess legitimate constitutional authority – he managed to draft a proposed constitution for the former colony and communicate it to the delegates in Williamsburg. In the end, however, Jefferson's contributions to the original state constitution were limited. The committee opted to work from a less ambitious plan devised by George Mason. But Jefferson's draft constitution, coupled with his subsequent discussion about it with Edmund Pendleton, candidly revealed the particular motivations and specific manners by which he hoped to establish an agrarian republic in Virginia – a project that he did not abandon after the adoption of the constitution.[16]

[14] *TB*, III: 79–81, 83–84, 90. Blackstone cited Selden as his source for the view that gavelkind was the once custom of the realm.

[15] Gregory S. Alexander, *Commodity & Propriety: Competing Visions of Property in American Legal Thought, 1776–1970* (Chicago: University of Chicago Press, 1997), 43–55.

[16] "The Virginia Constitution" in *TJP*, I: 329–337. On Jefferson's constitutional thought, see Dumas Malone, *Jefferson and His Time*, Volume I: *Jefferson the Virginian* (Boston: Little, Brown and Co., 1948), 235–240; and David N. Mayer, *The Constitutional Thought of Thomas Jefferson* (Charlottesville: University Press of Virginia, 1994).

Land tenure occupied a prominent position in Jefferson's draft constitution. His allodial scheme was included in it as a distinct article – Article Four – which immediately followed three other articles designed to ensure the separation of powers by establishing distinct legislative, executive, and judicial branches. The placement was telling; for Jefferson, individual land ownership would stand as a fourth tier in the separation of powers. Individual freeholders would constitute the fundamental politic units of the republic and would represent the primary basis of self-government. His constitution decreed that all lands previously held as socage tenures would hereafter be held "in full and absolute dominion," with "no superior whatever" and free from any condition of service. Under the authority of the executive branch, a land office would be established to administer any unappropriated or forfeited lands and redistribute them to "every male person" who did not already possess fifty acres of land. This freehold entitlement was designed to redress existing inequalities and to expand the franchise in order to create a material basis for republican equality. Jefferson did not go so far as to attempt to break up and redistribute existing estates, but he called for limiting future land grants to no more than 400 acres to inhibit the further acquisition of large estates. Finally, his draft constitution sought to disseminate land ownership widely over time as well, by rejecting primogeniture and prescribing that estates were to descend equally to all heirs – in partible inheritance – following the Kentish custom of gavelkind.[17]

Jefferson elaborated on the motivations informing his constitutional thought in a well-known series of letters written to Edmund Pendleton later that summer. Pendleton had been an established member of the colonial bar for four decades and a Burgess for two decades by the time of the Revolution. With the disintegration of royal government, Pendleton was chosen to preside over the Williamsburg Convention, and, more importantly, he chaired the Committee on Public Safety that governed insurgent Virginia when the Convention was not in session. Pendleton's disagreement with Jefferson over the appropriate basis of land tenure inaugurated an intense, but always congenial, debate between the two men concerning the fundamental principles of Virginia's republic. Their debate continued for a decade and culminated over the issue of the established Church. Their essential disagreement stemmed largely from their differing conceptions of human nature; Pendleton remained committed to a Christian perspective that recognized the power and pervasiveness of sin, whereas the younger Jefferson embraced Enlightenment beliefs in human reason and social improvement. Their adversarial relation thus reflected the important negotiations that occurred in the process of implementing an expressly liberal republic at the expense of a Christian one.[18]

[17] *TJP*, 1: 329–386, esp. 343–344, 352–353, and 362–363. Jefferson had originally proposed offering a freehold entitlement to "every person of full age," but the statement was revised to read "every male person" in his second draft.

[18] David Mays, *Edmund Pendleton, 1721–1803: A Biography*, 2 vols. (Cambridge, MA: Harvard University Press, 1952) and Thomas Buckley, *Church and State in Revolutionary Virginia, 1776–1787* (Charlottesville: University Press of Virginia, 1977).

Jefferson's letter to Pendleton dated August 13, 1776 remains a particularly intriguing text because it represented an attempt to justify allodial land ownership on the basis of its advantages for Virginia, and not merely on Saxon tradition. Jefferson explained to Pendleton that his legal readings had led him to the inescapable conclusion that Virginia's lands were rightly "allodial possessions," at least as far as they had been transplanted by the common law. He hoped to return to the historical sources in the future to prove the point definitively, but for the moment, he considered the question "a mere speculative point." He maintained that the sheer circumstances of revolution now made it possible for the Virginia Convention to make the land law whatever "it ought to be for the public good."[19]

Jefferson suggested that the constitutional basis for republican landholding was being considered from two different perspectives: land could act either as a source of revenue or continue as a system of tenure. He argued against both. He asserted that a demand for "perpetual revenue" derived from either the sale of land or the payment of quitrents was not merely inconsistent, but actually even harmful to the principles of republican government. He explained that a steady flow of income from quitrents contained the potential to "make the governing power" independent from revenue generated by taxation. Taxes, unlike quitrents, were preferable because they were levied by the elected representatives in the legislature and thus ultimately sanctioned by the people themselves. Here, Jefferson echoed the assertion made by Dalrymple, in his essay on feudal property, that historically, taxation had represented the distinguishing badge of freemen. Still, for this assertion to remain true, Jefferson believed that land had to be something other than a source of tax revenue; it had to be the vesting basis for political rights as well.

He also condemned contemporary proposals calling for the Continental Congress to assume control over the western lands. He was particularly dismayed by a proposal for the Congress to assume the western lands in order to then sell them for revenues to finance the government. On firmer ground of agreement with Pendleton on this point, Jefferson defended Virginia's charter rights and considered the proposal similar in design to the Dartmouth Plan. If such a plan were enacted, the Continental government would simply replace the British government as the source of usurping Virginia's legitimate claims to the western lands. He explained to Pendleton that he was opposed to the idea of selling land at all. A system of land sales, he believed, would place an undue burden on settlers and, consequently, would potentially serve to encourage squatting, tax evasion, and other forms of illegal behavior. He contended that, particularly in the case of Kentucky, such a policy, when coupled with the natural geographic divide and distance, would likely "cause an avulsion" among those settlers "from the common union."[20]

[19] Jefferson to Pendleton, August 13, 1776, *TJP*, 1: 491–492.
[20] Jefferson to Pendleton, August 13, 1776, *TJP*, 1: 491–492.

Jefferson preferred retaining the practice of issuing land grants from the local (i.e., state) government to the individual as the source of vesting title, but he rejected the corresponding practice of treating land granted in such a manner as a form of tenure. Once again, he declared that tenures represented a legal fiction that had been introduced to establish an antiquated military system and which, in time, had developed into "an engine of immense oppression." Somewhat questionably, he reminded Pendleton that "all other nations" (beside England) hold their lands in absolute dominion. And he made reference to the Restoration land reforms and asked whether or not Pendleton thought the British were better off for having previously abolished elements of the feudal system and restored the ancient "Saxon laws." Accordingly, Jefferson concluded by advocating that Virginia's best course of action was the full return to "that happy system of our ancestors," which he believed characterized the common law "before the 8th century," and which he deemed "the wisest and most perfect yet devised by the wit of man."[21]

The sheer vulgarity of individual land ownership in American culture today tends to obscure the profoundly radical nature of Jefferson's proposal. In many respects, his commitment to the allodial scheme was the most revolutionary aspect of his republican vision. Land ownership represented popular self-government *in extremis*. Independent individuals were deeded control over the actual territory of the polity with no apparent mechanism to guarantee that they would actually consent and participate in the affairs of government. The state would act only as a disseminator of its most precious natural resource; its territory, and its legislative and adjudicative powers would be confined to resolving issues of conflict. Otherwise, the land belonged to the people; not as a polity, not as a community, but as individuals. This allodial republican vision conceived of the body politic as being comprised of a collection of individual owners, each of whom possessed a tangible share in the polity. Hopefully, through their individual consent alone, they would agree to share in its fate as well. Land ownership, in Jefferson's constitutional thought, acted foremost as a political institution – indeed the most fundamental institution in what Donald Mayer has aptly characterized as the federal aspect of his constitutionalism. In governing the land, republican freeholders would actively participate in self-government on a daily basis, not merely through the act of exercising their right to elect representatives. Jeffersonian republicanism thus began with the individual freeholder. For this personal basis of self-government to work, however, land rights must be exclusively vested in the people – as individual owners, and protected against traditional claims of governmental interest such as quitrents and services.[22]

Despite Jefferson's passionate advocacy, Edmund Pendleton remained unconvinced. Having spent some time "beating [his] brain" about the idea of allodial

[21] Jefferson to Pendleton, August 13, 1776, *TJP*, 1: 491–492.

[22] Mayer, *Constitutional Thought*, xi, 53–88.

land tenure, Pendleton rejected it. He believed, instead, that the more prudent plan was to continue in the traditional manner of landholding and simply to transfer the customary rights of the Crown to the Commonwealth. Evincing his inclination toward political conservatism, he expressed serious concerns about making any alterations to "the terms of Our Original Institution." He found it incredible that Jefferson could consider that the payment of an annual quitrent to the Commonwealth would somehow compromise "the dignity of Freemen." Insightfully, Pendleton compared the liberal features of Jefferson's allodial scheme with Carter Braxton's proposal to sell unappropriated lands to the highest bidder for the immediate financial benefit of the Commonwealth. He remarked that both plans inherently encouraged a commercial conception of land and consequently shared a similar tendency to "throw" such lands "into the hands of men of property," who were interested in accumulating it merely for speculative purposes. He criticized Jefferson's optimistic evaluation that all individual land owners would be able to provide for themselves. Pendleton maintained that despite a universal freehold entitlement, inequality in terms of quantity and quality of acreage would persist. Not all land ownership was equal, nor were all land owners. Men farming poorer lands faced being excluded from the inherent commercial potential of allodial lands unless the Commonwealth restricted all land grants "to small quantities."[23]

Returning to the subject in another letter written a few weeks later, Pendleton still balked at Jefferson's allodial vision. He reiterated that he could see neither the disgrace nor the injury of tenants "holding of the commonwealth" and paying to their elected representatives a small quitrent for the "common benefit." Most significantly, however, Pendleton was troubled by the potential social consequences of giving individuals title to land without somehow otherwise "vesting them in the Community." Pendleton's conservatism encouraged him to distrust the forces of the commercial marketplace, and he therefore rejected out of hand the belief that private ownership could somehow guarantee republican virtue. He believed that it would only further facilitate self-interest. He concluded by questioning Jefferson's anachronistic commitment to the mythical Saxon Constitution. While he praised the "old Saxon laws in General," he thought them perhaps "better calculated for a few, Hardy, virtuous men" than for residents of a modern commercial society. And audaciously he supposed that these ancient laws might even be improved on "after an experience of so many Centuries."[24]

Pendleton's dissenting view of liberal property rights can be attributed to his persistent commitment to a Christian-inspired worldview. He considered the land and its products a gift from God, which could never be exclusively owned

[23] Pendleton to Jefferson, August 3, 1776, *LPEP*, 1: 195–197. Braxton offered his land sale proposal as part of his plan for government, delivered as *An Address to the Convention of the Colony and Ancient Dominion of Virginia; on the Subject of Government in General, and Recommending a Particular Form to their Consideration*, in *RV*, 6: 518–526.

[24] Pendleton to Jefferson, August 26, 1776, *LPEP*, I: 200.

by men. God's grant of dominion to Adam and Eve represented a charge of stewardship, not a license for individual indulgence. He clearly articulated this Christian theory of property rights in a contemporary petition he wrote to confirm the common fishing rights of his Caroline County constituents in the Rappahannock River. He noted that under colonial law, land grants "were bounded by the Edge of the Waters," whereas the waters themselves were "retained as the property of the Crown" in order to preserve them in common "for the benefit of all the members of the Community." With the breakdown of the colonial order, however, certain landholders on the western bank of the Rappahannock had challenged the right of the petitioners to fish in the "River Opposite to their shores" and raised doubts about the proper limits between "Landed property and the Common." He petitioned that the traditional common rights be extended and "not be ingrossed by a few Proprietors of Adjacent Lands in exclusion of all Others." Pendleton credited "the Bountiful Creator" as the source of the principle of the commons. He explained that God had placed this essential food source in waters that were "incapable" of being classified as "separate or individual Property." And he asserted that God had done so in order that fish "should ever remain in common to be caught indifferently by all whose necessity or other circumstances, should prompt to seek them."[25]

Pendleton's theology necessitated a worldview that considered men as essentially prone to sin and thus inherently corruptible. He believed that improvement and virtue arose through the grace of God and, accordingly, rejected the idea that republican government was going to change mankind's essential nature. Although Pendleton supported revolution and embraced republicanism, his republican vision was grounded firmly in the necessity of customary institutions like land tenures and an Established Church. Jefferson, on the other hand, as a disciple of the Enlightenment, thought that human progress was possible only by dismantling the oppressive institutions of Christendom, which, he believed, had shackled mankind's natural state of freedom for centuries. Renovation was premised on a return to a golden age of natural order – for Jefferson, the Saxon age. Throughout the decade of constitutional construction, the elder Pendleton proved ever patient with the precocious lawyer, but, at sundry moments in their correspondence, he chided Jefferson for his idealistic vision of the human potential. In commenting on a rumor that Jefferson intended to enact a liberal penal code, Pendleton remarked that if Jefferson truly intended to rely on "Virtue and the Public good" as sufficient

[25] "Caroline County Legislative Petition to Confirm and Ascertain the Common Right of Fishing in Rivers," [November 21, 1777] in *LPEP*, I: 237. For discussions of Christian conceptions of land tenure that were contemporary with and informed developing liberal ideas of ownership, see Laura Brace, *The Idea of Property in Seventeenth-Century England: Tithes and the Individual* (Manchester: Manchester University Press, 1998) and *The Politics of Property: Labour, Freedom, and Belonging* (Edinburgh: Edinburgh University Press, 2004); also Paschal Larkin, *Property in the Eighteenth Century: With a Special Reference to England and Locke* (Dublin and Cork: Cork University Press, 1930).

means to "promote Obedience to the Laws," than he would need to "find a new race of Men" to serve in such a republic.[26]

THE ALLODIAL REVOLUTION

Although Jefferson failed in his efforts to incorporate his allodial scheme into Virginia's constitution, the idea of individual ownership had already gained considerable traction by the time the new government was formed. The breakdown of Imperial authority had thrust the immediate problems of the disputed western lands into the hands of the insurgent government in Williamsburg. In the spring of 1775, two months after formally announcing the Dartmouth Plan, Governor Dunmore fled the capital in the face of legislative and popular resistance to his efforts to curtail the colonial insurgency, Thereafter, the Williamsburg Convention became the de facto governing authority over a geographic area of more than 100,000 squares miles stretching as far as Pittsburgh in the northwest to the confluence of the Ohio and Mississippi rivers in the west. By August, the Convention had appointed an eleven-member Committee of Safety, presided over by Edmund Pendleton, to act as an interim executive authority while the Convention was adjourned. Amid the pressing issues of raising and sustaining a revolutionary army, Virginia's provisional government also sought to remediate the conflicting claims to the western lands brought into their dominion by Dunmore's military actions the previous year. At the headwaters of the Ohio, in what was now designated the District of West Augusta, the boundary dispute between Virginia and Pennsylvania continued unabated. Downstream, in the lands of Kentucky, the settlement claims of the North Carolina–based Transylvania Company invasively challenged Virginia's charter right claims. Jefferson might adeptly refute the Crown's historical claim to dominion over these lands, but constructing an effective means of governing them would prove to be a different matter entirely. With the outbreak of revolution, Virginia's provisional government found itself in the unenviable position of not only having to consolidate its authority in the well-populated counties east of the Appalachian mountains, but also of having to establish it in the frontier lands of the Ohio River Valley.[27]

In this environment of questionable and contested authorities, the idea of allodial ownership quickly gained traction among those who were actually settling the land. It was not a sudden development; for more than a decade,

[26] Pendleton to Jefferson, August 10, 1776 in *TJP*, 1: 488–491. For a discussion of the revision of the criminal laws, see Kathryn Preyer, "Crime, the Criminal Law and Reform in Post-Revolutionary Virginia," *Law and History Review*, 1 (1983): 53–85. On the points of tension and synthesis between Christianity and republicanism, see Mark Noll, *America's God: From Jonathan Edwards to Abraham Lincoln* (New York: Oxford University Press, 2002).

[27] The territorial extent of Virginia can be viewed on John Willis's 1783 map of the United States. An interactive version is found in the American Memory collection of the Library of Congress at: http://memory.loc.gov/cgi-bin/query/r?ammem/gmd:@filreq(+@OR(@field(AUTHOR+@3(Wallis,+John,+1714+1793++))+@field(OTHER+@3(Wallis,+John,+1714+1793++)))+@field(COLLID+armap))

settlers who migrated illegally beyond the Proclamation line had refused to pay quitrents, much to the chagrin of colonial officials and land companies alike. By Christmas 1775, however, traditional claims of authority and right were being challenged by those who possessed legal status as well. In Loudoun County, and in surrounding Northern Neck localities, several tenants organized rent strikes to protest their landlords' demands for payment in hard money in lieu of the paper money printed by the provisional government. These protests arose as a consequence the economic hardships wrought by the British blockade of exports, but, as Woody Holton has observed, they were imbued with unusual elements of class conflict. Tenants associated their rent strikes with the calls for patriotic unity and the requirements for militia service. In February, James Cleveland, an employee of George Washington, orchestrated a demonstration on the steps of the Loudon county courthouse where he exhorted the crowd to consider their landlords "as much of an enemy as the British." In addition to encouraging the rent strike, Cleveland called for a policy of equal pay between officers and soldiers. He deemed it even more preferable for those landlords who also served as officers to receive no pay at all. Elsewhere in the old Fairfax estate, Richard Henry Lee's tenants demonstrated an unconventional amount of agency in negotiating their payment schedules and fees with his collector for their back rents. Meanwhile, occasional efforts by landlords to invoke their common-law right to distrain property for debts were met with threats of organized violence. Throughout that winter and spring of 1775, the customary rights of property in the Northern Neck were challenged and repudiated by those who actually occupied the land.[28]

The strongest popular appeals for allodial ownership emerged, however, from the new settlements in Kentucky. There, the feudalistic designs of Transylvania proprietors engendered popular protests and provoked appeals for land rights that were based on individual pre-occupancy and improvement. Judge Richard Henderson, the chief architect of the Transylvania Company, was a North Carolina land speculator who by 1774 had eyed the fertile lands of Kentucky for more than a decade. In a manner similar to Governor Dunmore, Henderson took advantage of the breakdown in imperial control over the western lands to broker a private agreement with the Cherokee to cede the lands between the Kentucky and the Cumberland Rivers to his company. Henderson did not seek authorization from London to do so but instead rested his claim on the Camden-Yorke opinion. In March 1775, Henderson met with the Cherokee assembly at Sycamore Shoals, transacted the treaty agreement, and established a proprietary settlement at Boonesborough. Yet the Transylvania settlement hardly stood alone in the Kentucky wilderness. Groups of migrants from both Virginia and Pennsylvania had moved into the fertile lands of the Ohio watershed and settled in squatter villages that spring as well.[29]

[28] "Petition of West Augustans," *RV*, 7: 161–163; "Proceedings of the Committee, 2 March 1776," *RV*, 6: 163–165, n. 8.

[29] For a detailed analysis of the Transylvania experiment in state formation, see Stephen Aron, *How the West Was Lost: The Transformation of Kentucky from Daniel Boone to Henry Clay*

In May, Henderson convened a congress of delegates from the various settlements to assert the Transylvania proprietor's authority over the region and to form a government under his leadership. Henderson began the convention by having representatives of the Cherokee participate with him in a ceremony of feudal investiture replete with livery of seisin, effectively making a public transfer of the lands to the Company. He then outlined a constitution for the new colony that included a land policy premised on the doctrine of tenures. The proprietors articulated the land policy during a September meeting, when they established the terms for granting lands. They reserved for themselves all the sources of salt and precious metals in the region and expressed their intention to collect quitrents from anyone who had settled there. They also decided to double the going price of land grants. Far from consolidating proprietary authority, the terms of the land policy fueled popular protest against the Transylvania Company. Kentucky squatters, led by the likes of Abraham Hite, James Harrod, and George Rogers Clark, refused to comply with the Transylvania policies and petitioned the Williamsburg Convention to protect them from the "rigorous demands and impositions of the gentlemen styling themselves Proprietors."[30]

The petitions from these squatters moved the Williamsburg Convention closer to embracing Jefferson's idea of allodial land rights. On June 24, 1776, the same day that the assembly first entertained the committee report for a new plan of government, they also addressed sundry petitions from the "inhabitants of the Western frontiers," who complained about the "exorbitant demands" that were being made on them by members of the Transylvania Company. Similar appeals for clarity of land tenures had been forward from settlers in West Augusta and Botetourt counties as well. Accordingly, even before taking up the plan for an independent government, the Convention delegates found it necessary to resolve the adversarial claims to the lands in the Kentucky and western Virginia regions – at least temporarily. As an expedient, they determined that anyone who was actually settled on western lands would continue to hold their property without having to make any payments to any private persons until the validity of the titles had been resolved by the legislature. Furthermore, they mandated that no land was to be purchased from any Indian nation without the prior approval of the legislature. Most significantly, however, they extended the right of preemption – squatter's rights – to anyone who was already settled on any lands to which there was not an existing legitimated claim. In so doing, they recognized the right to individual settlement in the absence of a grant or a documented right of entry and – on a temporary basis, at least – fostered the notion of private land ownership.[31]

(Baltimore: John Hopkins University Press, 1996); Abernathy, *Western Lands in the American Revolution*, 64–73, 123–135.

30 "Agreement of Convention and Proprietors of Transylvania," *RV*, 7: 755–756; "Petition of Aggrieved Transylvania Settlers," *RV*, 7: 780–781; For the Proprietors' rebuttal, see "John Williams to the Gentlemen Inhabitants in & about Harrodsburg," *RV*, 7: 778–779.

31 "Proceedings of Forty-second Day of Session [24 June, 1776] Fifth Virginia Convention," in *RV*, 7: 593, 600–601. See as well the response of the Transylvania Company in the petition of

The effort to establish a more permanent legal solution to the question of land tenure began in earnest four months later. In September, Jefferson declined an appointment to serve as a commissioner to France and resigned his seat in the Continental Congress. He decided to forego these offices expressly in order to return home to Virginia and work on the project of revising the colonial laws. At his behest, the Commonwealth's first legislative assembly recognized that many of the laws currently in force were "heterogeneous to the republican spirit." To address this problem, the assembly appointed a five-member commission composed of Jefferson, Pendleton, George Wythe, George Mason, and Thomas Ludwell Lee to conduct a thorough inspection of the laws, remove any "inconsistent with republicanism," and propose any necessary amendments to the legislature. Jefferson chaired the commission. He worked tirelessly on the project for the next two and a half years; drafting and proposing new legislation, ingratiating himself onto almost every major committee, and working outside the confines of the committee process when necessary in order to impose his distinct allodial vision on Virginia's political structure. In 1779, the commission delivered a full report on revising the laws to the legislature. Although some of its recommendations were passed in piecemeal fashion during various wartime sessions, the full body of the commission's recommended revisions was not taken up by the legislature until 1785.[32]

One historian of the period has aptly styled the work of the commission as the "Jeffersonian Revolution," although the agenda received significant assistance from his allies, especially George Mason, George Wythe, and James Madison. Equally, parts of it met with sustained opposition, especially from Pendleton, Carter Braxton, Robert Carter Nicholas, and Benjamin Harrison, who, despite being unsuccessful in stemming the general tide, imposed some significant amendments to the Jefferson agenda. Allodial land ownership became the standard, although without the universal freehold entitlement or the 400-acre limitation original to Jefferson's plan. Primogeniture, entail, and the established Church were dismantled, but questions over the land companies' claims to western lands and the glebe lands of the Church persisted well into the

June 26, 1776, 622–623. A detailed documentary history including depositions for particular claims is published in *TJP*, 2: 63–110.

[32] Jefferson, *Notes*, 136–137; *SAL*, 9: 175; 13: 130–131. Charles M. Cullen, "Completing the Revisal of the Laws in Post-Revolutionary Virginia," *Virginia Magazine of History and Biography*, 82 (1974), 84–99. Mason and Lee subsequently resigned from the commission, but, with some interruptions, the three remaining members completed the project and submitted it to the legislature in 1779. In 1789, the General Assembly again called a committee of revision and the following year appointed Edmund Pendleton, Henry Tazewell, St. George Tucker, Joseph Prentis, Arthur Lee, and William Nelson, Jr., charging them to review and revise the existing laws of the Commonwealth. Emphasis on this revision was on the inclusion of "such British statutes, if any there be, which are suited to this commonwealth and have not be enacted in the form of the Virginia laws." The committee was also charged with reducing multiple laws into single acts when possible and reporting which laws were unnecessary, but interestingly there was no mention of bringing the laws of the state into consilience with the new federal union. Their compilation was published in 1794 under the heading of *The Revised Code of 1792*.

nineteenth century. Nonetheless, the substance of Jefferson's constitutional vision was adopted and a secular-inclined liberal republic was constructed. The foundation of this liberal republic was grounded in the local governance exercised by freeholders in the county courts, which provided the principal institutional forum for the police of virtue and vice in republican Virginia.[33]

The five-member law commission first met in Fredericksburg in January 1777, to determine a plan of revision. The details of this meeting are transmitted to posterity exclusively through Jefferson's recounting in his *Autobiography* and, pending further research, its veracity should perhaps be accepted with a healthy dose of skepticism. According to Jefferson, the seminal question addressed by the commission concerned whether to "abolish the whole existing system of laws, and prepare a new and complete Institute," or instead simply to "preserve the general system, and only modify it to the present state of things." In Jefferson's recounting, Pendleton and Lee embraced the more radical position and proposed abrogating the common law and replacing it instead with a codified form of law modeled along the lines of Blackstone's *Commentaries*. Conversely, Jefferson maintained that he, Wythe, and Mason rejected codification and advocated the reception of as much of the common law and British statutes as possible into the law of Virginia. Jefferson's commitment to the common law is not surprising given his conservative view of the Revolution as an act to restore the purity of the common law, but Pendleton's stance seems inconsistent with his equally strong expressions in favor of the common law, including the tenurial system. Suspicion is warranted that Jefferson may have simplified Pendleton's argument into one that was more clearly antagonistic. Indeed, the subsequent publication of *Tucker's Blackstone* by St. George Tucker seemingly provided Virginians with the model proposed by Pendleton – a model that informed and organized, but did not replace, the common law. Irrespective of the details of the recounting, a majority of the members clearly favored retaining the common law as "the basis of the work" of revision. The committee divided the responsibilities for the revision, with Jefferson assigned to examine the British statutes through the Anglican Reformation in 1534, Pendleton reviewing the statutes passed from 1534 through the Glorious Revolution, and Wythe tasked with considering the remaining statutes "down to the present day." Mason undertook the examination of Virginia's colonial statutes, with a particular emphasis on the criminal and land laws, and Lee agreed to compile the laws pertaining to slavery and to identify potentially relevant laws from other colonies.[34]

[33] Boyd, "Editorial Note" in *TJP*, 2: 305–324. On the "Jeffersonian Revolution," see Mays, *Edmund Pendleton*, 2: 126–143. On the question of the church as the central political question of the postcolonial period, see Thomas Buckley, *Church and State*, and "Evangelicals Triumphant: The Baptists' Assault on the Virginia Glebes, 1786–1801," *WMQ*, Third Series (1988): 33–69.

[34] *GMP*, 1: 327–333; *TJP*, 2: 305–328. On Jefferson's subsequent characterization of the Fredericksburg meeting, see his *Autobiography* in Paul Leicester Ford, *The Writings of Thomas Jefferson* (New York: G. P. Putnam and Sons, 1892–1899), I: 58–59.

Despite eventually resigning from the committee, George Mason worked closely with Jefferson on the subject of the land laws. Their principal motivation seemed to focus on sorting out the crisis over western land claims and refuting the purchase claims of the Transylvania Company. Jefferson had gotten a head start in this respect. During the first weeks of the legislative session, he offered a bill to divide Fincastle County – a geographically vast area that extended all the way from the headwaters of the New River in southwestern Virginia to the Mississippi River as its western boundary. The measure was designed specifically to invalidate the claims of the Transylvania Company and to establish Virginia's juridical authority over the lands claimed by charter rights in Kentucky. In successfully maneuvering the bill through the legislature, however, Jefferson only attempted to resolve the disputed on a temporary basis. Fincastle County was divided into three separate counties – Montgomery, Washington, and Kentucky – and the petition from the Transylvania Company to the Virginia assembly to recognize the legitimacy of their claim was rejected.[35]

A more permanent solution was proposed the following year with the introduction of two bills specifically designed to establish an allodial land policy. These bills reflected the collaboration between Jefferson and Mason. The first bill called for the establishment of a land office and specified the arrangements by which vacant lands might be granted. The second bill sought to resolve the sundry controversies over existing titles in the western lands. The law commissioners had endorsed the plan in December 1777, and Mason introduced both bills in the legislature the following month. The bills met staunch political opposition, however, and it would take another year and a half for them to become law. The source of this opposition has often been attributed to rival legislators who were more vested in the grand designs of the land companies and thus sought to inhibit the more democratic aspects of Jefferson's allodial vision. Significantly, however, the leading opponents to the plan, Pendleton and Carter Braxton, also led the opposition against disestablishment of the Church. Given that both Jefferson and Mason were also well connected with the land companies, reconsidering the political opposition to the land bills as part of a larger debate over the fundamental nature of Virginia's republic might well be in order. Irrespective of oppositional motives, however, by the spring of 1779, serious concerns over the growing discontent of western settlers and a desperate need for a stable source of revenue forced the issue.[36]

The Land-Office bill detailing the process of granting lands in the Commonwealth reflected a joint effort in composition by Jefferson and Mason. It represented the culmination of their effort to construct allodial ownership as

[35] *TJP*, 1: 564–576, "A Bill to Divide Fincastle County."

[36] The legislative history of the two bills is detailed in Boyd, "Editorial Note," *TJP*, 2: 133–138 and *GMP*, 1: 408–409. The most detailed analysis of them is found in Abernathy, *Western Lands*, 217–229. For the legislative context, see Mason's assessment bill and the resolution authorizing an investigation of "disaffection in the western counties," in *GMP*, 1: 375–397, 398–399.

the basis of the republic. In one respect, it stands as a clear articulation of the fundamental principles of the agrarian vision that dominated Jefferson's republican thought. On the other hand, Mason prevailed in ensuring that land grants would be considered a source of public revenue and would be used to discharge the rapidly growing public debt. Faced with the corresponding problems of debt and wartime inflation, Mason devised a new system of public revenue that was premised on property taxes. His goal was to ensure that the expenses of government would be provided for "by assessments on the citizens in proportion to their property." Recognizing that a considerable amount of wealth existed in forms of personal property as well as land, Mason proposed levying taxes on slaves and personal income in addition to freeholds. Nevertheless, the largest extent of taxation necessarily descended on the freeholders because they outnumbered slaveholders and merchants. Mason advocated remedying the tax burden imposed on freeholders by abolishing the payment of quitrents, except for those on lands held in the Northern Neck. The Land-Office bill was designed in conjunction with the assessment bill – indeed the two were inseparable in concept – and it contained a provision for purchasing lands in the hopes that the revenue generated by these sales would further alleviate the tax burden on Virginia's freeholders. In the face of fiscal crisis, Jefferson recanted from his previous reluctance to sell lands and endorsed Mason's provisions.[37]

Still, revenue remained a tangential concern to creating an independent citizenry. Mason and Jefferson's bill began by calling for perpetuating "the ancient custom" of headrights to induce foreign immigration into the Commonwealth. Those who immigrated, or those who paid the costs of immigration, were entitled to a grant of fifty acres so long as the settler was older than sixteen and willingly professed an oath of fidelity to the Commonwealth. An important qualification to these customary rights prohibited any headright entitlements for the importation of slaves – a marked deviation from colonial policy. The bill also contained a provision awarding every freeborn child of the Commonwealth a grant of seventy-five acres upon his or her marriage and continued residence. The explicit purposes of these provisions were to ensure the "more equal distribution of lands" and to encourage marriage and reproduction in the new republic. Native women were entitled to the grant as well, but the certificate was to be deeded to their husband and his heirs, thus continuing to conform to the common-law practice of coverture. A third provision provided an allowance for bounty lands for those serving in the Continental army or Virginia militia as had been granted, or would be granted in the future, by state law.[38]

[37] See the draft land-office bills in *TJP*, 2: 139–154 and *GMP*, 1: 399–409. On Mason's assessment bills, see *GMP*, 1: 375–397. For Jefferson's subsequent characterization of the event see *Notes*, 137. A detailed analysis of the development of Virginia's taxation policy is provided in Robin L. Einhorn, *American Taxation, American Slavery* (Chicago: University of Chicago Press, 2006), 29– 52.

[38] Slightly differing drafts of the bill are provided in *GMP* 1: 400–401 and *TJP* 2: 139–141. Rutland believes that the Mason version represents an earlier draft of the bill than the Jefferson copy. Boyd provides extensive notes on the editorial process to the Jefferson draft, 2: 147–154.

Only after establishing the terms of these customary, native, and military grants did Jefferson and Mason detail the process of treasury rights. The sale of lands was designed specifically toward establishing a sinking fund for the discharge of the public debt. It was also considered a means to increase population. Warrants to survey unappropriated lands were to be made eligible to citizens of Virginia or "any other of the United States." Eventually, the purchase price was set at forty pounds per hundred acres. The process of purchase differed, however, depending on whether or not the warrant was more than 400 acres. Quantities in excess of 400 acres required direct payment to the state treasurer, but smaller acreages could be purchased from the clerk of the county court. Permission to purchase smaller lots directly from the county clerk represented an intended preference for independent settlers over speculators, but circumstances had forced Jefferson to reconsider his initial prohibition on grants of more than 400 acres as well. Julian Boyd, in his editorial notes on Jefferson's papers, observed that this particular clause was written in Jefferson's hand and affixed to the draft bill. Thus, despite a designed bias in favor of small owners, the Virginia land office would gladly accept the business of land companies too.[39]

Mason is credited with the primary composition of the second bill – a bill for settling land titles. In it he sought to assert Virginia's jurisdiction over the western lands and extinguish the numerous adversarial claims from the sundry land companies, which had now existed for more than a decade. Mason hoped to accomplish this by validating all claims that had been based on "Importation Rights" (headrights), treasury rights not exceeding 400 acres, or military grants that already had been surveyed by a licensed surveyor from the College of William & Mary. All other conducted surveys, particularly those of the Transylvania, Vandalia, and Indiana companies, were deemed "null and void." Military grants from the king, issued following the Proclamation of 1763, were also invalidated unless they had been obtained through the governor of Virginia. Those who had already settled on these lands, however, were entitled to make good a claim of 400 acres. This stipulation represented a clear effort to encourage the allegiance of squatters to the Virginia government through the legal process of validating their claims. Squatters were also allowed to claim preemption rights to purchase even greater quantities of land, but not to exceed 1,000 acres. Considerable restrictions were applied, however, in order to specify that these claimants were bona fide settlers who had improved the land, not mere speculators.[40]

Mason originally submitted the two land bills in January, 1778, but opponents delayed the necessary second reading by postponing it to the next legislative

[39] *TJP* 2: 140–141; 148. Boyd suggested that Jefferson was motivated by a preference for small, individual owners at the expense of the speculator but a thorough analysis of Jefferson dealings and involvement with Virginia's land companies contradicting Boyd can be found in Anthony F. C. Wallace, *Jefferson and the Indians: The Tragic Fate of the First Americans* (Cambridge and London: Belknap Press, 1999), 21–49.

[40] *GMP* 1:414–422; and *TJP* 2: 137–138, 155–167.

session. As discussed earlier, some larger issues informed the opposition to the bills, but most immediately, some delegates expressed concern about setting off a potential land rush, where soldiers and militia would leave the ranks to stake anticipatory claims on western lands. Mason responded to these concerns by ushering through a resolution prohibiting any further claims or settlements until after the land office had been opened. While the legislature delayed discussion of the bills, however, George Rogers Clark led a successful military campaign against the British outposts at Kaskaskia and Vincennes that effectively cleared the lands of Kentucky for settlement. By the spring of 1779, more settlers were moving into the Kentucky lands despite the lack of legal standing.[41]

Accordingly, the land bills were brought back up on the floor of the legislature in May 1779 and became law the following month. Mason's bill for settling titles passed through the assembly largely intact, but many of the provisions from the Land-Office bill were stricken or amended. The land office was established and quitrents were abolished, but the proposed rights to claim by headrights, immigration, nativity, and marriage were all were omitted. Only military bounties and treasury rights remained. Additionally, no limitation on the quantity of land purchased through treasury rights was made. The orientation of the laws clearly reflected the legislature's preference to protect the speculative interests of the land companies at the expense of individual settlers. Despite these significant alterations, however, the land acts established allodial ownership as the basis of land rights in the new Commonwealth. After five years of advocacy, Virginians finally accepted Jefferson's challenge to take notice of an error and to bring to an end to the system of tenure, which for five centuries had characterized landholding within the jurisdictions of the English common law.

REMOVING THE DEAD HAND

Correspondent with the efforts to establish allodial land ownership through the land acts, Jefferson worked to achieve similar ends by revising the laws of inheritance. In his draft constitution, he proposed implementing a system of partible inheritance where estates would descend equally to all heirs. In so doing, he desired to apply the principles of allodial ownership to lands that were acquired through inheritance as well as through grant. In addition to conforming to the ancient custom of gavelkind, Jefferson considered the implementation of partible inheritance essential to prevent the accumulation of vast estates that had characterized Europe's aristocracy. His subsequent time in France only confirmed this commitment. In a letter written to James Madison from Paris, Jefferson described the "wretchedness" he observed among the rural laboring classes. He attributed their decrepit condition to the grossly "unequal

[41] *GMP* 1: 422. On George Rogers Clark's Illinois Campaign see, Abernathy, *Western Lands*, 193–204 and Griffin, *American Leviathan*, 142–149.

distribution of property" that characterized the French landscape, where land was concentrated in the hands of a few who often kept large tracts idle merely "for the sake of game" while the masses remained landless. He expressed concern that "this enormous inequality," which was responsible for "so much misery to the bulk of mankind," had threatened to take root in Virginia too, but had been interrupted by the Revolution. He feared, however, that the threat would reemerge unless the practicable and "political measure" of enacting laws of partible inheritance was accomplished.[42]

Yet here, too, Jefferson's constitutional proposal was ignored. In the absence of a constitutional provision creating a scheme of partible inheritance, however, he believed that this political measure could be accomplished by abolishing the laws of primogeniture and entail. Both of these practices tended to consolidate lands by stipulating conditions of descent. Primogeniture – the requirement that an estate descend in its entirety to the oldest male heir – occurred in cases of a freeholder dying intestate. It represented a remnant of the original martial characteristics of feudal tenures where the demands for service needed to be met by someone physically capable. Entail acted as the legal handmaiden to primogeniture and encouraged the consolidation and preservation of estates through the stipulations of a will. It allowed for an individual to devise an estate to an heir for a limited term of life only, and by so doing prohibited the future alienation or disposal of that estate. It thus acted to prevent inheritors from dividing or selling an estate and preserved it "within the family." In legal terminology, such estates were known as being held in fee tail. During the colonial period, entailed land could be "docked" – released by an act of legislature – or by an edict from the county court if the value of the estate was less than 200 pounds sterling, but securing such releases often proved laborious to both heirs and creditors. Despite these bureaucratic frustrations, evidence suggests that the practice was expanding by the eve of the Revolution, stirred in part, perhaps, by the growing uncertainty over land tenures. Jefferson viewed these developments as dangerous and contrary to the general spirit of individual ownership. He characterized entailed lands using the old law-French term, "mortmain," which literally translated as "dead hand," and referred to an ancestor's ability to reach from beyond the grave and continue to exercise

[42] Letter from Jefferson to Madison, October 23, 1785, *TJP* 8: 681–683; also see Jefferson to Charles Bellini, September 30, 1785 reprinted in Merrill Peterson, ed., *The Portable Thomas Jefferson* (New York: Penguin, 1975). The inheritance revisions have attracted considerable commentary and analysis. In addition to most of the Jefferson biographies see, Stanley N. Katz, "Jefferson and the Right of Property," *Journal of Law & Economics*, 19 (1976), 467–488, and "Republicanism and the Law of Inheritance in the American Revolutionary Era," *Michigan Law Review*, 76 (1977) 1–29; Ray C. Keim, "Primogeniture and Entail in Colonial Virginia," *WMQ*, Third Series, (1968), 545–586; Gregory Alexander, "The Dead Hand and the Law of Trusts in the Nineteenth Century," *Stanford Law Review*, 37 (1985): 1189–1266. More recently, a significant contribution qualifying early interpretations has been made by Holly Brewer, "Entailing Aristocracy in Colonial Virginia: 'Ancient Feudal Restraints' and Revolutionary Reform," *WMQ*, Third Series (April 1997), 307–346.

control over an estate. Accordingly, Jefferson proposed that lands held in fee tail be declared by the legislature to be converted into lands in fee simple.[43]

Almost immediately upon the convening of the first legislative session of the Commonwealth, Jefferson sponsored a law that abolished entail in both land and slaves. He returned to the inheritance laws as part of the revision project and composed another bill directing the "course of descents" for an agrarian republic. The most salient feature of this bill was the abolition of primogeniture and the establishment of a system of partible inheritance analogous to gavelkind. As was the case with the allodial designation of the freehold, the implementation of partible inheritance represented an instance of conforming real property laws to those of personal property. In his *Autobiography*, Jefferson remarked on the opposition to his plan made by Edmund Pendleton. Pendleton, seeking greater stability in these necessary transfers of land, proposed adopting the "Hebrew principle," which would award a double allotment to the eldest son and single allotments to the other heirs. Despite the opposition, the bill passed without amendment in October 1785. The question of entail was also revisited at that time and a new statute was passed declaring that, after January 1787, all estates in lands that were granted, conveyed, or devised were considered as lands in fee simple unless otherwise specified. Jefferson considered these changes to inheritance as some of the most important revisions made to the laws of Virginia and showed little tolerance for any dissent from his view. Writing nearly two decades after Pendleton's death, Jefferson still felt compelled to mock the rival proposal that came to naught in favor of his parcenery scheme. St. George Tucker offered a more generous view but noted the exceptional qualities of Jefferson's changes by remarking that the new inheritance laws had "wholly changed the course of descents" and established "principles in direct opposition to those of the common law." He certainly was correct; yet the renovations had been informed by the practices of gavelkind and reflected Jefferson's desire to create new republican legal forms for Virginia premised on ancient custom.[44]

Land was not the only form of property entailed in colonial Virginia. Slaves could be entailed as well. As a moveable form of property, slaves generally were defined as chattels and were governed by the laws of personal property. But the peculiarity of human property and their importance in making colonial lands productive led to instances where slaves were considered in direct relations to assets of real property. Accordingly, in the British colonies were slavery existed, judges and legislators tried to reconcile the common law with slavery by treating slaves, in some instances, as a form of real property. The first example of this practice occurred in Barbados in 1688, where slaves were classified as real property for determining descent in cases of intestacy in order

[43] Brewer, "Entailing Aristocracy." Mortmain traditionally was associated with land held exclusively by the church.

[44] *TJP*, 1: 560–562 and 2: 391–393. See St. George Tucker's extended commentary in *TB*, 3: Appendix B, 12.

that widows and children would not be left without a labor force for their land. Virginia adopted a similar statute to address similar difficulties in 1705. Historian Thomas Morris has noted that, after the 1705 statute, "slaves were treated as chattels personal for some purposes and as real estate for others." Confusion reigned, however, as a result of this arrangement. In 1727, the Burgesses attempted to remedy some of this confusion by allowing slaves to be annexed to entailed lands. Still, the 1727 statue enabled creditors to force the sale of slaves in extreme situations of debt, and this ability fostered numerous instances of litigation during the eighteenth century. By 1748, the Burgesses had had enough and passed three acts that repealed the statues of 1705 and 1727 and declared slaves to be chattels personal once again. This effort to provide legal clarity failed, however, when the Crown refused to assent to this new definition. With the commencement of the Revolution, the legislature moved quickly to achieve what the Crown had heretofore denied, and Jefferson's 1776 law transforming estates held in fee tail into fee simple applied to slaves as well as lands. In 1792, an additional statute deemed slaves to be considered as personal estate, although some restriction remained on executors and administrators selling them. Jefferson praised these reforms and commented that the law making "slaves distributable" in the same manner as other forms of moveable property was among the most important revisions made during the republican reforms as well.[45]

A further indication of the postcolonial effort to bring slaves, and thus all forms of property, under an umbrella of allodial ownership was reflected in the 1782 Manumission Act. Prior to the Revolution, Virginia's slaveholders could only manumit slaves with the approval of the Burgesses. The 1782 Manumission act authorized the private emancipation of slaves and thus confirmed the absolute ownership rights of masters. This law sometimes has been used to demonstrate the presence of an "antislavery sentiment" in the wake of the American Revolution, and it did indeed expedite the process of emancipation, but it must be considered as a fundamental part of constituting an allodial property regime as well. Accordingly, the sanctification of the private right to manumit principally confirmed the absolute authority of the master over the slave and, in this manner, mirrored the new authority of the republican freeholder over his land.[46]

The climax of the allodial revolution came, however, in January 1786, with the resolution of the decade-long debate over the disestablishment of the church. The establishment issue proved to be the most contentious one in the construction of the Commonwealth. Thomas Buckley, the leading historian

[45] *SAL*, 3: 333; *TB*, 3: Appendix E: *Summary View of Laws Concerning Slaves as Property in Virginia*; Thomas D. Morris, *Southern Slavery and the Law, 1619–1860* (Chapel Hill: University of North Carolina Press, 1996), 66–71, 82–83; *SAL 1792–1806*, 1: 128; and Jefferson *Notes on the State of Virginia*, 131.

[46] *SAL*, 11: 39–41. On post-revolutionary emancipation, see Eva Sheppard Wolf, *Race and Liberty in the New Nation: Emancipation in Virginia from the Revolution to Nat Turner's Rebellion* (Baton Rouge: Louisiana State University Press, 2006).

of the debate, noted that this one issue trumped any other categorization of parties or factions that existed at the time. Furthermore, he demonstrated that members of the "Church party" – those in favor of maintaining an established church – spoke overwhelmingly in favor of religious toleration. The religious practice of dissenters was never at issue following the Revolution. Rather, the debate that emerged concerned the manner of distinguishing between toleration and religious freedom. Questions directed at resolving the issues of assessment and property holding were political, not theological, in orientation. James Madison's amendment to Virginia's Declaration of Rights, in which he substituted the phrase "free exercise of religion" for the word "toleration," established the parameters of a debate that lasted for more than a quarter-century. Jefferson's initial foray into this foundational debate occurred while serving on the Committee on Religion in November 1776, when he drafted resolutions for disestablishment and for exempting dissenters from paying tithes. These initial efforts crystallized into his "Bill for Establishing Religious Freedom," which was drafted in 1777 as part of the general plan of revision but was not adopted until 1786. The debate ebbed and flowed throughout the decade and culminated over the issue of whether or not the legislature should impose a general assessment that would establish a provision "for the Teachers of the Christian Religion." Despite some significant support for the measure, the eventual settlement rejected this idea as well and left all the churches to their own devices.[47]

The process of separating the church from the state represented the consummate phase in the process of constructing a liberal republican government. Rhys Isaac has suggested that Jefferson's Bill for Establishing Religious Freedom "did not stand alone" but was a component of the larger law reforms incumbent in the Report of the Committee of Revisors. Isaac focused on Jefferson's proposed educational reforms and demonstrated that his call for public education reflected an overarching desire to replace Virginia's colonial Anglican Christian establishment with a new "secular republican" one. Jefferson anticipated the argument for a general assessment to provide for religious education and countered it with his elaborate Bill for the More General Diffusion of Knowledge. Returning to his Saxon nostalgia, he called for the division of counties into smaller geographical units that the Saxons had called hundreds. The people of each hundred would be responsible for the construction and maintenance of a grammar school that would serve as the foundation of Jefferson's public education system. Hundreds were to be administered by select freeholders who would

[47] Thomas E. Buckley, *Church and State in Revolutionary Virginia, 1776–1787* (Charlottesville: University Press of Virginia, 1977); Rhys Isaac, *The Transformation of Virginia, 1740–1790* (Chapel Hill: University of North Carolina Press, 1982), 273–295; Merrill D. Peterson and Robert C. Vaughan, eds., *The Virginia Statute for Religious Freedom: Its Evolution and Consequences in American History* (New York: Cambridge University Press, 1988); H. J. Eckenrode, *Separation of Church and State in Virginia: A Study in the Development of the Revolution* (Richmond, 1910); Boyd, *TJ*, 1: 525–558.

hold office as aldermen and be tasked with providing a secular and enlightened education for the people of that hundred. It was to be a competitive system, with only the brightest students advancing to higher levels of education. Once again, however, his vision was frustrated and his plan for public education was set aside as inexpedient. Education in postcolonial Virginia, like religion, would be left to private interest. Although Jefferson lamented the failure of his plan, he preferred that education retain the sporadic qualities incumbent in a system dependent on private expense rather than for it to come under the nefarious domain of religious denominations.[48]

For Jefferson, disestablishment also represented an opportunity to purge the common law of the dangerous myth that it had been informed by Christianity. Writing in his commonplace book, Jefferson opined at length on the genealogy of the fiction and traced its origins to the earliest writing of English legal history. He lamented that the "alliance between Church and State in England" had perpetually made its "judges accomplices in the frauds of the clergy." Most egregiously, this alliance incorporated "the whole bible and testament" into the common law and, as a result, saddled the "English code" with "laws made for Jews alone," whereas correspondingly, "the precepts of the gospel, intended by their benevolent author as obligatory only *in foro conscientae*," were instead armed with the coercive power "of Municipal law." Jefferson attributed the original mistake to an instance of a poor translation from law-French, but he directed considerable ire at Matthew Hale for making a subsequent, unsubstantiated claim that Christianity was "parcel of the laws of England." Not surprisingly, Jefferson instead identified the circumstances of the Saxon "settlement in England" as the source of the common law, which he explained had occurred a full two centuries prior the introduction of Christianity on the island.[49]

Jefferson's crusade for establishing religious freedom was thus inseparable from his larger project to purify the common law through allodial reforms. Disestablishment wrested the traditional power of governing morality and spirituality away from the church. Admittedly, the institutional relationship between church and state in colonial Virginia existed in considerably more nuanced and ambiguous ways than it did in England. An ecclesiastical court system had never fully developed in the colony. Nor did the colony have a bishop invested as the constitutional representative of the established church in Virginia. Nonetheless, the colonial parish vestries exercised significant authority over matters of local government. They appointed, provided for, and maintained the parish rector, controlled church property (including the wealth-producing glebe lands), raised taxes for local improvement projects and the maintenance of the community poor, and policed the behavior of the parishioners. Disestablishment brought an abrupt end to the governing authority of the

[48] *TJP*, 2: 526–535, "A Bill for the More General Diffusion of Knowledge." See discussion in Notes, 146–149.

[49] Gilbert Chinard, ed., *The Commonplace Book of Thomas Jefferson*, 351–356, 359–363.

vestries and transferred each of these duties, except the selection of ministers, to the secular institutions of local government. Even more significantly, the Statute for Religious Freedom, by defining religion as a matter of conscience alone, transformed spiritual belief from a community activity into a form of private ownership as well. As had been the case in abolishing tenures, primogeniture, and entail, Jefferson considered the statute as a fundamental measure in the destroying the "dead hand" that had corrupted the purity of the ancient Saxon constitution.[50]

THE BOUNDS OF OWNERSHIP

The legal renovations enacted to give definition to Virginia's republican form of government revealed an effort to construct individual liberty exclusively on the basis of an economic independence achieved through the private ownership of land. This essential conflation of liberty with ownership wrought important consequences. Ownership became the foremost – in many cases the only – status for claiming a legitimate right. Unlike the multiplicity of status rights incumbent in the doctrine of tenures, the allodial revolution reduced property rights to the primacy of ownership. Indeed, in its aftermath, rights themselves came to be characterized as something owned by individuals. James Madison summarized this fundamental transformation when he explained that not only did man have a right to his property, but "he may be equally said to have a property in his rights." For Madison, "conscience [represented] the most sacred of all property," but within the Virginia Commonwealth, land remained politically privileged. Yet, the allodial revolution had unleashed a paradigm that emphasized the economic qualities of individual ownership and, increasingly, it fostered the tendency to consider land ownership as a particular right existing within an array of rights. This tendency conflated real property with other forms of property and eroded the traditional basis for considering land law as a separate branch of jurisprudence. The resulting contradictions between the political and economic considerations of ownership ultimately led to the undoing of the freeholder ideal as a viable source for political organization – and, correspondingly, subverted the foundational principles of the agrarian republic.[51]

[50] On the historical influence of the vestries, see Philip Alexander Bruce, *An Institutional History of Virginia in the Seventeenth Century*, 2 volumes (New York: G. P. Putnam and Sons, 1910): 1: 55–93. For the persistence of their authority in the late colonial period, see George Wythe's argument in the 1771 case of *Godwin v. Lunan* (1771), Jefferson 96; as well as Buckley, *Church and State*, 10–11; Isaacs, *Transformation*, 143–157; and John Gilman Kolp, *Gentlemen and Freeholders: Electoral Politics in Colonial Virginia* (Baltimore: Johns Hopkins University Press, 1998), 84–108.

[51] James Madison, *The National Gazette*, March 29, 1792. For discussion of this important essay, see Michael Kammen, "The Rights of Property, and the Property in Rights: The Problematic Nature of 'Property' in the Political Thought of the Founders and the Early Republic," in Ellen Frankel Paul and Howard Dickman, eds., *Liberty, Property, and the Foundations of the American Constitution* (Albany: SUNY Press, 1989). See as well Jennifer Nedelsky, *Private*

The litigious consequences arising from the 1779 Land Acts bear testimony to these contradictions. Despite Jefferson and Mason's expressed desire to protect the claims of squatters, the land companies ultimately benefited more from the settlement of the land question. Mason had attempted to vanquish the adversarial claims of the land companies, especially those with limited Virginia connections, but their claims remained a particular point of contention. Indeed, the organization of Virginia's land office simply caused a number of the land company representatives to redirect their petitions to the Confederation Congress and appeal for settlement from that body. Their cause was taken up by Thomas Paine, whose 1780 essay, *Public Good*, appeared as a detailed rebuttal to Virginia's charter right claims and advocated the organization of Kentucky as a new, independent state. Peter Onuf has detailed the significance of the subsequent negotiations between Virginia and the Congress over the cession of the former's charter claims to the lands north of the Ohio River. Onuf noted that Virginia was more than willing to cede these lands, but only on its own terms. These terms included recognition of the northwestern lands as part of Virginia's charter rights and a claim to military bounty lands on the northern bank. Virginia ceded the northwestern lands in 1784, but the problems of adversarial claims in the lands of Kentucky and western Virginia persisted well into the nineteenth century.[52]

Many of these adversarial claims sought resolution in the courts. In the wake of the Land Acts, some of Virginia's oldest land companies actively pursued litigation to validate their prior claims. The tenth section of the Land Title Act had prescribed that adversarial claims were to be brought before and determined by the Supreme Court of Appeals. In December 1779, Edmund Pendleton drafted a petition for the Loyal Company (of which he was a member) as well as the Greenbrier Company requesting that that court confirm the grants initially made by the Executive Council to those companies in 1749 and 1751, respectively. He revived the companies' argument from the colonial regime, contending that the French and Indian war and subsequent British policies had prevented them from completing all of the necessary surveys to perfect their titles. He also noted that some surveys had been conducted as late as 1774, at which time the governor and council had acted as if the initial grants remained in force

Property and the Limits of American Constitutionalism: The Madisonian Framework and Its Legacy (Chicago: University of Chicago Press, 1990) and Lance Banning, *The Sacred Fire of Liberty: James Madison and the Founding of the Federal Republic* (Ithaca, NY: Cornell University Press, 1995).

52 Thomas Paine, "Public Good: Being an Examination into the Claim of Virginia to the Vacant Territory, and the Right of the United States to the Same: to Which is Added Proposals for Laying off a New State, to be Applied as a Fund for Carrying on the War, or Redeeming the National Debt," reprinted in Moncure Daniel Conway, ed., *The Writings of Thomas Paine* (New York: G. P. Putnam's Sons, 1906), 2: 31–66. Peter Onuf, "Toward Federalism: Virginia, Congress, and the Western Lands," *WMQ*, Third series (1977) 34: 353–374 (and book). See, as well, Abernathy, *Western Lands*, 242–361; Clarence W. Alvord, "Virginia and the West" reprinted in David Curtis Skaggs, ed., *The Old Northwest in the American Revolution: An Anthology* (Madison: The State Historical Society of Wisconsin, 1977): 56–74.

by authorizing these surveys in anticipation of a favorable resolution from the colonial secretary. The Court of Appeals entertained the case immediately, but it did not issue a ruling until May 1783. Pendleton's protégé, John Taylor of Caroline, presented the argument on behalf of the Loyal and Greenbrier companies. He reiterated many of the points made in Pendleton's petition and contended that the companies' claims had never been forfeited, because "sufficient excuses were offered for all the delays." But Taylor also invoked specific sections of the Land Title Act to support the claims of the companies. He argued that the statute clearly intended to extend to any claimants – be they land companies or squatters – a spirit of preemption, which was based on the equitable rule of mortgages. Furthermore, he noted that the seventh section of the law explicitly referred to squatters who had purchased their claims from land companies and declared that these settlers "should have their titles confirmed, by the companies, upon payment of the original price with interest."[53]

Attorney General Edmund Randolph represented the Commonwealth in the case and rejected the arguments of the petitioners. He emphasized that because the original conditions of the grants had not been complied with, they had expired, and thus the companies' claims "could not be sustained." He explained that the original intention of the grant had been to effect the "speedy settlement" of the backcountry. The companies had failed to accomplish this fundamental responsibility. Indeed, Randolph challenged the core argument that the companies did not have sufficient time to conduct the surveys by noting that, in the instance of the Loyal Company, the specified allowance of four years had already elapsed by the time of the outbreak of the Indian war. He also rejected the petitioners' reading of the seventh section of the Land Act, suggesting instead that the reference to land companies in the section applied only to those companies who had already "fulfilled the conditions" of their grant and merely awaited the necessary forms "to complete the title." Randolph noted that such was not the case with the Loyal and Greenbrier companies, which he charged had been guilty of "the grossest negligence" and were now merely experiencing the consequences of it. Despite the vigor of Randolph's arguments, the Court of Appeals, presided over by Edmund Pendleton, ruled in favor of the companies and confirmed all of the surveys made by the Loyal and Greenbrier companies prior to the Revolution.[54]

The Court's ruling illuminated the practical difficulties of implementing an allodial scheme of individual land owning in the complex and confusing terrain of the western lands. Despite Jefferson's and Mason's preferences to deed the lands to squatters on the basis of preemption, the new land law forced a determination of ownership to all lands and, accordingly, opened the door to

[53] *The Case of the Loyal and Greenbrier Companies*, 4 Call 21 (1783). John Taylor was the nephew of Edmund Pendleton. Pendleton raised Taylor following the death of his father when Taylor was only three, and supervised his legal education at William & Mary and in his law office.

[54] 4 Call 21 (1783). For Pendleton's role in the case, see Robert Leroy Hilldrup, *The Life and Times of Edmund Pendleton* (Chapel Hill: University of North Carolina Press, 1939), 241–243.

adversarial claims. The status of squatters remained ambiguous unless they had evidence of purchase. And despite prior legislative efforts to extinguish the claims of the colonial land companies, the state found itself with no claim of its own ownership to ensure the execution of its policy. Instead, it could only adjudicate rival claims of ownership. The ruling in favor of the land companies opened the door for future litigation as well – with the Supreme Court issuing seven further rulings pertaining to Loyal Company lands over the course of the next decade in addition to a considerable number of cases decided in the lower courts. Only in 1834, in determining the case of *French v. Successors of Loyal Company*, did the Supreme Court prohibit the company from collecting any further revenues on the basis of the questionable colonial surveys.[55]

The particular case of James Maze illustrated the torturous process of determining ownership and the significant ramifications that the ruling in favor of the Loyal and Greenbrier claims had on settlers not affiliated with the companies. In 1764, Maze constructed a log cabin on land along the Greenbrier River, which he used for a while as a hunting cabin before placing a tenant on the land. In 1773, correspondent with the Greenbrier Company commissioning their previous grant lands to be surveyed, William and Andrew Hamilton made a claim of 1,100 acres, which included the land on which Maze's cabin was located. The Hamilton brothers evicted Maze's tenant by force, and the following year, Samuel Lewis, the surveyor for the company, made a survey of the 1,100 acres but acknowledged the adversarial claim and did not assign the grant to either party. Following the passage of the Land Acts, Maze claimed a right of settlement to 400 acres, which included his cabin, and a right of preemption to another, adjoining 1,000 acres. Section eight of the Land Title Act had established four-men commissions for the various western districts to immediately adjudicate and resolve rival claims, and in January 1780, the claims of Maze and Hamilton were brought before the commission. Owing in part to inclement weather, however, Maze was unable to attend the session, and the commissioners ruled in favor of Hamilton. Maze filed a caveat with the General Court, and in October 1782, that court reversed the decision of the commissioners and awarded ownership rights to Maze's claims based on settlement and preemption. The Hamilton brothers appealed on a writ of error, but the Court of Appeals quashed that writ and ruled that it had been issued on erroneous grounds.[56]

After that, the case really became complicated. Following the ruling of the General Court, Andrew Hamilton obtained the plat for the 1,100 acres surveyed by Samuel Lewis on the pretense that Hamilton was to purchase a grant to the land from the Greenbrier Company and register it with the land office. And in May 1783, the Court of Appeals issued its ruling recognizing the claims

[55] See especially *Hite v. Fairfax*, 4 Call 42 (1786); *Maze v. Hamilton*, 2 Wythe 51 (1789); *Burnsides v. Reid*, 2 Wash. 43 (1794); *Ross v. Keewood*, 2 Murf. 141 (1811). *French v. Successors of Loyal Company*, 5 Leigh 627 (1834).

[56] The original General Court case and the Court of Appeals ruling is cited as *Maze v. Hamilton*, 4 Call 33 (1782).

of the Loyal and Greenbrier companies. When Maze discovered Hamilton's intention, he filed a bill in the High Court of Chancery alleging that Hamilton was committing fraud. During the Chancery hearing, Hamilton asserted that John Maze and Thomas Spencer had claimed that they had purchased a "good will right" to the land from James Maze after he had abandoned the property and that one John Tacket also claimed a right to the land by moiety. Hamilton explained that he had purchased all these rights "for the sake of peace" and "to quiet all claims." His evidence failed to convince the Chancellor, George Wythe, that his claim of ownership through either survey or purchase should overturn the decree of the General Court in favor of Maze. Wythe determined that Hamilton's efforts "to frustrate and elude" the judgment of the court constituted fraud and ordered him to convey the patent for 1,100 acres to Maze as compensation for these actions. In delivering the opinion, Wythe argued that the immediate rights of settlement and preemption trumped the more abstract claims to possession through grant, which were advanced by the Greenbrier Company. The Greenbrier Company was entitled to survey and settle the lands according to its 1751 grant, except for those lands, like that of James Maze, that had been settled and improved through preoccupancy, as well as any additional lands claimed by the preemption provisions of the Land Acts.[57]

Hamilton made a final appeal of Wythe's ruling to the Court of Appeals. The court entertained the appeal in June 1791, with Edmund Pendleton once again presiding. John Taylor argued the appeal on behalf of Hamilton and explained that when the initial case was heard, all the facts were not before the General Court. Specifically, he noted that the Greenbrier Company's claim to the land "was not cognizable" at that time. John Marshall represented Maze and explained that the subsequent ruling on the land companies claims was irrelevant to this particular case: Whether the land belonged to the Commonwealth or to the Company did not matter because his claim was based on prior settlement and on a fair judicial decision, which was "anterior to" the judgment in favor of the land companies. In delivering the opinion for the court, Pendleton dismissed Marshall's arguments and contended that Maze "could not oppose the company" and, indeed, "must claim under them" because his settlement occurred thirteen years after the initial grant had been made to the company in 1751. Pendleton overturned the ruling of the Chancery Court, legitimated Hamilton's claim to the 1,100 acres, and ordered Maze to pay back the costs of the Chancery proceedings. He allowed Maze to retain the cabin and permitted him to mark off 400 acres out of the Hamilton claim. Pendleton denied Maze's adjacent claim, however, to 1,000 acres by right of preemption. He acknowledged that, by the terms of the 1779 Land Acts, a right to preemption existed in this case, but he stipulated that Maze would have to find 1,000 acres for which no prior claims from the land company existed.[58]

[57] *Maze v. Hamilton*, Wythe 51 (1789).

[58] *Hamilton v. Maze*, 4 Call 196 (1791). This case was the first of a number of cases where Pendleton reversed the prior ruling of George Wythe, causing the two to develop (or redeveloped) an openly antagonistic relationship. See David Mays, *Edmund Pendleton: A Biography*, 2: 290–302.

Questions of ownership surrounded property formerly held by the established church as well. The guarantee of freedom of conscience articulated in Virginia's Declaration of Rights, and the subsequent process of disestablishment culminating in the Statute for Religious Freedom, ushered in a mass exodus of congregants away from the established church and created immediate confusion over church property rights. New denominations – most especially the Baptist and the Presbyterians – raised questions about who was entitled to access and use the church buildings, which had been constructed by a tax imposed on all Virginia households. A law passed in the first months after independence exempting dissenters from the further payment of taxes also affirmed the property rights of the established church. By the end of the war, however, many of these churches had been abandoned by the congregants who affiliated themselves instead with one of the new denominations or, as was more often the case, simply disclaimed membership with any church. In some cases, Baptist and Methodists congregations simply took possession of the abandon churches and used for their own services. In other case, local ministers considered the churches as public property and simply arranged to share the church building for worship.[59]

The most prominent and protracted conflict over church property, however, concerned the disposition of the glebe lands. In 1661, as part of a general statute organizing the established church in Virginia, the Burgesses directed that glebe lands "be laid out" for every parish. Glebes were designed to serve as agricultural lands to produce food for the provision of the parish poor as well as to supplement the income and provide habitation of the parish minister. A subsequent statute, in 1727, stipulated that glebes should be no less than 200 acres and charged the parish vestries with levying a tax on the "titheable persons" to purchase and maintain glebe lands and buildings. In the wake of disestablishment, the disposition of these properties became the subject of a heated political debate that probed the essential meaning of the separation of church and state. Episcopalians asserted that they represented the remnants of the established church and argued that they therefore retained a private property right in the glebes, which had been vested in the colonial vestries. Rival denominations, led by the Baptist General Committee, dissented and contended that when disestablishment occurred, all church property rights dissolved and reverted to the people of the state, who had been the original donors of the property. They were supported in their argument by the fact the legislature had instructed vestries to sell the glebe lands in abandoned parishes since 1776. This procedure was formalized in 1802 when the legislature passed a statute

[59] Buckley, *Church and State*; H. J. Eckenrode, *Separation of Church and State in Virginia: A Study in the Development of the Revolution* (Richmond: Virginia State Library, 1910). The 1776 statute is found in *SAL*, 9: 164–167. For examples of rival denominations seizing church property, see George Carrington Moses, "The Colonial Churches of Surrey and Sussex County, Virginia," *WMQ* (1940): 285–305, and "The Colonial Churches of Nansemond County, Virginia," *WMQ* (1941): 37–54.

providing for the sale of all glebe lands that did not have an incumbent minister. The law dictated that the proceeds of the sales were to be distributed to the local Overseers of the Poor for the care of community widows, orphans, and destitute. The constitutionality of the statute was challenged by the Manchester vestry the following year in the case of *Turpin v. Locket*, but a split Court of Appeals upheld the lower-court's ruling in favor of the statute. The resumption of all the glebes thus was carried out over the next decades as the ministers died or removed. In disposing of the glebe lands, the state abolished any of the remaining powers of local government that traditionally had been exercised by the parish vestries. Of equal significance, the state asserted a claim to real property in the Commonwealth by establishing its authority to vest and divest claims through legislation and the adjudication of property rights.[60]

Beyond these difficult and controversial juridical determinations of ownership, other factors arising from the nature of allodial ownership undermined the agrarian ideal as well. Most significantly, freeholders once possessed of absolute control over their land proved unable to retain it. Personal debt proliferated and, correspondingly, mortgages and liens on estates grew more abundant. Admittedly, debt had created social problems in Virginia before. T. H. Breen has argued compellingly that the personal indebtedness of Tidewater planters during the late colonial period fueled the movement toward independence. The allodial revolution, however, democratized the problem of debt. Access to land gave individuals access to credit as well. And more often than not, credit was needed to purchase the tools, seeds, and labor to make the land productive. Furthermore, the new inheritance laws limited traditional forms of protecting real property rights of heirs against creditors, exacerbating the legal problems caused by personal debt. Freeholders encountered claims against their land from the Commonwealth too, when they failed to pay their taxes. As early as 1781, the legislature established a process by which the Commonwealth could distrain lands for the nonpayment of taxes. The process apparently raised more problems than it answered, because legislators continued to grapple with the issues of land registration and delinquency, passing more than twenty-five pieces of legislation on the subject during the next four decades. By the 1820s, the problem of indebtedness and the corresponding abandonment of property reached such a magnitude in the western lands that the legislature passed a series of Delinquent Land Acts to provide for a swifter process in disposing estates in default.[61]

[60] Buckley, "Evangelicals Triumphant" discusses the battle over the glebes in great detail. The legislative history of the glebes is presented in Tucker's, "Summary View of the Laws Relative to Glebes and Churches," in *TB*, 2: Appendix, Note M, 104–118, and his opinion in *Turpin v. Locket*, 6 Call 113 (1804). Buckley has tracked subsequent questions of Church property and the prohibition on denominational ownership into the nineteenth century in "After Disestablishment: Thomas Jefferson's Wall of Separation in Antebellum Virginia," *Journal of Southern History* (1995): 445–480.

[61] On the problem of debt in Jeffersonian Virginia, see Herbert Sloan, *Principle & Interest: Thomas Jefferson and the Problem of Debt* (Charlottesville: University Press of Virginia, 1995), and

Faced with an inability to meet the demands of creditors or the Commonwealth, many freeholders simply abandoned their lands. Vacated and forfeited lands fostered the practices of speculation and absentee ownership. Speculators with cash at hand could purchase forfeited lands cheaply through a sheriff's sale and seek short-term tenants as a means of quick revenue. Leasing became particularly common in the transmontane lands of western Virginia where many of the land owners were not even Virginians. Absentee ownership effectively divorced the relations of dominion, possession, and use that the transformation of the freehold into an allodial entity had idealistically attempted to achieve. Far from attaching an individual to a particular community, absentee land owning encouraged the perpetuation of a transient tenant class as well as the exploitation and neglect of the land on behalf of the absentee owner. Tenants who possessed and used the land, despite cultivating Jefferson's "germ of virtue," were not freeholders and thus were alienated from the body politic.[62]

THE ORIGINS OF REFORM

The social problems caused by the unintended consequences of the allodial vision appeared frequently in the literature of the postcolonial period. Less familiar today than Jefferson's profession of an agrarian utopia was the then-popular rebuttal depicting the agrarian reality, which was written by William Wirt. Born in Maryland, Wirt was adopted by the Virginia bar as a young man and became close friends with both Jefferson and St. George Tucker in the course of his influential career. In 1803, correspondent with the Louisiana Purchase, Wirt contributed a series of insightful essays under the guise of "a British Spy" that poked fun at the ubiquitous democratic rhetoric of the agrarian republic. His essays, written just two decades following independence, illuminated the sharp disparity between the ideals and the reality of Virginia's Commonwealth.[63]

Breen, *Tobacco Culture*, esp. 160–210. The legislative history of forfeited and escheated lands in detailed in Benjamin Watkins Leigh, et al., eds., *The Revised Code of the Laws of Virginia* (Richmond, 1819) 2: 484–561 with subsequent legislation printed in Shepherd's *Supplement to the Revised Code of the Laws of Virginia* (Richmond, 1833), 337–367.

[62] Barbara Rasmussen, *Absentee Landowning and Exploitation in West Virginia, 1760–1920* (Lexington: University Press of Kentucky, 1994). A number of historians have detailed some of the external forces that worked against this particular strand of republican ideology as well. Most notably, Drew McCoy has described how the disruption of Atlantic trade during the Napoleonic wars forced a reassessment of many of the economic assumptions that underlay the agrarian vision and ultimately encouraged the development of domestic manufactures for an emergent home market.

[63] William Wirt, *The Letters of the British Spy*, edited with an introduction by Richard Beale Davis (Chapel Hill: University of North Carolina Press, 1970). Wirt's essays were published originally in 1803. The Davis edition, from which all the citations here are drawn, is copied from an 1832 republication.

"The British spy" wryly noted that although Virginia's republicans often boasted of their equal liberties, they had far less to say "on the subject of equal property." Indeed, he believed it quite possible that there was no country where property was "more unequally distributed" than in Virginia. Upon touring various points along the lower Potomac, he had been struck by the contrast between the occasional "stately aristocratic palace" and, all around the surrounding countryside, "the smoky huts and log cabins of poor, laborious tenants." Even more disconcerting than these material conditions, however, were the patterns of behavior that resulted from them. He depicted the ridiculous spectacle of these tenants who regularly approached "*the great house*, cap in hand, with all the fearful, trembling submission of the lowest feudal vassals" but who, when they returned to their own, modest log-homes, boasted "with obstreperous exultation" that they lived as freemen in "a land of equal liberty and equal rights." To be sure, Wirt's comments, made from the posture of a British informant, were intended to be facetious. His observations rang true, however; despite the abolition of tenures and their inherent social hierarchy, the inequality incumbent in allodial ownership inevitably created its own "species of social rank" and introduced "a style of living and of conversation" beyond the means of many.[64]

Wirt also recognized that individual ownership failed to infuse freeholders with a sufficient interest in the community. Whether one referred to that interest in terms of virtue, patriotism, or public spirit, Wirt found Virginia sorely deficient. He decried that the state exhibited "no great public improvements...her roads and highways [were] frequently impassable" and the "very few public works" that were undertaken were "permitted to languish" for want of public spirit. He lamented that the only driving force throughout the countryside was the desire "*to grow rich*" – a passion that not only infected "private life" but had "poisoned every public body in the state" as well. Despite steady advancements in population and wealth, the spy confidently asserted that the Commonwealth lacked "the animating soul of a republic."[65]

John Taylor of Caroline joined Wirt in lamenting the "miserable" condition of Virginia's agrarian classes. Taylor, typically, has been associated politically with the "Quids," or "Old Republicans," a vanguard of conservative statesmen led by the likes of John Randolph, Littleton Waller Tazewell, and Phillip Pendleton Barbour. During the early decades of the nineteenth century, these Quids articulated a zealous defense of staunch republican principles in the context of national debates over the expanding powers of the federal government, particularly around the issues of the national bank and the federal tariff. Their position has been cast as essentially conservative, or even reactionary, and, correspondingly, Taylor's commitment to the agrarian economy has often

[64] Wirt, *British Spy*, 101–102. Wirt's characterization is echoed in the scholarly findings of Jackson Turner Main, "The Distribution of Property in Post-Revolutionary Virginia," *Mississippi Valley Historical Review*, 41 (1954): 241–258.

[65] Wirt, *British Spy*, 191–194.

been considered in the same light. But he was, foremost, a reformer. Although he criticized the federal government's trend toward policies that unevenly supported the manufacturing and commercial classes, his fundamental concern was directed at improving agricultural productivity in order to make that sector competitive with its urban rivals. His writings were steeped in the reform principles advocated by the English Board of Agriculture – the principal agent of the enclosure movement in Great Britain. Indeed, his evidence for depicting the degraded condition of agriculture in Virginia was drawn primarily from an essay composed by William Strickland, an English agricultural reformer. In 1795, Strickland, at the behest of the Board of Agriculture, traveled to New England and the Mid-Atlantic states to assess the current state of American farming and to prepare a report similar to the contemporary reports commissioned on many English counties for the purposes of justifying agricultural reforms.[66]

Noticeably absent from Taylor's agrarian writings, in this respect, were the Jeffersonian paeans to virtuous and industrious farmers. Instead, his *Arator* essays were premised on the belief that significant agricultural reforms were needed to restore both the economic and political primacy of agriculture. Improved husbandry, enclosure, manuring, draining, crop rotation, and diversification all were presented as necessary practices for enhancing agricultural production and creating more wealth. Still, Taylor did not hold the individual freeholders exclusively responsible for the "miserable" condition of agriculture in the Old Dominion. He attributed blame to the "baleful" influence of laws as well. Echoing the initial concerns of Edmund Pendleton, Taylor inferred that the allodial revolution had removed agricultural control from the authority of government and left its practice solely in the hands of the individual freeholders. And these allodial land owners had proven themselves incompetent to compete in an economy legally biased toward industry. Agricultural policies were needed. He called for "legislative cooperation with individual industry," which would facilitate agricultural reforms, and for the creation of agricultural societies, which would focus on electing legislators with "a genuine agricultural interest." Only by grasping political power could agrarians abrogate current policy, "which is the ruin of agricultural prosperity." His suggestion that

[66] Taylor's biographers include: Robert E. Shalhope, *John Taylor of Caroline: Pastoral Republican* (Columbia: University of South Carolina Press, 1980); Eugene T. Mudge, *The Social Philosophy of John Taylor of Caroline: A Study of Jeffersonian Democracy* (New York: Columbia University Press, 1939); Garret Ward Sheldon and C. Williams Hill, Jr., *The Liberal Republicanism of John Taylor of Caroline* (Teaneck, NJ: Farleigh Dickinson University Press, 2008). On the "Old Republicans," see Norman K. Risjord, *The Old Republicans: Southern Conservatism in the Age of Jefferson* (New York: Columbia University Press, 1965). Strickland's trip and report is detailed in G. Melvin Herndon, "Agriculture in America: An Englishmen's View," *Agricultural History*, 49 (1975): 505–516. The classic statement of Taylor as an agricultural reformer remains Avery Craven, *Soil Exhaustion as a Factor in the Agricultural History of Virginia and Maryland, 1606–1860*, reprinted with a new introduction by Louis A. Ferleger (Columbia: University of South Carolina Press, 2006).

laws and policies determined the distribution of wealth represented a clear inversion of classical Whig dictum that government should correspond to property. To reinvigorate agriculture, Taylor called on government to ensure its preservation.[67]

Taylor was not alone in criticizing the agriculture practices of the agrarian republic. In 1816, another series of letters appeared, similar to Wirt's, satirizing the customs and habits of the Commonwealth. These *Letters from Virginia, Translated from the French* were published anonymously but generally are attributed to George Tucker. Tucker, a nephew of St. George Tucker, had emigrated from Bermuda, studied law at William & Mary, and eventually became antebellum Virginia's leading political economist while serving as professor of Moral Philosophy at the University of Virginia. He wrote extensively, including the first full-length biography of Thomas Jefferson, and in most of these writings provided the most thorough critique of the agrarian republican ideals. At first, however, Tucker struggled as a lawyer. By 1807, he had abandoned his Richmond practice and taken a position serving as commissioner of bankruptcy. The position exposed him to an array of social problems caused by the ubiquity of indebtedness in Jeffersonian Virginia. Tucker did not need the office to become familiar with the problem, however, given that his personal life was affected by persistent indebtedness as well.[68]

In 1824, Tucker published *The Valley of Shenandoah*, what might appropriately be called the first plantation novel. The social consequences of ownership and debt provided the narrative tension for the story. Tucker explained that he wrote the novel to offer "a faithful picture of the manners and habits which lately prevailed in one of the most distinguished states of our confederacy." Richard Beale Davis, in his survey of intellectual life in Jeffersonian Virginia, described the book as "a conscious attempt to portray real Virginia life in fiction," and noted that other critics have praised Tucker's capacity "to portray characters from all levels of Shenandoah society," and not simply the planter class. The plot is set, however, around the misfortunes of the Graysons – a prominent Tidewater planter family that, upon the death of the patriarch Colonel Grayson, were forced to move their residence to their summer plantation in the Valley because of debts incurred against the estate. Tucker narrates the story largely through the experiences of Edward Grayson, the young heir. Edward was soon to complete his degree at William & Mary and embark on a promising legal career that would enable the family to escape from its situation. He arrives home for the summer recess with his New York schoolmate, James Gildon, who quickly becomes romantically involved with Edward's

[67] John Taylor, *Arator: Being a Series of Agricultural Essays, Practical and Political; in Sixty-Four Numbers*, edited and introduction by M. E. Bradford (Indianapolis, IN: Liberty Fund, 1977), 53–57.

[68] Robert C. McLean, *George Tucker: Moral Philosopher and Man of Letters* (Chapel Hill: University of North Carolina Press, 1961); Tipton Snavely, *George Tucker as Political Economist* (Charlottesville: University Press of Virginia, 1964).

younger sister, Louisa. The ill-advised romance was conducted poorly from the start, affording Tucker the opportunity to provide an "instructive moral to the youth of both sexes." In many respects, however, the romantic relationship remains tangential at best to Tucker's primary commentary on the manners and customs of Virginia's republican society. Yet his "faithful picture" of Virginia's agrarian republic is a tragedy. Louisa is compromised by Gildon, who then refuses to marry her in favor of a rich New York heiress that has been his family's intended bride all along. Edward dies in a duel with Gildon to avenge his sister. Any hopes to reverse the family's economic misfortunes die with Edward. Tucker concludes the fable with the once grand estate laying in arrears. The slaves are auctioned and separated, and Colonel Grayson's widow and shamed daughter are forced to take refuge in a small cabin provided for them by the family lawyer.[69]

Although Tucker's literary prowess is often dismissed, he manifested a certain amount of creativity in making the deceased Colonel Grayson one of the more intriguing characters in the novel. The Colonel appeared only in the references of other characters, but his untimely death created the fundamental circumstances of debt that caused the rapid decline of the family. Yet Tucker portrayed the deceased as neither the intemperate sluggard nor the spendthrift aristocrat common elsewhere in the genre. Instead, Colonel Grayson embodied the ideal of the republican freeholder; productive, honorable, and imbued with public spirit. Indeed, civic virtue proved to be his undoing. Not content to see only himself succeed, he readily guaranteed the debts of less capable citizens who, more often than not, failed him and fled for Kentucky. Tucker's novel thus presented a critique of Virginia's republican society and was not simply an indictment against individual misbehavior. Grayson placed his family in a precarious position because he acted on republican ideals in a society that awarded marketplace shrewdness instead.

In the story, Tucker juxtaposed the fate of the Grayson family against that of the miserly Fawkners, their *nouveau riche* neighbors in the Valley. Major Fawkner exhibited a prudent business sense, acting foremost on self-interest, perpetually suspicious of his less-fortunate neighbors, and disinclined toward the passions of politics. Tucker presents Fawkner as the model farmer in a rationalized system of agricultural production. Fawkner supervises and manages his own fields, he diversifies and rotates his crops, and he shuns slave labor. Most significantly, unlike Grayson, he recognized that debt and forfeiture represented the real consequences of mismanaged allodial property and that within this new order, economic security necessarily took precedence over public spirit and communal involvement.

[69] George Tucker, *The Valley of Shenandoah, or Memoirs of the Graysons* (New York: Charles Wiley, 1824; reprinted by the University of North Carolina Press, 1970). For literary analyses, see the introduction by Donald R. Noble, Jr. in the North Carolina reprint edition and Richard Beal Davis, *Intellectual Life in Jefferson's Virginia, 1790–1830* (Chapel Hill: University of North Carolina Press, 1964), 305–309.

Tucker's portrait of the freeholders' republic reflected a deep ambivalence. It conveyed tremendous respect for the influence and power of capitalist social relations and thus revealed that Tucker proved more willing than Jefferson to accept its features as permanent. Nonetheless, they both shared a mistrust of avarice and recognized that the pursuit of wealth for its own ends contradicted the foundational premises of a self-governing polity. The Yankee Gildon was the villain of the novel. The problem for Tucker then – indeed the problem for Virginia – was how to preserve the republican ideals of the landed gentry when the freehold itself had become an agent of marketplace habits. Tucker articulated this ambivalence in a passage where the widow Grayson foreshadowed her own undoing. Tacitly acknowledging the precariousness of her economic position, she commented that "estates change hand much oftener than they used to do" but, as a good republican, she allowed that it probably was "right it should be so." Widow Grayson faced a dilemma: The dynamic transfer of land made possible by the allodial reforms directly threatened her very security, but to protest against them risked disowning the recognized triumphs of the American Revolution and thus, correspondingly, to be suspected of yearning for aristocracy.[70]

The agricultural vision advanced by George Tucker and by John Taylor departed significantly from Jefferson's allodial vision. For Jefferson, land ownership both reflected and ensured the fundamental basis of self-government. The widespread distribution of land ownership meant greater equality and expanded popular involvement in the quintessential republican act of self-government. For Tucker and Taylor, however, the land represented too important a resource to be trusted to the many. Their rationalized approach to land ownership called for only those with demonstrated ability to manage the essential tasks of agricultural production. And their economic perspective subsequently carried the day. Increasingly, Virginia's landscape was presented as one of stagnation and decay in contrast to places were modern doctrines of improvement and scientific agriculture prevailed. A prominent editorial published in the inaugural issue of the *Southern Planter*, a Richmond-based journal devoted to disseminating modern agricultural practices, sought to demonstrate how a farmer was but a manufacturer in rural habit. The editorial, significantly entitled "Capital," took the form of a paternal letter of advice to a son who had declared his intentions to pursue "agriculture as a profession." The epistle conveyed a strong sense of disdain for the rustic yeoman while, conversely, praising those farmers who embraced the ethics of manufacturers and small businessman. He told the story of an encounter with a simple farmer who could not afford to invest in "a decided and admitted improvement" in agricultural machinery, and he explained that he had been inclined to ask in response what that farmer might think of a blacksmith who had to "blow his fire with his mouth, because he could not afford to buy a pair of bellows." The moral was clear: "One of the greatest errors committed in farming," the

[70] Tucker, *Valley*, 8.

writer warned, arose "from the erroneous impression that this business may be undertaken with less capital than most others."[71]

By the first decades of the nineteenth century, Jefferson himself had acknowledged the limits of the freeholder's republic and had adopted the mantle of reform. In his correspondence with noted French economist Du Pont de Nemours, Jefferson discussed the limitations of the doctrines of agricultural wealth in the face of the increasing shift toward manufacturing. He lamented that despite "sufficient means in the hands of our citizens," the American economy was "foundering" in the midst of "unproductive and ruinous" expedients adopted to serve as economic policy. He attributed this piecemeal approach to an ignorance of the "sound principles of political economy" first developed by the French Physiocrats, which Du Pont had elaborated in his preceding letters. Jefferson's praise was qualified immediately, however, by associating those doctrines with the commercial theories of Adam Smith and Jean-Baptiste Say, which, he asserted, "commended and dilated" the original agrarian perspective. To be sure, the tensions between the emerging theories of capitalism and Jefferson's agrarianism existed from the outset, but his correspondence with Du Pont reveals an attitude of resignation and accommodation. A year later, in a letter to Benjamin Austin, Jefferson was more explicit. He candidly admitted that in the years since the publication of *Notes on the State of Virginia*, the circumstances of "rapid depravity" that rendered the "close of the century the disgrace of the history of man" forced a serious reconsideration of his agrarian philosophy. He believed that "we must now place the manufacturer by the side of the agriculturalist" and acknowledged that the national experience had clearly shown "that manufacturers" were as "necessary to our independence as to our comfort." Jefferson now suggested that anyone who opposed developing domestic manufactures "must be for reducing us either to dependence on that foreign nation, or to be clothed in skins, and live like wild beasts in dens and caverns."[72]

Beyond making these necessary economic reforms, however, Jefferson also contemplated a new republican political model for Virginia – one based on the New England township system. In a series of letters written to John Adams,

[71] *The Southern Planter: devoted to agriculture, horticulture, and the household arts* (Richmond: P. D. Bernard), January 1841. Edmund Ruffin emerged as the dominant figure for agricultural reform in Virginia. See David F. Allmendinger, Jr., ed., *Incidents of My Life: Edmund Ruffin's Autobiographical Essays* (Charlottesville: University Press of Virginia, 1990).

[72] Thomas Jefferson to Du Punt de Nemours, February 28, 1815, in Gilbert Chinard, *The Correspondence of Jefferson and Du Pont de Nemours* (Baltimore: Johns Hopkins University Press, 1931), 210–212; and Thomas Jefferson to Benjamin Austin, January 9, 1816, in Peterson, *Portable Thomas Jefferson*, 547–550. Du Pont articulated his economic thought to Jefferson relative to the particular context of America in letters written on April 10 and September 14, 1810, December 12, 1811, and January 25, April 14, and May 17, 1812. Jefferson also appears to have read a similar letter written to James Madison on January 20, 1810. Jefferson responded on April 15, 1811 and November 29, 1813, in addition to the February 1815 letter cited earlier. Du Pont's letters can be found, respectively, on the following pages in Chinard: 157–158, 158–159, 172–177, 179–193, 193–196, 196–199, and 155–157 (to Madison); Jefferson's replies are found on 163–164 and 206–212.

Joseph C. Cabell, and Samuel Kercheval, Jefferson laid out a program for constitutional revision in Virginia. Even before then, Jefferson expressed his frustration at the defeat of his proposal for a freehold entitlement that would have guaranteed the franchise and direct representation and, in 1785, along with James Madison, had sought a constitutional convention to remedy these defects. By 1813, however, a more comprehensive plan of reform emerged in Jefferson's correspondence. Expanded suffrage, more equitable representation, public education, an elected judiciary, and the construction of a ward system stood as the centerpieces of this reformed republic. The ward system in particular, which Jefferson characterized as "the wisest invention ever devised...for the perfect exercise of self-government," signaled his own acknowledgment that individual land ownership had failed to provide a sufficient means of cultivating civic virtue – the essential public attachment to local government. Wards were to be drawn out of the counties and were designed to relieve what Jefferson now perceived as the oligarchic county court "of nearly all its business." Wards would replace the freehold as the fundamental unit of his four-tiered system of republican government, which culminated with the federal union. "Every citizen," according to Jefferson, would participate as "an acting member of the government" by fulfilling the offices "most interesting to him" and in this manner "attach him by his strongest feelings to the independence of his country."[73]

Jefferson's plan for a ward system for Virginia did not garner much immediate enthusiasm. The recognized failure of the allodial freehold to cultivate republican behavior, however, demanded an ideological revision. Virginians reacted by making sundry calls for social, legal, and political reforms. Such calls incorporated diverse and oftentimes antagonistic positions about the appropriate manner of change, but their central motivation remained consistent: Institutional changes were needed to reconcile republican government with the ubiquitous habits of the capitalist marketplace. Over the course of the ensuing decade, a growing popular mandate for reform gained momentum. It climaxed in 1828 with a plebiscite voting in favor of convening a constitutional assembly. Jefferson's conversion loomed large in the minds of many of the reform delegates who gathered in Richmond the following year. They embraced his proposals for expanded suffrage, equitable representation, and curtailing the powers of the county courts. Once again, however, as had been the case with his agrarian republican vision, Jefferson's latest political ideas created unforeseen consequences.

[73] TJ to Samuel Kercheval, July 12, 1816, in Ford 10: 39–41. See his letters to Joseph C. Cabell, January 31, 1814 and February 2, 1816, as well in Joyce Appleby and Terence Ball, eds., *Jefferson: Political Writings* (Cambridge: Cambridge University Press, 1999), 195–197, 202–206, and Mayer, *Constitutional Thought*, 308–319. An example of Jefferson's criticism of the county courts is TJ to John Taylor, May 28, 1816 in Appleby and Ball, 206–210. In Jefferson's letter to John Adams, October 28, 1813, he suggested that he had elaborated this idea of a ward system in his "Bill for the More General Diffusion of Knowledge (1779)," but the existing evidence does not support this assertion. Boyd notes, however, that the drafts and the annotations for that particular bill were unusually absent.

PART II

REFORMATIO

I detested all the fruits of my labor under the sun, because I must leave them to a man who is to come after me. And who knows whether he will be a wise man or a fool? Yet he will have control over all the fruits of my wise labor under the sun. This too is vanity.

Ecclesiastes 2: 18–19

3

An Invidious and Anti-Republican Test

In autumn of 1829, a group of Richmond merchants gathered to draft a petition to the delegates of the upcoming state constitutional convention. These merchants were frustrated by their disfranchisement, and they hoped the constitutional revision would remedy their situation by extending the right of suffrage to all white, male citizens. Identifying themselves as "non-freeholders," they described themselves as members of a class of citizens who did not have "the good fortune to possess a certain portion of land" and, for that reason alone, they were "debarred" from enjoying "the right of suffrage." The tone of their petition contrasted sharply with the Jeffersonian rhetoric of virtuous, republican freeholders. Instead, they spoke of Virginia's freeholders as members of a privileged and tyrannical aristocracy who had created "an odious distinction between members of the same community." Freeholders excluded men from the government, treating them "like aliens or slaves, as if destitute of interest, or unworthy of a voice." Far from serving as the embodiment of self-government, freeholders had effectively "seized upon the sovereign authority" and vested themselves with political power solely on the basis of their private possessions and "not in consideration of their public services."[1]

When the assembly convened a few weeks later, many of the delegates sympathetic to democratic reform quickly adopted the language of these merchants. Richard Henderson, a lawyer from the town of Leesburg, stood Jefferson's revolutionary rhetoric on its head when he invoked the terminology of feudalism and characterized those merchants denied the right of suffrage as being reduced to "political villinage [sic]." Winchester lawyer John Rogers Cooke rejected the premise that the freehold qualification had undergone any republican reconciliation. He contended instead that it had been "imposed upon the

[1] *Proceedings and Debates of the Virginia State Convention of 1829–30* (Richmond, 1830), 25–25. (Hereafter *PDVSC.*) The Richmond merchants were not alone; the Convention received several other petitions from counties with large urban populations also calling for the extension of suffrage. See *PDVSC*, 31–33 for petitions from Fairfax, Rockingham, and Shenandoah as well.

Colony" by the king and enforced by the dispatch of "two regiments of British soldiers" in 1677. He maintained that "no grosser error" existed than to think that Virginia's constitution had been formed in 1776. Rather, he asserted, its most distinctive features – "the sectional and aristocratic" – had been devised a full century earlier. Faintly echoing the invocation of the Norman Yoke, Cooke argued that these aristocratic devices persisted merely because the people had become reconciled to them through "long habit." Lucas P. Thompson from Amherst, a future judge of the General Court, pleaded for a revised suffrage law that would "abolish forever the freehold qualification," which he characterized as something that had "always appeared an invidious and anti-republican test."[2]

The convening of delegates to revise the state constitution represented an open acknowledgment that new political and social conditions had undermined the ideological premises of Virginia's agrarian republic. The pastoral image of a polity composed of independent farmers and the corresponding idea that land ownership could serve as the basis of republican citizenship came under sharp public scrutiny as Virginians evaluated the suitability of their institutions in a modern, commercial world. Over the course of four years, beginning with the constitutional convention in October 1829, Virginians engaged in a series of divisive public debates that examined the fundamental relations of property ownership, law, and self-government. In addition to addressing fundamental constitutional questions of suffrage and representation, these debates grappled with key political issues about the appropriate structures of an independent judiciary and local governance, the best manner of funding public improvement projects, the nature of relations with the federal government, and, most famously, in the wake of the 1831 Nat Turner rebellion, the future of slavery.[3]

[2] *PDVSC*, 361 (Henderson); 57 (Cooke); 410 (Thompson).

[3] The Virginia Debates have received a considerable share of scholarly attention already, although seldom as a comprehensive episode in political development. And although scholars have sometimes disagreed over their significance, they have differed very little over interpretation. The prevailing consensus maintains that the debates represented a failure for the reform-minded, non-slaveholding Western Virginias and therefore a triumph for the conservative slaveholders of the East. This interpretation initially was advanced by the substantive work of Charles Ambler, *Sectionalism in Virginia from 1776 to 1860* (Chicago: University of Chicago Press, 1901); Theodore M. Whitfield, *Slavery Agitation in Virginia, 1829–1832* (Baltimore: Johns Hopkins University Press, 1930); William Sumner Jenkins, *Proslavery Thought in the Old South* (Chapel Hill: University of North Carolina Press, 1935); Clement Eaton, *Freedom of Thought in the Old South* (Durham, NC: Duke University Press, 1940); Joseph Clarke Robert, *The Road from Monticello: A Study of the Virginia Slavery Debate of 1832* (Durham, NC: Duke University Press, 1941); J. R. Pole, "Representation and Authority in Virginia from the Revolution to Reform," *JSH* (1958): 16–50; and Merrill Peterson, *Democracy, Liberty, and Property: The State Constitutional Conventions of the 1820s* (Indianapolis, IN: Bobbs-Merrill, 1966), 271–285. See too, however, the important contrasting interpretation offered by Fletcher M. Green, "Democracy in the Old South," republished in J. Isaac Copeland, ed., *Democracy in the Old South and Other Essays by Fletcher Melvin Green* (Nashville, TN: Vanderbilt University Press, 1969), 65–86. More recent interpretations have offered qualifications but the general "rejection of democracy" theme persists. They include: Dickson D. Bruce, Jr., *The Rhetoric of*

The principal consequence of these debates was a reconceptualization of republican political ideals. The traditional common-law concept of freehold citizenship was replaced by a more democratic belief that diverse forms of property ownership, most notably property in labor, also possessed substantial political value. This idea that the productive capacity of labor created an ownership right in one's labor transformed both politics and jurisprudence throughout nineteenth-century Anglo-American society. In Virginia, however, the issue of property in labor was complicated by the ownership of slaves. If merchants, artisans, and even wage earners could stake a claim for political representation on the basis of their control over their labor, then the owners of slaves could make similar claims too – only exponentially. In this manner, property rights to slaves became a key ingredient of Virginia's legal and political reformation. The Virginia debates thus reflected a sea change in republican political thought whereby the ownership of labor replaced the ownership of land as the fundamental property relation signifying the capacity for self-government.[4]

Virginia did not experience this reformation in isolation. The constitutional realignments marking the emergence of democracy in American politics have been well documented by many historians of the era. Changes in political language, electoral processes and voter mobilization, as well as the emergence of nationally recognized candidates with ideologically oriented platforms, all were reflected in a corresponding commitment to mass political parties and white-manhood suffrage. This realignment thus created the essential mechanisms for the establishment of modern representative democracies, in which political

Conservatism: The Virginia Convention of 1829–30 and the Conservative Tradition in the South (San Marino, CA: Huntington Library, 1982), xi–xii; Alison Goodyear Freehling, *Drift Toward Dissolution: The Virginia Slavery Debate of 1831–1832* (Baton Rouge: Louisiana State University Press, 1982); Robert Sutton, *Revolution to Secession: Constitution Making in the Old Dominion* (Charlottesville: University Press of Virginia, 1989); William W. Freehling, *The Road to Disunion: Secessionists at Bay, 1776–1854* (New York: Oxford University Press, 1990), 162–177; William Shade, *Democratizing the Old Dominion: Virginia and the Second Party System, 1824–1861* (Charlottesville: University Press of Virginia, 1997); and Laura J. Scalia, *America's Jeffersonian Experiment: Remaking State Constitutions, 1820–1850* (Dekalb: Northern Illinois University Press, 1999). Since Charles Ambler, however, no scholar has contemplated the important 1833 legislative debate over federal relations and nullification as part of this larger constitutional episode. For preliminary explorations of the theses advanced here and in the next chapter, see Christopher M. Curtis, "Reconsidering Suffrage Reform in the 1829–1830 Virginia Constitutional Convention," *Journal of Southern History*, 74 (February 2008): 89–124, and "*Partus Sequitur Ventrem:* Slavery, Property Rights, and the Language of Republicanism in Virginia's House of Delegates, 1831–1832," *Australian Journal of Legal History*, 6 (2000): 93–114.

[4] E. P. Thompson, *The Making of the English Working Class* (New York: Vintage Books, 1963); Sean Wilentz, *Chants Democratic: New York City & the Rise of the American Working Class, 1788–1850* (New York: Oxford University Press, 1984); Harry L. Watson, *Liberty and Power: The Politics of Jacksonian America* (New York: Oxford University Press, 1990); Robert J. Steinfeld, *The Invention of Free Labor: The Employment Relation in English & American Law and Culture, 1350–1870* (Chapel Hill: University of North Carolina Press, 1991); and Christopher L. Tomlins, *Law, Labor, and Ideology in the Early American Republic* (Cambridge: Cambridge University Press, 1993).

rights were vested in individual personhood. Virginia experienced many aspects of these political reforms, especially the development of the party system, in ways very similar to that of other states. In other ways, however, Virginia's experience diverged sharply from national trends. Two instances are particularly notable in this respect. First, the process of democratization in Virginia, as in the remainder of the South, was colored distinctively by the presence of slavery. And second, because of the centrality of the freehold to Virginia's original understanding of republican government, the Commonwealth proved more reluctant than other states to abandon all real property qualifications and adopt white-manhood suffrage. Nevertheless, by mid-century, the core principal of modern democracy – that political rights and representation were vested in individual persons – was realized in Virginia. Paradoxically, however, this vision of democratic citizenship reached fruition simultaneously with an increasingly ardent commitment to the preservation of slavery.[5]

"ALL OTHER REPUBLICS HAVE FAILED"

Popular calls for constitutional reform had begun in earnest in the years following the end of the War of 1812. In addition to the recognized unsuitability of a freehold-based polity, the rapid population growth in the counties west of the Blue Ridge Mountains and the corresponding development of the region's grain production informed the circumstances of dissent. Coming on the heels of war, questions of the franchise and of taxation loomed in the minds of many who had served in the militia or paid increased taxes to repel the British invasions. On July 4, 1815, residents of Harrisonburg issued an address calling for suffrage reform that conformed to the profession of inalienable rights found in Jefferson's Declaration of Independence. More than any other issue, however, concerns over the inequity of legislative apportionment between the eastern and western counties inspired popular appeals for constitutional reform. In August and September 1816, Shenandoah Valley farmers convened meetings in Winchester and Staunton and drafted petitions calling for a convention to revise the state constitution. These Valley reformers expressed frustration at their inability to get the necessary appropriations for desired internal improvement projects from a state legislature where they were notoriously underrepresented. The system of apportionment established by the 1776 Constitution awarded each county two representatives to the House of Delegates, irrespective

[5] William Shade, *Democratizing the Old Dominion: Virginia and the Second Party System, 1824–1861* (Charlottesville: University Press of Virginia, 1997); Ronald Formisano, *The Transformation of Political Culture: Massachusetts Politics, 1790s–1840s* (New York: Oxford University Press, 1983); Harry Watson, *Liberty and Power: The Politics of Jacksonian America* (New York: Hill and Wang, 1990); Richard McCormick, *The Second American Party System: Party Formation in the Jacksonian Era* (Chapel Hill: University of North Carolina Press, 1966); and, more recently, Bruce Ackerman, *The Failure of the Founding Fathers: Jefferson, Marshall, and the Rise of Presidential Democracy* (Cambridge, MA: The Belknap Press of Harvard University Press, 2005).

of the geographical size or the population of the county. State senators were selected from designated senatorial districts that were drawn on a historical basis. Overall, it was a system that greatly favored the older (and smaller) eastern counties of the Tidewater at the expense of the increasingly populous transmontane counties. Subsequent petitions and ad hoc county conventions persisted in calling for changing this system by way of a constitutional convention. In 1817, the General Assembly responded by reapportioning the Senate districts as a means to rectify some of the apportionment inequity.[6]

More change was desired, however. In 1825, another convention held in Staunton managed to bring together westerners interested in apportionment reform with eastern merchants who wanted suffrage reform. Thirty-one counties sent more than a hundred reform-minded delegates who promptly adopted a resolution decrying Virginia's freeholders as "an odious landed aristocracy." Their public appeals for equitable representation, expanded suffrage, greater access to bank credit, and a state-sponsored program of internal improvements were broadcast throughout the state by sympathetic newspaper editors. The construction of this public discourse generated substantial popular clamor for reform and finally pressured legislators to call for a plebiscite on the question of revising the constitution during the 1827–1828 session. That spring, a majority of Virginia's freeholders voted in favor of a constitutional convention; a year later, they elected delegates to represent them in convention.[7]

The delegates convened in Richmond in October 1829, and remained in session for more than three months, until the middle of January. It was Virginia's first state constitutional convention and it attracted considerable notoriety because of the participation of former Presidents James Madison and James Monroe, Chief Justice John Marshall, former Governor William Branch Giles, and the irascible former Senator John Randolph; all of whom were elected as delegates. Merrill Peterson has labeled the meeting "the last of the great constituent assemblies in American history," echoing similar sentiments made at the time. These political giants all made significant contributions during the process of constitutional revision, but they did not dominate the proceedings. Instead, a generation of delegates who came of age after the Revolution orchestrated the principal maneuverings and crafted the substance of the new document. The movement for reform was led by the likes of John Rogers Cooke, Charles Fenton Mercer, Lucas Thompson, Chapman Johnson, Archibald Stuart, Jr., and Briscoe Baldwin, while Benjamin Watkins Leigh, Robert Stanard, Littleton Waller Tazewell, and Abel Parker Upshur anchored the conservative line. Despite taking opposing sides on the issues, these men shared the common experience of being members of the Virginia bar. One historian has calculated

[6] Shade, *Democratizing*, 57–60; Sutton, *Revolution to Secession*, 62–64.

[7] For details on the movement for constitutional reform and the circumstances of the Convention, see Shade, *Democratizing*, 57–60; Bruce, *Rhetoric of Conservatism*, 19–26; Sutton, *Revolution to Secession*, 62–67; and Charles Ambler, *Thomas Ritchie: A Study in Virginia Politics* (Richmond: Bell Book and Stationary Co., 1913).

that three-quarters of the convention delegates were lawyers. Yet the experience of the bar was changing too. The younger generation of delegates represented an increasingly professionalized group who were less likely to have read law under the tutelage of the local country magistrate but who had attended one of Virginia's new proprietary law schools. Still, their education had been steeped in the common law and their speeches, resolutions, and amendments reflected this excessive familiarity with its intricacies and nuances. Indeed, their political opinions proved inseparable from their understanding of the law. As a result, the constitution they produced has been characterized by at least one scholar as an exercise in legal "obscurantism."[8]

The core elements of democratic reform were thus critically examined from a common-law perspective during the convention debates. And they were done so in the context of the generally recognized failure of Jefferson's common-law-inspired vision of an allodial republic. Accordingly, the convention debates necessarily engaged the fundamental question of how to best negotiate the competing interests between property and persons in order to assign status, in the absence of the centuries-old freehold qualification. The debates raised crucial questions concerning the nature of representation, the social origins of political rights, and the authority of office. Questions about the constitution of citizenship, however, stood at the core of the engagement and informed all of its corollary issues. What status would now make someone a citizen? And what did citizenship now imply? Eugenius Wilson, a merchant and former Federalist from Monongalia County, framed the fundamental problem faced by the Convention when he asked: "What test shall we apply" to determine what constituted a "permanent, common interest" for a republican citizen? Philip Doddridge put it even more succinctly: "Who is the Commonwealth?" he asked.[9]

From the outset, then, most of the delegates recognized that the principal agenda of the convention was reform. Despite subsequent historiographical characterizations of an entrenched conservative opposition, few delegates, aside from John Randolph, offered anything near an impassioned plea for perpetuating the status quo. In convening the assembly, its president, James Monroe, charged the delegates with devising "a new support to our system of free government." He warily reminded them that "all other republics had failed"; that the landscapes of the once mighty Roman and Grecian republics were now dominated by the "ruins of ancient buildings," and that the present inhabitants of those lands now languished in "a state of decrepitude

[8] Peterson, *Democracy, Liberty, and Property*, 271; Shade, *Democratizing*, 64; Chilton Williamson, *American Suffrage from Property to Democracy, 1760–1860* (Princeton, NJ: Princeton University Press, 1960), 233.

[9] *PDVSC*, 351 (Wilson). On the questions concerning the development of democratic citizenship, see Williamson, *American Suffrage*; James H. Kettner, *The Development of American Citizenship, 1608–1870* (Chapel Hill: University of North Carolina Press, 1978); and Douglas Bradburn, *The Citizenship Revolution: Politics & the Creation of the American Union, 1774–1804* (Charlottesville: University of Virginia Press, 2009).

and wretchedness." He called on the convention to reflect on the historic examples of these failed republics, as well as Virginia's own experiences after five decades of self-government, in order to enact the reforms needed to preserve republican rule.[10]

Beyond the fundamental issues of citizenship and representation, the convention addressed other significant questions pertaining to executive power, establishing a procedure for constitutional amendment, public education, and the authority of the county courts. The delegates divided themselves into four subcommittees in order to examine the separate sections of the Constitution: the legislative, the executive, the judiciary, and the Declaration of Rights. Each committee proposed recommendations with the exception of those reviewing the Declaration of Rights. Efforts had been made to include rights to white manhood suffrage and proportional representation in the Declaration, but they failed in committee. Discussions in the Executive Committee centered around the future of the Executive Council, a consulting body that represented a holdover from the colonial government, and the mode of electing the governor. Reformers sought to abolish the Executive Council and make the office of governor popularly elected. Significant debate occurred in the Judiciary Committee over the authority and composition of the county courts. There, and on the floor of the convention, the county courts were characterized as bastions of the "freehold oligarchy" by reformers who desired an elected judiciary.[11]

The issue of establishing an appropriate basis for legislative representation dominated the course of the Convention, however. Reform delegates sought an apportionment on the basis of the white population of each county, but opponents balked. They emphasized the association between apportionment and the power of taxation and expressed concerns about the need to represent property as well as persons. An explicit effort to protect slave property from excessive taxation motivated much of this opposition to the white-basis agenda. The numerical division between the groups was close, however, and encouraged a sustained, intense debate throughout the convention. Debate erupted over the issue when James Madison delivered the legislative committee report favor white-basis representation in late October. The subsequent debate over apportionment held the exclusive focus of the delegates for nearly three weeks. Rival schemes were proposed that provided for representation on the basis of taxation and the three-fifths formula used in computing federal representation. But part of the problem encountered in trying to find an acceptable basis for apportionment was the corresponding question about the right of suffrage. When the debate over representation devolved into a stalemate, the delegates turned their attention to the more fundamental issue concerning the source of the franchise in anticipation of replacing the freehold qualification.[12]

[10] *PDVSC*, 1–2.

[11] Peterson, *Liberty, Property, Democracy*, 271–285; Sutton, *Revolution to Secession*, 72–102 is a more detailed but less satisfactory account.

[12] Peterson, *Liberty, Property, Democracy*, 275–279.

The franchise had originated as a circumstance of freehold tenure. In England, by the eighteenth century, however, the franchise no longer exclusively determined suffrage rights. Different qualifications existed for different elections. For example, the necessary qualifications to vote for Parliament often differed significantly from the more expansive suffrage rights granted to select vestries. New qualifications also arose as the borough system developed, creating increasing definitional ambiguity over the basis of the franchise. In general, the right to vote in England was dependent on local custom. An effort to standardize the franchise during the fifteenth century had resulted in the establishment of the forty-shilling freehold qualification for Parliamentary elections, but in point of fact, this merely became the standard on which to base numerous exceptions. By the seventeenth and eighteenth centuries, the capacity to be economically independent appeared as the most determinative feature in establishing suffrage practices.[13]

Despite the ambiguity in England, the freehold qualification was established as the explicit criteria for suffrage and office holding in colonial Virginia, except for the vestry elections. Following the suppression of the Bacon's Rebellion, in 1676, the king instructed Governor Berkeley and the House of Burgesses to prescribe a freehold qualification for suffrage to ensure more orderly elections. They did so without providing any specific definition of a freehold in the colony, however, and this oversight quickly proved detrimental to the intent of the qualification. In a colony where the initial landholdings had developed largely as a result of customary agreements, and where copyholds and other forms of tenure that served to provide definition of a freehold did not exist, the imposition of a freehold qualification only confused an already ambiguous issue of determining the franchise status of landholders.[14]

Throughout the eighteenth century, the Burgesses sought to correct this problem by attempting to provide adequate definitions through sundry statutes. These statutory definitions were driven by a need to reform electoral abuses in the colony and did not reflect dissatisfaction with the common law. In 1705, the General Assembly incorporated the common-law definition of a freeholder into a statute regarding the franchise, specifying a freeholder as a tenant possessing an estate for life. This general definition – merely echoing the common law – did little, however, to resolve the problems of electoral corruption. Three decades later, in 1736, the burgesses tried once again to define the

[13] Williamson, *American Suffrage*, 5–12; John Phillip Reid, *The Concept of Representation in the Age of the American Revolution* (Chicago: University of Chicago Press, 1989), 39–42, 53–62; James H. Kettner, *The Development of American Citizenship, 1608–1870* (Chapel Hill: University of North Carolina Press, 1978); and J. R. Pole, *Political Representation in England and the Origins of the American Republic* (Berkeley: University of California Press, 1971).

[14] Chandler, *Suffrage in Virginia*, 18–20; Charles Sydnor, *Gentlemen Freeholders*, 34–43; A. E. Dick Howard, *Commentaries on the Constitution of Virginia* (Charlottesville: University Press of Virginia, 1974), 317–321; Giles Jacob, *The General Laws of Estates; or Freeholder's Companion* (London, 1740).

parameters of the freehold qualification for suffrage. Legislators augmented the common-law definition by stipulating that a freehold necessarily consisted of twenty-five acres of cultivated land with a house, or one hundred acres of uncultivated land. In addition to the acreage qualifications, the statute placed restrictions on women, free and enslaved African Americans, children, and religious dissenters. The exception proved the rule, however, in regards to making the freehold the sole source of the franchise. To extend the right to vote to some substantial merchants who lived inside the incorporated towns of Williamsburg and Norfolk, a house built on a lot of relative value in one of those towns was declared to be a freehold.[15]

Furthermore, the statute removed the requirement of actual residency and allowed a man to vote in any county where he possessed a freehold. The abolition of a residency requirement imbued suffrage in Virginia with a distinctive feature that would come to be considered by many as its defining characteristic. Virginians were entitled to vote in each county in which they possessed a freehold and therefore could vote more than once in an election. Given that colonial elections were often held on separate days, or lasted for several days, and the original Tidewater counties were geographically small, it was not uncommon for a Virginia freeholder to ride from county to county and cast a vote in multiple elections. By the nineteenth century, this practice of multiple voting became particularly notorious in the face of modern democratic ideas of one man, one vote. It was exacerbated further by the consequences of the fact that the geographically clustered counties of the Tidewater region stood in stark contrast to the larger western counties of the upper Piedmont and Mountains. Despite vociferous public criticism, this distinctive aspect of suffrage persisted as an anomaly of Virginia politics until 1851.

The 1736 statute remained the definitional standard until after the Revolution. As part of the postcolonial legal revisions, the acreage requirement was reduced from one hundred to fifty uncultivated acres. Otherwise, all other qualifications of the statute remained in force. Virginia lawmakers had attempted to amend the acreage qualification twice previously, in 1762 and again in 1769. On both occasions, the House of Burgesses had passed statutes defining the freehold by the fifty-acre qualification. The amendment reflected their desire to bring the law into correspondence with the customary patterns of headright grants, which customarily were made in fifty-acre parcels. In 1769, as a freshman delegate, Jefferson had acted as a principal agent in advocating this definitional amendment. But the king refused to approve the legislation. Consequently, the issue was left for the postcolonial legislature

[15] Chandler, *Suffrage in Virginia*, 18–20; Sydnor, *Gentlemen Freeholders: Political Practices in Washington's Virginia* (Chapel Hill: University of North Carolina Press, 1952), 34–43; Howard, *Commentaries on the Constitution of Virginia*, 317–321; J. R. Pole, *Political Representation in England and the Origins of the American Republic* (London: Macmillan, 1966); Robert E. Brown and Katherine Brown, *Virginia 1705–1786: Democracy or Aristocracy?* (East Lansing: Michigan State University Press, 1964). Evidence suggests that the law excluding dissenters was rarely enforced.

to rectify. Jefferson again supported the amendment in 1785, but this time, in addition to the argument of custom, he understood it as a way to expand the franchise in a manner closer to his original proposal for a general freehold entitlement. Correspondent with the revisions, Jefferson and James Madison were arguing for a constitutional convention to redress the inequities in popular suffrage and representation that they believed were imbedded in the 1776 Constitution and were inconsistent with republican principles. The statutory redefinition significantly expanded the franchise without changing its fundamental form as a right emanating from one's relationship to the land. As in the other key areas of the postcolonial revision, the new acreage qualification for the freehold represented a reconciliation of republican values with a commitment to an idealized form of custom.[16]

THE MUSTER ROLL OF ISRAEL

By the time of the Constitutional Convention, however, the language of reform had changed significantly. Arguments for democratic reform were premised on a conceptualization of rights vested in individual persons. Many of the speeches delivered by reform delegates were embedded in a juristic language of natural rights, which was distinct from the common-law terminology that had characterized previous republican discourse. Unlike Jefferson, they did not seek to ground their natural-rights philosophy in any specific historical narrative. Instead, they repeatedly cited Virginia's Declaration of Rights – a document independent of but complementary to the state constitution – as the ideological basis for their reforms. They contended that the Declaration of Rights, more than the constitution, more than the laws, embodied the liberal spirit of Virginia's republicanism and should serve as the guidepost for determining political privileges. They especially invoked the first article declaring "That all men are by nature equally free" and the sixth article stipulating "That elections…ought to be free; and that all men, having sufficient evidence of permanent, common interest with, and attachment to, the community, have the right to suffrage." John Rogers Cooke referred to the declaration of rights as "a sacred instrument" from which emanated the fundamental principles of popular sovereignty and the natural right of majority rule, which he championed as "the essential character of free government." These common-law-educated reformers consistently employed the Latin-based term *suffrage* in lieu of the traditional reference to *franchise*. Eugenius Wilson professed his

[16] *SAL*, 12: 102–121 (1785); Julius F. Prufer, "The Franchise in Virginia from Jefferson through the Convention of 1829," *WMQ*, 2nd series, 7 (1927): 255–270 and 8 (1928): 17–32. To my knowledge, no attempt to quantify the number of voters enfranchised by this statutory redefinition has been attempted. In the late colonial period, Robert and Katherine Brown estimated that only 25% of landholders possessed the necessary hundred acres in mid-century and suggest that this number may have waned by the time of the Revolution. The decreased acreage requirement ought to have made the franchise available to a considerable number of farmers.

belief that "Nature, or Nature's God" had conferred "certain original rights upon man" among which he included the "undeniable" right to "appoint our own agents."[17]

It was Cooke, however, who, throughout the convention, led the cause for democratic reforms premised on a natural-rights philosophy. The Frederick County lawyer had been born in Bermuda but migrated to Virginia and settled in Martinsburg as a young man. By the time of the Convention, he was an established and very successful lawyer in Winchester and had been a leading voice for reform in the Shenandoah Valley for more than a decade. His critique of the freehold republic was premised on his commitment to the principle of majority rule, which he believed had been violated by the 1776 Constitution in two different ways. First, he noted, it vested power exclusively in freeholders who composed a "minority of the people"; and second, it did not delineate between counties with small populations and counties with large populations for purposes of representation. He acknowledged that under Virginia's Constitution, freeholds represented "real political units" that served foundational purposes and enabled freeholders to exercise "the essential elements of political power." But he rejected as myth the idea that the 1776 Constitution represented an effort to construct a truly republican form of government. He suggested, instead, that in the midst of the Revolution, Virginia's statesmen found themselves in a situation where the threat of enemy canon made it impossible to "pull down and erect anew, the whole fabric of government." Accordingly, the actual creation of the Commonwealth represented a haphazard and accidental affair in which the decision to leave "the freeholders and the counties as they found them" merely reflected the prudence of pragmatic statesmen bowing "to the supreme law of necessity."[18]

In advancing the cause of reform, Cooke embraced a particularly positivist view of history as a linear movement toward expanded liberty. He explained that it was imperative to avoid the "retrograde movement in the science of government," which he considered incumbent in maintaining the status quo. To do nothing was to stand in the face of historical progress. Accordingly, he demanded that Virginia keep "pace with improvements" in political science by extending the principle of popular sovereignty to "its full extent," or risk sinking into declension and decay. His arguments reveal the increasing influence of a utilitarian conception of republican politics and a liberal historical theory of human progress. From Cooke's perspective, the American Revolution had represented a radical catalyst for a social improvement and human progress, not a historical event marking the restoration of ancient Saxon liberties.[19]

[17] *PDVSC*, 54–55 (Cooke); 351 (Wilson); 411 (Thompson).

[18] Diary of John Rogers Cooke, Virginia Historical Society, (Mss55:1 C7754:1); Sutton, *Revolution to Secession*, 198; *PDVSC*, 55–57. Cooke married Maria Pendleton Cooke, and two of their sons, Philip Pendleton Cooke and John Esten Cooke, achieved literary acclaim as romantic poets.

[19] *PDVSC*, 54–56 (Cooke).

Not all reformers appealed to a philosophy of natural right. Lucas Thompson, one of the more able lawyers in the assembly, spoke of his indifference toward regarding suffrage "as a natural, a social, a civil, or a political" right. He maintained that such an inquiry only satisfied curiosity and served no useful purpose. He contended instead that the argument for suffrage reform rested on expediency and boldly proclaimed that "if it be a valuable right," its original basis did not matter. Alexander Campbell, on the other hand, sought to ground his argument for expanded suffrage on Holy Scripture. Campbell, an outspoken reformer from Brooke County in the far northwestern portion of Virginia, was an evangelical minister who founded the Disciples of Christ soon after the Convention. Perhaps not surprisingly, he chastised delegates for championing Virginia's constitution as the first written constitution and for miscrediting Oliver Cromwell with the origins of general suffrage. He referred them instead to the Old Testament, where, he contended, "the God of Israel first proposed a social compact." In Hebrew, this compact was called *Berith*, which Campbell maintained was "precisely equivalent to our English word *Constitution*." He suggested that this seminal Hebrew constitution had been written and then "submitted to every man on the muster roll of Israel" – not just the land owners – for ratification. This historical episode, Campbell contended, represented the venerable "origin of General Suffrage."[20]

Indeed, many of the most revealing invocations of democratic language emerged in the debates over suffrage reform. Delegates who advocated manhood suffrage often professed the creed of an emergent democratic culture. They characterized the right to vote as the absolute form of political expression and the guarantor of all other civil rights. The petition submitted by the Richmond merchants candidly articulated these sentiments, positing that suffrage was "the highest prerogative of freemen" and warning that "experience has but too clearly evinced" the fragility of all other rights for those denied the franchise. One reform delegate referred to the right of suffrage as "the paramount right" on which all other rights rest for "protection, preservation, and safety." Another maintained that of all the original rights conferred by "Nature, or Nature's God," none appeared "more clear and undeniable, than the right of appointing our own agents." Democratic reformers contemplated suffrage not in the confined sense of merely "the right to vote for public functionaries," but in an enlarged sense as the right that signified their membership in a government found on a social compact – "the means by which that same man gives expression of his will in the formation of that compact, his consent to, or his veto upon, measures of the Government in legislation."[21]

This expanded conceptualization of the right to vote, however, reflected a significant narrowing of republican understandings of political participation in general and citizenship in particular. It emphasized the virtues of political expression through the occasional right to vote rather than through the more

[20] *PDVSC*, 411 (Thompson); 388 (Campbell).

[21] *PDVSC*, 25–26 (Richmond Petition), 412 (Thompson), 351 (Wilson).

demanding and ordinary responsibilities of local office, such as serving on a jury. The civic obligation inherent in the duties of office had originated in the reciprocity embedded in the doctrine of tenures and framed the traditional understanding of the franchise. Across the centuries, the principle function of the franchise had been to assign the responsibility of local governance to freeholders. Voting represented one aspect of this governance, but it was not the sole or arguably even the most important aspect. The allodial revisions to the land law transformed the original structure but retained the duties of governance in the franchise as a means to ground republican citizenship. Significantly, then, democratic proposals for suffrage reform rejected this orthodoxy and fostered a conception of citizenship and self-government that demanded only casual affiliations between the citizen and the polity. Alexander Campbell's comments reflected this new democratic vision when he defined a citizen as "a freeman, who has a voice in the Government under which he lives, [and] who has the privilege of being heard in the councils of his country, by his agent, or representative." Unlike the elaborate mechanisms designed to balance self-interest and civic duty in the republic, advocates of democracy believed that citizens would be vested in a polity simply by their desire to participate in it.[22]

At the core of this democratic impulse was the idea that citizenship should be vested in individual persons whose consent and allegiance to the state expressed their necessary social affiliation, irrespective of any property holdings or tangible attachment to a specific community. The logical consequence of this idea was universal suffrage – an idea at which even the most ardent reform delegates in the convention balked. Ultimately, it was this inability to reconcile their desire for limited democratic reform with their argument for democracy that frustrated their efforts. Indeed, conservatives repeatedly chided reform delegates about their inconsistency in arguing that suffrage was a natural right while explicitly denying it to women, children, paupers, free blacks, and slaves. Judge Abel Parker Upshur challenged reform delegates by asking them why, if natural equality was the basis for political rights, were "women, children, and paupers [not] admitted to the polls?" And he noted that if majority rule was the determining principle of free government, women and children must necessarily rule in any society deemed free because they composed the natural majority.[23]

Reformers were not so easily deterred, however, and – at the outset of the convention, at least – not prone to significant compromise of their democratic principles. On November 17, the legislative committee presented its report with recommendations for expanding suffrage. It included plans to extend the franchise to those leaseholders who were tenants for at least five years, heads of households who resided in towns and cities, and those who had recognized

[22] *PDVSC*, 383 (Campbell).

[23] *PDVSC*, 67–68 (Upshur). For a sophisticated treatment of how women did involve themselves in antebellum Virginia politics, see Elizabeth Varon, *We Mean to Be Counted: White Women and Politics in Antebellum Virginia* (Chapel Hill: University of North Carolina Press, 1998).

future rights to freehold estates. More significantly, the plan proposed redefining the freehold from a concept that was defined in terms of acreage to one that was considered, instead, in terms of assessed monetary value. The change was designed to promote equity between landowners who owned lands of differing productive value, and to ensure that freeholds of wasteland could not be established for political purposes. But it effectively divorced the freehold of its common-law moorings and reduced it to the cash nexus of commercial society. By expanding the franchise and redefining the freehold, the legislative committee's proposal for suffrage reform reflected a consensus that considered a freehold estate specifically, and land ownership in general, simply as one of a myriad of property interests. Land ownership would no longer be entitled to a privileged political status.

Many democratic reformers were initially dissatisfied, by the recommendations of the legislative committee. They protested the persistence of real property qualifications and sought to expand the right even further. In response to the committee report, reformers offered three separate proposals to extend suffrage beyond a landed qualification in order to approach their desired result for white-male suffrage. Amendments to the committee report were offered by Eugenius Wilson, Alexander Campbell, and John Rogers Cooke. Wilson proposed enfranchising every free white male who had resided in the Commonwealth for two years, had fulfilled his militia obligations, and had paid his taxes in the year of the election. In advancing his resolution, Wilson rhetorically asked how delegates should ascertain where a man's "interest and attachments are centered?" He answered by suggesting that "when you have a man's person, you will, in general, have his property also, and this together with every thing dear to him, will bind him to the country, and deeply interest him in its welfare." Wilson hoped to extend suffrage to those who participated in the burdens of government through taxation, required road service, and militia duty. Campbell's amendment, in contrast, proposed extending suffrage solely on the bases of age and residency. It stands as the most democratic plan for suffrage offered in the assembly. Nevertheless, the majority of delegates liked neither, and both amendments were defeated.[24]

Cooke's proposal was tendered much later in the debate and reflected a sense of exasperation in the reform camp. In a desperate act of ingenuity, Cooke proposed an argument for white male suffrage that was cloaked in an array of extensive disqualifying clauses. Admittedly, all the proposals contained various exclusionary clauses. Cooke, however, explicitly called for the enfranchisement

[24] *PDVSC*, 351, 353 (Wilson). Wilson's proposal was advanced by Richard Henderson, 354–361, and Thomas Bayly, 371–376. Wilson's initial resolution was amended by Henderson to allow for commissioned officers in the military or naval services to exercise the right of suffrage. Noncommissioned officers and enlisted men on regular duty in the armed services were still excluded. Wilson accepted this friendly amendment, 354. It was voted down; Ayes 37, Noes 53. Campbell's resolution was reported as having "failed by a very large majority, [with] eleven only rising in the affirmative" (390)

of "all white male citizens of the United States, of the age of twenty-one years, or upwards, and resident in the county, city, or borough or other electoral district, where they shall respectively offer to vote, at the time of the election," and then made subsequent qualifications and disqualifications the norm and not the exception. Qualifications included a residency requirement for nonnative Virginians, a freehold requirement for naturalized citizens, and a record of paying taxes for two years prior to any election. Criminals, paupers, those of unsound mind, and any enlisted servicemen were explicitly disqualified. In short, Cooke deigned to vest the right of suffrage in all white men and then restrict it based on the particular needs of the polity. The proposal flowed logically from his view of history as a story of human progress: Suffrage would be recognized in personhood and the qualifications would be repudiated over time. Conservatives were not deceived, however, and, even after Cooke had substantially amended his resolution, they voted down his proposal as well.[25]

Democratic reformers failed in their efforts in large part because they could not demonstrate the suitability of any other test to replace the freehold. The argument that residency evinced the necessary social attachment proved unconvincing in the face of a host of qualifiers pertaining to the amount of time needed to establish residency. Such qualifiers were also indicative of a highly mobile society where frequent changes in residence were normal. Furthermore, residency, as with forms of mobile property, offered no mechanism to bind individuals to the fate of a particular community, for better or worse. The particulars of Virginia's tax policy also made the payment of taxes an inadequate standard for suffrage. Taxes were paid on land, slaves, carriages, and horses and were subject to levels set by the legislature. Even John Rogers Cooke recognized that a franchise resting on the payment of a certain amount of taxes was subject to the caprice of the legislature. Whole classes of voters could be enfranchised or disenfranchised simply by changing the laws of assessment. Accordingly, the effort to abandon real property qualifications and to situate citizenship in individual persons was frustrated by an inability to justify a sense of permanent attachment on the basis of anything more substantial than patriotism or consent. Ironically, the provision stated in the Declaration of Rights stipulating that suffrage should be extended to those with a "permanent interest" ultimately stymied the efforts to democratically reform voting rights.[26]

IMAGINARY FREEHOLDS

Although reformers failed in their ultimate objective to impose democratic citizenship, they succeeded in launching a devastating attack on the franchise principle of the freehold. They did so by emphasizing the problems posed by the consequences of allodial ownership, with its inherent consideration of land

[25] *PDVSC*, 432. Cooke's resolution was defeated narrowly; Ayes 43, Noes 49 (441).

[26] *PDVSC*, 362–368. Nicholas offered a direct critique of Wilson's proposal, and see 434 for Cooke's discussion of the problems of a taxation mechanism.

as a commodity and subject to market values. Eugenius Wilson, in offering his reform resolution, explained that his proposal not only intended to rectify the inequity of the suffrage laws, but also attempted to avoid "the difficulties which must ever attend to any scheme of property qualification." He suggested that it was generally admitted among the delegates that limiting suffrage rights to those owners of a "fixed number of acres of land" was both "absurd and unjust, because of the inequality of the value of land." He noted too that, in a market society, the value of land was "too fluctuating, and its tenure too uncertain" to furnish sufficient evidence of a permanent attachment. He provided a hypothetical example of a "virtuous and intelligent man" who held the franchise by virtue of his freehold but who, "by one of those sudden reverses of fortune, which…are continually occurring," should lose his farm. He asked if this former virtuous citizen should now be deprived of his vote as well. Wilson, of course, concluded that the man should not, and argued that because he had been deprived of his source of wealth, he would be even "more concerned in the procurement of equal and just laws," which stood as his only defense against oppression. Charles Morgan spoke of the ease of alienating land titles in Virginia in order to challenge the premise that it was more difficult to divest oneself of land than it was of bank stocks. Alexander Campbell agreed and exclaimed that if a freehold estate was proof of a "permanent interest in the State," then this interest was "fixed upon as great an uncertainty as can be well conceived."[27]

Lucas Thompson attacked the freehold qualification from a different perspective. He emphasized that conservative arguments advocating the natural independence of freeholders were subverted by the problem of widespread indebtedness. He suggested that "at least one half or three-fourths" of all Virginia's freeholders were financially beholden through mortgages or other debts and thereby reduced to the status of tenants who paid rent. He provocatively contended that if economic independence was essential for the franchise, then government ought to be put exclusively "in the hands of the creditor class of the community." Alexander Campbell elaborated on this point by noting that for all practical purposes, within a rational understanding of Virginia's land laws, both a landlord and a tenant might possess "the same permanency of interest" in the same estate. Another reformer criticized the myth of the independent freeholder by commenting that, in Virginia, where land was cheap, a freehold could be purchased for as little as twenty-five dollars. From this fact he asserted that a millionaire like Stephen Girard could create "a whole Commonwealth" of freeholders who would be loyal to him without materially impairing his financial resources. Thompson argued passionately that all standards contained a measure of imperfection, "except those of age and residence." He chided his conservative counterparts who derided universal suffrage by suggesting that any test of independence "founded on the possession of property is equally Utopian, equally unjust, and equally fallacious."[28]

[27] *PDVSC*, 351–352 (Wilson); 377 (Morgan); 386 (Campbell).
[28] *PDVSC*, 415 (Thompson); 357 (Henderson); 386 (Campbell).

Conservative delegates easily dismissed charges of a freehold aristocracy as "ludicrous" and indicative of "a confusion of ideas." Responding to criticisms of the efficacy of the freehold qualification proved more difficult, however, particularly given that those who opposed democratic reforms were divided over the issue. Conservative delegates Philip Nicholas and John Randolph argued vociferously for maintaining the traditional freehold qualification as the very best basis for establishing suffrage. Their speeches were replete with Jeffersonian images of freehold cultivators as the "chosen people of God" and the guarantors of civic virtue. Others, however, like John Williams Green, Robert Stanard, and James Monroe, advocated for enhancing the landed qualification so that it could include long-term leaseholders, house-keepers, and those with future legal claims to a freehold estate through remainder or revision. Their vision recognized the historical authority of the *paterfamilias* – the head of the household – and they sought to make this convention the basis for citizenship. This moderate group of conservative delegates also advocated redefining the standards used to determine a freehold estate. They actively sought to replace the acreage requirement with a qualification based on a minimum assessed monetary value. It was this group of moderates that had influenced the initial recommendation on suffrage in the legislative committee. Their new definitions marked a substantial departure from previous understandings of the freehold that had considered its agricultural productive capacity as the sole source of economic independence. In the end, their vision of an enhanced landed qualification prevailed mostly because the more staunchly conservative delegates needed the allegiance of these moderates to thwart the more substantial proposals of democratic reformers.[29]

The fact that previous historians have overlooked this schism between conservative factions can largely be attributed to the herculean efforts of Benjamin Watkins Leigh to maintain an antidemocratic consensus throughout the debate. Leigh was a prominent Richmond lawyer who had achieved notoriety in revising the State Code in 1819. His career would include two terms in the state legislature, an appointment as the reporter for the Virginia Supreme Court of Appeals, and a brief but outspoken stint as a U.S. Senator. During the two weeks that the debate over suffrage raged, he orchestrated the conservative opposition to democratic reform. The energy he expended in coordinating the opposition largely masked the internal divisions among the conservative delegates. Personally, Leigh professed an inclination toward preserving the traditional freehold qualification, but he acknowledged the likely futility of the cause, not because "it ought to fail," but simply because people believed it would fail. Frustrated with such an impending prospect, he lamented that "in almost every instance," when other states had "departed from the landed qualification," they had proceeded almost "instantaneously" to the concept of universal suffrage and embraced "those extremes of democracy" that had

[29] Critical responses to the charges of a freehold aristocracy can be found in *PDVSC*, 365–366, 402, and 436–437.

historically devolved into despotism. In an effort to prevent such a fate for Virginia, he proposed a compromise plan that maintained the original spirit of the freehold basis but extended the franchise to those who he described as being "within the equity of the original principle." In brief, Leigh sought to establish the franchise on the basis of ownership rights. He believed that the initial report of the legislative committee, with some important amendments, could serve as the basis for establishing the franchise on an equitable basis that reflected the changing economic conditions of the state. He offered his own plan for reform along such lines.[30]

Although Leigh's own initiative was ultimately defeated, the effort to establish an enhanced landed qualification characterized the antidemocratic argument throughout the remainder of the debate over voting rights. The embrace of an expanded property qualification reflected the belief that landed status remained the best test of a permanent attachment but otherwise, did not possess any politically significant attributes and did not merit special privilege. Gone were discussions of the interconnectedness of economic independence, vicinage, and civic virtue that provided a conception of republican citizenship in the post-colonial Commonwealth. Land remained the best test for citizenship, but both conceptions of land and of citizenship had fundamentally changed. These new principles formed the core of the new suffrage provisions of the revised constitution. The franchise was extended to leaseholders, house-keepers, and those with an abstract future right to an estate. Ultimately, however, the strongest evidence of change was reflected in abandoning the language that spoke of freeholds in terms of acreage. Thereafter, freeholds would be considered as were all other forms of property in Virginia, except slaves, merely in terms of the cash nexus.

The initiative to create a monetary-based freehold had been advanced in the legislative committee by moderate delegate Judge John Williams Green and reflected an effort to resolve the problem of "imaginary freeholds" in the western lands. In response to initial protests from Leigh and John Randolph about the fact that such a redefinition could potentially disenfranchise some freeholders, Judge Green explained that he had introduced the monetary proviso to counteract the disparity of land values between the eastern and western portions of the state. He noted that "it was a notorious fact, that in the Western part of the State there were bodies of land not worth a cent an acre," and which, he suggested, were not being occupied by independent farmers but were instead in the hands of speculators. He explained that if the freehold continued to be defined by the quantity of acreage alone, with no prescribed assessment value, then any "one of these large land-holders would be able to create at will, as many freeholders" as he pleased, when he pleased.[31]

[30] *PDVSC*, 393–394, also 345–346. Leigh also accepted the extension of suffrage to tenants who were "in circumstances to vote independently of their landlords." *cf.* The speech of Philip N. Nicholas, a Richmond banker, reflected traditional arguments for the freehold franchise. *PDVSC*, 363–367.

[31] *PDVSC*, 345–346. The term "imaginary freeholds" was employed during the debate by delegate Robert Stanard of Spotsylvania County.

Warnings by reform delegates about the potentially nefarious consequences of land acquisition by someone like Stephen Girard – the richest man in America – revealed that delegates on both sides of the issue were concerned with the ability to create freeholds by purchase and grant. Abundant access to cheap land could easily lead – if it had not already – to the establishment of a land-based system of hierarchical dependency similar to forms of tenancy found in New York's Hudson River valley. Such dependency, in turn, threatened to corrupt the integrity of the vote by facilitating political machines, which acted to achieve a factional interest. Robert Stanard, despite his stated opposition to the monetary value qualification, confirmed Judge Green's concerns by noting that "no one could cast his eye over the Western part of Virginia" without recognizing that the physical condition of the country was such that it allowed anyone who could afford "the price of the paper on which a deed could be executed, to qualify himself as a voter." He noted that western mountain lands were overrun with "rocks and shrubbery" and that in some western counties, the average value of all land "was less than five cents an acre, good and bad." In the most remote mountainous regions, Stanard contended that much of the land "was fit only for lairs for wild beasts" and "not worth one mill per acre." He suggested that these circumstances fostered the ability of certain well-off individuals to create imaginary freeholds and "qualify voters by the hundred." This recognized consensus thus proved a revealing moment in the debate; Jefferson's allodial vision, intended to secure economic and political independence, had been turned in on itself and now was considered a mechanism of dependency.[32]

Although acknowledging the extent of the problem, conservative delegates nevertheless opposed the plan to assign a monetary valuation on a freehold. Leigh protested the incongruity in the committee recommendations to place an assessment valuation on freeholders, yet not apply a similar standard to enfranchised house-keepers. He asked if the delegates seriously intended not only "to abolish the freehold qualification, but to make it a *less* qualification than the payment of the very smallest tax?" He offered an example of a freeholder whose estate was assessed at a dollar less than the projected valuation and in whose house resided a tenant who owned a single horse. "The result," Leigh exclaimed, would be "that the landlord, who owns the house, is forbidden to vote, while the tenant who pays a tax of four cents on his horse, is admitted to the polls." John Randolph offered a more traditional defense of the freehold. He expressed shock that a convention, which had been called because of popular outrage over the limitations on suffrage, could now propose to disfranchise the poorer classes of freeholders. Robert Stanard took a more moderate stance but still opposed the monetary valuation because it merely altered the formula;

[32] *PDVSC*, 346–347. Conservative Philip Nicholas also expressed concerns that characterizing land exclusively as a form of wealth would encourage the creation of vast estates and corrupt the "independence of character" traditionally associated with land ownership. Nicholas asked if anyone had ever heard of a Virginia freeholder being called the equivalent name of "a Livingston man, or a Clinton man" as was common in New York (366).

it did not actually rectify the inequality caused by a market determination of land values. He explained that "in the West, a certain quantity of land, not worth five cents in all, was sufficient to make a man a voter, while in the East, the smallest quantity of land communicating the same privilege, was worth from fifty to one hundred dollars."[33]

Despite the protests, a monetary proviso valuing a freehold at twenty-five dollars received sufficient support in the convention to be incorporated into the revised suffrage law. The new provisions provided that every white male citizen, twenty-one years old and resident in the Commonwealth who either possessed or whose tenant possessed a freehold estate in "value of twenty-five dollars," as assessed by law, was entitled to vote. In response to criticism made by John Randolph, that the definitional change would disenfranchise existing freeholders, the revised law explicitly affirmed the right of suffrage to all of those who were already qualified under the "former Constitution and laws." The franchise was also extended to those joint tenants, tenants in common, and parceners who met the twenty-five dollar valuation of the freehold. This additional amendment enfranchised those who held a portion of land as members of a corporation, those who possessed title in equity, and those who held mortgages, so long as their interest in a particular plot of land was equivalent to at least twenty-five dollars in assessed value.[34]

The convention's embrace of a commodity conception of land meant that henceforth, freeholders were defined by the monetary value of their interest in a piece of land. Freeholds could be easily divided into shares in a manner similar to stocks and bonds without undermining the principal of ownership. On one hand, the reform represented an effort to revive the multiplicity of individual rights to a freehold, which, traditionally, in the common law, had been addressed by the doctrine of tenures. On the other hand, the traditional conception of status was now articulated principally in terms of mere pecuniary interest. Indeed, an individual no longer actually had to own a freehold outright in order to vote; rather he just needed to meet the minimum level of interest to claim a right of freehold, as it was defined by law. The redefinition thus reflected a significant movement away from the tangible notions of individual ownership that had informed the allodial revolution. Ideological commitments to independence, self-sufficiency, and vicinage disappeared and were replaced by a commitment to an abstract right of ownership, which was expressed in terms of value and investment. This fundamental reconceptualization of the freehold thus facilitated significant reforms to the franchise and, by extension, recast fundamental beliefs about citizenship and self-government in Virginia's republic.

[33] *PDVSC*, 346–347 (Leigh, Randolph, Stanard), 900 (Revised Constitution).

[34] *PDVSC*, 900. A parcener (or coparcener) is a joint heir, or someone who inherits an estate with others, whereas a joint tenant is someone who holds lands for a term of life, years, or at will with at least one other person. Joint tenants have one common interest in the land and hold by the same title. Tenants in common, on the other hand, hold the same land but by separate and distinct titles.

COMPROMISE: SUFFRAGE AND PATERNAL AUTHORITY

Whereas the implementation of a monetary value-based definition of a freehold provoked substantial debate, the corresponding effort to enfranchise those who had future claims to a freehold went forth largely uncontested. The revised constitution extended the franchise to every white, male citizen entitled "to a reversion or vested remainder in fee" that was expected on a real estate for life and whose assessed value was at least fifty dollars. Reversion and remainder were specific common-law concepts extending from the doctrine of estates that signified a potential or eventual right to a property. Accordingly, the revised constitution extended suffrage to anyone who had a legally recognizable future claim to a freehold as part of an inheritance or long-term grant. Similar to the monetary revision that awarded a freehold right to someone who had a sufficient pecuniary interest, this reform was premised on the idea that multiple parties could share ownership rights in a particular freehold.[35]

Henry St. George Tucker, the son of St. George Tucker and a contemporary of the convention delegates, explained the twin concepts of reversions and remainders in his law school lectures, which he published as *Commentaries on the Laws of Virginia*. The younger Tucker noted that under the common law, freehold estates may be considered either in a state of possession or in a state of expectancy. He further explained that whereas it was often commonplace to assume a status of possession when discussing general rules of law, the "doctrine of estates in expectancy contain[ed] some of the nicest and most abstruse learning in English law." These two categories of expectancy were distinguished from actual possession by delineating possession as a state that began when the "time of enjoyment" began, after which the owner received "the rents and other advantages arising therefrom [i.e., the estate]." Possession thus indicated a status in which the present interest resided in the owner and did not depend on any other "subsequent circumstance or contingency." Others typically shared a legal interest in a particular estate, however, and these interests were vested by the doctrine of expectancies. The doctrine distinguished between two different forms of expectancy: a remainder, which arose from an agreement between parties; and a reversion, which was created specifically by an act of law.[36]

Remainders were essentially contractual in nature and signified an agreement concerning the present and future disposition of an estate. Quoting directly from Blackstone, Henry St. George Tucker defined a remainder as "an estate limited to take effect and be enjoyed after another estate is

[35] *PDVSC*, 900.

[36] Henry St. George Tucker, *Commentaries on the Laws of Virginia: Comprising the Substance of a Course of Lectures Delivered to the Winchester Law School*, 2 volumes (Reprint of the Third Edition, 1846: Lawbook Exchange, 1998), 1: 124–163. Tucker was the son of jurist St. George Tucker, the brother of Nathaniel Beverley Tucker, and the half-brother of John Randolph of Roanoke. He opened a law school in Winchester, served as the President of the Supreme Court of Appeals, and toward the end of his life taught law at the University of Virginia.

determined." As an example, he offered the case of a freeholder who granted his lands to Smith for twenty years and then, at the expiration of that term, to Jones and his heirs forever: Under such an arrangement, Smith would be considered as a tenant for years while Jones would have a remainder in fee. Accordingly, the doctrine of remainders facilitated the widespread use of extended tenancy without prohibiting subsequent grants or subverting the intended pattern of inheritance. The revised suffrage laws thus enabled Jones to vote during the twenty years that Smith occupied the freehold – even though Jones had not yet taken possession of the estate. Reversions, on the other hand, established a similar process through the law in cases of a freeholder dying intestate – without a will. Tucker described a reversion as "the returning of land to the grantor or his heirs after the grant is over." The most common form of reversion was the legal settlement of dower. Dower represented a remedy to the common-law principle of coverture – the principle that denied married women status to real property. Dower traditionally entitled a widow to one-third of her husband's estate, and the profits arising from it, following his death. It was a life estate, meaning that the dower remained in force for as long as the widow survived or did not remarry. Upon her death or remarriage, however, the estate passed to the lawful heir through the doctrine of reversion. Endowed lands were protected from creditors in a manner that the remaining lands of the estate were not. Extending suffrage to reversioners did not enfranchise widows, but it did allow the reversioner through descent – normally the heir, who would assume the freehold after the dower lapsed – the ability to exercise his franchise irrespective of the credit status of the remainder of the estate.[37]

The expansion of suffrage to those who had a future interest in the lands of the Commonwealth accordingly represented an attempt to correct some of the inherent instabilities experienced by the gentry in a dynamic, market society that considered land as a commodity. The effort to so amend suffrage implied a concern over the rampant problems of debt among freeholders and reflected an attempt to alleviate some of the pressures on transferring lands to adult offspring. Reform delegate William McCoy, a U.S. Congressman and merchant from Pendleton County, elaborated on the problem. He suggested that it was not uncommon for a father to grant the use of a plantation to each of his sons as they came of age but to retain the titles to each estate in his own hands. Because of the large debts incurred in starting up a new plantation, this method of retaining the title was a particularly effective way of avoiding forfeiture in case of misfortune or a bad harvest during the initial years of planting. Creditors were prevented from putting a lien on the land if the sons fell into problems with excessive debt because the land was not the property of the son, but the father. McCoy contended that "many of the most respectable farmers

[37] Tucker, *Commentaries*, 125, 161. On dower, see Marylynn Salmon, *Women and the Law of Property in Early America* (Chapel Hill: University of North Carolina Press, 1986).

in Virginia resided on land that was not yet theirs, but which they expected to get title for."[38]

Thomas Bayly, a delegate from Accomack County of Virginia's Eastern Shore, offered another example by explaining that in Accomack, many freeholders had already divided their farms into smaller freeholds to "give their sons the right of voting." On the confined space of the Eastern Shore, the practice had reached the point where they could "lop off no more, without depriving themselves of the privilege." He inferred that the scarcity of land was leading to a de facto return to the practice of primogeniture. Farms were divided and subdivided to the point where they could no longer be "done to any advantage" and could "only be given to one son...generally the first born," necessitating that the other sons be sent from home "to learn useful mechanical trades." The experience of Bayly's constituents may have been exceptional, but still, his remarks detailing the generational problems of partible inheritance when dealing with a finite amount of land foreshadowed the future of other Virginia counties. His comments, like those of McCoy, illuminated some of the subversive tendencies that an allodial conception of land ownership exercised on the stability and preservation of the traditional household. Enfranchising those landholders who held their estates in expectancy was thus a means of conforming voting rights to the complex landholding patterns of Virginia's gentry and diffusing the franchise among family members and others who shared an interest in the land.[39]

This new political conception of the freehold as an abstract right facilitated the enfranchisement of leaseholders as well. Leaseholders, by virtue of their extended leases and shared interest in an estate, evinced an adequate level of permanency to exercise political rights as well. Given that allodial ownership by itself had proven too uncertain a principle, extending the landed qualification to include leaseholders seemed logical. Their tenure provided a compatible level of stability with the actual conditions of Virginia's freeholders. The convention consequently extended suffrage to leaseholders who held leases for at least five years and paid an annual rent of at least twenty dollars, which, it was argued, sufficiently reflected a permanent attachment to the political community. Leasehold suffrage reflected a tacit recognition of an equivalency of interests between owners and long-term tenants, at least within the dynamics of a commercial society where land was considered principally as a transferable commodity.

The extension of the franchise to leaseholders clearly demonstrated the influence of antidemocratic moderates who had advocated for an expanded landed qualification. James Monroe had argued strongly for just such a qualification and had characterized the moderate position by noting that "our Country" was nothing "more than our territory," and that the best evidence

[38] *PDVSC*, 347 (McCoy).
[39] *PDVSC*, 373 (Bayly).

of attachment could be found in "some interest of moderate value" in the soil of the Commonwealth. Leasehold suffrage signaled the extent by which the concept of an interest in the land had replaced the ideal of land ownership as the necessary litmus of attachment to the community. In this particular aspect of revision, Virginia anticipated the enfranchisement of copyholders in Great Britain as part of the process of land reform there. It also reflected a retreat from much of the postcolonial rhetoric that maintained that economic independence was an essential component of republican citizenship. Certainly dependency remained a concern; the final section of the new suffrage provisions excluded paupers, any "person of unsound mind," anyone convicted of "any infamous offence," and any enlisted men or noncommissioned officers in the armed services. These exclusions were directed specifically at those persons who were perpetually in a state of dependence or, in the case of convicts and servicemen, had ostracized themselves from the interests of a specific community. Nonetheless, the idea of dependency itself had been transformed from a test of the ability to produce one's own food into a test of relative social productivity.[40]

This fundamental transformation in the conceptualization of the landed qualification facilitated even further reform. Following the adoption of the leasehold qualification, Charles Fenton Mercer offered an amendment to enfranchise those house-keepers, or heads of a family, who paid taxes and met a twelve-month residency requirement. This amendment was directed largely at the enfranchisement of those men, like the merchants of Richmond, who did not work the land but who, through their trades and amalgamated forms of property, were considered productive members of society with a common interest in the fate of the Commonwealth. Mercer's argument was grounded in the idea that land was simply one form of capital. Personal property, too, acted as "an essential ingredient in the wealth of the country," and those property rights were equivalent to those "of the land-owner to the land." Mercer believed that political rights should correspond to social productivity and this productivity was evaluated by one's relation to capital. This was especially true, he continued, given that the right to vote in Virginia was never vested in the land itself, but in "the relation in which the proprietor stands to it." He suggested that because land and capital actually represented one and the same thing, it might be said that house-keepers too possessed an "interest in the soil."[41]

Initially, Mercer's proposal passed with very little discussion. It was revisited, however, when the legislature returned to the suffrage question to set the property values for freehold and leasehold estates. At that point, conservatives sought to remove the house-keeper provision. Benjamin Watkins Leigh reacted sharply against the proposal; indeed, the subsequent debate stirred up feelings of personal animosity between the two men. Leigh protested that

[40] *PDVSC*, 428 (Monroe); 638.

[41] *PDVSC*, 441–442 (Mercer). Douglas R. Egerton, *Charles Fenton Mercer and the Trial of National Conservatism* (Jackson and London: University of Mississippi Press, 1989).

the ambiguity of the term "house-keeper" would effectually impose universal suffrage. Furthermore, he reiterated the argument that any qualification premised on the payment of tax simply transferred the powers of enfranchisement and disfranchisement to the legislature. Finally he referred to his previous invocation of Jefferson's old adage in complaining that tradesmen and merchants were "the last class of men (except paupers) who ought to be admitted to the polls" because of their inherent dependency. Weary from fending off the repeated attempts at democratic reform, however, Leigh proposed that if Mercer could "fix upon any forms of words" that would enfranchise house-keepers but prohibit "Universal Suffrage," he would support such an amendment. Still, he believed such an effort "wholly impracticable."[42]

Despite conservative dissent, the provision enfranchising house-keepers was retained. Certainly, Mercer's resolution was helped in no small part by a favorable endorsement from James Madison. Madison was reticent throughout the convention, making only one speech on the subject of representation. But he weighed in on the subject of house-keeper suffrage by circulating a memorandum to the delegates that explained his reasons for expanding suffrage beyond a landed basis. He acknowledged that merely expanding the franchise to a more liberal landed qualification would suit the current conditions of the Commonwealth, but he reminded the delegates that they had been tasked with preparing "a system of [government] for a period which it is hoped will be a long one." Hence he encouraged the delegates to contemplate "the prospective changes in the condition and composition of society" that the times were "rapidly producing." Madison justified enfranchising house-keepers on the basis of Malthusian population theory; he believed that improvements in agricultural production inevitably resulted in a rise in the number of landless wage laborers. This proletarian specter haunted Madison. He was well aware that a class of men "without property, or the hope of acquiring it" could never "be expected to sympathize sufficiently with its rights," and so he asked the delegates what was "to be done with this unfavored class of the community?" He considered it essential for the future of republican government that members of this class be admitted into the "partnership of power" so that they too had a vested stake in the interests of the community. He believed that house-keepers and heads of families, representing those types who had made themselves "hostages to fortune," would give themselves "to their Country" as well.[43]

Madison's argument for expanding suffrage beyond a landed qualification reflected the recognition that the dictates of the commercial marketplace

[42] *PDVSC*, 638–641; 398, 442 (Leigh). On the animosity between Mercer and Leigh, see Egerton, 228–233.

[43] Gaillard Hunt, ed., *The Writings of James Madison* (New York: G. P. Putnam's Sons, 1910), 9: 358–360. Madison had expressed similar sentiments as early as 1821. For analysis, see Drew McCoy, *The Last of the Fathers: James Madison and the Republican Legacy* (Cambridge: Cambridge University Press, 1989), 192–198.

imbued men with a sense of responsibility. Significantly, his argument was not one for manhood suffrage: bachelors, journeymen, and day laborers would still be excluded by this final provision. Instead, those who exercised paternal authority over their households were considered imbued with the permanent attachment to the community necessary to exercise the franchise. Of equal significance, Madison's assertion that extending the right to vote to this class would vest them in the community turned traditional understandings of the franchise on its head. Freeholders had possessed the franchise because their circumstances better connected them with the community; henceforth, Madison contended, house-keepers would be better attached to the community by possession of the franchise. His letter went to the very heart of the issue of reform, but it was essentially conservative, rejecting pietistic references to natural rights in favor of an argument for political expedience and public order.

CONVERGENCE: CONSTRUCTING A NEW REPUBLICAN THEORY OF PROPERTY

In addition to Madison's endorsement, Charles Fenton Mercer's effort to enfranchise house-keepers was facilitated by its premise that labor, as well as land, provided an important source of capital in Virginia. By defining productive labor as a form of capital, and by suggesting that capital should serve as the basis of political rights, Mercer articulated a reconceptualized vision of property that bridged the antagonistic arguments of democratic and conservative delegates. Property remained the litmus. It continued to serve as the principal means of expressing the permanent attachment to the community necessary for the exercise of political rights. But it was a particular understanding of property, one that emphasized its economic qualities as productive capital. This more expansive conceptualization allowed the productive capacity of labor to be considered as a form of property ownership and, therefore, to be seen in an equivalent light as the traditional productive capacity of land. Extending property rights to those who had capital in labor thus served as a means of reforming suffrage without undermining the conservative commitment to a property qualification. Furthermore, and perhaps more significantly, Mercer's proposal to expand suffrage to house-keepers on the basis of their productive labor buttressed conservative arguments for a scheme of legislative apportionment that adequately represented property – especially their property in slaves.

Abel Parker Upshur, a leading antidemocratic delegate from Accomack, advanced a series of arguments during the convention that, while conservative in nature, sought to establish a new political basis for property rights, and which converged with the reform proposals made by Mercer. Upshur served as a judge on the General Court. He had been born into a prominent Eastern Shore planter family with strong Federalist affiliations. As a young man he matriculated at Princeton until he was expelled for participating in a student-riot and then studied at Yale for a time before ultimately reading law under the tutelage of William Wirt. His speeches during the convention highlighted the traditional commitment to property rights while simultaneously reflecting their changing meaning. Despite his staunchly conservative professions, he favored making any reforms he considered necessary and appropriate. Not so surprisingly, then, he endorsed the revisions to suffrage but remained adamantly opposed to a white-basis system of representation. Upshur particularly criticized the natural-rights arguments of the reformers. He rejected the liberal myth of a state of nature, explaining instead that men were born into existing societies and historically constituted governments. Anticipating Tocqueville, he disdained reformers' embrace of the principle of majority rule as an attempt to establish a despotic democracy through a tyranny of numbers. Furthermore, he contended that democratic reformers had "fallen into a great error" in considering the convention "as if we were now for the first time, entering into a social compact." Quite to the contrary, he asserted, the Commonwealth had operated effectively for "fifty-four years" during which time rights had been defined and property had been preserved. This assembly represented a moment of constitutional amendment, not revolution.[44]

Upshur maintained that property, as well as persons, comprised the "constituent elements of society." He contended that true representative government took this dualism into account and constructed mechanisms to represent property interests as well as persons. Nevertheless, he explicitly acknowledged the complexity of modern property relations and considered them the principal catalyst for reform. He explained that property rights had become "infinite" and could only be determined by adjudication or by reading "volume upon volume" of the "leading principles relating to them." The sheer pluralism of property rights in a commercial society created new sets of relations that demanded the "continual imposition of the Legislative power" on a daily basis. Most notably, he noted the difficulty inherent in the common law in grappling with the pervasive influence of mobile species of property, especially money and stocks. Certainly, Upshur's own experiences as lawyer and judge had facilitated an internalization of this new dynamic vision of property. His life was rooted in the law, not in the soil. Revealingly, in responding to democratic criticisms of property-based representation, he offered the delegates an example of how property rights were actually represented by speaking of a "bag of guineas," not an estate in land. He explained that to suggest that the bag of guineas "was a constituent entitled to representation" was "grossly absurd"; rather, it

[44] *PDVSC*, 69–74 (Upshur). Claude H. Hall, *Abel Parker Upshur: Conservative Virginian, 1790–1844* (Madison: State Historical Society of Wisconsin, 1964). In many respects, Upshur typifies the conservative profile suggested by Dickson Bruce in *Rhetoric of Conservatism*, who has observed that conservative arguments seeking to protect the representation of property in government were consistent with contemporary conservative positions taken on both sides of the Atlantic. Bruce argued that Virginia's conservatives should not be characterized as eccentric reactionaries looking to recreate a feudal order, but instead as a group of serious thinkers who wanted to establish a new basis for property rights amid the changing nature of property relations. He noted, too, that in Virginia, and throughout the American South, this conservative position was being increasingly informed by the commitment to slavery.

was "the rights and interests which spring from the possession of money" that he proposed needed representation.[45]

Significantly for the future of republican political thought in Virginia, Upshur advanced an argument maintaining that these multiple species of modern property contributed to government in different ways. In agricultural Virginia, he explained, "a great, and important, and leading interest" was represented by the ownership of slaves. He emphasized that in addition to supplying more than half of the productive labor force, slaves were also the basis for 30 percent of the "revenue derived from taxation." Slaves, he contended further, were an anomalous species of property because the government taxed not only the "slaves as property," but also the fruits of the labor earned by slaves. He offered as an example the circumstances of a slave owner who paid taxes on his slaves and then paid taxes on his horse or a carriage, which had been purchased from profits produced by slave labor. He provocatively maintained that under the existing laws of taxation, no such tax was imposed on the white laborer. Upshur suggested that this "double imposition" was chiefly responsible for the "striking peculiarity" of slave property. It served as the source for the demand for "a double security" in the form of legislative apportionment that would protect that species of property from the increasingly populous, non-slaveholding electorate.[46]

Judge Upshur's comments are revealing in many respects. Like those of Charles Fenton Mercer, they define an interest in society through a test of relative social productivity, which both men understood in terms of capital. House-keepers deserved political rights because their paternal responsibility imposed on them the necessity of consistent production. Certainly James Madison's characterization that family life made those heads of households "hostages to fortune" could easily serve as a clarion call for the American middle class, resonating across the centuries. Lacking tangible property in land, however, these house-keepers would be forced to seek that fortune by employing the productive capacity of the only asset they possessed – their labor. Similarly, slave owners argued for a distribution of political rights on the basis of the productive labor that they employed. They sought a mechanism for the representation of the dual interests in property and persons because of their exponential capacity to produce and the double imposition of taxes on that production. Despite staunch ideological differences during the convention, the arguments of both reform and conservative delegates converged around the recognized value of productive labor in sustaining the Commonwealth. In the end, both sides accepted the failure of the allodial land ownership in general and the freehold in particular to provide an adequate foundation for republican citizenship. In its wake, they embraced a series of constitutional reforms that reflected the changing social values of property ownership: The ownership of land was

[45] *PDVSC*, 70–71.
[46] *PDVSC*, 74–75.

replaced by the ownership of productive property, or capital, as the litmus of civic attachment.

Significantly, then, the ideological shift to consider all property foremost as a form of capital fostered the development of a complex political argument for the primacy of slavery within Virginia's republican polity. In the opinion of Upshur, as well as those of many of his fellow conservatives, slaves, not freeholds, represented a special form of property with a recognized civic value and thus in need of specific constitutional protections. Certainly slave property had always been important in Virginia; as a preferred form of labor, it had served as an instrumental component of the Commonwealth's agrarian vision. But the idea advanced by Upshur – that the ownership of slaves provided the necessary economic productivity for stable republican government – reflected the substantial change wrought to republican political thought by the consideration that all species of property served principally as sundry forms of capital. At the outset of the convention, former President James Monroe had charged delegates to fashion a new form of republican government to replace the original freeholder ideal. In this effort they were tragically successful; henceforth, the new foundation for republican government in Virginia would be the institution of slavery.

4

Can These be the Sons of Their Fathers?

One can fairly well surmise that Nat Turner never had the privilege of reading Blackstone's *Commentaries*. Like most Virginians, however, he had read the King James Bible and this reading fostered in him a very strong conception of justice. So much so that in the early morning hours of August 22, 1831, Turner and six of his fellow slaves launched a violent raid against the white population of Southampton County to strike a blow against the injustice of human bondage. The attack was brutal. Using the weapons initially at hand – axes, hatchets, and a dulled broadsword that could only maim – Turner and his compatriots snuck into local households and murdered their occupants, sparing neither women nor children. As the morning advanced, Turner's force grew to fifty or sixty men. Confiscating firearms and horses from their victims, they terrorized a schoolhouse in the Cross Keys community, killing the teacher and ten of her pupils. The uprising waned that afternoon following an unsuccessful attack on the town of Jerusalem – Southampton's county seat. In the face of growing white resistance, Turner took refuge in a local barn and attempted to reorganize his force, but he was unable to revive the attack the next morning. Most of the insurgents scattered after a halfhearted assault on a nearby farmhouse during the early morning hours. By daybreak, fifty-five white residents were dead and Turner and his few remaining compatriots were on the lam. But the violence was only beginning. Armed vigilantes scoured the local swamps arresting and executing alleged insurgents. Reprisals were indiscriminate. Distinctions between free and enslaved were erased as race became the only meaningful badge of status. By nightfall, and for the next few days, a wave of militia men descended on the county and their repression equaled the brutality of the revolt. A North Carolina militia company affixed the decapitated heads of their black victims to posts along the roadsides of Southampton. Witness to the slaughter must have challenged even the most idealistic to question mankind's capacity for self-government. On August 28, after nearly a week of terror, General Richard Eppes, at the behest of the governor, arrived on the scene, declared martial law, and restored order to the community.[1]

Nat Turner evaded capture for another two months until he was apprehended at the end of October. Given the subsequent history of southern race relations, it is a point of profound significance that he was not lynched following his arrest. Despite his rampant act of terror, he was neither summarily executed nor incarcerated without legal recourse. Rather, pursuant to the law of Virginia, he was publicly sentenced and tried before the local Court of Oyer and Terminer – a special incarnation of the County Courts designed to hear cases involving slaves and free blacks. Indeed, Turner stood as the final defendant in the fifty-one cases heard by the court determining verdicts against the indicted conspirators. Turner and eighteen others were convicted and sentenced to be executed. Others were convicted and transported outside the Commonwealth, whereas twenty-three of those arrested were either acquitted or, lacking sufficient evidence, simply released from custody.

These slave trials hardly met contemporary constitutional standards of "fair." Certainly, none of the defendants was able to present evidence or interrogate witnesses on their behalf. Nor was their fate determined by a jury of their peers. Moreover, an initial presumption of guilt affected all their testimony. Still, the trials were significant because they represented the community's desire to impose legitimacy on an episode of sheer violence. Certainly, at a fundamental level, such a desire exists in every judicial proceeding, but these slave trials reflected a particular effort to restore the complex relations of paternalism that had come undone and had been exposed as resting on brute force. Additionally, they occurred at a time when slavery was becoming increasingly prominent in discussions of constitutional and legal reform in Virginia. Indeed, each of the critical events that arose as a consequence of the uprising – the trials, the publication and dissemination of Nat Turner's "Confessions" by lawyer Thomas Gray, and the subsequent Virginia slavery debate – all can be considered as efforts to reconstruct a legitimate basis for slavery.[2]

[1] *The Confessions of Nat Turner and Related Documents*, edited with an Introduction by Kenneth S. Greenberg (Boston and New York: Bedford Books, 1996) and Greenberg, ed., *Nat Turner: A Slave Rebellion in History and Memory* (New York: Oxford University Press, 2003); Stephen B. Oates, *The Fires of Jubilee: Nat Turner's Fierce Rebellion* (New York: New American Library, 1976); Herbert Aptheker, *Nat Turner's Slave Rebellion* (New York: Humanities Press, 1966); Henry Irving Tragle, ed., *The Southampton Slave Revolt of 1831: A Compilation of Source Material* (Amherst: University of Massachusetts Press, 1971).

[2] See the summation of trial results in Tragle, ed., *Southampton Slave Revolt*, 229–245; Daniel Fabricant, "Thomas R. Gray and William Styron: Finally, A Critical Look at the 1831 Confessions of Nat Turner," *American Journal of Legal History*, 37 (1993): 332–361; and David Almendinger, Jr., "The Construction of *The Confessions of Nat Turner*," in Greenberg, ed., *Nat Turner*, 24–42. On the relation between law and paternalism, see Eugene Genovese, *Roll, Jordan, Roll: The World the Slaves Made* (New York: Pantheon Press, 1974); Mark Tushnet, *The American Law of Slavery 1818–1860: Considerations of Humanity and Interest* (Princeton, NJ: Princeton University Press, 1981); Ariela Gross, *Double Character: Slavery and Mastery in the Antebellum Courtroom* (Princeton, NJ: Princeton University Press, 2000); and

Admittedly, when compared in terms of size, duration, and casualties to other slave revolts in the Atlantic World, Nat Turner's revolt seems a relatively minor affair. But it had tremendous resonance. In 1831, Virginia was the largest slaveholding state in the Union. Many slaves continued to be involved in the production and distribution of tobacco, but the institution extended far beyond the tobacco fields of the Southside plantations. Slave labor was used heavily in the grain economy, with slaves planting and harvesting cereal crops and working in gristmills. Enslaved artisans could be found working in the iron forges and in textile production. The coal mines of Chesterfield and the salt mines of Kanawha were manned by slaves. Slaves built and maintained the state's roads, canals, and railroads. Virginians in every region of the state benefited, either directly or indirectly, from the produce of slave labor. Turner's actions thus struck at the economic base of the entire Commonwealth.[3]

More significantly, the revolt shook the ideological pillar of Virginia's republican polity – the idea of the rule of law. Considered from this perspective, the violent slave revolt and its brutal aftermath forced Virginians to address a question that, heretofore, had been somewhat more easily ignored: the question of slavery's legitimacy – its lawfulness. Since the Revolution, Virginia's legal culture had tacitly ascribed to Blackstone's criticisms of those legal writers, most notably Justinian, who had grounded justifications for slavery in the natural law. Instead, postcolonial Virginians generally attributed the legal basis of slavery as arising from the mere circumstantial construction of positive laws under the colonial government. In the wake of the Turner's insurrection, the significant effort to abolish slavery in the Virginia legislature forced defenders of slavery to abandon this orthodoxy and develop new arguments to legitimate slavery as an institution arising from the natural order.

Turner's uprising inaugurated an extended debate about the future of slavery in Virginia. Early public discussions culminated that winter in the House of Delegates where Thomas Jefferson Randolph, the grandson of his namesake, proposed a plan of gradual emancipation modeled after the successful efforts in Pennsylvania and New York. The debate that ensued focused almost exclusively on the legitimacy of slave ownership. Emancipationists raised questions

Sally Hadden, *Slave Patrols: Law and Violence in Virginia and the Carolinas* (Cambridge, MA: Harvard University Press, 2001).

[3] U.S. Census Office, Fifth Census, Tables [10]-[13]. The 1830 census listed Virginia's slave population at 469,755. This figure was 38.7% of the state's total population. On the diverse characteristic of slavery in antebellum Virginia, see Robert McColley, *Slavery in Jeffersonian Virginia* (2nd edition, Urbana: University of Illinois Press, 1964); Charles B. Dew, *Bond of Iron: Master and Slave at Buffalo Forge* (New York: W. W. Norton, 1994); J. C. Ballagh, *A History of Slavery in Virginia* (Baltimore: Johns Hopkins University Press, 1902); and Joseph Clarke Robert, *Tobacco Kingdom: Plantation, Market, and Factory in Virginia and North Carolina, 1800–1860* (Durham, NC: Duke University Press, 1938). On Nat Turner in a comparative perspective, see Eugene Genovese, *From Rebellion to Revolution: Afro-American Slave Revolts in the Making of the Modern World* (Baton Rouge: Louisiana State University Press, 1979), and Douglas Egerton, "Nat Turner in a Hemispheric Context," in Greenberg, ed., *Nat Turner*, 134–147.

about the social origins of property rights, the doctrines of eminent domain and police powers, and the general effectiveness of classifying slaves in the same manner as other forms of personal property. In the midst of the debate, these legislators ultimately abandoned the legal fiction of allodial property rights and, instead, embraced contemporary dogmas of legal positivism and governmental police powers. Defenders of slavery, on the other hand, discovered that their traditional arguments about the inviolability of private property rang hollow in the wake of a slave uprising. Yet after weeks of intense public debate and political maneuvering, the emancipationists failed to persuade a majority of delegates to effect any substantial antislavery legislation. In the end, the indecisive legislature passed a resolution by a mere seven votes that expressed a desire for the eventual removal of the state's entire black population but declared any "action for the removal of slaves" at that time to be inexpedient.[4]

The debate did not end there, however. The emancipationist challenge compelled a more thorough conservative response that transformed the idea of slave ownership within republican political thought. In the following months, defenders of slavery published a series of essays that reiterated and developed the proslavery arguments articulated in the legislature, contextualized them within a republican political discourse, and legitimated slavery as a historical institution. The most notable of these essays were written by three lawyers who did not participate in the legislative debate: Benjamin Watkins Leigh, Nathaniel Beverley Tucker (a son of St. George Tucker), and Thomas Roderick Dew, a young professor of political law at the College of William & Mary, whose contribution became a particularly seminal expression of modern proslavery arguments. Together, these essays marked the articulation of a profound shift in republican political thought in the Commonwealth. Similar to contemporary reforms in the industrializing northern states, these Virginia's lawyers necessarily reconceptualized republicanism. They abandoned the classical formulation of land tenure as the basis for republican citizenship and replaced

[4] *Journal of the House of Delegates in the Virginia Legislature, 1831–1832*, 99. Hereafter cited as *House Journal*. I explore the legislative debate in more detail in "*Partus Sequitur Ventrem:* Slavery, Property Rights, and the Language of Republicanism in Virginia's House of Delegates, 1831–1832," *Australian Journal of Legal History*, 6 (2000): 93–114. On the debate, see Joseph Clarke Robert, *Road From Monticello* (Durham, NC: Duke University Press, 1941); Theodore M. Whitfield, *Slavery Agitation in Virginia, 1829–1832* (Baltimore: Johns Hopkins University Press, 1930); Alison Goodyear Freehling, *Drift Toward Dissolution: The Virginia Slavery Debate of 1831–1832* (Baton Rouge: Louisiana State University Press, 1982); and William Shade, *Democratizing the Old Dominion: Virginia and the Second Party System, 1824–1861* (Charlottesville: University Press of Virginia, 1996). Douglass R. Egerton, *Gabriel's Rebellion: The Virginia Slave Conspiracies of 1800 and 1802* (Chapel Hill: University of North Carolina Press, 1993) has argued that the legislative sessions following Gabriel's Rebellion were much more significant and decisive than the 1831–1832 session, as there was still a chance for an "elite-led" abolition effort to succeed that he suggests no longer existed by 1832 because of the increasing domestic slave trade to the cotton states.

it by situating their privileged labor relationship – slavery – at the core of republican values.[5]

Although the substantial consequences of these reforms have sometimes eluded historians of the debate, most of the contemporary participants easily recognized the profound changes to conceptions of law and property rights that were in the making. James Gholson, a future judge of the General Court, articulated this awareness when he lamented that "when the distant reader shall discover, that the Virginia legislature, in 1832, was engaged in solemn debate on the questions, [of] whether 'private property can be taken for public use without compensation,' [and] whether 'slaves are property'...he will be lost in amazement, and will be ready to exclaim of us, can these be the sons of their fathers?"[6]

SLAVERY, REPUBLICANISM, AND LEGAL AMBIGUITY

The tensions existing between slavery and republican ideology manifested themselves in differing ways and in distinct expressions. Republican ideology grounded in allodial property simultaneously supported and undermined slavery. Attempting to make any summary characterization of Virginia's commonwealth men as either proslavery or antislavery proves to be an exceptionally difficult proposition, and probably more confusing than enlightening. Indeed the imposition of such a dichotomy on the ambience of labor relations during the postcolonial period has been, in many respects, a mere historiographical artifice given that such distinctions were only just emerging at the time. Only after the divorce of labor from the land, and the "invention of free labor," would it become possible to categorize someone accurately as either proslavery or antislavery. In any event, most Virginians of the period certainly would have considered such an either-or proposition reductive. Suffice it to say that slavery posed serious problems for republican government, and this recognition fostered a degree of consensus on several key points. Most importantly, postcolonial

[5] The most influential of these essays were: Benjamin Watkins Leigh, *A Letter from Appomattox to the People of Virginia* (Richmond, 1832); Thomas Roderick Dew, *A Review of the Debate in the Virginia Legislature of 1831 and 1832* (Richmond, 1832); Jesse Burton Harrison, "The Slavery Question in Virginia," *American Quarterly Review* (December 1832); and Nathaniel Beverley Tucker, "A Note on Blackstone's Commentaries," *Southern Literary Messenger* (January 1835). Leigh's essay originally appeared in the *Richmond Enquirer* on February 4, 1832, and elicited some letters to the editor in response on February 16 and 28, 1832. Leigh responded further on February 28, 1832 as well. Similar letters to the editor addressing the legislative debate appeared in other Virginia papers as well. On the adaptation of republican values and language to meet the needs of an industrial labor force, see Sean Wilentz, *Chants Democratic: New York City & the Rise of the American Working Class, 1788–1850* (New York: Oxford University Press, 1984). For a preliminary statement that addresses these reforms in the South, see Eugene D. Genovese and Elizabeth Fox-Genovese, "Slavery, Economic Development, and the Law: The Dilemma of the Southern Political Economists, 1800–1860," *Washington and Lee Law Review*, 41 (1984): 1–29.

[6] *Richmond Enquirer*, January 21, 1832.

Virginians uniformly considered slavery as an inherited burden that had been imposed on the colony by British merchant capitalists and slave traders.[7]

The inheritance of slavery created constitutional problems for a republic dedicated to allodial ownership. The recognition of these problems fostered expressions of lamentation that often have been construed as antislavery sentiments. Admittedly a few individuals, like St. George Tucker, decried the inherent incongruity between espoused ideals of republican equality and an unabashed commitment to slavery. Most, however, considered the problem from a different perspective. They anguished over how slavery corrupted the daily habits of slave owners and eroded the necessary qualities of virtue in these republican citizens. Most notably, Thomas Jefferson referred to slavery as a daily exercise "in tyranny" and commented that "the whole commerce between master and slave is a perpetual exercise of the most boisterous passions" reflecting characteristics of "the most unremitting despotism." He concluded that a slave owner would have to be a "prodigy" in order to "retain his manners and morals undepraved by such circumstances." George Mason agreed. He charged slaves with producing "the most pernicious effect on manners" and lamented that "every master of slaves is born a petty tyrant."[8]

Besides the pernicious effects that the enslaved seemingly imposed on the virtue of their masters, Virginia's jurists were also aware that slavery posed some particular problems within the jurisprudence of the common law. The English common law did not expressly legitimate slavery. Since it had developed in the colonies, the question of its legitimacy was entwined with the larger question of whether or not the common law was transmitted to the colonial possessions. Some commentators maintained that slavery existed only through the construction of positive laws, but the property rights claimed in slaves typically were adjudicated according to common-law categories. The local and customary nature of the common law facilitated this practice as well. By the eighteenth century, however, more and more British lawyers and magistrates maintained that a "spirit of liberty" was presumed in the common law, making slavery repugnant to the British constitution.[9]

[7] Robert J. Steinfeld, *The Invention of Free Labor: The Employment Relation in English & American Law and Culture, 1350–1870* (Chapel Hill: University of North Carolina Press, 1991) details the complexity of labor relations in early America. On the tensions between republicanism, race, and slavery in Virginia, see Eva Sheppard Wolf, *Race and Liberty in the New Nation: Emancipation in Virginia from the Revolution to Nat Turner's Rebellion* (Baton Rouge: Louisiana State University Press, 2006). On the latter theme more generally, see David Brion Davis, *The Problem of Slavery in the Age of Revolution 1776–1823* (Ithaca, NY: Cornell University Press, 1976).

[8] Jefferson, *Notes on the State of Virginia*; Robert Rutland, ed., *Papers of George Mason, 1725–1792* (Chapel Hill: University of North Carolina Press, 1970), 965–966. cf. St. George Tucker, *A Dissertation on Slavery: with a Proposal for the Gradual Abolition of It in the State of Virginia* (Philadelphia, 1796).

[9] Thomas D. Morris, *Southern Slavery and the Law, 1619–1860* (Chapel Hill: University of North Carolina Press, 1996), 37–57. For the application of common-law concepts onto the law of slavery, see David Brion Davis, *The Problem of Slavery in Western Culture*

This belief was adopted formally as a matter of English law following the ruling by the Court of King's Bench in the famous *Somerset* case in 1772. The case centered on the question of whether or not slavery could legally exist in England. James Somerset had been enslaved and sold to Charles Steuart, a British customs officer serving in Norfolk. In 1769, Somerset traveled to England with Steuart and managed to escape while there. He was recaptured, however, and destined to be sold back into slavery when his cause was taken up by Granville Sharp, a leading British abolitionist. Sharp obtained a writ of habeas corpus from the Court of King's Bench to determine Somerset's status. The case was debated for more than six months before the court ruled that Somerset must be released. In announcing the ruling for the court, Chief Justice Lord Mansfield commented that slavery was "so odious, that nothing can be suffered to support it, but positive law." Still, as historian James Walvin has noted, Mansfield's decision did not free all the slaves in England; indeed, he took "great pains" to circumscribe the *Somerset* decision to the specifics of the case and thus merely perpetuated the long-standing tension between slavery and the common law.[10]

Prior to the *Somerset* ruling, Blackstone had conveyed similar antislavery sentiments in critiquing Justinian's commentary on the natural origins of slavery. In the *Commentaries*, Blackstone engaged the "flawed foundations" of Justinian's explanation as to the sources of slavery. Justinian had suggested that slavery arose naturally either from a state of war, from contract, or by heredity. Much of Blackstone's argument was borrowed from Montesquieu and built on the explicit Christian belief that life itself was a gift from God. He argued that one man's power – or the state's power – over another was intrinsically limited by this divine donation. This principle of life appeared most evident in Blackstone's challenge to Justinian's contention that slavery resulted from the absolute right of the conqueror, in a state of war, over the lives of those captured. He refuted this assertion by rejecting as "an untrue position" that either the "law of nature or nations" allowed that a man "may kill his enemy" in any circumstance. Rather, he maintained that a combatant only had the right to kill in "particular cases," which were demanded by self-defense. Blackstone invoked the Augustinian just-war doctrine in holding that war itself was only justifiable "on principles of self-preservation." Such a principle, he contended,

(New York: Oxford University Press, 1966), 207–209; Mark Tushnet, *The American Law of Slavery, 1810–1860: Considerations of Humanity and Interest* (Princeton, NJ: Princeton University Press, 1981); Jenny Bourne Wahl, *The Bondsman's Burden: An Economic Analysis of the Common Law of Southern Slavery* (Cambridge: Cambridge University Press, 1998); and Michael Craton, "Property and Propriety: Land Tenure and Slave Property in the Creation of the British West Indian Plantocracy, 1612–1740," in John Brewer and Susan Staves, eds., *Early Modern Conceptions of Property* (London: Routledge, 1996), 497–529.

[10] *Somerset v. Stewart, ex parte Somerset* (1772) Lofft 1–18. James Walvin, *Black Ivory: Slavery in the British Empire* (2nd edition, Oxford: Blackwell Publishing, 2001), 12–14, 262; and George Van Cleve, Daniel J. Hulsebosch, and Ruth Paley, "Forum: *Somerset's Case* Revisited," *LHR*, 24 (2006): 601–671.

necessarily disappeared at the point of capture, and he emphasized that any "right of making slaves by captivity" must necessarily depend on "a supposed right of slaughter," which, he maintained, could never exist under a divinely inspired natural law.[11]

He took further issue with Justinian's premise that slavery could also arise contractually, with one man selling himself to another. He asserted that every sale implied an equivalent price – "a *quid pro quo*," that the seller received in exchange for "what he transfers to the buyer." Accordingly, he questioned what equivalent existed in exchange "for life, and liberty?" As with Justinian's state-of-war justification, Blackstone suggested that the relationship broke down at the point of enslavement – "the buyer gives nothing, and the seller receives nothing." Any contract was false and any sale invalidated. Finally, he rejected out of hand Justinian's supposition that heredity served as a source of slavery – that a person could be determined a slave at birth based on the status of one or both of their parents – on the grounds that any such contention necessarily derived from either of the other two previous sources. Given that the martial and contractual origins of slavery proved false, anyone born into the condition arising from these circumstances must be held contrary to the natural law.[12]

In Virginia, St. George Tucker elaborated on Blackstone's critique in an influential essay on the state of slavery in Virginia, which was appended to his edition of the *Commentaries*. One of the more ardent critics of slavery in the Commonwealth, Tucker opened his essay by declaring that whereas America had proven a "land of promise" for those of European descent, it had served as "the vale of death to millions of the wretched sons of Africa." Believing that slavery was incompatible with the principles of Virginia's revolution and its republican government, Tucker called for its end and proposed a detailed plan of gradual abolition. His essay was designed to facilitate such a plan by comprehensively considering the "rise, progress, and present state" of slavery in order to demonstrate its general "nature...properties, attendants, and consequences." He began by defining different forms of both liberty and slavery – political, civil, and domestic – before turning his attention exclusively to the circumstances of domestic slavery. Tucker endorsed Blackstone's repudiation of Justinian, reprinting the passage verbatim in the appendix, and then extended his commentary by analyzing the nature and historical circumstances of slavery in Virginia and elsewhere. In addressing each particular theme – origins, runaways, homicides, and manumissions – he interspersed his analysis with abundant examples of the development of statutory laws in the Virginia colony. In the end, he had compiled a comprehensive legal history of slavery in the colony and through the Revolution. Not surprisingly, he concluded his analysis by portraying slavery as a human institution, legitimated only by the circumstantial construction of positive laws. He elegantly noted that upon concluding a survey of the legal basis of slavery, "we are unavoidably led to remark, how

11 *TB*, II: 124–138.
12 *TB*, II: 423–424.

frequently the laws of nature have been set aside in favour of institutions," reflecting the pure circumstances "of prejudice, usurpation, and tyranny."[13]

Affixed to the leading legal primer in the Commonwealth, St. George Tucker's characterization of slavery possessed tremendous influence over Virginia's bench and bar. The comprehensiveness and accessibility of the narrative made it the definitive source on the legal basis of slavery throughout the early decades of the nineteenth century. It also evinced strong antislavery biases, especially because Tucker's previously published plan for gradual emancipation was included at the close of the essay. But Tucker was a gradualist in matters of race relations. Invoking the recent "melancholy picture" of emancipation in the French West Indies, he counseled prudence and caution in dealing with the problem of slavery. Tucker acknowledged the incongruity between slavery and the common law but suggested a pragmatic approach to the problem of emancipation. Such counsel enabled Virginians to postpone serious discussion of emancipation and delay efforts to reconcile the persistence of slavery within its common-law jurisprudence on the basis of temporary expediency.

PARTUS SEQUITUR VENTREM

Nat Turner brought an end to any inclination to postpone discussion of slavery. His insurrection ensured that the question of slavery was to be the unequivocal priority for the legislature when it convened in December 1831. In the months following the revolt, expressions of panic, anxiety, and pessimism had proliferated throughout the Old Dominion. County militias made urgent requests for muskets to the governor's office, and, on repeated occasions, residents of the slave-rich Southside counties reacted to false alarms of slave uprisings by fleeing from their homes. Newspaper editorials reported a "dark and growing evil at our doors," and at least one young Virginian anxiously hoped that the governor would "recommend some important measures... [during] this momentous crisis... in the affairs of our State." From across the state, Virginians petitioned the General Assembly to enact more strident restrictions on the black population. Some of these petitions called for the removal of the entire free black population, and a few even suggested the abolition of slavery itself. When the delegates convened in Richmond, Governor John Floyd inaugurated the session and, for the first time, publicly detailed the events of the August insurrection. He recommended that the delegates strengthen existing slave codes and called for the necessary appropriations to deport the state's free black population.[14]

[13] Tucker, "Of the State of Slavery in Virginia," *TB*, II: Appendix H, 31–32, 63.

[14] Legislative Petitions, 1831–1832, Library of Virginia. Numerous requests for muskets as well as accounts of panics and false alarms are found in the letters to the governor from September to October 1831. Governor's Papers, Library of Virginia, *viz.*, Leesburg, September 18, 1831; the Inhabitants of Chesterfield [N.D. September 1831]; Samuel Diggs, September 26, 1831; and Benjamin Cabell, October 1, 1831 and October 19, 1831. *Richmond Enquirer*, December 17, 1831; Philip St. George Cocke to General John Hartwell Cocke, December 14, 1831, Cocke

The content of the governor's annual message and the reception of the numerous petitions inspired legislators to create a special committee tasked with addressing the questions raised by the insurrection. Of the delegates initially appointed to this committee, eleven out of twelve owned slaves, with the majority of them representing Tidewater and Piedmont counties where the greatest density of slaves in the state existed. The chairman of the committee, William Brodnax, was himself a slave owner from Dinwiddie County, which bordered Southampton. He had served as a militia general and played a key role in implementing martial law after the insurrection. Brodnax represented the consensus opinion of delegates in the House. He referred to slavery as "a transcendent evil" but believed that the right to own slaves was "as perfect and inviolable as that to any other property." Embracing the social orthodoxy, he regarded the removal of Virginia's free black population as a necessary precondition to any plan for abolishing slavery. Accordingly, upon convening the select committee, he directed them to restrict their discussions to the possible removal of the free black population while tabling any petitions that openly discussed emancipation.[15]

Proslavery delegates feared that any open legislative debate over the future of slavery would only encourage further insurrections. Accordingly, they attempted to confine the discussions to the closed-door sessions of the select committee. Their strategy initially proved successful except for a brief procedural debate over the reading of the legislative petitions during the first month of the session. On January 2, however, delegate Charles Faulkner submitted a proposal for gradual emancipation of Virginia's slaves to the committee. Reports of Faulkner's proposal were leaked to the newspapers. With this encouragement from the newspapers, the public discussion over slavery, which had been quelled by the convening of the legislature, now erupted again with more force. Defenders of slavery became increasingly concerned that this public forum would "stimulate…fresh acts of violence," and they lashed out at the newspapers for disregarding "the safety and property of others." For several days, they remained determined to suppress open debate and engaged in a tirade against the newspapers sympathetic to such a public drama. Yet events seemed to conspire against them. By the end of a week, while rumors of emancipation schemes reached a crescendo in the state newspapers, word of another attempted slave insurrection in nearby Goochland County reached Richmond. Under these portentous circumstances, conservative proslavery spokesman, William Goode, made a motion to discharge the select committee "from the consideration of all petitions," that pertained to emancipation.[16]

Family Papers, Alderman Library, University of Virginia. Governor's Message in *House Journal*, 1831–1832, 9–14.

[15] William Brodnax, *Speech of William Brodnax, In the House of Delegates of Virginia on the Policy of the State with Respect to the Colored Population* (Richmond, 1832), 4–5, 6–8, 10.

[16] Charles Ambler, ed., *The Life and Diary of John Floyd* (Richmond, VA: Richmond Press, 1918); see especially the entry for January 9, 1832. *Richmond Enquirer*, January 7, 1832. *Richmond Enquirer*, January 19, 1832 [Speech of William Goode]. On the Goochland insurrection:

Ironically, Goode's motion launched the public debate that proslavery delegates had long been trying to avoid. He justified his motion on the grounds that he believed that the delegates were "considering whether they would confiscate the property of the citizens" – a question that he believed the legislature "had no right to act upon or consider." Emphasizing the market value of human property, he contended that merely by discussing the subject of emancipation, the select committee had impaired the property value of slaves. Slave owners, in anticipating legislation requiring emancipation, might suddenly flood the domestic slave market in a preemptive maneuver that would greatly increase the supply of slaves in the market and thus lower the price. He also forecasted (correctly) that other states, fearing an influx of slaves from Virginia, would prohibit the introduction of new slaves into their territory.[17]

Goode's comments reveal a defense of slavery grounded in a traditional commitment to the allodial theory of property, which considered the master-slave relation secured within a the realm of private ownership, and which increasingly allowed for slaves to be treated as elements of wealth and capital. Initial proslavery efforts to suppress discussion of emancipation had been motivated by the orthodox view that slave property was a matter of individual ownership, essentially a private institution, and that any public discussion threatened to erase the important distinction between public and private spheres. Thus, despite the recognized failure of the allodial freehold to serve as an effective republican political institution, these initial proslavery arguments maintained that preserving the absolute right of private property remained an essential precondition for the existence of republican liberty. Paradoxically then, Goode found himself in the position of inaugurating a legislative debate to refute legislative authority to engage in just such a debate.[18]

Thomas Jefferson Randolph proposed his plan of emancipation as an antithetical amendment in immediate response to Goode's motion. Randolph's amendment called for the select committee to "inquire into the expediency of submitting to the...voters" a plan of emancipation *post nati* (following birth).

Ambler, *Diary*, 174; John B. Floyd, Executive Papers, January 9, 1832, Library of Virginia. Council Journal, January 11, 1832, Library of Virginia. Goode's motion was reprinted in the *House Journal*, 93. For discussion, see Robert, *Road from Monticello*, 17 and Alison Freehling, 123, 127–28.

17 *Richmond Enquirer*, January 19, 1832. Louisiana and Pennsylvania passed restrictive laws in the aftermath of Southampton; another one had been defeated by close margin in Kentucky.

18 In 1806, following the slave insurrections in 1800 and 1802, the legislature passed a removal act mandating that all freed blacks must leave the state within a year of their manumission unless they received a special dispensation from the legislature. It is important to note that while the Removal Act signaled the legislature's willingness to enact laws concerning freed persons, they still refused to impose themselves on master-slave relation during the process of manumission. Specifically, the Removal Act did not charge the manumitting slaveholder with any responsibility (financial or otherwise) for overseeing the eventual removal. In practice, this act seems to have been sporadically enforced. See Luther Porter Jackson, *Free Negro Labor and Property Holding in Virginia, 1830–1860* (New York: D. Appleton, 1942), and Ira Berlin, *Slaves without Masters: The Free Negro in the Antebellum South* (New York: New Press, 1974).

Under this plan, the children of all female slaves born on or after July 4, 1840 would become the property of the Commonwealth when they came of age; males when they turned twenty-one, females at eighteen. Randolph believed that his emancipation plan allowed abolition to occur on grounds favorable to slave owners. They would not forfeit any of their existing slaves, nor would they lose any slaves born within the next eight years. Similar to the emancipation programs in Pennsylvania and New York that preceded it, his plan encouraged slave owners to transfer or sell their slaves out of state before the mandated emancipation date. Randolph did not consider his plan for gradual emancipation as original. He believed that he was following in the wake of the successful emancipationist programs carried out in other Mid-Atlantic States. More significantly, he contemplated his proposal as realizing the emancipationists' designs of both his grandfather, Thomas Jefferson, and his father, Thomas Mann Randolph, who had also proposed a plan of emancipation while serving as governor.[19]

Yet, despite invoking his grandfather's legacy, Randolph's plan differed in fundamental ways, reflecting a sharp discontinuity from previous emancipation proposals in Virginia. Jefferson had ruminated about an emancipation plan conditioned on the subsequent removal of freedmen on three separate occasions, but he had never presented his musings as an actionable plan, leaving it instead for "the next generation." He believed that the financial burdens imposed by the necessary costs of removal and compensatory payments to slave owners effectively inhibited state-sponsored emancipation. Randolph circumvented much of this funding problem by forgoing any consideration of compensatory payments to slave owners. Another difference in his plan was the manner in which emancipated slaves would be disposed while pending removal. Jefferson had simply spoken of slaves being raised at the public expense. Under Randolph's plan, emancipated slaves would work as the state's property until sufficient funds for their removal were raised. The state government would become an active agent in the emancipation process by serving as an intermediary between slavery and freedom.[20]

[19] *House Journal*, 93. *The Speech of Thomas Jefferson Randolph, in the House of Delegates, on the Abolition of Slavery* (Richmond, 1832). If these offspring were detained in Virginia until they came of age, they would "be hired out until" they raised enough funds "to defray the expense of their removal." Arthur Zilversmit, *The First Emancipation: The Abolition of Slavery in the North* (Chicago: University of Chicago Press, 1967), and Leon Litwick, *North of Slavery: The Negro in the Free States, 1790–1860* (Chicago: University of Chicago Press, 1961).

[20] Jefferson reflected on emancipation in his Draft Constitution (1783), *Notes on the State of Virginia*, and in an 1824 letter to Jared Sparks. It should be noted that following the 1806 Manumission Act, the removal of freedmen was not merely Jefferson's preference but was the law in Virginia. Despite a plethora of writings on Jefferson and slavery in recent years, the best treatments of his complicated perspective remain Winthrop Jordan, *White Over Black* (Chapel Hill: University of North Carolina Press, 1968); David Brion Davis, *The Problem of Slavery in the Age of Revolution, 1776–1823* (Ithaca, NY: Cornell University Press, 1976); John C. Miller, *The Wolf by Its Ears: Thomas Jefferson and Slavery* (Charlottesville: University Press of Virginia, 1991); and Annette Gordon-Reed, *Thomas Jefferson and Sally Hemings: An American Controversy* (Charlottesville: University of Virginia Press, 1998).

These divergent aspects of Randolph's plan were recognized immediately by proslavery delegates. James Gholson called the proposal a "monstrous and unconstitutional" violation of property rights, while James Bruce declared it "the most extraordinary doctrine that has ever broached this Hall." Nor were they alone in expressing their sentiments. Committee chairman William Brodnax disapprovingly scolded the heir, commenting that "were Mr. Jefferson now alive, I cannot for a moment believe, that he would approve...such a proposition as this." He explained that Jefferson's plan "contained features essentially different from this," and particularly noted that he did not believe that Jefferson ever recommended that "the off-spring of slaves should be torn from their owners without compensation." Randolph's plan was "fraught...with incalculable mischiefs" that would "subvert principles" that had been "constructed by the wisdom of ages." It would destroy "every barrier with which [the] constitution and laws have fenced the security of private property."[21]

In response, Brodnax submitted his own emancipation proposal that he believed to be more Jeffersonian than Randolph's. He called for the removal of approximately 6,000 people and their transfer to the colony of Liberia. This number was equivalent to the annual percentage of increase in Virginia's black population. Brodnax's plan was one of attrition. He wanted to concentrate on removing the increase in population and let the natural process extinguish slavery. He stipulated, however, that removal should begin with the free black population in order to avoid paying any necessary compensation to slave owners. He allowed, however, that slave owners could, at their own discretion, manumit their slaves who would then be subject to deportation.[22]

Proslavery delegates rejected Randolph's plan because it failed to recognize the future progeny of slaves as vested property. They had embraced Justinian's hereditary basis for slavery and ignored the traditional critiques offered by Blackstone and St. George Tucker. Significantly, they argued that Randolph's scheme ignored the common-law dictum of *partus sequitur ventrem*. This dictum had persisted as a useful remnant of feudal law and referred to the condition of the offspring naturally following the status of the progenitor. It had originally been used to prescribe status based on paternity, but during the seventeenth century, Virginia courts inverted the principle, making it matrilineal and ruling that the condition of an offspring was determined by the status of its mother. The device, once inverted, became an effective principle to determine status in a colony where paternity was not always definitive, and it represented one of the successful means by which common-law jurisprudence was adapted to a slave society.[23]

[21] *Richmond Enquirer*, January 21, 1832 [Speech of Gholson], and January 26, 1832 [Speech of Bruce]. *Speech of Brodnax*, 26–34, 17, 6.

[22] Brodnax's plan was later adopted by the House of Delegates as a guide for an appropriation bill designated for the removal of Virginia's free blacks, but it was defeated in the Senate. *House Journal* (1831–1832), Bills 7 and 12 (amended).

[23] Thomas D. Morris, *Southern Slavery and the Law, 1619–1860* (Chapel Hill: University of North Carolina Press, 1996), 43–49.

Legislators who defended slavery against Randolph's plan on the basis of *partus sequitur ventrem* seemed blissfully unconcerned about its significant historical reinterpretation. They characterized the maxim as part of the ancient wisdom of the common law. James Gholson explained the proslavery interpretation simply and harshly: "[T]he owner of land had a reasonable right to its annual profits; the owner of orchards, to their annual fruits; the owner of brood mares, to their product; and the owner of female slaves, to their *increase*." James Bruce noted that that if *partus sequitur ventrem* was not a rule of law and if slave owners had "no property in the future increase" of their slaves, than they certainly had no claim to those now living, because "the property in both must necessarily be derived the same way." Brodnax further added that such a "probability of increase [was] an essential constituent in the value of the female slave" and posited that the age-old maxim was not simply a rule of common law but a "dictate of common reason and common sense."[24]

The rule represented decided law, but it was complicated by some clearly defined limitations. In 1824, the Virginia Supreme Court had ruled on the complex matters of emancipation *in futuro* in the case of *Maria and Others v. Surbaugh*. The *Maria* case both resolved and raised some of the difficult questions surrounding the concept of *partus sequitur ventrem* by addressing the status of slaves emancipated by their owner's will at a future date. The case concerned the status of Maria, who was the child of the slave Mary. Mary, when she herself was a child, had been bequeathed to William Holliday by his father on the condition that she would become free on her thirty-first birthday. Holliday eventually sold Mary and – indicative of the consequences of allodial property – she was bought and sold another four times before she turned thirty-one. By 1818, when she came of age for freedom, Mary had four children. Maria was the oldest. Once emancipated, Mary brought an action for the freedom of her children against their current owner, David Surbaugh, on the grounds that following *partus sequitur ventrem*, her children should attain freedom correspondent with the status of their mother. The question before the court was thus whether or not Mary's children were to be freed as a consequence of her own emancipation. Judge John Williams Green, building on earlier precedent, ruled that the act of emancipation did not represent a transfer of property rights from the master to the slave, but instead signaled the mere abrogation of the owner's property rights. Accordingly, for Judge Green, the determinative issue in the case was not the condition of the mother but the intent of the testator in drafting the will. Given that Mary was the only person specified in the will, her children remained in bondage. The case testified to the flexibility of the common law in dealing with matters of slavery, but this same flexibility consequentially fostered an uncertainty inherent in resolving such issues before the bench. Green's ruling demonstrated that

[24] *Richmond Enquirer*, January 21, 1832; *Richmond Enquirer*, January 26, 1832; *Speech of Brodnax*, 13–14, 22.

partus sequitur ventrem stood as a rule only as long as it served the public good. In this instance, the public good was identified in the persona of the slave owner.[25]

Given these limitations imposed on *partus sequitur ventrem*, it was not so surprising that defenders of slavery proved reluctant to rely exclusively on the doctrine or the ruling in the *Maria* case during the legislative debate. On perceptibly more tangible ground, they also criticized Randolph's plan as subversive because it proposed to appropriate private property without awarding just compensation. They admitted that the government had the right to assume private property, but that it could do so only in instances of absolute necessity, "when the public safety and prosperity, obviously required the deprivation of private property." Even then, however, they maintained that any such appropriation required just compensation. Brodnax explained that whether or not "public necessities" required "the surrender" of private property, it still arrived at the same logical end; it could not be "taken against our consent, but on paying to us its value." Any such an action, they contended, violated both custom and constitution. James Gholson noted that the assembly had already followed the customary process of compensating slave owners – in this instance, for those slaves executed during Nat Turner's insurrection. Other proslavery delegates cited guarantees of just compensation not only in state constitution, but in the Fifth Amendment to the Federal Constitution as well. Exercising eminent-domain powers without compensation would dismantle the institutional mechanisms of allodial property.[26]

This emphasis on the doctrine of eminent domain reflected the intrusion of contemporary legal debates over government taking powers into questions of emancipation. The slavery debate took place at a time when eminent domain was undergoing a substantial reconceptualization. The principle was being used expansively, particularly by the state governments, to finance and construct internal improvement projects. While just compensation had been a regular component of eminent domain since the seventeenth century, state legislatures and courts were increasingly seeking new ways to circumvent compensation to meet the financial demands of material progress. One popular innovation was reflected in the practice of off-setting compensation. Compensation paid to an individual was adjusted by the value gained by the improvement made. For example, the value of land submerged as a result of a new mill-dam being constructed downstream would be considered in light of its proximity to the

[25] *Maria and Others v. Surbaugh* (1824) 2 Randolph 228. See the important discussion of this case in Thomas D. Morris, *Southern Slavery and the Law, 1619–1860* (Chapel Hill: University of North Carolina Press, 1996), 404–412. On the importance of the concept of the public welfare in nineteenth-century judicial interpretation, see Peter Karsten, *Heart of Head: Judge Made Law in Nineteenth-Century America* (Chapel Hill: University of North Carolina Press, 1997), and William Novak, *The People's Welfare: Law and Regulation in Nineteenth-Century America* (Chapel Hill: University of North Carolina Press, 1996).

[26] *Speech of Brodnax*, 23, 13–14; *Richmond Enquirer*, January 21, 1832.

new mill. The projected increase in the value of such land would compose part of the tenant's compensation for the taking.[27]

At a basic level, this theory of adjustment was reflected in Randolph's emancipation proposal. The absence of direct compensation was predicated on the notion that emancipation would foster both security and economic growth for Virginia's slave owners. At the time of the slavery debate, however, Virginia had been reluctant to embrace such a liberal interpretation of compensation. Four years earlier, the state Supreme Court had ruled explicitly against it in the case of *Crenshaw and Crenshaw v. Slate River Company*. The case involved promoting the navigational improvement of waterways at the expense of mill owners. As in the *Maria* case, however, the decision rested largely on judicial interpretations of the public good – the very doctrine that elsewhere was being used to promote takings. In the aftermath of the case, Virginia had included an amendment prohibiting uncompensated takings in the Revised Constitution of 1830; something that had hardly seemed necessary in the original constitution. Nonetheless, Randolph was advancing a familiar argument to a sympathetic crowd of western delegates who advocated internal improvement projects and who were well aware of how liberal judicial interpretations had facilitated them in other states.[28]

His plan for gradual emancipation ultimately failed, however, because it contradicted allodial conceptions of property, which essentially understood the ownership of private property as an exclusionary right. If enacted, government-imposed emancipation would have breached the dominion of slave owners by confiscating the children of slaves, thus causing the owners to forfeit a portion of their property without any compensation. Within the traditional republican theory of property, any exercise of eminent domain without compensation represented an absurdity that contradicted the very premises of free government. Brodnax effectively summarized this position by noting property stood as "the very ligament which [bound] society together....Without this principle, there was no civilization – no government." Delegate James Bruce offered a eulogy for Randolph's proposal by stating that "its glaring...defects serve to show us the difficulty, or rather the impossibility, of devising any scheme of emancipation which shall be practicable, and not at the same time" directly violate the rights of property ownership.[29]

[27] A. E. Dick Howard, *Commentaries on the Constitution of Virginia*, 2 vols., (Charlottesville: University Press of Virginia, 1974), 1: 210–229; Harry Scheiber, "The Road to Munn: Eminent Domain and the Concept of Public Purpose in the State Courts," *Perspectives in American History*, 5 (1971), 372–402; Tony Freyer, "Reassessing the Impact of Eminent Domain in Early American Economic Development," *Wisconsin Law Review* (1981): 1263–1286; and James W. Ely, Jr., "That Due Satisfaction May Be Made': The Fifth Amendment and the Origins of the Compensation Principle," in James W. Ely, Jr., ed., *Property Rights in the Colonial Era and Early Republic* (New York: Garland Publishers, 1997): 67–84.

[28] *Crenshaw and Crenshaw v. Slate River Company*, 6 Randolph 245 (1828).

[29] *Speech of Brodnax*, 13; *Richmond Enquirer*, January 26, 1832.

TWO ROADS FROM MONTICELLO

Had Virginia's emancipationists facing this predicament simply "sat down in silent despair," the slavery debate would have ended then and there. But they did not. They understood that for slave owners "to contend that *full value* shall be paid for slaves" was to deny any form of action on the subject. They thus attempted to subvert the proslavery commitment to allodial ownership by advancing a new and more radical argument grounded in a positivist theory of law and an instrumental conception of property rights. Their new discourse of property emphasized the government's inherent right to exercise its police powers. They argued that when a species of property became so harmful that it threatened the public safety, the state had a superior responsibility to confiscate or destroy that property. Instead of acknowledging that property was either a natural or vested right, emancipationist delegates declared that all property rights were created only through positive laws and were merely sanctified through social convention. Charles Faulkner referred to property as a "creature of civil society" and explained that slave owners held their slaves "not by any law of nature...but solely by...the acquiescence and consent of the society in which they live." William Ballard Preston, speaking on behalf of a new motion calling for abolition, proclaimed that the power possessed by the Legislature in "declaring what shall be property" also enabled it to declare what was not property. Preston noted that the Virginia Constitution did not specify slaves as property, and he claimed that the constitutional provision that guaranteed property referred exclusively to the common-law definition of property. Slaves, however, were exceptional because they "were not property by common law but were made so by statutory enactments." Accordingly, he posited that slavery could be abolished during this very "session of the General Assembly simply by repealing the existing statutes that upheld slavery."[30]

Emancipationists also challenged the proslavery mandate for compensation by rejecting traditional liberal beliefs that suggested that governments existed foremost to secure property. James McDowell affirmed that both "the rights of private property and of personal security existed under every government, but they were not equal." Preferring the political doctrines of Hobbes over Locke, he argued that security was "the primary purpose for which men entered into government" and that the protection of property was only a secondary incident. Both McDowell and Charles Faulkner allowed that as long as a "property was not dangerous to the good order of society, it...would be tolerated." But if a property became pernicious and jeopardized the social tranquility, then any right by which individuals held their property was abdicated: "[S]ociety ceased to give its consent." They maintained that this "supreme law of society" stood alone as a law existing "above and paramount to all other laws." In such

[30] *The Speech of Charles Jas. Faulkner (of Berkeley) in the House of Delegates of Virginia on the Slave Question* (Richmond: T. W. White, 1832), 14–15. (Preston) *Richmond Enquirer*, February 9, 1832.

instances of public welfare, the exercise of the government's police powers nullified any inferior claims to compensation.[31]

William Ballard Preston, who would go on to have a successful political career as a Whig, also argued against compensation by forcefully rejecting the argument that slaves were protected by the just compensation clause in the Bill of Rights. Foreshadowing the Marshall Court's opinion in *Barron v. Baltimore* the following year, he contended that the Fifth Amendment only applied to cases in which the federal government directly confiscated property. It did not extend protection to citizens from takings that originated from state or municipal governments. This more radical argument for emancipation thus rested on the premise that when private property was determined to be "a positive wrong to society," there existed no legitimate basis for its continuation and no logical requirement for compensation.[32]

In challenging the orthodoxy of allodial property rights in slaves, the comments of McDowell, Faulkner, and Preston interjected ideas of analytical modes of jurisprudence and positivist theories of property rights, which had characterized other contemporary law reforms throughout the common-law diaspora. In this sense, the emancipationist effort should be considered within the context of a larger intellectual endeavor to legally reconceptualize property, which occurred as reformers sought to reconcile the traditional precepts of the common law with modern commercial and industrial practices. Their arguments reflected the influence of previous criticisms of natural-law property theory, most often credited to Jean-Jacques Rousseau, but subsequently adapted to condemn the common law as well by Jeremy Bentham and John Austin. Foremost, these reforms rejected traditional considerations of the law as a remedial system and instead sought to standardize and formalize the law under a system of analytical jurisprudence. They represented the embrace of the utilitarian principal that governments should strive to provide for "the greatest happiness for the greatest number of people." From this principal, they crafted a theory of democratic jurisprudence, which preferred positive legislation over specific judicial interpretations as the primary source of law. They also considered property rights an ambiguous concept that was subject to social conventions and statutory definitions.[33]

[31] *Speech of James M'Dowell of Rockbridge in the House of Delegates of Virginia, on the Slave Question: January 21, 1832* (Richmond, 1832), 15. *Speech of Faulkner*, 14.

[32] *Richmond Enquirer*, February 9, 1832. On *Barron v. Baltimore*, see 7 Peters 243 (1833). *Speech of Faulkner*, 14.

[33] Jeremy Bentham, *A Fragment on Government: Being an Examination of what is delivered, on the Subject of Government, in General in the Introduction to Sir William Blackstone's Commentaries: with a Preface in which is given a Critique of the Work At Large* (London, 1776) in *The Works of Jeremy Bentham*, Volume I, edited by John Bowring (Edinburgh, 1843). David Lieberman, "From Bentham to Benthamism," *The Historical Journal*, 28 (1985): 199–224; Michael Lobban, *Common Law and English Jurisprudence 1760–1850* (New York: Oxford University Press, 1991).

Significantly, then, within the context of the legislative debate, this language of law reform emerged initially in opposition to slavery. Nevertheless, it forced defenders of slavery to respond and to reconcile it with contemporary ideas of human progress. The speeches of Faulkner, McDowell, and Preston clearly appeared radical within the context of the legislative session. These radical inclinations were made evident by the absence of any historical references to emancipation in their speeches – a point that distinguished them from the rhetoric of Thomas Jefferson Randolph. Yet the ideas of law and property they espoused where becoming increasingly accepted within common-law communities. In the wake of a slave insurrection, and on the heels of the recent constitutional reforms, their pleas for substantial law reform and their desire to reconceptualize property laws along such instrumentalist lines had contemporary precedents and thus real political viability.

William Ballard Preston eloquently argued that "so great and overshadowing [were] the evils of slavery" that the immediate removal of the entire slave population was justified by "the great law of state necessity." Consequently, emancipationist delegates could readily contend that Randolph's emancipation *post nati* proposal represented the most reasonable compromise available to proslavery delegates. Delegates who defended slavery should willingly accept this compromise because it deferred immediate emancipation and guaranteed slave owners their current slave property. Charles Faulkner declared that Randolph's plan did not violate any rights of property that the legislature was bound to respect given the existing "public danger in this commonwealth." He suggested that if slavery was "conceded to be an evil" – and he reminded the assembly that "no one had yet asserted otherwise" – then he asked, could "the *equity* of such a compromise be questioned?"[34]

Proslavery delegates responded immediately to this reformist challenge by proclaiming that slavery, as it existed in Virginia, was not evil. Alexander Knox, a representative from tobacco-rich Mecklenburg County, argued that slavery was indispensable "in order to preserve... Republican Government." He evoked the grandeur of classical Greece and Rome as examples of magnificent republics that had flourished by slave labor. Additionally, Knox asserted, "the slave in Virginia, reared as he is to the knowledge of moral principle, is in a more happy condition than the African, wandering as he does in ignorance and wretchedness." Petersburg delegate John Thompson Brown, who, at the outset of the session, had referred to slavery as the greatest evil of an "angry Providence," now argued that emancipation and colonization could only be considered a cruel alternative. He pleaded to let the slaves remain in bondage in Virginia because "they are happier than they would be in any other situation." Brown also emphasized the paternalistic qualities of the master-slave relation and, ironically, argued that only quixotic condemnations of slavery had caused the slaves to forsake their otherwise contented station and rise in rebellion. He warned

[34] Preston Amendment, *House Journal*, 99; *Richmond Enquirer*, February 9, 1832; *Speech of Faulkner*, 15.

delegates against making political decisions in a climate of fear and assured them that slavery did not threaten public safety. "Throughout the world," he proclaimed, "there is not a spot where life is more secure than in Virginia."[35]

Despite efforts by some to adopt a conciliatory tone, after two weeks of intense debate in the legislature, hostility between the proslavery and emancipationists factions had increased tremendously. Governor Floyd expressed concern in his diary that the debate was "engendering bad…feelings" and "must be checked in erratic tendencies." As the debate grew more intense, delegates increasingly revived the intrastate sectional divisions that had characterized the constitutional debates of legislative apportionment. They began identifying themselves as easterners and westerners regardless of their position on slavery. On the floor of the House, proslavery delegate John Shell warned that if the amended motion calling for abolition was enacted, it would "immediately be met by a proposition to divide this State." Under these conditions, continuation of the debate potentially threatened the dissolution of the government. On January 25, George Wilson called for an immediate vote on both the current proslavery and emancipationist motions that had been submitted to the delegates. Neither motion was able to attain a majority of votes, reflecting both the divisiveness of the legislature and the presence of a strong moderate faction hoping for some type of reform. Archibald Bryce, an old and respected lawyer from Spotsylvania, proposed a new motion that expressed a desire to remove the entire black population of the state but declared that any action for the removal of slaves from Virginia was at this time "inexpedient." Bryce's compromise motion was approved by a vote of sixty-five delegates in favor against fifty-eight opposed, marking an end of the legislative debate over emancipation.[36]

In the following days, the delegates proved more successful in passing legislation restricting the activities of free blacks and slaves. Bills were passed prohibiting black Virginians from attending nighttime religious assemblies, and black preachers were banned from conducting religious services. The state militia was strengthened and authorized to conduct nightly patrols throughout the eastern counties. In the spirit of Bryce's compromise, the House of Delegates managed to pass a bill appropriating money for the removal of Virginia's free blacks that reflected the colonization proposal detailed during the debate by William Brodnax. It appropriated money to pay for the removal of free blacks for the next two years, but the bill failed to get through the Senate.

By upholding the status quo ante, proslavery delegates claimed victory in the legislative debate. Still, they lost ground in some significant areas. They failed in their primary effort to prevent an open discussion of emancipation and, accordingly, they were forced to defend slavery on the basis of the

[35] *Richmond Enquirer*, February 11, 1832. For Brown's change of position, see *Richmond Enquirer*, December 17, 1831 and *The Speech of John Thompson Brown, in the House of Delegates, on the Abolition of Slavery* (Richmond, VA: T. W. White, 1832), 20–23, 30–31.

[36] Charles Ambler, *Diary of John Floyd*, 174–175; *Constitutional Whig*, February 16, 1832; *House Journal*, 103.

Commonwealth's traditional commitment to allodial ownership. This proslavery position, however, caused the theory of allodial property itself to come under attack, as emancipationists adopted a rhetoric that advocated an instrumental theory of property and appealed to the state's police powers. The framework of the debate changed. Discussion of a plan for emancipation quickly enlarged into a fundamental debate concerning the nature of the right of property and its relation to republican government. Instrumental conceptions of property expressly challenged both slavery and the foundational principles of Virginia's republican government. Although these emancipation efforts were defeated, this new vision of property rights remained to be rebuked. With the close of the legislative debate, conservative Virginians still felt compelled to repudiate the positivist legal and political theories whose very persistence threatened the allodial conception of property on which slavery was legitimized.

REVIEWING THE DEBATE

As the legislative debate came to an end, its issues, arguments, and proposals were broadcasted by the publication of the speeches and corresponding editorials in the newspapers and in pamphlets. Two essays in particular, written by Benjamin Watkins Leigh and Thomas Roderick Dew, significantly developed the necessary themes for a refined proslavery argument that could adequately engage contemporary legal theories of property rights. Neither of these essayists participated in the legislative debate. Nor did they abandon professions about the sanctity of private property in liberal government, but both Dew and Leigh now championed the master-slave relationship, not the ownership of land, as the foundational relation on which to manifest the principal qualities of republican virtue. Leigh's comments are particularly revealing, given his expressed preference for freehold-citizenship only two years earlier in the constitutional convention. They clearly reflect the essential changes to republican political thought mandated by the slavery debate. Dew's essay proved more influential, however, largely because he offered a sophisticated repudiation of Blackstone's critique of Justinian and thus paved the way for the development of modern natural-law theories of slavery. To be sure, he was not the first to characterize slavery as a positive good, as once had been suggested; but he situated a positive-good argument into detailed historical narrative of legal and social development that emphasized the master-slave relation as vital to the progress of Western civilization. In this manner, both Leigh and Dew substantially contributed to reorienting the proprietary characteristics of self-government originally associated with land ownership and directing them instead toward a reformed model of republican political thought that was premised on the distinctive relationships of southern slavery.[37]

[37] Evidence of prior arguments characterizing slavery as a positive good are presented in Fredrika Teute Schmidt and Barbara Ripel Wilhelm, "Early Proslavery Petitions in Virginia," *WMQ* 30, Third Series (1973): 133-146. Interpretations advancing a "Great Reaction" in southern thought concerning slavery around the Virginia debates are found in Clemont Eaton, *Freedom of Thought in the Old South* (Durham:Duke University Press, 1940) and William Sumner Jenkins, *Proslavery Thought in the Old South* (Chapel Hill: University of North Carolina Press, 1935).

Immediately following the conclusion of the legislative debate, an extended review of its issues appeared in the *Richmond Enquirer* in a letter signed by Appomattox – the name of a local indigenous tribe long vanquished. It was recognized as a pseudonym for Benjamin Watkins Leigh. The *Letter from Appomattox* was written hastily. It probably had been drafted before the vote on Bryce's compromise amendment and was intended to summarize the proslavery position and emphasize its key points. Indeed, it appeared in print before many of the speeches had been published in the Richmond newspapers. Leigh directed his response to discrediting the more radical emancipationist arguments calling for the exercise of police powers to ensure public safety. He considered these sentiments reflective of Jacobin democracy and believed that the arguments themselves were inherently dangerous. Echoing points that arose in the recent constitutional convention, he reminded his readers that if the will of the majority transcended constitutional principles, tyranny reigned. To avert such tyranny in Virginia, Leigh asserted that the popular majority must never violate the fundamental principles of the original contract, which, in this instance, had sanctified the right of private property. Accordingly, he contended that emancipationist calls to confiscate slaves in order to preserve public safety were revolutionary in themselves. They violated the principles of the written constitution and, in that manner, were subversive of the public welfare in their own right.[38]

Yet Leigh refused to place the blame solely on the shoulders of the emancipationists. He chided those proslavery delegates who had "indulged in some flourishes of rhetoric" decrying the evils of slavery, which had encouraged emancipationists' claims of the need to act in the interest of public safety. He provocatively suggested that any further slave insurrections would not be traced to either the "divine visions" of another Nat Turner, or even the incendiary writings of northern abolitionists; rather, they would be incited by the "measures proposed, and ... speeches delivered, in our own Legislature." Traditional apologies, lamenting slavery as a necessary evil, had been co-opted and perverted by the emancipationists for their own use. Presaging the national debate over the "gag rule," Leigh opined that such a situation must never occur again in the state legislature. Slavery must never again become a public issue. Furthermore, he contended that in the future, those who defended slavery must champion the positive characteristics of slavery and reject the traditional apology of slavery as an evil. Slavery was

[38] *Richmond Enquirer*, February 4, 28, 1832. Leigh wrote two letters to the *Enquirer* that subsequently were published in pamphlet form as *A Letter From Appomattox to the People of Virginia* (Richmond, 1832). His initial letter was published on February 4 and advanced his argument in detail. Two vigorous rebuttals to Leigh's initial letter were printed in the February 16 *Enquirer* under the pseudonyms Jefferson and A Subscriber. Leigh responded directly to these rebuttals in the February 28 edition. "Jefferson" accused "Appomattox" of merely recasting, in a less convincing manner, the principles already expressed in John Thompson Brown's speech. Appomattox replied to the charge by endorsing Brown's speech and recommending "the perusal of the speech to the whole public." Brown's speech was subsequently published as a pamphlet. For an excellent analysis of Leigh's position within the context of transatlantic conservatism, see Dickson Bruce, *Rhetoric of Conservatism*, 73–88.

indeed a necessity, Leigh acknowledged, but "a necessity imposed upon us by Providence," and thus to argue against slavery was to question the plan of God himself.[39]

Leigh's *Letter from Appomattox* consolidated the proslavery arguments advanced during the legislative debate. He wrote while the legislature was still in session, when proposals to divide the state where still being threatened and when proslavery delegates were still unsure of their victory. Leigh hoped to influence public sentiment against abolition by disseminating a uniform and comprehensive justification for slavery. His aims, however, were only partially met. Still, Leigh managed to establish the contours of a new proslavery discourse, one that championed slavery as a positive source of republican virtue. Indeed, scriptural justifications had long proclaimed slavery as a positive good, sanctified by the Bible and in accordance with Divine providence – but Leigh's essay represented a preliminary effort to incorporate this particular religious theme directly into Virginia's republican ideology. His efforts were built on in the following months by subsequent proslavery theorists.[40]

Most immediately, the argument was taken up by Thomas Roderick Dew. Dew was a thirty-year-old professor of political law at the College of William & Mary. He did not participate in the debate in the House of Delegates; indeed, he never held political office or owned any slaves. Following the conclusion of the legislative session, however, Governor Floyd asked him to address the themes of the recent debate. Two years previous, Dew had published an essay extolling the virtues of free trade and criticizing the federal "tariff of abominations." The resultant publicity involved him in some efforts to work out a compromise between the nullifiers in South Carolina and the Jackson administration. During his short life (he died at the age of forty-four), he published numerous other essays on an array of topics, but the essay commissioned by Floyd – the *Review of the Debates in the Virginia Legislature* – established Dew's reputation as one of the leading political philosophers of the South.

The reputation was merited, but Dew has proven somewhat enigmatic to historians. Recognized immediately as a staunch defender of slavery, he was also an adherent to the social teachings of the Scottish Enlightenment thinkers, especially Adam Smith, and considered one of the leading liberal political economists of his day. This blend of influences was manifested clearly in his sentiments about slavery in Virginia. Embracing slavery as a positive good that had facilitated the Neolithic Revolution, Dew nevertheless believed that because Virginia's climate and soils did not facilitate an extensive plantation economy, market mechanisms would bring an eventual end to slavery and impose a more

[39] Leigh, *Letter from Appomattox*.

[40] On the scriptural justifications for slavery, see Jenkins, *Pro-Slavery Thought*, 200–241; Larry Tise, *Proslavery: A History of the Defense of Slavery in America, 1701–1840* (Athens: University of Georgia Press, 1987), esp. 3–40. Mitchell Snay, *Gospel of Disunion: Religion and Separation in the Antebellum South* (Chapel Hill: University of North Carolina Press, 1997) explores the consequences of these reforms to proslavery ideology on Southern churches.

efficient free-labor system. At various times then, Dew has been depicted as both the spokesmen for "a group of propertied reactionaries," committed to maintaining an aristocracy, and as a progressive-liberal – an articulator of "free-soilism," who, had he lived long enough, would have found communion within the Republican Party. More recently, Michael O'Brien and Eugene Genovese have shown that he was instead at the same time both and neither; he was an insightful man of his own time and place. Genovese has aptly portrayed him as facing the horns of the dilemma of freedom and progress that imperiled southern slave society during those antebellum decades.[41]

Dew's *Review of the Debate* represented an effort to resolve this dilemma. It presented a sophisticated synthesis of Christian and liberal views portraying slavery as an instrument of human progress. His essay thus served to meet the intellectual demands made on slavery by contemporary notions of historical materialism and social progress. In so doing, he constructed a much-needed historical basis for a modern slaveholding republic. He began his essay by framing it within the question of whether or not "two distinct races of people, now living together as master and servant," could ever be separated. He sought his answer in history. Dew investigated the historical circumstances of slavery before directly engaging the merits and demerits of the various emancipation and colonization arguments levied in the legislative debates. Noting that slavery had been widely pronounced, "in the abstract, at least," as contradicting natural law, he proposed undertaking a "hasty" examination of the origin of slavery to demonstrate the influences it had "exerted on the progress of civilization." Dew cautioned his readers with a critique of Enlightenment universalism by acknowledging that although "the man born and matured in the lap of freedom, looks upon slavery as unnatural and horrible," the nature of man was essentially circumstantial and that "his habits and sentiments are…the growth of adventitious causes – hence the endless variety and condition of our species." To understand slavery, he suggested, one must attain a level of cultural and historical empathy with those actors from other places and times. Dew also emphasized the fact that, to the best of man's ability to discern, slavery was sanctioned by divine authority. He posited that Abraham had owned hundreds

[41] For interpretation of Dew's thought, see Eugene Genovese, *Western Civilization Through Slaveholding Eyes: The Social and Historical Thought of Thomas Roderick Dew* (New Orleans, LA: Graduate School of Tulane University, 1985), and *The Slaveholders' Dilemma: Freedom and Progress in Southern Conservative Thought, 1820–1860* (Columbia: University of South Carolina Press, 1992), 13–19; Allen Kaufman, *Capitalism, Slavery, and Republican Values: American Political Economists, 1819–1848* (Austin: University of Texas Press, 1982), chapters 5–6; and Michael O'Brien, ed., *All Clever Men, Who Make Their Way: Critical Discourse in the Old South* (Fayetteville: University of Arkansas Press, 1982), 125–127. An abridged version of this essay was first published as "The Abolition of Negro Slavery" in the September 1832 edition of the *American Quarterly Review*. Later that year, Dew published the entire version in pamphlet form under its more common title. The essay was subsequently republished three decades later as part of E. N. Elliot's, *The Proslavery Argument*. For the genealogy of the text, see Drew Gilpin Faust, *Ideology of Proslavery: Proslavery Thought in the Antebellum South, 1830–1860* (Baton Rouge: Louisiana State University Press, 1981), 22.

of slaves and that Solomon's temple had been built by slave labor. Furthermore, evidence of slavery could be found in all of the ancient civilizations, and he connected the institution of slavery with the historical moment at which societies acknowledged the right of private property. The relationship between slavery and the legal basis of property had thus been entwined from the beginning. Antislavery ideas were the new force in the world, and Dew's examination sought to demonstrate that the critique of slavery was itself a product of social progress.[42]

In identifying the origins of slavery, Dew revived much of the Justinian explanation that had been rejected by Blackstone and St. George Tucker. In so doing, he explicitly challenged the intellectual orthodoxy that held that slavery was contrary to natural law. Dew offered four methods by which slavery had originated: the laws of war, the state of property and feebleness of government, bargain and sale (contract), and crime. He contended that warfare represented "the most fruitful source of slavery" and echoed the Justinian precepts that slavery signaled a "mild" form of punishment when compared to the conqueror's absolute right over life. The establishment of slavery mitigated the harsh brutality of primitive warfare and thus marked the transition to an advanced stage of human society in at least one of the belligerents. Informed by theories of the Scottish Historical School, Dew identified four distinct stages of society: hunting and fishing, pastoral, agricultural, and commercial. He accordingly repudiated Blackstone's criticism of Justinian because it applied ethical principles emanating from "laws of modern war" to people who had lived in "earlier stages of civilization." He also charged that Blackstone had misunderstood the intellectual grounds on which Justinian had rooted "the justification of slavery as arising from the laws of war." Blackstone, Dew suggested, had mistakenly supposed that slavery had arisen from the circumstances of combat and capture – instead, he contended, slavery arose in response to an inherent fear of retaliation, from which, he maintained, sprang forth "most of the horrors of war." Dew attributed these errors to Blackstone's basic characterization of slavery in "its pure, unmitigated form," which – as both Rousseau and Locke had described it – was merely "the continuance of a state of war."[43]

Dew also refuted Blackstone by asserting that slavery did indeed arise from cases of bargain and sale – the contract theory of slavery. He recalled Blackstone's familiar maxim that because every sale implied a quid pro quo, no equivalent could exist in the case of slavery, and he used this statement as a foil against which to pose his criticism. Dew chided Blackstone for fixing his attention "exclusively on those countries" where people could procure the basic necessities of life and where, consequently, a man's life could "never be in jeopardy from want." He suggested that such security was not the case in "semi-barbarous or densely populated countries." In cases of famine, when the

[42] Thomas Roderick Dew, *Review of the Debate in the Virginia Legislature, 1831–32* (Richmond: T. W. White, 1832), 5–6.

[43] Dew, *Review of the Debate*, 19.

afflicted were driven to desperation, it appeared that life itself was a suitable equivalent for liberty; and he offered the biblical example of Esau trading his birthright for a bowl of soup. Dew contended that in most nations, slaves received basic legal protections over life and limb and that their "nourishment and subsistence [were] positively enjoined." In such cases, Dew imagined "many instances in which liberty might" find an equivalent. He contrasted the secure circumstances of slaves with deplorable conditions of Chinese laborers. He provocatively asserted that the reason why people did not sell themselves into slavery more frequently was simply because they were either "forbidden by the laws, or [could] find no purchasers." He provocatively noted that the price of nourishment, support, and protection of slaves was seemingly beyond what could be afforded even by "the capitalist in Great Britain." And he concluded by suggesting that if the laws of Great Britain allowed slavery, then there would doubtless be more sellers than persons willing to buy.[44]

Dew maintained that slavery could also arise from crime as well as from the circumstances of property relations within in a society. These were sources of slavery that were neither included in Justinian's explanation nor addressed by Blackstone, but Dew thought them important contributions, especially his analysis of slavery as arising from the "state of property and feebleness of government" in particular societies. He offered the example of the relationships of dependency arising in feudal Europe as an instance in which a form of slavery arose "from the poor distribution of property and a lack of opportunity." Invoking Harrington's classical Whig formulation of material determinism, Dew argued that "the character of government" depended "more on the condition of property than on any one circumstance beside," and he noted that in Europe, the laws of primogeniture and entail had consolidated the land into the hands of the few. Echoing Jefferson, Dew believed the existence of these laws reflected the inherent weakness of aristocratic government and, in later writings, he championed their removal.[45]

Following his narrative on the origin of slavery and a brief criticism of the African slave trade, in which he excused Virginians from any culpability, Dew engaged the specific emancipationist arguments of the legislative debate. Most notably, he refuted the various proposals for emancipation and colonization. He argued that because the inviolability of property required compensation to the slaveholder, the cost of any plan for emancipation and removal was beyond the current means of Virginians to accomplish it. He reiterated arguments made by proslavery delegates that estimated total costs of compensation and deportation for the annual increase of slave population alone at more than a million dollars, and concluded that any scheme of abolition dependent on removal was totally impractical. Furthermore, he suggested that the difficulties in colonization were

[44] Dew, *Review of the Debate*, 6–23, 25–26.

[45] See Dew's historical lectures on feudalism, the English Constitution, and the French Revolution in his *A Digest of the Laws, Customs, Manners, and Institutions of the Ancient and Modern Nations* (New York: D. Appleton, 1852).

far greater than imagined. He maintained that white Virginians not only faced the financial concerns about the cost of removing the black population, but also had a moral obligation to assure the continued well-being of the deportees in Africa. In Dew's mind, this moral obligation was complicated by the history of slavery: As the subjects of bondage for centuries, Virginia's black population had become exceedingly dependent and would face tremendous difficulties if simply left to their own devices. He rejected the notion that the capacity for self-government was simply inherent in all men. Rather, it was something that could only be prepared for through the process of history. Because every conceivable plan for emancipation and removal was impracticable, he concluded that even those who found slavery disagreeable must acknowledge the inherent irresponsibility in subverting the established rights of property.[46]

Confident that he had dispelled the emancipationist schemes, Dew presented a justification that situated slavery as an instrument of human progress and as providing the appropriate social foundation for a republican government. Evoking a theological justification for slavery, he claimed that its persistent and universal presence signaled that it was "*the necessary result of the laws of mind and matter…and was intended by our Creator for some useful purpose*" (emphasis in the original). Dew believed that, when considered as part of a divine plan, one could reasonably understand that slavery had been "perhaps the principal means for impelling forward the civilization of mankind." Slavery had mitigated the natural horrific conduct of war and destroyed the migratory spirit of pastoral peoples. The structure of slavery abrogated habits of indolence, sloth, and carelessness that restricted "independent savages" to an existence similar to that of the "beasts of the forests." Furthermore, he contended, slavery was facilitating the transformation to a liberal age of self-government and commercial prosperity. The circumstances of American slavery guaranteed the persistence of the republican spirit by preserving a realm of liberty for white Virginians. He suggested that "color alone is here the badge of distinction, the true mark of aristocracy, and all who are white are equal in spite of the variety of occupation." In Virginia, he explained, "the poorest white person seems to consider himself nearly on the level with the richest." Dew also rejected the lamentations of earlier generations who maintained that slavery corrupted the manners and morals of the master class. To the contrary, he proclaimed that long exposure to the master-slave relation developed benevolent habits of stewardship and provided an effective model for republican virtue. He cited "well-known fact" that the cruelest masters were "those who have been unaccustomed to slavery," specifically those "northern gentlemen who marry southern heiresses." In Dew's mind, and from the long perspective of

[46] Dew, *Review of the Debate*, 40–55, 60–76. Dew repeated almost verbatim the estimates of the cost of emancipation from the speech of John Thompson Brown of Petersburg. Dew also challenged emancipationists' arguments about uncompensated takings as well and suggested that delegates had failed to demonstrate how a rebellion of twenty-five of the Commonwealth's half-million slaves constituted a state of "real exigency," 56–60.

history, such an institution could not be a bane on society – indeed, it served instead as a positive good.[47]

The *Review of the Debate* represented a significant episode in the development of proslavery thought in Virginia. Admittedly, Dew was not the first to proclaim slavery a positive good, but his essay revised the fundamental principles of jurisprudential and republican thought pertaining to slavery. He refuted the conventions embraced by both Blackstone and St. George Tucker that maintained that slavery existed only through positive law and contradicted the principles of natural law. Although Dew did not himself offer an argument for a natural-law basis for slavery, it was implied by his placement of slavery at the core of historical progress. In this manner, he set the stage for subsequent natural-law justifications for slavery. He also reconciled slavery, republican political thought, and contemporary ideas of human progress. He accomplished this in part by first abandoning the cyclical theory of history, which had characterized the civic humanist discourses of early modern republican ideas, and then supplanting it with the developmental-stage theory of the Scottish Historical School. Unlike the cyclical theory, the historical-stage theory cohered with traditional Christian eschatological historical thought and allowed for a synthesis between Christian and republican justifications for slavery. This synthesis resulted in a historical narrative in which the absolute dominion of the master over the slave was no longer considered as a dangerous source of potential corruption. Instead, when informed by traditional Christian doctrines of kindness and charity, the master-slave relation represented a model of stewardship and of virtue.

Grounding the defense of slavery in an argument that advocated slavery's exceptional qualities in a republican government had profound ramifications for future political and legal thought in antebellum Virginia. Certainly, the proslavery reaction in the legislative debate reflected a growing ambivalence toward liberal modernity, with its dogmas of political equality and economic progress, and the tensions it inspired in the effort to preserve slavery. Where previous justifications for slavery often had acknowledged the potentially corrupting characteristics of the master-slave relation, the speeches of Brown and Knox and the essays of Leigh and Dew revealed an emergent proslavery discourse founded on the idea that the ownership of slaves served as a guarantor of republican liberty and virtue. The argument that slavery fostered virtue was not original. It had appeared in scriptural justifications for slavery for decades. During the winter of 1832, however, it had become the only tenable justification in the face of antislavery arguments grounded in positivist conceptions of property and an instrumental view of law. Once a coherent republican political language that championed slavery emerged, Virginia's conservatives no longer had any need for the freehold. The proslavery response thus further facilitated the displacement of land ownership as the natural source of republican citizenship and substituted it instead with the ownership of slaves.

[47] Dew, *Review of the Debate*, 23–24, 97–99.

A NOTE ON BLACKSTONE'S COMMENTARIES

The American Colonization Society, upset by the harsh treatment they received from Dew, commissioned a response from expatriated Virginian, Jesse Burton Harrison. Harrison's rebuttal was published in the *American Quarterly Review* in December 1832, a year after the debate in the legislature. Harrison had grown up in Bedford County, Virginia, and had attended Hampden-Sydney College before he studied law under the tutelage of Joseph Story at Harvard. By the time of the debate, however, he had moved to New Orleans and practiced law there. His essay contributed nothing original to the debate. For the most part, it simply reiterated the moderate emancipationist position of Thomas Marshall, the son of the Chief Justice, delivered in a speech during the first week of the legislative debate. Harrison himself rejected Randolph's proposal for emancipation *post nati* and maintained that any emancipation plan had to include compensation for the slave owners. In this respect, Harrison's essay simply revived the postcolonial justifications for slaveholding found in the writings of Jefferson and St. George Tucker. He lamented the evils that slavery wrought on the white population and associated Virginia's economic malaise with its persistent reliance on slave labor. He hoped to replace slaves with industrious, free, white laborers through a process of gradual emancipation and colonization, but he was unwilling to contest the inviolability of allodial ownership as Faulkner, McDowell, and Preston had done. To the contrary, he specifically declared the fallacy of their radical views. Harrison believed, as did Dew, that because Virginia's geography was unfavorable to the continuation of slavery, the state would eventually shift to a system of free labor when the necessary economic conditions could be met. Until that day came, Harrison advocated implementing William Brodnax's proposal to remove the annual increase of the state's black population. Toward that end, he called for substantial public funding to support the mission of the Colonization Society.[48]

Unlike Harrison's inability to advance the antislavery position, defenders of slavery continued to elaborate and consolidate their arguments. Two years after Dew's essay was published, his colleague at the College of William & Mary, Nathaniel Beverley Tucker, delivered a lecture to his students that justified slavery on the basis of natural law. He published the lecture a month later in the *Southern Literary Messenger* under the expansive title: "A Note to Blackstone's Commentaries: Being the Substance of Remarks on the Subject of Domestic Slavery." It was not the younger Tucker's first public engagement on the question of slavery and gradual emancipation. Years earlier, as a young judge in Missouri, he had published a series of essays with fellow expatriate Virginian Edward Bates denouncing the proposed Tallmadge Amendment to the Missouri admission bill. Beverley Tucker and Bates, writing under the

[48] Harrison, "The Slavery Question in Virginia," reprinted in Fairfax Harrison, ed., *Aris Sonis Focisque: Being a Memoir of an American Family, The Harrisons of Skimino* (Privately Printed for the Harrison Family, 1910), 337–400. See O'Brien, ed., *All Clever Men*, 55–57 for biographical information.

pseudonyms Hampden and Sydney, presented strong constitutional arguments against the plan of gradual emancipation included in the amendment. Tucker's essays were proslavery in essence but they addressed the constitutional issues more explicitly. He defended slavery because it legally existed as a recognized form of property and therefore conformed to the constitutional compact that had established the American Union. In the wake of Nat Turner and the Virginia debate, however, Tucker embraced the natural-law justification for slavery. His "Note on Blackstone's Commentaries" represented an explicit repudiation of his father's legal reasoning on the subject of slavery in Virginia.[49]

Beverley Tucker dismissed Blackstone's efforts to prove that slavery arose from unlawful origins as a mere exercise in sophistry. He referred his students to Dew's essay as sufficiently exposing the "specious fallacy" of Blackstone's repudiation of a compact theory of slavery and took issue himself with the argument that slavery could not legitimately originate from a state of war. Most significantly, however, Tucker sought to ground the legitimacy of slavery in the natural conditions that made "labor the price of subsistence." His argument essentially echoed Aristotle's maxim that some were born masters and some slaves. Tucker noted that in every society there were "rich and poor"; some men "rise in affluence," whereas others remain "as they began." For those who remained, the only thing available for them was to labor for their subsistence. Forms of labor varied depending on the circumstances of particular societies, and in Virginia, those required to labor the earth were frequently slaves. Tucker then laid out the reasons why the master-slave relationship was preferred to the social relations that characterized employers and wage laborers. Foremost, he contended that the master-slave relation was an affiliation between recognized individuals, which he contrasted with the impersonal class relations of the wage system. Furthermore, he suggested that because of the natural condition requiring men to labor for subsistence, even those men that a society might designate as "free laborers" were actually subject to the compulsion of the natural order. Although his brief essay did not represent a comprehensive natural-law justification for slavery, it laid the intellectual groundwork for subsequent proslavery apologists, most notably Albert Taylor Bledsoe, James Philemon Holcombe, James Henry Hammond, and T. R. R. Cobb, who also repudiated Blackstone's interpretation and sought to find a legitimate basis for slavery not in positive laws or custom, but in nature.[50]

[49] *Southern Literary Messenger*, January 1835, 227–231. Tucker's Hampden essays and his early view on slavery are analyzed and discussed in Robert Brugger, *Beverley Tucker: Heart over Head in the Old South* (Baltimore: Johns Hopkins University Press, 1978), 52–57. His Hampden essays appeared in the *Missouri Gazette & Public Advertiser*, April 21 and May 5 and 19, 1819.

[50] *Southern Literary Messenger*, January 1835, 227–231. A well-argued rebuttal to Tucker appeared under the pseudonym "A Virginian" the following month, reaffirming the Blackstonian orthodoxy and chiding Tucker for failing to demonstrate any lawful origins for slavery. *Southern Literary Messenger*, February 1835, 266–270.

Nat Turner forced Virginians to try to answer a question that they had long ignored. His brief rebellion inaugurated a more lasting and more influential debate over the legitimate basis for slavery within Virginia's republican government and over the theory of property rights best designed to serve it. Coming on the heels of the democratic reforms enacted during the constitutional convention, the question of emancipation raised old problems in a new political context. The positivist theory of property rights, although invoked by radical emancipationist during the debate, possessed an increasingly popular appeal among many state legislators of all political stripes who believed it vital to the process of economic development. Given this popularity, and the corresponding ideas of an instrumental approach to law itself, those who defended slavery not only needed to legitimize it in a way they never before seriously needed to do; they needed to place it on a higher ground than the traditional common-law understanding of *partus sequitur ventrem* allowed. In doing so, they abandoned common-law justifications and embraced a natural-law basis that fostered the idea of slavery as an exceptional – or "peculiar" – species of property.

The Virginia slavery debate stands, therefore, as a watershed event within the contemporary reforms to reconcile common-law property rights with the changing social relations of modern industrial society. Arguments for both emancipation and retaining slavery generated new discourses about the nature of a modern republic in a slave society emphasizing the role of property rights in such a society. Similar to the case in the industrializing northern states, labor relations in Virginia emerged as the focal point in reforming legal and political institutions. Yet, it was a very different form of labor relations in Virginia – as Nat Turner had reminded everyone. Ironically, then, the debate that he inspired completed the process of political reformation, which had begun during the constitutional revision, and signaled the death knell for the Jeffersonian republican vision of allodial land ownership. Henceforth, the freehold appeared as an increasingly archaic form of property and its historic political value was readily dismissed by the democratic and economic sensibilities of the day. In its stead, the property rights of Virginia's slave owners emerged as the privileged form of property in the Commonwealth.

5

Doubt Seems to Have Arisen

Since the Revolution, the freehold had maintained a precarious balance between the attributes of allodial ownership and the common-law juridical structure on which it had been perched. By the middle decades of the nineteenth century, however, the scales were tipped heavily in favor of the economic attributes of private ownership. Nonetheless, notable traditional characteristics of the freehold persisted. Most especially, the freehold qualification for holding office remained the litmus for the exercise of political power. Nowhere was the persistence of this traditional practice more evident than in the county courts. There, freeholders continued to administer and adjudicate the local issues of police, justice, and taxation. Despite reforms to the court system, the freehold qualification persisted as the sole determining standard for the offices of justices of the peace, sheriff, coroner, as well as for grand and petit jurors. In addition to determining when a crime had been committed and which creditor would be repaid first, these county officers also appointed commodity inspectors, authorized civic projects such as the repair of roads and the construction of public buildings, and determined the appropriate county levy for them. In their capacity as local officials, then, freeholders arguably did more to shape public policy and exercised more political agency than they did through the right of suffrage. Not surprisingly, then, the freeholder-dominated county courts emerged at the crux of social tensions between the republican desire for the local determination of police and justice and the demands for an uniform interpretation of the law that was required by the expanding capitalist marketplace.[1]

[1] The classic examination of Virginia's freehold gentry as a ruling class is Charles Sydnor, *Gentlemen Freeholders: Political Practices in Washington's Virginia* (Chapel Hill: University of North Carolina Press for the Institute of Early American History and Culture, 1952). Sydnor argued that the legal and institutional mechanisms of eighteenth- and nineteenth-century Virginia fostered superior leadership qualities in the landed gentry. Most especially, Sydnor credited the influence of the county court system, where he noted, "in most cases the first upward step in a political career was admission to the office of justice of the peace and thus to a seat on the bench of the county court" (100). Richard R. Beeman, *The Old Dominion and the New Nation, 1788–1801* (Lexington: University Press of Kentucky, 1972) expanded on Sydnor's thesis and

The political power of these courts attracted the ire of reform delegates during the 1829 Constitutional Convention. Lewis Summers, a reform delegate from Kanawha, introduced a series of resolutions designed to marginalize the county courts by creating a ward system similar to the proposal advanced by Thomas Jefferson. Summers called for the counties to be divided into wards and for the voters of each ward to elect a Commissioner of Police. The elected commissioners were to form a Board of Police for the county, which would be charged with the "power to assess, levy, and...[collect], all local, county, or ward taxes" and to oversee their distribution "for the support of the poor"; the building and repair of "public roads and highways"; and the construction of "bridges, and other public structures." As evident from these prescribed duties, Summers sought to remove the power of taxation from the county courts and place it in the hands of elected officials. He explained that he had no intention of interfering with "Judicial powers" of the courts and contended that they "administered justice as cheaply, and as satisfactorily" as any other practicable tribunal. But he protested against vesting the powers of taxation and disbursement in an institution that possessed the inherent power to perpetuate itself and did not have to answer directly to the people it served.[2]

Summers's proposal was defeated in the convention. Still, his comments reveal much about the changing conceptualization of office in the minds of democratic reformers. Expressions of local office holding as a form of political participation – a civic duty – were largely absent from this discourse. Instead, the political power incumbent in an office was emphasized and needed to be circumscribed through popular election. Similarly, Summers clearly delineated between what he considered the judicial and the governing powers of the courts; in effect, divorcing law from politics and relegating judicial proceedings into the private sphere. Implicit in this distinction was an ideal that judicial opinions – and, indeed, judges themselves – were to be apolitical in their decisions. Cases were best decided on the merits of the law, as it was commonly (not particularly) understood, and accordingly, the best judges would prove themselves able technicians of this legal formalism. This core distinction between the judicial and the governmental represented the hallmark of democratic efforts at legal reform.[3]

Ultimately, however, these calls for democratic legal reform achieved little success in Virginia. Reform did occur, but the balance between the economic

suggested that the "gentlemen freeholders" accommodated themselves to the emerging party system in a successful effort to preserve their rule. See also T. H. Breen, *Tobacco Culture: The Mentality of the Great Tidewater Planters on the Eve of Revolution* (Princeton, NJ: Princeton University Press,1985), and John Gilman Kolp, *Gentlemen and Freeholders: Electoral Politics in Colonial Virginia* (Baltimore: Johns Hopkins University Press, 1998).

[2] *PDVSC*, 626–631.

[3] Perry Miller, *The Life of the Mind in America from the Revolution to the Civil War* (New York: Harvest Book, 1965), 99–265; Morton Horwitz, *The Transformation of American Law, 1780–1860* (Cambridge, MA: Harvard University Press, 1975); and Grant Gilmore, *The Ages of American Law* (New Haven, CT: Yale University Press, 1977).

and political characteristics of the freehold was upset, not by political reformers, but by judicial efforts to define and clarify proliferating forms of commercial land transfers. From this perspective, Virginia's legal reformation appears as part and parcel of a larger, transnational effort to resolve problems with the substantive elements of the common law itself. Similar reform efforts took place contemporaneously in Great Britain and throughout the common-law diaspora. These reforms sought to correct the inability of traditional common-law jurisprudence to conform to the changing system of property relations that characterized modern commercial society. As one contemporary commentator explained, "the system of British law was built upon real property," and modern-day judges frequently found themselves "at a loss for precedents, and even principles" to provide for the adjudicative demands arising from the prolific transfer of "these new elements of national wealth," which were grounded in personal property and dedicated to the "accumulations of capital." Issues relative to the currency, bonds, and certificates that comprised these new elements of wealth generally belonged to the realm of mercantile law, a derivative branch of property law devised to address the inadequacies of common-law remedies in commercial exchanges. Now, however, this historical subset threatened to become the norm as the exchange of currency and certificates increasingly was interwoven with the transfer of land.[4]

Accordingly, the commodification of land and its dynamic transferability inspired by that process did more to undermine the traditional privileges of the freehold than did any professions of democratic ideals or constitutional reforms. During the decades of the 1830s and the 1840s, Virginia's courts grappled repeatedly with the social consequences of allodial land ownership. The rulings in this series of cases tended to privilege the economic reality of land ownership over its traditional political attributes and thus undermined them. In their wake, the idea of the freehold as a fundamental political element appeared more and more archaic. In this manner, the decisions in the courts set the stage, and even necessitated, the more comprehensive legislative reforms that occurred as part of the process to revise the civil and criminal codes at the end of the decade.

REPUBLICAN POLICE AND JUSTICE

Virginia's revolutionaries had inherited a decentralized colonial court system that vested considerable police authority in the hands of local freeholders and prized communally adjudicated justice. It was premised initially on the English shire system but quickly took on its own characteristics to meet the unique situations of the colony. Phillip Alexander Bruce, in his seminal study of the colony's institutions during the seventeenth century, identified six different

[4] *Southern Literary Messenger*, vol. 16 (Richmond, 1850), 322. These passages were written specifically to detail the process of law reform in England but were actually used to contextualize the revision of the Code in Virginia.

courts in operation: "the Magistrate's Court; the Parish Court; the Monthly or County Court; the General Court; the General Assembly; and the Court of Admiralty." From these, the two most important colonial courts to develop relative to the regular matters of law and justice were the county courts and the General Court.[5]

County courts provided for the administration of local justice. They were organized during the earliest decades of settlement and followed the English practice of convening grand juries on a monthly basis. They had original jurisdiction over cases at both law and equity. Justices of the Peace were to be chosen from "the most able, honest, and judicious" freeholders in the county and appointed by the governor. In practice, the appointments actually became the customary offices of select planter families in each county. The efficiency of the county courts rested in the local familiarity of the participants and causes were often determined less on matters of law than on a general acquaintance with the issues and personages involved. The freeholder-justices who adjudicated these cases, and the freeholder-juries who determined them, thus possessed significant communal influence, irrespective of their knowledge or ignorance of the law.

As the colony prospered and extensive networks of trade developed, litigation multiplied and demands for more consistent jurisprudence increased the stature of the General Court. During the colonial period, the General Court consisted of the governor and the Privy Council. They served as an appellate court and a court of original jurisdiction in criminal cases where capital or corporal punishments could be awarded and in civil cases involving more than 1,600 pounds of tobacco. Until 1683, the House of Burgesses possessed the authority to act as the final appellate authority. Thereafter, the General Court served in that capacity as well. Despite its increased stature, the provincial nature of the colony in the seventeenth century encouraged procedural informality in cases brought before the General Court. By the end of the century, however, procedural matters became more significant as more colonial lawyers and barristers were educated in England. Most of these formally educated attorneys settled within a convenient distance of the General Court in Williamsburg. In the early years of the eighteenth century, as the volume and financial significance of litigation increased, many of these barristers and attorneys turned a critical eye toward the informal procedures of Virginia's courts and expressed a preference for a formal system of legal education that reflected outright intellectual contempt for the planter-justices.[6]

[5] Phillip Alexander Bruce, *Institutional History of Virginia in the Seventeenth Century*, 2 vols. (New York: G. P. Putnam and Sons, 1910), 463, 478, 482–483. He identified only one parish court authorized in Virginia – Bristol parish in 1656. The General Assembly was the final court of appeal until the end of the seventeenth century, when this prerogative was denied. See 690–696 and 697–707 for the complex procedures of the Admiralty Court.

[6] Bruce, *Institutional*, 665, 570–587. Bruce noted that the figure limiting the Court's jurisdiction in civil cases changed over time. The 1,600 pound limit was in force at the end of the seventeenth century. Apparently, very few cases came before the court under its original jurisdiction in civil cases. A. G. Roeber, *Faithful Magistrates and Republican Lawyers: Creators of Virginia Legal*

Historian A.G. Roeber has suggested that these tensions between the professionally biased General Court and planter-dominated county courts simply mirrored the paradigm of conflict between court and country ideologies, which purportedly shaped that confluence of eighteenth-century British politics.[7] He has posited that country planters, committed to local autonomy, mistrusted the relatively obscure procedures of the common law as well as the lawyers themselves, who traditionally were aligned with the Court and perceived to act in the interest of centralizing tendencies. They considered the devotion of an emergent legal culture to the obscure technicalities of published law treatises an instrument by which the governor could subvert their local autonomy. These antagonisms came to a head in the midst of the imperial crisis when, in 1774, the county courts were closed because continuing resolution that provided the fee schedule for attorneys expired. Many local lawyers and litigants boycotted the scheduled sessions of the General Court as well. For all practical purposes, the colonial judicial system was shut down. Accordingly, the establishment of a working court system became a priority for the new republican regime.[8]

Following independence, Virginians struggled to devise an efficient court system that would conform to both the ideological and practical needs of the republic. Ideologically committed to establishing the rule of law, they zealously advanced a concept of an independent judiciary liberated from legislative influences and grounded in the common-law tradition of local justice. Such a judiciary was intended to be free from the corruptions of patronage and intrigue, which had characterized the politics of office holding during the eighteenth century. The traditional independence and parochial familiarity embodied in the county courts seemed a much more appropriate model for a republican legal system. Once the institutional structure of the republican court system was established, however, the desired judicial independence seemingly contradicted the corresponding republican ideal that unchecked power would inevitably dissolve into tyranny. Furthermore, the specialized nature of the law, and the corresponding need for a class of specially educated practitioners, exacerbated this concern that lawyers and judges would gain control of the republican institutions and create a judicial oligarchy. Thus, Virginians endeavored to strike a balance between the competing needs to administer the rule of law by an emergent legal hierarchy and the inherent egalitarian impulse of a republican system of justice.[9]

Culture, 1680–1810 (Chapel Hill: University of North Carolina, 1981). See especially the chart provided on pages 54–55.

7 Roeber, *Faithful Magistrates*. The court-versus-country paradigm used to depict eighteenth-century British politics is articulated in Isaac Kramnick, *Bolingbroke and His Circle: The Politics of Nostalgia in the Age of Walpole* (Cambridge, MA: Harvard University Press, 1968).

8 Roeber, *Faithful Magistrates*, 160–171; Woody Holton, *Forced Founders*, 115–132; and George M. Curtis, III, *The Role of the Courts in the Making of the Revolution in Virginia* (Madison: State Historical Society of Wisconsin, 1976).

9 On the issues surrounding the creation of republican courts in Virginia, see Roeber, *Faithful Magistrates*, 160–202, and F. Thornton Miller, *Juries and Judges Versus the Law: Virginia's*

This effort was marked by a series of revisions to the courts during the early years of the Commonwealth. Initially, attention was focused on constraining the influence of the General Court and divorcing it from its traditional affiliation with the executive branch of government. The 1776 Constitution removed the governor and the executive council from the General Court and granted authority to the General Assembly to make judicial appointments to the Court in an express effort to limit the patronage power of the governor. Under this system, the governor commissioned the General Court judges, but their appointment was determined by election in a joint ballot in the legislature. Additionally, the General Court's appellate jurisdiction was limited to felony cases whereas jurisdiction over cases of admiralty, equity, and civil proceedings was divided among other established superior courts. This restructuring limited the central authority of the General Court, thus checking the most serious historical threat to a judicial grab for power in the new Commonwealth and, theoretically at least, vesting greater authority in the local courts of the counties. Correspondent with the limitations placed on the General Court, however, an intermediate level of district courts was created to serve as a check on the power of the county courts. These district courts were established to handle cases outside the realm of and on appeal from the county courts. In establishing this intermediate tier, the professional knowledge of the general court would now be brought into the countryside to supervise and inform the practice of the county justices.[10]

Subsequent assertions of a judicial oligarchy to the contrary, many of the most nefarious abuses of the colonial courts were alleviated during the construction of the Commonwealth. The fourth section of the Declaration of Rights prohibited the hereditary transfer of office. It stated explicitly that "no man, or set of men, are entitled to exclusive and separate emoluments or privileges from the community, but in consideration of public services, which not being descendible, neither ought the offices of Magistrate, Legislator, or Judge, to be hereditary." Neither could these offices be sold or transferred, as had been the practice in much of eighteenth-century Europe. In this manner, judicial offices took on a uniquely republican bent – even if they were lifetime appointments.[11]

Provincial Legal Perspective, 1783–1828 (Charlottesville: University Press of Virginia, 1994). For larger issues concerning judicial independence, see Robert E. Ellis, *The Jeffersonian Crisis: Courts and Politics in the Young Republic* (New York: Oxford University Press, 1971); Kathryn Preyer, "Crime, the Criminal Law and Reform in Post-Revolutionary Virginia," *LHR*, 1 (1983): 53–85; and David Konig, "Legal Fictions and the Rule(s) of Law: The Jeffersonian Critique of Common-Law Adjudication," in Christopher Tomlins and Bruce Mann, eds., *The Many Legalities of Early America* (Chapel Hill: University of North Carolina Press, 2001), 97–117, and "Jurisprudence and Social Policy in the New Republic," in David Thomas Konig, ed., *Devising Liberty: Preserving and Creating Freedom in the New American Republic* (Stanford, CA: Stanford University Press, 1995): 178–216.

[10] Roeber, *Faithful Magistrates*, 160–230.

[11] *SAL*, 9: 109; A. E. Dick Howard, *Commentaries on the Constitution of Virginia*, 2 vols. (Charlottesville: University Press of Virginia, 1974), 1: 77–80. On the customary sale of offices elsewhere, see William Doyle, *Venality: The Sale of Offices in Eighteenth-Century France* (Oxford: Oxford University Press, 1996).

Despite this new judicial structure, the county courts remained integral to the conduct of local government in the Commonwealth. Supreme Court Judge William Brockenbrough remarked that the county courts managed "the most important duties in matters of police and economy." His sketch of the composition and jurisdiction of Virginia's courts, written in 1828, attested to the continued vigor manifested by these freeholder-dominated institutions in the administration of republican justice. He explained that the county courts had general jurisdiction to hear and determine most of the cases at law arising within the county. Civil cases needed to exceed a value of either "twenty dollars, or four hundred pounds of tobacco" to qualify for a jury trial; otherwise, a case of less value could be decided by a Justice of the Peace at an informal hearing. Their jurisdiction was limited in criminal cases, however, where conviction might lead to a sentence of death, dismemberment, or imprisonment in a penitentiary. The legislature had imposed this restriction in 1823, in an attempt to vest jurisdiction over criminal matters exclusively in the circuit courts. Initially, the statute had assigned cases of petit larceny to the circuit courts as well, but in 1831, this restriction was removed and criminal jurisdiction over cases of petit larceny was restored to the county courts. This restoration reflected a particular effort to crack down on illegal gaming operations and recognized the effectiveness of the local courts in this regard. Additionally, even in criminal cases to be tried by the district courts, the county courts acted as examining courts of "free persons charged with offences." They heard and determined any preliminary motions, entertained presentments from grand juries, and decided whether the case warranted acquittal or indictment, and if the latter, in what court the case was to be tried.[12]

County courts also had general jurisdiction over all matters of equity within their respective county. Equity represented a remedial system of justice designed to correct inequities in the body of the common law. If justice could not be found in the law, then a party had recourse in equity. Since the sixteenth century, a corpus of equity jurisprudence had developed symbiotically with the common law. James Philemon Holcombe, in his treatise on equity jurisprudence, noted that the principles of equity should not be considered in opposition to the common law, but as complementary to it. He asserted that every civilized country contained "some such tribunal" in order to ensure that the principles of natural justice would be upheld when the law, "by reason of its [universal application]," failed to do so. Equity remained a fundamental component of Virginia's jurisprudence, with both the county courts and the circuit courts acting as chancery courts (the courts of equity) because of their concurrent jurisdiction.[13]

[12] William Brockenbrough, *Brief Sketch of the Courts of this Commonwealth*, in 2 Virginia Cases (1826), v; Conway Robinson, *Practice in the Courts of Law and Equity in Virginia*, vol. 1 (Richmond, 1832), 1–5; *1849 Code of Virginia*, 616. This hearing procedure replicated that of the colonial magistrate's courts. Determining the qualification in terms of tobacco was removed from the law during the 1849 revision to the Code.

[13] On equity, see James Philemon Holcombe, *An Introduction to Equity Jurisprudence, on the basis of Story's Commentaries with Notes and References to English and American Cases,*

The assignment of original jurisdiction in equity allowed the county courts to retain considerable power even at the expense of the appellate authority of the circuit courts. Conway Robinson noted that "so general are the words giving chancery jurisdiction" that a county court had jurisdiction to "try the validity of a will, which a circuit court, sitting as a court of probate, may have admitted to record." In such suit, Robinson explained, a county court might direct it "to be tried at its own bar" in order to determine whether or not "the writing be the true will of the testator." The authority to issue injunctions stood as the lone exception to this otherwise broad jurisdiction. County courts were unable to issue an injunction to "stay proceedings at law upon a judgment obtained in a circuit court." Still, they could issue injunctions in other cases, even against the judgment of other county courts when a particular defendant did not reside in the county where the case was being heard. Debtors who lived outside of the Commonwealth, but who possessed lands within the state, were also subject to suits in chancery in the county courts.[14]

Additionally, the county courts served as Courts of Oyer and Terminer for the trials of slaves and free blacks. Trials of slaves were not conducted as jury trials, but required a quorum of five justices who ruled exclusively on the legal evidence presented. Conviction of a slave required a unanimous guilty verdict. Slaves charged with felony offenses were to be tried not less than five days but no more than ten day following incarceration. Slaves were not allowed to be tried in the circuit courts and, therefore, their only source of appeal resided in the governor. Free blacks were tried in the same manner as slaves, except in cases of homicide.[15]

Corporation courts acted as the equivalent to the county courts in Virginia's towns and cities. The first corporation courts had been established in Williamsburg and Richmond by the House of Burgesses early in the eighteenth century. By 1845, nine such courts existed in the towns of Richmond, Norfolk, Petersburg, Fredericksburg, Lynchburg, Staunton, Williamsburg, Winchester, and Danville. Corporation courts possessed similar jurisdiction except in civil suits, where their jurisdiction was confined to cases among citizens and inhabitants of the corporation exclusively. If a civil suit involving participants who were not citizens or inhabitants of the corporation, but were Virginians, the corporation court deferred to the appropriate county court or to the circuit

adapted to the use of Students (Cincinnati, 1846), 9–10; and Joseph Story, *Commentaries on Equity Jurisprudence*. The original text from Holcombe reads "universality." On the issues surrounding equity and law reform in the nineteenth century, see the forum on Chancery Reform in *Law and History Review*, 22 (2004): 389–427, 565–599, and 601–617. The forum features the following contributions: Michael Lobban, "Preparing for the Fusion: Reforming the Nineteenth-Century Court of Chancery" (Part 1 and Part 2); Joshua Getzler, "Chancery Reform and Law Reform"; James Oldham, "A Profusion of Chancery Reform"; and Lobban's response, "The Chancellor, the Chancery, and the History of Law Reform."

[14] Robinson, *Practice*, 1: 2–3; See, for instance, *Ford v. Gardner*, 1 Hening & Munford, 72; *Paul v. Paul*, 2 Hening & Munford, 525.

[15] Brockenbrough, *Brief Sketch*, v. and Robinson, *Practice*, 1: 8.

court. Unlike their county brethren, corporation courts were not composed of justices but of a tribunal that included the mayor, a recorder, and aldermen. The method of appointment and tenure in office for the selectmen of the corporation courts depended on the specifications of the respective town charter.[16]

Beyond their adjudicative responsibilities, the county courts were responsible for appointing and sustaining local offices. They possessed direct appointment authority over the offices of county constables and surveyors, and nominated candidates for sheriffs, coroners, and militia officers below the rank of brigadier to the governor. They also nominated and appointed commodity inspectors. Laws governing the inspection of tobacco and other agricultural products had existed in Virginia since 1630, when a law was enacted to address the problem of exporting poorly cured tobacco. Although the initial regulations concerned tobacco, inspection laws proliferated as the colonial economy diversified. By the time of the Revolution, commodities inspections were required for flour, cornmeal, bread, salt, fish, pork, beef, tar, pitch, turpentine, lumber, lime, hemp, and lard. For each of these commodities the method of appointing inspectors varied significantly, because the laws had been enacted at different times to address different needs. In the case of tobacco inspectors, those county courts with a tobacco warehouse in their jurisdiction were charged with nominating four men every August or September to serve as inspectors. From the list of four, the governor would appoint a first and second inspector who served for a term of one year. County courts appointed all inspectors for flour, meal, and bread without confirmation from the governor, although he was entitled to make the appointment if the court failed to do so. Lumber inspectors, on the other hand, were appointed exclusively by the governor, whereas laws pertaining to inspectors of salt, fish, beef, and pork tasked only the courts and made no provision for the executive.[17]

County courts convened four times a year in designated quarterly sessions. In these sessions, presentments were made, criminal trials conducted, and suits in law and equity were heard. Additionally, any caveats against land grants within the county were determined during these sessions. In the months not designated for quarterly sessions, the county courts convened to record deeds and wills, grant probate and privy examination certificates, and attend to any other necessary business. Both the quarterly and monthly sessions were administered by justices of the peace. Justices were required to be freeholders. They were nominated by the court and commissioned by the governor. The commission was a lifetime appointment, unless they moved from the county or held a

[16] Brockenbrough, *Brief Sketch*, v–vi.

[17] *SAL*, 1: 152. Joseph Clarke Robert, *The Tobacco Kingdom: Plantation, Market, and Factory in Virginia and North Carolina, 1800–1860* (Durham, NC: Duke University Press, 1938), 76–93. *Reports of the Revisors*, 476; Bruce, *Economic History of Virginia in the Seventeenth Century*, I: 302–308. Tobacco inspectors could not be owners of any tobacco warehouses, hold any other state or local office, or be an ordinary keeper "at or near the warehouse where he is inspector." Local variations on the process developed especially in cases distinguishing between publicly owned and private warehouses.

federal office. It was not salaried, although limited compensation came from fees, particularly when a justice served his term as sheriff. Each justice of a county served as sheriff for two years on a rotational basis.[18]

The number of justices per county was a recurring source of concern in Virginia. In the seventeenth century, the House of Burgesses had noted that the "great number of commissioners in each county hath rendered the place contemptible and raised factions among themselves, rather than preserved the peace of the people." In response, in 1662, the Burgesses enacted a statute that limited each county to eight justices. Following the Revolution, the standard was discarded. Candidates for justice of the peace were nominated to either replace or to expand the office because of an increasing workload. The 1776 Constitution had responded to the corresponding growth in population and litigation by conferring on the governor the discretion to expand the number of justices as necessary. In practice, however, the number of justices in any given county was determined by the discretion of the court itself, because the governors consistently found it difficult to refuse these nominations in what, for all practical purposes, was a system of bottom-up patronage.[19]

Baltimore lawyer John Pendleton Kennedy featured the freehold-based judicial system as the locus of social authority and community activity in his novel, *Swallow Barn*. The county courts, along with the lawyers and the country gentlemen who populated them, occupied a prominent place in Kennedy's portrait of the Old Dominion. Most notably, Tidewater planter Frank Merriwether provided an archetype of the republican freeholder replete with all the mythical characteristics of independence, local attachment, and community consciousness inherent in the ownership ideal. Naturally, he served as a justice of the peace in the county courts where he kept "the peace as if he commanded a garrison, and administer[ed] justice like a Cadi." Significantly, Kennedy did not depict Merriwether as a rustic farmer ignorant of legal learning; rather he emerges as man who understood both the advantages and the limitations of the law and who, in the end, preferred local adjudication over legal principles as a method of resolution. Indeed, in the matter of resolving a dispute over his own land claims, Merriwether opted to devise a settlement outside the bounds of the courthouse – a "trial by view," in Kennedy's parlance.[20]

The theory of law articulated in these passages reflected a projection of a pure common law – a law recognized by common custom and common sense.

[18] Some claimed that the compensation received in performing the office of sheriff was indicative of compensation for the whole, but, Brockenbrough noted, "experience shews that the profits of the Shrievality are hardly equal to its responsibility." Brockenbrough, *Brief Sketch*, v.

[19] *SAL*, 2: 21; See the historical commentary provided in the *Virginia Code* 1849, 243, note.

[20] John Pendleton Kennedy, *Swallow Barn; or, a Sojourn in the Old Dominion* (Originally published in 1832; republished with an introduction by Lucinda H. MacKethan, Baton Rouge: Louisiana State University Press, 1986), citation found on 32–33. For a scholarly interpretation of the nineteenth-century justices that reaches similar conclusions, see W. Hamilton Bryson, "Introduction," in *Essays on Legal Education in Nineteenth Century Virginia* (Buffalo: William S. Hein & Co., 1998), 9–34.

Juxtaposed against this idealized form of community justice are references to the technical, procedural, and substantive elements of jurisprudence informed by the realities of the modern commercial economy. These references provide the narrative tensions that allow the county court system to be portrayed from a nostalgic perspective. Kennedy surrounds Merriwether with a host of legal personalities that amplify these tensions: Talliferro Hedges, the young squire of the court and bon vivant of the bar; Philpot Wart, the learned sage of the law, who Kennedy openly modeled as a caricature of William Wirt; and the irrepressible Singleton Oglethorpe Swansdown, pettifogger extraordinaire. Admittedly, Kennedy portrayed this legal system in a state of decay. The courthouse itself is depicted as an isolated brick building, "entirely unornamented," with its "ample windows covered with dust and cobwebs." The county seat is a small village, hardly worth the name, whose economic activities centered solely on the convening of the court. The only trial of note focused on a case of disorderly conduct from a well-known disorderly, and the pace of the proceedings was languid. It was a portrait of decay – but it was natural decay, and thus one that evoked sentiments of nostalgia.[21]

THE QUINTESSENCE OF THE FREEHOLD DIGNITY

In many respects, the English common law's two-tiered jury system stood as the most salient feature of continuity between the colonial and republican periods. Within this system, trial by jury meant that an initial jury – the grand jury – contemplated charges and made presentments to the court, whereas a secondary jury – the petit jury – heard arguments and rendered a verdict. The postcolonial law revisions easily accommodated this historic process to a republican model that remained committed to the ideals of local justice and trial by peers. In these republican courts, freeholders remained obliged to perform their conventional jury duties of arbitrating disputes, determining and enforcing public policies, defining community standards, and maintaining the peace. Freeholders were specifically tasked with making presentments and indictments, as well as conveying any information to the bench about all felonies and misdemeanors committed within their jurisdiction. They accomplished these duties during each session of the county and corporation courts, as well as during the select sessions of the circuit courts that heard criminal cases. For each judicial session, twenty-four freeholders were summoned to serve as grand jurors. At least sixteen needed to be present to form a competent grand jury, and the concurrence of twelve grand jurors was needed to make a presentment or bring an indictment. John Pendleton Kennedy, in characterizing the duties of the office, referred to the civic virtue exercised in this very public forum as "the quintessence of the freehold dignity."[22]

[21] Kennedy, *Swallow Barn*, 166–174.

[22] Conway Robinson, *The Practice in the Courts of Law and Equity*, 3 volumes (Richmond: Samuel Shepard, 1832–1839), 3: 82–83. Also see the *Virginia Code 1849*, 767. Kennedy, *Swallow Barn*, 170–171.

The history of this dignity long preceded its exercise in Virginia's republic. It was popularly understood that the office had been the traditional preserve of the English freeholder since time immemorial, and they repeatedly acknowledged that the performance of the office embodied the liberties historically guaranteed by the common-law system. The origins of the grand jury were rooted in the ecclesiastical courts. A twelfth-century document, the Assize of Clarendon, contained a specific reference requiring an inquest to be conducted by twelve lawful men of the hundred and it is generally acknowledged to mark the seminal moment that the practice was incorporated into the emerging body of the English common law. Further evidence suggests that grand juries developed along with the practice of the trial by jury, which replaced trials by ordeal during the thirteenth century. The office of grand juror became considerably more important following the Fourth Lateran Council, in 1215, when the Church prohibited the clergy from participating in trials by ordeal. The two-tiered jury system developed in the wake of this decree, with the grand jury determining whether or not the evidence was sufficient to enter a *billa vera*, and the petit jury charged with determining innocence or guilt. The freehold qualification for grand jurors appears to have been present from the beginning. Thomas Green, the leading historian of the English criminal jury, has found the explicit references from sheriffs for freeholders to be empanelled as jurors in 1288 and 1289. And as the jury system developed, the freehold qualification became imbedded in the lore of the common law. Blackstone identified the qualification as arising from the feudal ceremony of *homagium*, when freeholders pledged their fealty and agreed to attend the court of their lord, where they were charged with bringing and answering complaints concerning their tenures as well as acting as jurors in "the trials of the fellow tenants."[23]

The freehold qualification was transplanted to the Virginia colony, but the exact moment when the qualification was institutionalized remains obscure. In 1632, the county courts were formally organized (although then referred to as monthly courts) and the appointed commissioners were charged with conducting the courts in a manner "as near to the common laws of England" as was possible. Admittedly, however, it is difficult to establish undeniably whether

[23] Thomas A. Green, *Verdict According to Conscience: Perspectives on the English Criminal Jury Trial 1200–1800* (Chicago: University of Chicago Press, 1985), 52. *Tucker's Blackstone*, 3: 54. On the history of the grand jury in English law see Barbara J. Shapiro, "*Beyond Reasonable Doubt" and "Probable Cause:" Historical Perspectives on the Anglo-American Law of Evidence* (Berkeley: University of California, 1991), esp. chapter 2; R. H. Helmholz, "The Early History of the Grand Jury and the Canon Law," *University of Chicago Law Review*, 50 (1983): 613–627; Roger D. Groot, "The Jury of Presentment before 1215," *American Journal of Legal History*, 26 (1982): 1–24; *cf.* Naomi Hurnard, "The Jury of Presentment and the Assizes of Clarendon," *English Historical Review* 61 (1941): 371–410. In addition to the work of Thomas Green, the origins of trial by jury is discussed in Leonard Levy, *The Palladium of Justice: Origins of the Trial by Jury* (Chicago: I. R. Dee, 1999), and Harold J. Berman, *Law and Revolution: The Formation of the Western Legal Tradition* (Cambridge, MA: Harvard University Press, 1983), esp. 447–461. On the importance of the trial by jury in the Commonwealth, see Miller, *Juries and Judges*.

or not the freehold qualification was used exclusively in the colony during the first decades of settlement. Philip Alexander Bruce, in his comprehensive study on the origins of Virginia's institutions, noted that presentments were made by churchwardens, but he also maintained that grand jurors assumed a prominent role in determining justice from the colony's earliest days. Thirteen years later, in 1645, another statute granted jurisdiction to the county courts for all causes of common law and equity and specified that jurors should be empanelled from "the most able men of the country." It was not until the Restoration legal reforms, in 1662, however, that an explicit effort was made to make judicial trial procedure in Virginia correspond, as nearly as possible, to the laws of England. These reforms instructed county sheriffs to empanel grand juries at least twice a year to "enquire of the breach of all penall laws in their severall countyes, and…make presentment thereof." No mention was made, however, about the qualifications for grand jurors. It is perhaps reasonable, nevertheless, to expect that the contemporary statutory definitions for freehold suffrage paralleled the determination for office as well. Not until the end of the century, however, was the freehold qualification specifically mentioned in a series of statutes pertaining to the practices of the courts. Yet this act required that jurors for the General Court must, in addition to being freeholders, also possess visible land and goods valued at one hundred pounds sterling. Jurors for the county courts had to possess a visible estate of fifty pounds sterling according to the statute. Certainly, the property caveat suggests that the freehold qualification was already in force and that the statute, like those pertaining to suffrage, was attempting to further define the freehold on the colonial landscape. A more comprehensive 1705 statute addressing the procedures for summoning, empanelling, and fining jurors retained these prescribed qualifications for grand jurors.[24]

In 1748, a series of legislative reforms made two significant changes to the requirements for jurors and grand jurors. The first change amended the estate value requirement from "pounds sterling" to "pounds current money," which during that period often meant tobacco. Indeed, the same act listed the fines for absent jurors in pounds of tobacco. Accordingly, this amendment probably can be construed as an effort to expand the pool of grand jurors, given that one hundred pounds of tobacco was typically much easier to come by in the colony than one hundred pounds sterling. The second change, however, was exclusionary in nature and prohibited empanelling ordinary keepers, constables, surveyors of highways, and mill owners from serving as jurors. The exclusion of acting constables and surveyors from any form of jury duty

[24] Philip Alexander Bruce, *Institutional History of Virginia in the Seventeenth Century*, 2 vols. (New York: G. P. Putnam's Sons, 1910), 79–93, 605. Bruce discussed the role of churchwardens in making presentments and their eventual relationship with freeholders in exercising this task. He noted that the monthly or county courts were instituted in 1619. William Waller Hening, *The New Virginia Justice*, 3rd edition (Richmond: Cochran, 1820), 406. *SAL*, 1: 169, 303; 2: 73–74, 175. On the colonial development of freehold suffrage, see Julian A. C. Chandler, *History of Suffrage in Virginia* (Baltimore: Johns Hopkins University Press, 1901), 9–16.

reflected the fact that both offices were already affiliated with the business of the court. It probably represented an instance of the law following existing practice. Ordinary keepers had a reputation as purveyors of vice, but, more pragmatically, most ordinaries in colonial Virginia were located in proximity to the courthouse and did their best business when the court was in session. It was probably difficult to get keepers to close up shop in order to sit as a jury member. Furthermore, the actual ownership of ordinaries was often cloaked in secrecy, and many in the community suspected that, in some instances, they were owned by some of the county justices themselves.[25]

On the other hand, the exclusion of the mill owners was intended to isolate a specific commercial interest that potentially compromised the disinterested ideal of the republican freeholder. The prohibition recognized that mill owners possessed special interests, which were often in conflict with the general interest of the community. The exclusion corresponded with the development of the grain and flour industry in the colony and suggests the emergence of significant social tensions arising from a diversifying economy. Nearly a century later, Judge Lewis Summers explained that "the mischief to be remedied" by the 1748 statute was the potential influence of mill owners serving as grand jurors and "having jurisdiction of their peculiar cases."[26]

Wheat had been grown in Virginia since the early seventeenth century and maize, of course, was indigenous, but neither was deemed sufficiently profitable to merit development into a cash-crop industry. By the middle of the eighteenth century, however, circumstances had begun to change. By 1790, grain exports represented a significant component of Virginia's economy. Wheat production was concentrated principally in the counties of the Northern Neck and in the Shenandoah Valley. Subsequently, as tobacco demanded fresh soil and moved westward into the south-central Piedmont, wheat supplanted it as the

[25] *SAL*, 6: 201. The social perceptions of ordinary keepers are discussed in Roeber, *Faithful Magistrates*, 139, and in Rhys Isaac, *The Transformation of Virginia* (Chapel Hill: University of North Carolina Press, 1982), 94–98. In the wake of the Revolution, Virginians preserved the freehold qualification but made subsequent amendments to it to meet the demands of a republican juridical model. The historical disqualifications to mill owners, ordinary keepers, and aliens were maintained, although the question of alien landholding and office holding became more confusing in the absence of a monarchical model of tenures. During the statute compilation project leading to the 1819 *Revised Code*, legislators removed the supplemental property qualification for grand jurors but maintained one requiring a visible estate of $300 for petit jurors in the superior courts and $150 for the county courts. The 1819 *Revised Code* also mandated that no one under twenty years of age could serve as a juror. Over the next decades, however, Virginia's courts found frequent occasion to contemplate the purpose of the qualification and to necessarily clarify the statutes, particularly pertaining to the disqualifications for office of alien landholders, joint owners, nonresidents, and mill owners. *The Revised Code...of Virginia*, B. W. Leigh, comp. (Richmond: T. Ritchie, 1819), 264–266. *Commonwealth v. Long*, 2 Va. Cas. 318; *Moran v. Commonwealth*, 9 Leigh 651; *Commonwealth v. Cherry*, 2 Va. Cas. 20. The court also addressed the question of joint ownership in the case of *Commonwealth v. Willson* (1830), 2 Leigh 739.

[26] *Moran v. Commonwealth*, 9 Leigh 654.

principal crop in the lower Tidewater as well. Both Richmond and Alexandria were considered important grain ports during the early nineteenth century. This expansion of the grain industry and the subsequent increased acreage dedicated to cereals necessitated an expansion in the number of mills throughout the Old Dominion. And, at least until the 1840s, Virginians expressed a preference for local mills over larger factories, undoubtedly to allay transportation costs. Consequently, roughly two-thirds of the flour manufacturing occurred in small, local establishments.[27]

Other legal historians have focused on the emergence of milldams and canals in New England as a means to examine the tensions wrought on traditional notions of property and social value during the early stages of industrialization. Most notably, Morton Horwitz has argued that these tensions indicated a "fundamental transformation" in the idea of property – "from a static agrarian conception entitling the owner to undisturbed enjoyment, to a dynamic, instrumental, and more abstract view of property that emphasized the newly paramount virtues of productive use and development." Horwitz examined a series of court cases involving the rights of mill owners and has provocatively suggested that they demonstrate that the doctrines of natural and prior use – which traditionally were antidevelopmental in orientation – were, in fact, transformed in the courts to support the developmental preferences of entrepreneurs and capitalists. He argued that this transformation happened at the expense of the rights of private ownership. Gary Kulik complemented Horwitz's findings by noting that legal dispensations for mills eroded traditional public rights, most notably fishing rights, as well as individual property rights in general. Both of these studies have described the intricate means by which an ideological preference for industrial development was accommodated by the legal system.[28]

Things were different in Virginia, however. Unlike the issues raised in a region where industrialization was seen in a favorable light, Virginians had to negotiate the problems posed by mills in an economy that remained dedicated to agriculture. Within that economy, waterways served as the principal means of powering gristmills but also were the principal means of transporting tobacco hogsheads by bateaux to the coastal port cities. Any attempt to refashion the doctrine of prior use met with different and stauncher obstacles

[27] On Virginia's mills see: Arthur G. Peterson, "Flour and Grist Milling in Virginia: A Brief History," *Virginia Magazine of History and Biography*, 63 (1935): 97–108; Thomas S. Berry, "The Rise of Flour Milling in Richmond," *Virginia Magazine of History and Biography*, 78 (1970): 387–408; and David D. Plater, "Building the North Wales Mill of William Allason," *Virginia Magazine of History and Biography*, 85 (1977): 45–50.

[28] Morton Horwitz, *The Transformation of American Law, 1780–1860* (Cambridge, MA: Harvard University Press, 1977), 46–54; Gary Kulik, "Dams, Fish, and Farmers: Defense of Public Rights in Eighteenth-Century Rhode Island," in Steven Hahn and Jonathan Prude, eds., *The Countryside in the Age of Capitalist Transformation* (Chapel Hill: University of North Carolina, 1985), 25–50. Horwitz argued that this intellectual transformation of the concept of use corresponded with a legal reconceptualization of property law in the decades following independence.

in Virginia where the waterways were already functioning toward economic development. Consequently, Virginia's tobacco planters could just as easily find legal sanctuary in a "modern" reading of prior use, and so the question of mill construction appeared in the form of a negotiation over the preferred form of economic development in a particular instance. Any proposed obstructions or alterations to a watercourse necessarily raised questions regarding whether it potentially contributed more to the community as a source of energy, as a highway, or – if possible – as both.[29]

Throughout the first half of the nineteenth century, Virginia's laws remained biased toward inhibiting the obstruction of watercourses. Water was held in common under the common law, and Virginia law declared that all navigable waterways were specified as public highways. Once a watercourse was declared a public highway by law, the courts were prohibited from granting permission to build any dam that would obstruct "ordinary navigation, or the passage of fish." Special statutes further classified many lesser tributaries and estuaries that were not navigable as public highways as well. Even in tributaries not declared public highways, any dam or other obstruction that limited navigation or the passage of fish was considered a public nuisance unless it was for a mill or manufacture that was deemed "useful to the public" and permitted by a court order. To erect a dam, or to cut a canal, an individual was required to apply for a writ of *ad quod damnum*, and an inquest into the probable damages was to be conducted by a grand jury of twelve freeholders of the county. The grand jury determined whether approval would be granted and, if so, what compensation was to be paid for any lands that might be overflowed or any property that would be destroyed by the alteration. Compensation was to be paid before the project commenced. Once all the assigned compensation had been paid, the applicant was seized in fee simple over the lands identified by the inquest, in effect giving him legal title over the lands in question. But if the applicant did not begin his work within a year, or finish the project within three years, the title to these lands reverted to its former owners.[30]

Despite these requirements, mills proliferated throughout the nineteenth-century Virginia countryside. The courts articulated a clear standard of reasonable use, which, in the tradition of the common law, adjudicated rulings on a case-by-case basis and attempted to balance competing visions of economic development. The circumstances surrounding the ruling by the Supreme

[29] For a detailed look at Virginia's postcolonial economy, see Joseph Clarke Robert, *The Tobacco Kingdom: Plantation, Market, and Factory in Virginia and North Carolina, 1800–1860* (Durham, NC: Duke University Press, 1938), and Robert McColley, *Slavery in Jeffersonian Virginia* (2nd edition, Urbana: University of Illinois Press, 1964).

[30] *Virginia Code 1849*, 325–330; *Revised Code, 1819*, 2: 231–232; *SAL*, 6: 70, 12: 189; *TB*, 3: 14, 18. The list of specific statutory provisions from 1819 through 1847 was listed in Conway Robinson and James Patton, *Reports of the Revisors*, 2: 367, note. The writ of *ad quod damnum* technically commanded the sheriff to make inquiry "to what damage" a specified act, if done, will tend. In practice, in Virginia, the writ charged the sheriff with empanelling the jury of freeholders to make the inquiry.

Court of Appeals in *Asbury Crenshaw and Thomas B. Crenshaw v. Slate River Company* provided a clear example of how these standards were recognized and applied by the bench. In 1824, the Crenshaw brothers purchased a plot of land straddling the Slate River in Buckingham County that already had an operating water gristmill on it. Their title was excellent; they were able to trace an "undisturbed possession" on the land for nearly a hundred years and the authorized mill had been operating for sixty of those years. They soon found it necessary, however, to request a Bill of Injunction to prevent the Slate River Company from declaring their milldam a public nuisance and destroying it. The Slate River Company, a joint-stock corporation, had been created by the General Assembly in 1819 and tasked with improving the navigation of the river "from its junction with the James River" to the "highest practicable point" of navigation "by vessels drawing one foot of water." When this improvement was accomplished, the legislature intended to declare the river a public highway and granted the Company a license to receive profits from tolls as a means to compensate stockholders for their investment. To make the river navigable, however, the statute authorizing the project also required that mill owners along the river construct and maintain sufficient locks or canals at their own expense. If they failed to do so, the Company was authorized to clear away the milldams and charge the owners for the cost.[31]

The Crenshaw brothers refused to subscribe to this plan of internal improvement. They took their case to court and, in March 1828, the four-member Supreme Court of Appeals contemplated the tangled issues of private and public rights, eminent domain, and economic development. The Court ruled unanimously in favor of the Crenshaws and prohibited the implementation of the Slate River improvement statute. Writing a concurring opinion, Judge John Williams Green explained that he did not believe the legislature intended "to invade private rights" but had proceeded on the conviction that the rights of mill owners "were subordinate to the public right of navigation." He acknowledged that a difference of opinion could exist over such an issue but believed that the appropriate determination of such a contest were "emphatically Judicial in their nature." In this instance, like their New England brethren, Virginia judges ruled in favor of the mill owners. Yet, they did so to protect private property rights in the face of an apparent public improvement and recognized the traditional reading of prior use to preserve a manufacturer at the expense of agriculture.[32]

The case reflects the complexity surrounding the role of mills in Virginia's economic development. Not surprisingly, ambivalence emerged periodically in regards to the policy of disqualifying mill owners as grand jurors. In 1795, as part of the republican revisions, the disqualification of mill owners (along with tavern keepers and surveyors) was removed for grand jurors serving the district

[31] *Crenshaw and Crenshaw v. The Slate River Company* (1828), 6 Randolph 245–284. *cf.* Horwitz, 47–49.

[32] *Ibid.*

and appellate courts. Because the disqualification had always been premised on local concerns, logic seemingly dictated that these parties should only be excluded from participation in the county court sessions. By 1814, however, the restriction was reimplemented by a legislature committed to creating uniform practices and procedures at all levels of the courts. This reform reflected the growing influence of an increasingly professionalized bench and bar. Given the ubiquity of judicial circuit riding, both lawyers and judges sought reforms that standardized procedures throughout the juridical system. By the 1830s, however, with the development of mills powered by coal burning, the worm had turned again and many of the issues of potential conflict were becoming moot. In 1836, the General Assembly revised the disqualification to exclude only those owners of "water grist mills" from serving as grand jurors.[33]

Three years later, the General Court reexamined the historic disqualification of mill owners in the case of *Moran v. Commonwealth*. Peter Moran, a resident of Petersburg, had been indicted for manslaughter, but he entered two pleas to challenge the grand juror qualification of Francis Follett, the owner of a water-powered gristmill. The pleas actually represented the same charge, but were couched in different terms in order to elucidate a clear ruling on the disqualification. In the first plea, the defense argued that Follett owned and occupied a water gristmill in the adjacent county of Chesterfield at the time when he was summoned to serve as a grand juror. In the other plea, they charged that Follett was the owner and occupier of a gristmill when the grand jury made the indictment, but in this plea they did not specify the location of the mill. The General Court rejected both pleas and overturned Moran's petition for abatement on a writ of error. Nearly a decade after trying to establish a ward system, Judge Lewis Summers delivered the majority opinion for a divided court. He explained that the customary "privilege of a freeholder" to serve as a grand juror was inherent in the common law and posited that any subsequent constraint to it devised for the public interest should be construed by the courts in the manner least likely to "abridge the general privilege." He noted that the public purposes of the disqualification were satisfied simply by limiting it to apply to the specific jurisdiction within which the mill was situated. Summers emphasized that the reasons underlying both the qualifications and disqualifications for grand jurors were premised on the incidence of vicinage. Accordingly, he controversially proclaimed that this ruling held that "residence, as well as freehold, within the county" were necessary to meet the qualification for grand jurors. Although the stipulation of a residency requirement was not contested in the case, Summers managed to incorporate it into the opinion. The ruling thus represented an important shift in interpreting the freehold qualification, foreshadowing the trends of the legal reforms enacted during the decade that followed.[34]

[33] *Virginia Code 1849*, 767.

[34] *Commonwealth v. Moran*, 9 Leigh 651, 654–656 (1839). Judges John B. Clopton, John Christian, and Lucas Thompson dissented, but they did not write any opinions.

Like the freehold qualification itself, the disqualification of mill owners represented a commitment to the principals of vicinage and parochialism that informed the desire for the administration of local police and justice. During the colonial period and the early decades of the republic, mill owners represented one of the strongest threats to the customary rights of local communities. Their disqualification, however, was not aimed at prohibiting the development of mills. Rather, it reflected an effort to control development within the purview of the public good – a public good administered by a grand jury of disinterested freeholders. In theory at least, republican freeholders embodied the qualities of vicinage and virtue that made local self-government possible.

By the middle decades of the nineteenth century, however, the sheer ability to pursue these ideals was rapidly coming undone. Mill owners increasingly represented only one of an array of special interest groups that potentially stood poised to intrude on the private rights of individuals as well as the public rights of a community. The case of *Crenshaw and Crenshaw v. the Slate River Company* proved an ironic example of this diversity, with the court rescuing mill owners from the ambitious designs of a joint-stock corporation, doubtlessly composed of freeholders. Beyond this confusion of interests, however, the freehold qualification for grand jurors was being subverted by the changing conceptualization of the freehold itself. During the Constitutional Convention, conservatives along with democratic reformers had acknowledged the inadequacy of the freehold, as it existed in daily social practices, to ensure the integrity of the right of suffrage. Now, after five centuries of routine performance, similar problems affected the exercise of office as well.

CESTUIS QUE USE

The freehold qualification for grand jurors was subverted neither from an unsuitable definition of the freehold nor from an inconsistent conception of the qualification. Rather, it was undone by the question of how to interpret the qualification in the face of more complicated patterns of possession and transfer that had their origins in the principles of equity, but which were becoming ubiquitous on the commercial landscape of the nineteenth century. Specifically, the practices of transferring lands through mortgages and trusts inherently blurred the legal boundaries and ideological precepts that defined allodial ownership. In December 1843, Virginia's General Court entertained the case of *Commonwealth v. Burcher*, which posed the question of whether or not an individual could be considered a valid grand juror if he did not actually possess the legal title to a freehold, but instead based his claim on the principle of an equity of redemption. In other words, was a right of trust or mortgage equivalent to the characteristics of independence and vicinage predicated in allodial ownership – at least so far as to meet the qualification for office?[35]

[35] *Commonwealth v. Burcher*, 2 Robinson 326 (1843).

The case was brought forth by James Burcher, a rather dubious character who had been arrested and charged by the Petersburg circuit superior court for running an illegal roulette table. He contested the charge, however, on a procedural technicality by questioning whether or not one of the grand jurors, who made the presentment, was actually a freeholder. Burcher contended that William Lea did not possess a deed in fee simple on his house and lot in Petersburg and, therefore, could not be considered a qualified grand juror. In this instance, the ambiguity of Lea's status arose from the particular methods by which he has purchased the estate and by which the title was conveyed. Lea had purchased the house and the lot for the price of $4,360 from John Grammer, who held good and valid title to the property. Lea did not pay the full purchase price, however, nor did he execute a deed of trust on the property in order to borrow the purchase money. Instead, he agreed that the fee-simple deed would be held by a third party until he had paid Grammer the entire purchase price through a series of installments. Accordingly, Grammer and his wife signed and sealed the deed conveying the property to William Lea and, as was agreed to by both parties, "placed it in the keeping of William Pannill," who promised to deliver it when Lea completed making all the payments due. Lea took possession of the property, continued to pay his installments on time, and, by the time of the case, had made about $800 worth of improvement to the property.[36]

In the eyes of the law, Lea remained a vendee – someone who was still in the process of purchasing – and, accordingly, until the title was actually conveyed, he was considered merely as a tenant-at-will, not a freeholder. Significantly, however, despite the absence of legal title, the principles of equity jurisprudence protected his possession from any adversarial claims under the doctrine of *cestuis que use*. This medieval doctrine acknowledged that Lea held his property as a trust, which, although distinct from legal ownership, conferred to him an equitable title that ensured that he received any profits arising from the estate and protected him from eviction. In a court of equity, Lea was considered a trustee to use, and this status entitled him to the rights and privileges of the freehold. Yet his title in equity confused the allodial definition of a freeholder and thus raised questions concerning his validity to perform the office of grand juror.

Learned jurists recognized that the practice by which Lea had procured his land was not necessarily new. *Cestuis que use* had been devised by the monasteries during the thirteenth century as an extralegal form of landholding. James Philemon Holcombe, one of the more erudite members of the Virginia bar on matters of equity jurisprudence, explained that the Church had created the practice to evade the 1279 Statute of Mortmain, which prohibited the acquisition of land by religious orders. Parliament had enacted mortmain in the interest of the feudal barons, who found themselves in competition with the monasteries over land. And the Church had responded in kind.

[36] *Ibid.*

The process of establishing a *cestuis que use* was simple; an individual legally conveyed his estate to another, who was actually a third party representing the interests of the religious order. The conveyance expressly stipulated that the estate would be used by a particular religious order and, in so doing, created a legal loophole. The third party (known as the feofee for the use) possessed legal title to the estate, but the religious order had unlimited and perpetual use of the property. Since common-law courts were concerned exclusively with the legal transfer and tenure of the estate, they necessarily recognized the legitimacy of the conveyance. The title, or seisin, to the estate had been transferred to an individual, not to the monastery, and thus conformed to the Statute of Mortmain. As had been the rule with the practice of sub-infeudation, the law was concerned with the condition of service attached to the estate, not how it was used. Common-law courts considered the particular clause in the deed directing that the person should hold the conveyed property for the use of other persons, the *cestuis que use*, "as a nullity – as nothing." It did not affect the tenure. In the Chancery Courts, however, which were courts of conscience where the principles of equity reigned, the clause expressed the substantive spirit of the contract and, accordingly, was looked on "as everything." Henry St. George Tucker, in his law school lectures, explained that a Chancellor would regard the stipulation of use as "the *essential* part of the deed," and that, therefore, chancery courts would enforce "its scrupulous observance," because "no real benefit was intended by the conveyance to the individual to whom the deed was made." Indeed, because equity was committed foremost to justice, it would be considered an iniquity for someone to appropriate property deeded to him under these circumstances and then "refuse to permit its enjoyment by those for whom it was really intended."[37]

Another Virginia commentator, Judge John Tayloe Lomax, offered jurists a more detailed history of the doctrine. Lomax noted that *cestuis que use* was "a species of property totally unknown" to the original elegance of the common law and identified it as a doctrine of the Roman civil law. He maintained that it had developed from a specific inheritance practice of giving a gift of property to another, in confidence, with instructions that it should be conveyed or disposed of in a certain manner. This practice was known as a *fidei commissum*. Because such a donation represented a gift, it acquired features of permanence that were necessarily legitimated by civil law. Lomax contended that the introduction of this practice into the English law had produced "a revolution in the system of real property." He noted that it particularly subverted the law of primogeniture because it permitted the landholder

[37] James P. Holcombe, *An Introduction to Equity Jurisprudence, on the basis of Story's Commentaries* (Cincinnati, OH: Derby, Bradley, & Co., 1846), 2–18; Henry St. George Tucker, *Commentaries on the Laws of Virginia, Comprising the Substance of a Course of Lectures Delivered to the Winchester Law School*, 2 vols. (3rd edition, Richmond: Shepherd and Colin, 1846), 1: 31–32. Tucker's account was drawn principally from Blackstone. Simpson, *History of the Land Law*, 2nd edition, 173–207.

to designate future uses and profits of an estate during his own lifetime at the expense of the heir.[38]

Parliament had sought to close this loophole during the reign of Henry VIII. The Statute of Uses was designed to abolish the secret conveyances of use that created a "double property in land," and to bring all transfers under the realm of law. It was also intended to restore many of the king's prerogatives, and associated revenues, which had been perceived to have been weakened by the practice of equitable use. The statute stipulated that the possession of an estate was transferred whenever the use of it was transferred, thereby erasing the conceptual differences between possession and use and collapsing the distinction between legal and equitable title. In the end, however, the Statute of Uses failed to achieve these ends. Despite collapsing these fundamental distinctions, the wording of the statute did not prefer one over the other and, consequently, both the beneficiary of the use and the feoffee were able to legally convey the estate. Confusion ensued. In the end, by adopting a strict construction of the statute, it was manipulated to foster the opposite effect, and the advantages gained enabled *cestuis que use* to persist and become incorporated into the practices of trusts.[39]

The practices of trusts and mortgages expanded in England during the seventeenth century as a means to preserve estates from indebtedness. An important aspect of this expansion was the jurisprudential development of the equity of redemption – a right that entitled a mortgagor to redeem or recover his property if he failed to repay his loan on time. David Sugarman and Ronnie Warrington, in their insightful essay on the concept, traced not only the legal development of the right, but assessed it political ramifications as well. They emphasized that the equity of redemption played an important role in maintaining the privileged position of the landed class at a time when its political and economic future appeared uncertain. In so doing, the concept preserved and even advanced certain core cultural attributes of "property, justice, citizenship," which fostered a very specific idea of "Englishness" that was intrinsically connected to the development of a national jurisprudence.[40]

Both the Statute of Uses and the equity of redemption had been transmitted to the colonies and, subsequently, received into American law as part and parcel of the English common law. In Virginia, the Statute of Uses was repealed

[38] John Tayloe Lomax, *Digest of the Laws Respecting Real Property* (Philadelphia: John S. Little, 1839), 200, 202. His entire account of the doctrines of use and trust are found on 199–286.

[39] Lomax, *Digest*, 1: 212–214. Simpson, *History of the Land Law*, 2nd edition, 184–188, 200–201.

[40] David Sugarman and Ronnie Warrington, "Land Law, Citizenship, and the Invention of 'Englishness': The Strange World of the Equity of Eedemption," in John Brewer and Susan Staves, eds., *Early Modern Conceptions of Property* (London: Routledge, 1996): 111–143. *Equity of Redemption*: The right of the mortgagor of property to redeem the same (i.e., save from foreclosure) after it has been forfeited, at law, by a breach of the condition of the mortgage (i.e., default in mortgage payments), upon paying the amount of the debt, interests, and costs. *Black's Law Dictionary*, 541.

in 1792, however, as part of the postcolonial law revisions. The republican legislature chose not to enact a similar general statute regarding the practice, but it did pass a specific law concerning contractual exchanges, which collapsed any distinction between use and possession in the instances of bargain, sale, release, or covenant. In other circumstances, however, most notably in those instances of conveyances through inheritance, use remained something distinct from possession and legal title. In the 1834 case of *Bass v. Scott*, Judge William Cabell explained that the absence of a general Statute of Uses in Virginia meant that those particular instances where a use was devised by a will created an equitable estate only. Legal title was not executed by the transfer. Equitable title thus persisted in Virginia after the allodial reforms and even became more commonplace. Mortgages, trusts, and the equity of redemption expanded as creative methods to finance land purchases and as a way to protect estates from creditors.[41]

Two previous cases had addressed the question of equitable tile and grand juror qualifications prior to *Commonwealth v. Burcher*. Neither of these cases proved definitive, but their rulings informed the subsequent arguments made in *Burcher* and suggest that it marked the culmination of a recognized juridical problem. Ten years earlier, in 1833, the case of *Commonwealth v. Reynolds* addressed a challenge to the freehold status of grand juror Smith. Prior to being summoned as a grand juror, Smith had conveyed his lands conditionally to Monroe on the stipulation that he would perform "certain covenants" before taking legal seisin, or title. The "certain covenants" had not been completed by the time the Reynolds was brought to trial, and the question posed before the court was: At what point, in such a conditional transaction, did the actual transfer of ownership take place? Reynolds's attorneys claimed that the parcel of land had been transferred when the bargain and sale agreement had been reached between Smith and Monroe. Accordingly, they argued that Smith held "naked legal title" to the land only, and that he should not be permitted to enjoy the privileges of a freeholder. In an interesting twist, the General Court refused to hear the arguments in the case because of a procedural technicality, but they delivered a *per curiam* opinion declaring that if they had entertained the case, Smith would have been considered a proper grand juror.[42]

Three years later, in 1836, the General Court engaged the issue again in *Kerby v. Commonwealth*. This time, the case proved considerably more complicated. Kerby had been indicted in the Albemarle Circuit Court for selling "ardent spirits" without a license. He challenged the indictment on the assertion that the freehold title of grand juror Boswell Yates was insufficient. In

[41] *Bass v. Scott*, 2 Leigh 356 (1834). On the reception of the equity of redemption, see *Clayborn v. Hill*, 1 Wash. 177 (1793) and *Cadwallader v. Mason*, Wythe 188 (1793), which also contains a monographic note on Deeds of Trusts. Accordingly, at a time when other states sought to erase the distinction between law and equity and unify their doctrines under one formal model of jurisprudence, Virginia did not.

[42] *Commonwealth v. Reynolds*, 4 Leigh 663 (1833).

1828, Yates purchased a tract of land from William Garland, who was the executor of the estate from which the land originated. Yates took possession of the land and paid all of the purchase money except for the last installment. Prior to making the final payment, however, Yates became aware of an adversarial claim against the estate. Garland had prepared a deed in fee simple, but Yates refused it, claiming that Garland could not convey a sufficiently clear title to the land. At the time that Yates was empanelled as a grand juror in the *Kerby* case, he had obtained an injunction preventing Garland from demanding the final installment, and their dispute was pending in Chancery. The Albemarle Circuit Court was aware of these circumstances but considered Yates to be a valid grand juror anyway. The General Court disagreed; they reversed the judgment, set aside the verdict, and quashed the indictment.[43]

Judge Edwin Duncan delivered the majority opinion in the case. He acknowledged that solid reasons existed to presume that Yates met the freehold qualification. He cited a Coke's *Institutes* as specifying an instance of *cestuis que use*, where an individual was determined to be a competent juror because he received the "whole profits" from the estate and "in equity and conscience" the land belonged to him. He also referenced an earlier ruling that had extended the freehold qualification to a juror who had mortgaged his land to pay his debts. This practice represented the contemporary standard for mortgages (mortgages were not originally used for purchase) and fell well within the expectation of the equity of redemption. Duncan differentiated between the issues in that case, however, where the juror possessed legal title before the mortgage, and the question posed in the *Kerby* case, where legal title had never actually been conveyed. Seeking a determinative ruling, he asked the fundamental question of whether or not the freehold qualification embraced "a mere vendee in possession": someone who had paid purchase money and had an equitable right to "call for the legal title," but who had yet to attain such title. Duncan hoped to establish a formal rule to deal with such matters in the future, but he was disappointed and the court contented itself with issuing a narrow ruling. The judges agreed that, even though the title could be construed to meet the requirements of *cestuis que use*, and Yates held an equity of redemption in the land, he could not "be considered as a freeholder within the equity of the statute," because the estate was unsatisfactory to him. In other words, the land had to be his in conscience for an equitable title to exist.[44]

Duncan's unanswered question about whether or not a person who had never received title could serve as a grand juror anticipated the fundamental issue arising in *Commonwealth v. Burcher*. It further reflected the principal challenge in determining grand juror qualifications in the wake of the market revolution. Land transfers had become routine and more people were engaged

[43] *Kerby v. Commonwealth*, 7 Leigh 749 (1836). Judges Daniel and Thompson dissented but did not offer an opinion.

[44] 7 Leigh 749–751; the earlier ruling was *Commonwealth v. Carter* 2 Virginia Cases, 319–320 (1822).

in them. By the middle of the nineteenth century, an individual did not need to belong to a land company to engage in speculative activity. Once transactions were reduced to the cash nexus, the modes of financing them proliferated and more purchasers had access to more purchasing options. The certainty of ownership eroded. In this dynamic environment, the customs of local justice unraveled. Freeholders originally had been tasked with making presentments because they represented the collective memory of the community. This principle of vicinage grounded the idea of trial by a jury of peers – who were not just anonymous people, but neighbors. Now, communities were not even sure who was qualified as a freeholder. The necessary intimacy of local government, which characterized the customary jurisprudence of the common law, had been subverted by the social mobility of commercial society. The ideal was stood on its head, and the courts were called on to determine status within the community.

Despite the fact that similar issues had arisen in prior cases, both sides in *Commonwealth v. Burcher* acknowledged that the validity of William Lea's claim to freehold status remained an ambiguous and unsettled legal question. Burcher's attorneys, led by Richmond lawyer William Macfarland, argued against Lea's status by endeavoring to persuade the court to accept an expansive reading of *Kerby*. He contended that that decision could be construed to have rejected the premise that equitable title met the standard for a freehold qualification. Macfarland also cited the ruling in the *Reynolds* case in an effort to establish that the possession of legal title served as the determinative factor in adjudicating freehold status. Yet he failed to convince.

A decade after his fiery defense of slavery in the legislature, James Gholson once again engaged the question of property rights – this time as a judge on the General Court. In delivering the majority opinion, Gholson rejected an expansive reading of *Kerby* and explained that it had only addressed the question of an estate where the title was actively disputed. He reminded the defense that the General Court had refused to pronounce Boswell Yates a freeholder "not only because he had disclaimed the ownership and title to the land, but because it was deemed improper to decide in a collateral way a question which was then the subject of judicial investigation in another forum." Gholson also dismissed the argument that the *Reynolds* ruling applied in *Burcher*. He emphasized the disparities between the two situations and refuted the suggestion that any legal precedent had been established by either *Kerby* or *Reynolds*, which necessarily would determine the grand juror status of William Lea.[45]

Instead, Gholson contemplated Lea's claim to freehold status relative to historical practices in both England and Virginia. He acknowledged that *cestuis que use* traditionally met the freehold qualification for grand jurors in England. Citing Lord Coke, he noted that legal title was "clearly not necessary" to establish Lea's competency. And he recalled that "mortgagors, or grantors in deeds

[45] 2 Robinson 829.

of trust made to secure debts, while in possession and entitled to equity of redemption," were considered good jurors in Virginia. But the gist of Gholson's opinion dealt with the fact that Lea had a better claim to the title than any other party. Gholson described Lea as "the tenant of the freehold." Not only did he receive the profits from it, but his possession was so secured "that no one could oust him from it." Lea had made every installment of his payments to date, and was not in default, so his condition was such that "a court of equity would have kept him there against the world." Even if Lea failed to pay the remainder of the installments, an equity court could not evict him but "would direct the property to be sold as his," with any profits in excess of the balance due on the mortgage remaining with Lea. Gholson also emphasized that the previous owner and conveyor of the land, John Grammer, had parted completely with the legal title and neither retained any claim nor any "way to recall it." In conclusion, Gholson likened Lea "to that of a mortgagor in possession, where the mortgagee has no right to call for a foreclosure of the equity of redemption." Gholson explained that because no one else possessed an equitable or legal claim to the property, the status attached to the freehold estate fell to the possessor and, accordingly, Lea was qualified as a good grand juror.[46]

The majority opinion was contested, however, and a dissenting opinion was delivered by Judge Edwin Duncan, the author of the *Kerby* ruling. Duncan, a western lawyer from Clarksburg, was the brother-in-law of Judge John Allen, who was President of the Supreme Court of Appeals, and had been a staunch advocate of reform during the constitutional convention. Paradoxically, Duncan's dissent was grounded in a traditional commitment to the principles of independence and vicinage that underlay the historical justification for the freehold qualification. He explained that the qualification was founded on "the idea that men having a fixed and permanent interests in the soil could be more safely entrusted with the delicate and important duty of bringing offenders against the laws to justice." He further emphasized that both in England, where the practice originated, and in Virginia, legislators had chosen a freehold qualification because they considered "the degree and permanency of the estate, rather than the amount or value of it," the determinative factor in achieving "the ends of public policy." Duncan acknowledged that the question arising in this particular case was unique in many ways. He attributed this uniqueness to the consequences of changing social arrangements and financial practices, which had created ambiguity in the orthodox understanding of a freehold. He imagined that those who devised the qualification never would have anticipated such confusion, but it appeared now that "doubt . . . seems to have arisen" over "the precise meaning of the term" freehold – at least as far as it pertained to grand juror qualifications.[47]

[46] 2 Robinson 828–829.

[47] 2 Robinson 830–831. For biographical information on Judge Duncan, see Henry Hammond, "Judge E.S. Duncan," *West Virginia Historical Magazine*, 2 (1902): 74–76, as well as the Papers of John James Allen, *VHS*, Mss2 AL5375b. Judges Benjamin Estill and James E. Brown also dissented but did not file opinions.

Duncan offered an alternative opinion of how to determine the validity of the freehold qualification. His dissent emphasized the process of transferring legal title as it was specified in statutory law. He reminded the majority of the "well settled rule in the construction of statutes," that when terms used in a statute had a specific common-law definition, "that signification is intended to be adopted" for the purposes of the law. Rather pedantically, Duncan explained that the freehold, at common law, was "an estate in lands for not less than term of life" and that, in feudal times, "a livery of seisin" – the ceremonial transfer and investing of the estate – was a necessary ritual to establish the freehold. In modern times, he noted, other forms of conveyances specified by the statute of uses had also become recognized as acceptable means to create a freehold. In Virginia, the most common form of these modern conveyances was the deed of bargain and sale. Duncan posited that these deeds simply replaced the ceremonial act of investiture, contending that "the delivery of the deed supersed[ed] the formula of livery of seisin."[48]

Of equal significance, he noted that the use and the possession of the land needed to be united in order to create a freehold estate. Use could not be created legally except by a written deed that was "sealed and delivered." Duncan believed that in this particular instance, William Lea had not been conferred the use of the estate because the deed had never been delivered. He suggested instead that Lea had acquired possession through an "act of pais" – a local, nonlegal agreement between parties "in the country." Duncan reiterated that it was the act of deed delivery that served as "the medium by which the title passes out of the bargainor to the bargainee." He offered the actual delivery as the litmus for determining freehold status, and, of course, this ritual had not occurred in this instance.[49]

In attempting to restore a semblance of certainty to ownership, Duncan thus rejected Gholson's reading of the case as one concerning adversarial claims. Far from being a case of adversarial possession, Duncan considered William Lea's relationship with John Grammer as "under the vendor"; it reflected a trust between the vendor and vendee. Lea's possession existed under the supervision and cognizance of the vendor, and until the deed was delivered, Grammer maintained legal title. Lea would receive the deed if and when he satisfied the obligations of the conveyor. Duncan argued that if Grammer decided to convey the lot to a third person and passed the title to him, Lea might be "evicted in an action of ejectment by the last purchaser." Any adversarial claim against the estate would have to take the form of a suit against Grammer, not Lea. That said, Duncan acknowledged that Lea held an equity of redemption in the land and that it would protect him from the vendor's heirs in the event of death before the full payment of the purchase money. But he emphasized that

[48] *Ibid.*

[49] 2 Robinson 831. An act of pais is "an assurance transacted between two or more persons, 'in the country' that is, upon the very spot transferred," and not in court. *Black's Law Dictionary*, 1110.

Lea had no right to obtain the legal title from a court of equity, and he might never obtain that right because it depended exclusively "upon his ability and his will to pay."[50]

Duncan concluded by seeking to illuminate the potential social problems posed by the majority reading. From a practical standpoint, he noted that "a relaxation of the statute will involve the courts in innumerable questions of difficulty as to the qualifications" not only of grand jurors but of petit jurors as well. Every contested juror would have to undergo the scrutiny of any potential adversarial claims to the estate. Furthermore, he reminded his audience that the freehold qualification had been devised to protect "the rights of the public, and the safety of the persons and property of its citizens" by providing "that the jurymen who present for crimes, and the jurymen who try the offenders, shall have that fixed and permanent interest in the country, which will place their independence…out of the reach of power, or the influence produced by fear, favour or affection." The possession of an estate merely through equitable title did not confer on William Lea these requisite characteristics of permanency or independence. His possession was dependent on the goodwill of another. And yet, Duncan mused, by the ruling of the General Court, William Lea was "said to be a freeholder."[51]

JUSTICE WAS NOT FULLY RECOGNIZED IN VIRGINIA

The General Court's ruling in *Commonwealth v. Burcher* neither informed nor confused judicial practices in Virginia for very long. By the end of the decade, the decision was made moot by a series of reforms that recrafted judicial procedures and offices. Modern commercial society required that the standards of holding office be transformed. As had been the case with freehold suffrage, the concept of office, too, was divorced from its traditional association with the land and vested instead in the individual person. Freehold status remained an inappropriate determination in a democratic age.

Fostered by cases like William Lea's, where traditional measures to discern qualifications proved inadequate, reformers called for new methods of selecting grand and petit jurors. Indeed, by the time of the *Burcher* opinion, the freehold qualification for petit jurors had already been effectively eroded by the customary practice of ignoring it in the county courts. The amount of litigation heard in these courts often required six- or seven-day quarterly sessions. Freeholders proved to be apathetic in their civic duty and refused to devote so much time to legal matters. Self-government required too many weekdays. Accordingly, to clear the docket, jurors were empanelled who were not freeholders. In some instances, juries were comprised of those who had their own cases to be adjudicated later on the docket and needed to be in attendance anyway. It was not unusual for a person to sit on a jury in the morning, and then, to appear

[50] 2 Robinson 832–833.
[51] 2 Robinson 833–835.

as a defendant in the afternoon; sometimes, particularly in instances of debt collection, against the same plaintiff. Not surprisingly, complaints against the judicial process in general, and trial by jury in particular, proliferated.

Issues of juror qualifications and the jury process naturally dovetailed into the larger discussions of judicial reform. As part of the project to reform Virginia's civil code, Conway Robinson and John Mercer Patton, two prominent lawyers assigned to the project, recommended abolishing the freehold requirement for petit jurors and replacing it with a qualification based on property, age, and the right of suffrage. In 1849, when the new Code was enrolled by the legislator, the freehold qualification for petit jurors was abolished and replaced by an age requirement of twenty-one and a property qualification of owning the equivalent of one hundred dollars of real or personal property. The freehold qualification for grand jurors lingered for another few months until the constitutional convention in 1850, known as the Reform Convention. During that convention, Virginians adopted white manhood suffrage and embraced the idea of an elected judiciary. The abandonment of the last vestiges of the franchise signaled the end of the freehold qualification for grand jurors. The 1852 Judiciary Act explicitly abolished the centuries-old qualification and mandated the random selection of grand jurors from a list of registered voters instead. Yet, the abolition of the freehold qualification represented merely one part of the larger reformation of Virginia judicial institutions.[52]

Conway Robinson was the chief architect of this reformation. He was born to John and Agnes Conway Moncure Robinson in 1805. His father served as the clerk of the Henrico circuit court, and he grew up immersed in the law. He began his legal education at the age of thirteen by becoming an assistant clerk in Richmond's municipal courts and, within six years, was appointed clerk of the most prominent court in the city. He also served as assistant clerk for the General Court. In 1827, as soon as he came of age, Robinson was admitted to the bar and, the next year, was appointed chief clerk of the General Court. In 1831, he resigned his duties as clerk to pursue the business of his growing practice and to begin writing legal treatises. The next year, he published the first volume of his three-volume work detailing procedural law, which established his reputation as one of the most learned members of the bar. Robinson enhanced his professional and social reputation even more when he married Mary Susan Selden Leigh, the daughter of prominent Richmond attorney and U.S. Senator Benjamin Watkins Leigh. In 1842, Robinson succeeded his father-in-law as the reporter for the Virginia Supreme Court of Appeals. He published two volumes of court reports during his tenure in that office.[53]

[52] Robinson and Patton, *Reports of the Revisors* (February 1847), 813–814; *1849 Code*, 628; Robert Ruffin Collier, *Some Observations on the Law Affairs of Virginia, which are Respectfully Inscribed to the Committee on Courts of Justice* (Petersburg, VA: 1846).

[53] Richard A. Claybrook, Jr., "Conway Robinson," in W. Hamilton Bryson, ed., *The Virginia Law Reporters Before 1880* (Charlottesville: University Press of Virginia, 1977). In addition to his two volumes of the *Virginia Reports* (1843, 1844), Robinson's principle works include: *Practice*

Robinson issued a formal call for immediate legal reform in the prefatory section to the 1844 edition of the *Virginia Reports*. He emphasized the inadequacy of current processes of appeal and found it intolerable that it should take seven or eight years for a case to be decided by the General Court. Perhaps more troubling was the fact that the problem was compounding with each session, because the General Court typically decided fewer cases in each session than the "number of new appeals...[they] awarded." Although he criticized the inexpediency of the appellate courts and the lack of professionalism within the judiciary, he emphasized the pernicious influence of systemic problems with the legal process as well. Robinson directed much of the blame at the state legislators too, contending that they fostered many problems by refusing to pay judges adequate salaries and by infusing party politics into the process of judicial appointments. He chided partisan legislators for the grievous practice of selecting judges in a manner similar to the demagogic litmus used to choose "an elector for the office of President of the United States." He remonstrated that it represented meager consolation to a litigant who had had his particular case "delayed or erroneously decided" that the judge who had presided over it shared an opinion with him as to who might be "the most suitable person to be elected president." Given such a state of affairs, Robinson believed that Virginia's freehold-based system of law and justice was broken. He gravely lamented that the foundational principle of Anglo-American law, as articulated in *Magna Carta*, "that justice or right shall not be sold, denied, or deferred to any man," was not, at that time, "fully recognized in Virginia."[54]

He compared the troubled experienced of Virginia with similar difficulties recently resolved in New York. He explained that, over the past four years, the justices of that state had cleared a large docket of pending cases simply by increasing their standard case load and by simultaneously preventing an accumulation of new cases. Robinson challenged Virginia's bench and bar to pursue a similar "energetic course of action," calling for attorneys to bring forth a greater number of cases in each session and spend less time arguing the merits of each case. He proposed that this could be readily done by augmenting oral pleadings with printed arguments, which would be circulated in advance

in the Courts of Law and Equity in Virginia, 3 volumes (1832–1839); *Forms Adapted to the Practice in Virginia* (1841); *An Essay upon the Constitutional Rights as to Slave Property* (1840); *Account of Discoveries in the West Until 1519, and of Voyages to and Along the Atlantic Coast of North America from 1520 to 1573* (1848); *Views of the Constitution of Virginia* (1850); *Practice in the Courts of Justice in England and the United States*, 7 volumes (1854–1874); and *History of the High Court of Chancery and Other Institutions of England* (1882).

54 Conway Robinson, "Preface" to *Reports of the Virginia Supreme Court of Appeals for the 1843 Term* (Richmond, 1844), iii–iv (hereafter cited as 2 Robinson); Collier, *Some Observations on the Law*, 13–14; an example of the complexity facing litigants in negotiating the judicial system is provided in the correspondence between William Daniel, Jr. and Mrs. Elizabeth S. Cabell, July 7, 1843 and August 19, 1846, Bouldin Family Papers, Virginia Historical Society.

among the parties. He also suggested extending session times by an hour, from noon until four in the afternoon, as opposed to the traditional adjournment at three. He noted that even in England, the Court of the Queen's Bench now sat in session from ten in the morning until at least four in the afternoon, and often continued until five or six o'clock in the evening.[55]

Some of his recommendations were adopted immediately by the Supreme Court of Appeals. A few months after Robinson published his report, the court issued a revised digest of the rules of conduct and procedure. In them, the court mandated that "a clear and concise" written statement of each case, replete with points of argument, had to be presented to the judges of the court prior to the session. Any errors that appeared in this preliminary statement would not be grounds for argument during the hearing, unless reason to do so could be established by either party. This qualification was specifically designed to address further appeals arising from typographical, spelling, or grammatical errors in the written record and to confine the arguments of counsel to matters of law and fact. In chancery cases, the reading of the case record was deemed unnecessary, and arguments over the testimony of expert witnesses were confined to matters of law only. Further procedural revisions stipulated that each attorney was limited to one argument in cases where there were multiple counsels for one party, along with the strongly expressed recommendation that "gentlemen of the bar" should "cite only the most pertinent authorities" in presenting their arguments.[56]

Beyond these procedural measures, Robinson's vision of reform also included making significant institutional changes as well. Most notably, he encouraged abandoning the common-law model of judicial office, which had been grounded in the reciprocity of the freehold tenure, and replacing it with a professionally educated and trained judiciary whose technical expertise separated them from laymen. Here as elsewhere in his proposed reforms, Robinson was not so much inventing a new judicial system as responding to ongoing social changes. Over the course of the previous two decades, law schools had supplanted the apprenticeship model of reading for the bar as the preferred means of obtaining a legal education. The College of William & Mary had named George Wythe as Professor of Law and Police as early as 1779, and the University of Virginia established a faculty of law in 1826, but even more influential was the creation of proprietary law schools across the state. These schools typically were established and directed by leading jurists as a means to supplement their judicial salaries. Creed Taylor's Needham Law School, Henry St. George Tucker's school in Winchester, as well as John Tayloe Lomax's in Fredericksburg and Briscoe Baldwin's in Staunton, all

55 2 Robinson, iii–v.

56 Peachy Ridgeway Grattan, *Reports of the Virginia Supreme Court of Appeals for the 1844 Term*, (Richmond, 1845), xix–xx. (Hereafter cited as 1 Grattan). For the persistent recurrence of this debate over written records in Virginia's legal culture, see A. G. Roeber, *Faithful Magistrates and Republican Lawyers* (Chapel Hill: University of North Carolina Press, 1981).

had graduated an impressive number of Virginia's lawyers by the time of Robinson's appeal for reform.[57]

A professional judiciary demanded both time for the essential scholarship of the office and independence from the necessary labors of life. Robinson correspondingly urged the legislature to pay the Supreme Court justices a sufficient salary, one that would allow them to live with and support their families in Richmond during the six months of the year they were required to be in session. As it stood, time on the court took them away from their necessary private practices, and in some instances, from the farms and plantations on which they were dependent for economic sufficiency. The office also demanded separation from their families, frequently encouraging the appointed to spend as little time in Richmond as possible and deterring others from aspiring to such positions. Similar problems permeated the General Court. The 1831 Judiciary Act had divided the state into ten judicial districts, each of which was subdivided further into two circuits, which formed the Circuit Superior Courts of Law and Chancery. General Court judges were assigned to ride each of these circuits and hear the respective cases within their jurisdiction. Accordingly, these judges rode circuit for several months of the year and, potentially, were required to convene the General Court in Richmond twice a year in June and December. All of the circuit court judges were members of the General Court, but the five senior judges were designated to actually conduct the session. The burden of the incessant travel often caused these judges to forego their General Court duties, however, leaving the younger and most inexperience judges to handle the appellate sessions. Robinson called on the legislature to remedy the situation, arguing that an independent judiciary should be both financially and emotionally independent to ensure that the judges' focus remained on the expedient administration of justice.[58]

Robinson also proposed a plan to separate cases of law and equity heard on appeal. The 1831 Judiciary Act had assigned the Circuit Superior Courts both original and appellate jurisdiction over cases of law and equity. The arrangement largely replicated the jurisdiction of the county courts, although, in both forums, any exercise of these distinct jurisdictions was to be conducted "separately and distinctly" from one another, despite the fact that the cases were heard and decided by the same judges. The Supreme Court of Appeals served as the final appellate court, receiving cases from the circuits, and thus also held jurisdiction at both law and equity. The result was a growing backlog of cases to be decided faster than the courts could manage. From October 1844

[57] W. Hamilton Bryson, *Legal Education in Virginia, 1779–1979: A Biographical Approach* (Charlottesville: University Press of Virginia, 1982), 1–41 and Appendix II, "The Known Alumni of the Proprietary Law Schools," compiled by E. Lee Shepard, 762–774.

[58] James Allen to John James Allen, September 7, 1829, Allen Family Correspondence, Virginia Historical Society; Thomas R. Morris, *The Virginia Supreme Court: an Institutional and Political Analysis* (Charlottesville: University Press of Virginia, 1975); 2 Robinson, vi; Legislative Session Acts, 1830–31, chapter 11, 42.

until May 1845, the Court of Appeals decided 123 cases, but 144 cases had commenced during the session and another 506 cases were still pending. Robinson blamed much of the litigation backlog on this shared jurisdiction at the final appellate level and, as he was wont to do in many instances, recommended adopting the New York method to resolve the problem. He proposed creating an office of Chancellor, one for the eastern and one for the western portion of the state. The chancellors would hear appeals at equity arising from the Circuit Courts before they went to the Supreme Court of Appeals.[59]

The proposal reflects Robinson's desire to maintain a sharp distinction between law and equity jurisprudence at a time when many of his contemporaries sought to merge together these complementary doctrines. In so doing, Robinson endorsed the view expounded by his colleague, James Philemon Holcombe. And he praised the English common law for having historically established "two distinct tribunals for the administration of law and equity" and further contended that this segregation was the most successful means to ensure equitable remedies. Although opposed to efforts to merge these two distinct forms of remedy, both Holcombe and Robinson approved a substantial reform of equity jurisprudence through the formalization of its principles.[60]

Robinson desired to restore order between these two branches of jurisprudence in Virginia. He believed that if well-qualified, well-compensated individuals were appointed to the position of Chancellor, most equity cases would never go beyond them. As had been the case following the similar reform in New York, rarely would the Supreme Court of Appeals hear an equity case "except in cases presenting very novel questions, or cases of great magnitude." Relieved from the mundane appeals at equity, the Supreme Court of Appeals would concentrate on matters of common law. In addition to easily disposing of the appeals from the circuits, Robinson hoped that the chancellors might even provide relief for overwhelmed circuits by transferring some of their equity cases on the docket. He also anticipated legislative concerns about increasing the size of the judiciary and recommended that appropriate salaries for the chancellors could be easily attained by reducing the number of Supreme Court justices from five to three, and using the offset difference to compensate the new chancellors.[61]

Robinson continued to pursue the idea of judicial consolidation during the process of revising the Code when he, along with his partner, John Mercer Patton, proposed limiting the number of justices of the peace appointed to the

[59] 2 Robinson, vi–vii; George W. Munford, "Abstract from the Reports of the Clerks of the Court of Appeals and of the Circuit Superior Courts of Law and Chancery, for the Year ending 30th August, 1845," published as Document 6 in the *House Journal, 1845–1846*.

[60] Morton Horwitz, *Transformation of American Law, 1780–1860* (Cambridge, MA: Harvard University Press, 1975), 265–266; Lawrence Friedman, *A History of American Law* (2nd edition, New York: Touchstone, 1985), 393–395; and Charles E. Clark, "The Union of Law and Equity," 25 *Columbia Law Review* 1 (1925), 1–10. Friedman acknowledged dissent to the idea of merging law and equity but categorized it stemming from "stubborn judges."

[61] 2 Robinson, vi–vii.

county courts. As it then stood, justices were still required to be freeholders and, technically at least, were appointed to serve by the governor. Typically, however, justices were nominated by the other members of the court and the appointing power of the governor was a mere formality. Robinson and Patton acknowledged that although the governor possessed the authority to refuse appointments, it was a power "both delicate and difficult to be exercised" without upsetting the nominating justices themselves, and thus rarely employed. Furthermore, the number of justices for each county court was itself discretionary upon the respective court. Such discretion tended toward a "multiplication of justices beyond the wants of the county." Robinson and Patton identified this tendency as "a great and growing evil" that undermined the office by cheapening its status, encouraging a cavalier attitude toward the necessary knowledge and duties or the position, and generally impairing the efficient functioning of Virginia's historic "administrative and executive system." Accordingly, they proposed setting a limit on the number of justices in each county that corresponded to its number of delegates to the General Assembly. They also sought to reduce the requirement for a quorum in the county courts from four justices to three, noting that such a reduction would avoid the frequent embarrassments and delays that arose from split decisions between the justices in deciding a case.[62]

The images that emerge from Conway Robinson's proposed reforms reflect a sharp contrast from the casual portrait of court days depicted by John Pendleton Kennedy in *Swallow Barn*. Robinson's advocacy for an elite cadre of well-educated, efficient, professional judges represented a clear departure from the freehold model of judicial office, which the Commonwealth had inherited and had adapted to meet the needs of republican justice. Furthermore, unlike prior efforts at reform, such as the ward system proposed by Thomas Jefferson and Lewis Summers, Robinson's focus was less on creating more democratic institutions than on establishing the appropriate procedural and institutional forms in which legal technicians could do their work. In this respect, Robinson believed that education and experience were the best determining qualifications for office. Although debate about the nature of the judiciary was hardly new, these reforms led to the resolution of the conflict between legal professionalism and the desire for local justice. Despite articulating a clear preference for a technically proficient judiciary that would be able to sort through the complex matters of law and equity and pronounce authoritative decisions grounded in the principles of common law, Robinson embraced popular conceptions of

[62] Robinson and Patton, *Reports of the Revisors* (March 1848), 265–266 and (May 1849), 797, note. Robinson and Patton engaged the idea of judicial consolidation to argue for the establishment of a Special Court of Appeals as well. See Erwin Surrency, "An Unusual Judicial Proposal: A Proposed Reduction in the Number of Judges – The Report of the Virginia Revisors on the Circuit Superior Courts – 1848," *The American Journal of Legal History*, 13 (1969): 145–164.

justice that were imbedded in the local institutions of the county courts and the trial by jury. He envisioned a class of learned professionals, who, by serving on the high courts and teaching in the law schools, would, in a very paternalist fashion, inspire and instruct a class of aspirants who conducted the mundane deliberations of modern democracy in the county courts.

Yet Robinson did not intend to leave the instruction of young lawyers and county magistrates solely in the hands of a cadre of legal professionals. At the core of his vision for legal reform in Virginia stood a "concise, plain, and intelligible" revised code of laws. Such a code would be something more than the mere compilation of statutes that previously had passed under that guise. Instead, it would take the form of a systematic primer on laws of the state and, although not entirely comprehensive in itself, would serve to inform and elucidate those attorneys, clerks, and legislators regularly engaged in the subject. In February 1846, he undertook such a project, and his efforts would have lasting consequences for the future of common law in Virginia.

6

A New System of Jurisprudence

The adoption of the 1849 *Code of Virginia* marked the end of the freehold as an exceptional form of property in the Commonwealth. Land tenure ceased to be considered as a source of political rights and, for all practical purposes, the historical distinction between real property and personal property as separate legal categories was erased. Codification standardized all forms of property under the purview of commercial contract relations. In so doing, it also replaced the traditional remedial conception of law with a more rule-based understanding of law as a positive statement of authority. This positivist understanding of law demanded a formalized system of jurisprudence, which was grounded in consistent and predictable articulations of the law, and necessarily favored the pronouncements of a centralized legislative body over the sundry adjudications of independent judges. Statutes were preferred to precedent and opinion because they more easily fostered a homogenous juridical system. Judicial authority persisted, to be sure, but it was increasingly guided and circumscribed by the codified law. Consequently, the 1849 Code became the principle source to explicate the law and assumed the place of the inherited English common law as the fountainhead of jurisprudential interpretation. Thus, ironically, despite serious efforts by the revisors to characterize codification as a conservative means to reform, the successful course of that reform fostered a rejection of the common-law orthodoxy, which had defined the legal culture since colonial times, and promulgated instead a "a new system of jurisprudence" for Virginia.[1]

This legal change wrought a political reformation as well. The Special Session of the General Assembly that convened in May 1849 to enroll the Code and its companion assembly, the Constitutional Convention, which followed on its heels a year later, signaled the ultimate repudiation of the agrarian

[1] *The Quarterly Law Journal*, vol. 1 (Richmond, 1856): 9. The origins of codification in Virginia are explained more fully in my article, "Codification in Virginia: Conway Robinson, John Mercer Patton, and the Politics of Law Reform," *VMHB*, 117 (2009): 141–180. For consistency, I have retained the contemporary spelling of the word "revisors" throughout.

republican ideal. Virginians rejected the Jeffersonian image of self-government through individual autonomy that had been embodied in the commitment to allodial ownership. Instead, they embraced an alternative model of representative government, one that posited a democratic concept of citizenship premised on the idea of rights vested in one's personhood.

This political reformation was by no means unique to Virginia. Prior to the Civil War, each American state underwent its own particular experience of democratic development, following its own path and constructing democratic institutions in its respective fashion. Yet the consequences of this democratic reformation in Virginia were radical. Divorced from the tangible substance of place that the freehold qualification had provided, the traditional mechanisms of local self-government became obsolete and were subsumed into the bureaucratic apparatus of the newly constituted state government. The county courts were diminished in authority as local offices became mere positions of patronage, while the governor, as the consummate representative of all the people and the dispenser of this expanded patronage, grew in stature and power. New efficient institutions, capable of manipulating both the representative legislature and the bureaucracy, became necessary, and this need was filled quickly by the extra-constitutional national political parties – most notably, the Whigs and the Democrats – that emerged in correspondence with democratic reforms. By channeling avenues of political participation, controlling patronage, and determining the relevance of political issues, these organizations sought to nationalize state and local political structures under the auspices of party ideology.[2]

The Reform Convention has long been recognized as the seminal moment when Virginia fully embraced these fundamental tenets of modern democracy. During the Convention, the remaining institutional structures of the freeholder's republic were dismantled. Property qualifications for suffrage were removed in favor of a general white manhood suffrage, albeit one limited by age, residence, and the payment of a $200 capitation tax. Correspondingly, by

[2] William Shade, *Democratizing the Old Dominion: Virginia and the Second Party System, 1824–1861* (Charlottesville: University Press of Virginia, 1997); Ronald Formisano, *The Transformation of Political Culture: Massachusetts Politics, 1790s–1840s* (New York: Oxford University Press, 1983); Richard McCormick, *The Second American Party System: Party Formation in the Jacksonian Era* (Chapel Hill: University of North Carolina Press, 1966); Joel Silbey, *The American Political Nation, 1838–1893* (Stanford, CA: Stanford University Press, 1991); and Harry Watson, *Liberty and Power: The Politics of Jacksonian America* (New York: Hill and Wang, 1990). Shade has argued that the changes embodied by Virginia's reform constitution were similar to the constitutional reforms in other states and "reflected an Americanized version of the model of liberal democracy articulated in the writing of English utilitarians and philosophical radicals in which the expansion of suffrage was designed to protect the governed from the government." He suggested that this justification of the suffrage signaled a shift away from "the republican idea of a stake in society," which had grounded the Commonwealth vision, and instead, expressed a "democratic faith in the people's natural competence to govern themselves" in effect standing the republican formula on its head by insisting "that the practice of democracy would promote civic virtue."

implementing the residency requirement, the right to vote was restricted to the "one-man, one-vote" principle, irrespective of the extent and locations of an individual's landed property. In many respects, this particular reform most candidly revealed the transformative aspects of modern democracy. Traditionally, under the common-law conception of rights, the right to vote – the franchise – had emerged from the stewardship responsibilities of landholding and reflected the actual representation of the estates of the realm. With the advent of modern democracy, the right to vote was awarded on the basis of consensually established qualifications of citizenship, which bore little or no connection to an individual's interests in a specific locality, but instead premised on the idea of self-ownership. No longer grounded in status, citizenship itself became an act of imagination and thus provided a necessary precondition for constituting in and participation in what Benedict Anderson has termed an imagined community. Anderson's classic study was directed at the development of nationalism, but similar patterns were manifested in the reconstruction of more local identities as well – in this particular case, Virginia.[3]

The constitutional changes made by the Convention went well beyond the suffrage reforms. The county courts – the institutional locus of self-government in the freeholder's republic – were subjected to some of the most substantial changes. The freehold qualification was removed for all local offices and judicial offices became open to popular election. Juries and grand juries would be selected by ballot from a list of all white male inhabitants of a county between the ages of twenty-one and sixty, who were not exempted based on legislatively prescribed criteria. Judges for the Circuit Courts and the Supreme Court of Appeals also were subject to popular election for fixed terms of tenure. And after more than two centuries of service, the General Court and the Executive Council were abolished. These two institutions had originated as one – the Council was the General Court – so there was some symmetry in retiring them together. The abolition of the Council represented the unquestioned embrace of the federal model of a chief executive in lieu of the colonial model that had persisted for seven decades. This new-model governor was to be elected by the people and his term was extended from three to four years, although the prohibition on a successive term was maintained. The legislature was also restructured. The contentious issue of representation again dominated debate, and a particularistic plan of apportionment, which gave the western counties a majority in the House and the eastern counties a majority in the Senate, was agreed on. Reapportionment would occur every ten years, and if the issue proved irresolvable in the legislature, the governor would submit two plans to the people for a plebiscite. Actual representation would prove less meaningful, however, because the power of the legislature was also constricted when the

[3] Robert J. Steinfeld, "Property and Suffrage in the Early American Republic," *Stanford Law Review*, 41 (1989): 335–376; Benedict Anderson, *Imagined Communities: Reflections on the Origin and Spread of Nationalism* (Revised Edition, London: Verso Press, 1991).

Convention determined that the state legislature would henceforth convene biennially instead of annually.[4]

Most significantly, the Reform Convention explicitly embedded slavery into the constitution. Slaves were deemed a special form of property for purposes of taxation, and slave owners received protection from future tax increases on their human property. The state constitution now recognized slavery as a matter of public policy. The constitutional provision represented the culmination of discussions on other areas of law and politics too, in which the public-interest aspects of slavery dominated the debate. Certainly, it was not coincidental that slavery became constitutional in the midst of the fierce national debates over the question of its legality in the new federal territories. By 1850, Virginia had a decision to make about its commitment to slavery. The Reform Constitution reflected that decision and thus represented the point at which Virginia formally became a slave state – a state in which slavery was incorporated as a fundamental component of its constitution.

In contrast to these constitutional reforms, however, the necessary episodes of law reform that immediately preceded it have largely eluded scholarly focus. Yet this legal reformation demands attention too if one wishes to understand the intricate process by which Virginia's ruling class embraced democratic institutions while simultaneously entrenching their commitment to slavery. Neither democratic principles nor the legal apparatus of slavery could simply be grafted onto the juridical structure of the common law; its core concepts and institutions needed to be restructured before any substantial political or constitutional reforms could take place. The comprehensive process of revising the laws that began in legislative session of 1845–1846 and culminated with enrolling the new Civil and Criminal Code during the summer of 1849 was particularly notable in this respect. Codification provided an opportunity to reorder the social priority attached to different forms of property in Virginia. On one hand, the Code implemented a legal conception of land ownership that considered it a purely economic activity. The new conceptualization was designed to facilitate the commercial exchange of land as a positive means of fostering economic development. Divested of its political responsibilities, land ownership served simply to promote the wealth and happiness of the individual. On the other hand, codification also resulted in increased governmental

[4] William G. Bishop, reporter, *Register of the Debates and Proceedings of the Virginia Reform Convention* (Richmond, 1851); Charles Ambler, *Sectionalism in Virginia from 1776 to 1861* (Chicago: University of Chicago Press, 1901); Fletcher Green, *Constitutional Development in the South Atlantic States, 1776–1860: A Study in the Evolution of Democracy* (Chapel Hill: University of North Carolina Press, 1930); A. E. Dick Howard, "'For the Common Benefit': Constitutional History in Virginia as a Casebook for the Modern Constitution-Maker," *Virginia Law Review*, 54 (1968); William Link, *Roots of Secession: Slavery and Politics in Antebellum Virginia* (Chapel Hill: University of North Carolina Press, 2003); Robert P. Sutton, *Revolution to Secession: Constitution Making in the Old Dominion* (Charlottesville: University Press of Virginia, 1989); Francis Pendleton Gaines, Jr., "The Virginia Constitutional Convention of 1850–51: A Study in Sectionalism" (PhD dissertation, University of Virginia, 1950).

authority and more explicit regulation over slave owners as well as over those who had temporary possession and authority over slaves. These regulations reflected an anxiety about the encroachment of marketplace forces on the master-slave relationship and a growing awareness that the ownership of slaves in a commercial society required public supervision as a matter of public policy.[5]

PUTTING THE CONSTITUTION IN HARNESS

In February 1846, the Virginia legislature appointed Conway Robinson and John Mercer Patton to revise the state's thirty-year-old Civil Code. Within a year, they had taken over a stalled project to reform the Criminal Code as well. Over the course of the next three years, they examined every section of the old Code and attempted to reconcile them with three decades of additional statutes, judicial decisions, and, when applicable, with similar reforms in other common-law jurisdictions. From the outset, Robinson and Patton considered their task as one that differed markedly from previous revision projects. They contrasted their charge with that of the last major effort to compile a code three decades earlier, in 1817, and emphasized the disappointing consequences of the legislature's timid commitment to that project in order to advocate for greater authority. They justified the need for such a substantial revision by explaining that, as things stood, judges and lawyers were required to examine the 1819 Code and then the separate acts of thirty subsequent legislative sessions simply to determine which laws were now "in force." And they suggested that this lofty requirement for legal research was "only one of many inconveniences" that resulted from the present conditions of the laws. Frequent contradictions between different sections of various acts bred uncertainty, confusion, and litigation.[6]

[5] A contemporary map of Virginia, drafted by state engineer Claudius Crozet in 1848, can be found as part of in the Library of Congress map collections and viewed at: http://memory.loc.gov/cgi-bin/query/h?ammem/gmd:@field(NUMBER+@band(g3880+rr003070))

[6] *Journal of the House of Delegates of Virginia, 1845–1846* (Richmond: Samuel Shepherd, 1846), Bill 142 (Hereafter *House Journal*). Conway Robinson and John Mercer Patton, *Report of the Revisors of the Civil Code of Virginia, Made to the General Assembly at December Session 1846* (Richmond: Samuel Shepherd, 1847), iii, vi–vii. (Hereafter *Report of the Revisors*). Benjamin Watkins Leigh, ed., *The Revised Code of Virginia, 1819* (Richmond: T. Ritchie, 1819). The legislature appointed five legal luminaries to serve as a revision committee: Judges Spencer Roane, John Coalter, William Brockenbrough, and attorneys Robert White and Benjamin Watkins Leigh. These revisers brought lofty ambitions to the project. They had aspired to reconcile contradictions among sundry statutes and to remove the obsolescence from the extant edition, an amended version of the 1792 code republished three years earlier by Samuel Pleasants. They were largely disappointed, however, owing to the fact that, as a whole, the House of Delegates was not interested in pursuing such a substantial project of reform. Writing for the committee, Leigh expressed his regret that they were allowed neither sufficient time nor funds to examine and assess Virginia's body of laws and to perform the comprehensive revision they had believed necessary. Instead, they simply assembled the existing statutes into a two-volume collection thereafter known as the *Revised Code of 1819*. This work was later amended in 1833 when

If Virginia's previous effort at law reform represented a model of what not to do, recent reforms in other jurisdictions provided Robinson and Patton with ample positive examples of how to proceed. Contemporary reform projects had occurred in Great Britain, Nova Scotia, New South Wales, and several other states as common-law lawyers sought to reconcile the common law with modern commercial practices. Virginia's revisors noted that New York had carried out a comprehensive statutory revision during the legal reforms of 1829–1830. They also acknowledged the influence of recent reforms in Great Britain, especially the recommendations made by the Brougham Commission on Real Property to make land transfers simpler. And they sought to incorporate similar reforms into the Virginia project. The report by the Massachusetts Committee on Revision, however, proved most influential source. It was crafted by Joseph Story and offered Robinson and Patton a template for constructing a modern code.[7]

Codification proved a controversial idea in the nineteenth century. Typically, it was associated with the radical utilitarian philosophy of English legal theorist Jeremy Bentham. Bentham initially had proposed codification as a more uniform and efficient alternative to the apparently haphazard character of the common law, which he believed needed to be destroyed. As with his political philosophy, his codification plan was premised on the idea of scientific social progress and thus evinced an inherent disdain for existing common-law judicial structures. His new legal vision appealed to reformers who embraced the

Samuel Shepherd published a supplement that contained the pertinent legislative acts that had been passed since 1819. The original work was not revisited, however, and Shepherd's volume simply stood as an essential supplemental text.

7 *Report of the Revisors* (February 1847), vi. Michael Lobban, *The Common Law and English Jurisprudence, 1760–1850* (Oxford: Clarendon Press, 1991); J. Stuart Anderson, *Lawyers and the Making of English Land Law, 1832–1940* (Oxford: Clarendon Press, 1992); Peter Karsten, *Between Law and Custom: 'High' and 'Low' Legal Cultures in the Lands of the British Diaspora – The United States, Canada, Australia, and New Zealand, 1600–1900* (Cambridge: Cambridge University Press, 2002); Phillip Girard, "Married Women's Property, Chancery Abolition, and Insolvency Law: Law Reform in Nova Scotia, 1820–1867," in Girard and Jim Phillips, eds., *Essays in the History of Canadian Law, Volume 3: Nova Scotia* (Toronto: Osgoode Society for Canadian Legal History, 1990), 106–113; Andrew R. Buck, "'This Remnant of Feudalism': Primogeniture and Political Culture in Colonial New South Wales, with Some Canadian Comparisons," in John McLaren, Andrew R. Buck, and Nancy E. Wright, eds., *Despotic Dominion: Property Rights in British Settler Societies* (Vancouver: UBC Press, 2005), 169–189; Charles M. Cook, *The American Codification Movement: A Study of Antebellum Legal Reform* (Westport, CT: Greenwood Press, 1981); Perry Miller, *The Life of the Mind in America from the Revolution to the Civil War* (New York: A Harvest Book, Harcourt, Brace & World, Inc., 1965); and Gregory S. Alexander, *Commodity and Propriety: Competing Visions of Property in American Legal Thought, 1776–1970* (Chicago: University of Chicago Press, 1997). The New York law reforms are examined in the context of state politics in Charles McCurdy, *The Anti-Rent Era in New York Law and Politics, 1839–1845* (Chapel Hill: University of North Carolina Press, 1986); and Reeve Huston, *Land and Freedom: Rural Society, Popular Protest, and Party Politics in Antebellum New York* (New York: Oxford University Press, 2000).

democratic tendencies of the age and attracted disciples in both England and America. These codifiers preferred legislative enactments over the discretionary rulings of the judiciary as the pure basis of law. They emphasized principles of uniformity and clarity in order to attain a standard of legal certainty that was nigh impossible within the particularistic customs of judge-made precedent and remedial justice through equity. Perhaps the most outspoken proponent for codification in America was Massachusetts lawyer Robert Rantoul. A staunch Jacksonian democrat, Rantoul considered judges as nothing more than bankers in robes in exercising despotic power over the fate of others. Rantoul called for the elimination of the common law and its replacement with "a positive and unbending" code, enacted by a popularly elected legislature, that would "speak the public voice" in articulating the law and deprive judges of their oppressive power.[8]

In the Massachusetts report, Story attempted to belay these concerns and proposed another perspective from which codification could be considered as a handmaiden, not as an alternative, to the common law. He contended that, at the time, "all the known rules and doctrines of the common law" were scattered among sundry treatises, digests, and reports encompassing several hundred "ponderous volumes," which could be understood by only the most eminent lawyers and judges. This diffusion of essential information fostered uncertainty and caused frequent errors among the many lawyers and judges who did have access to adequate law libraries. Story believed that this problem could be rectified rather easily, however, by creating a systematic "code of the common law." Such a code would not presume to address all aspects of the law, but it would reduce its general principles into a coherent volume that would be characterized by brevity, clarity, and uniformity. Story's vision of codification focused on the intrinsic instrumental capabilities of knowledgeable, well-written legislation to purge the law of its archaic features, to reconcile any contradictory elements, and to present it in an accessible manner.[9]

Robinson and Patton fully embraced Story's concept of codification and used it to guide their revision project. They estimated that the entire project would take about three years, and in the interim, they asked the General Assembly to refrain from passing any new legislation unless circumstances rendered it imperative. They organized the Code into four major sections: the opening section

[8] Jeremy Bentham, *A Fragment on Government: Being an Examination of what is delivered, on the Subject of Government, in General in the Introduction to Sir William Blackstone's Commentaries: with a Preface in which is given a Critique of the Work At Large* (London, 1776); David Lieberman, "From Bentham to Benthamism," *The Historical Journal*, 28 (1985): 199–224; Cook, *American Codification*; Alexander, *Commodity and Propriety*, 104–114; Peter Stein, *Legal Evolution: The Story of an Idea* (Cambridge: Cambridge University Press, 1980).

[9] Joseph Story, "Codification of the Common Law," in William W. Story, ed., *Miscellaneous Writings of Joseph Story* (Boston, 1852), 722–725. R. Kent Newmeyer, *Supreme Court Justice Joseph Story: Statesman of the Old Republic* (Chapel Hill: University of North Carolina Press, 1985), 271–281.

addressed the essential matters of government and public administration; the second section focused exclusively on laws pertaining to "the acquisition, enjoyment, and transmission of property," including the laws of "domestic relations" and "private rights"; the third section explained judicial procedure and organization; and section four contained the Criminal Code. They explained that the revised Code was not intended to either replace the common law or to encompass its entirety. Instead, it would simply make the common usages more clear, intelligible, and efficient. To attain such a level of clarity, however, uniformity was demanded – uniformity that could not emerge from the multiple voices of the judicial bench, but necessarily ought to emanate from the centralized position of the legislature. Indeed, like Joseph Story, Robinson and Patton believed that this form of codification answered the criticism of reformers who called for a more democratic jurisprudence. Story had gone so far as to assert that under his scheme, it would be the democratically elected legislature, not the judiciary, that would "proclaim the common law."[10]

When the General Assembly convened for its session in December 1848, Robinson and Patton had already submitted two sections of their revisions to that body and were close to completing the third. In January, the legislature decided to establish a special joint committee to examine the revised code in detail and to prepare it, in the form of several bills, for enrollment by the full assembly. The twelve-man committee was composed of seven members from the House of Delegates and five members from the Senate. Given the long history of sectional divisiveness in state politics, the composition of the committee was remarkable for its near absence of western Virginians. Only two senators – Thomas Sloan and Vincent Witcher – represented constituencies from the western regions of the state. Even more remarkable was an apparent lack of discussion about the geographical imbalance – particularly given the reappearance of an outspoken "western interest" in the Constitutional Convention the following year. Significantly, however, a greater balance seems to have been achieved between Whig and Democrat members.[11]

By March, Robinson and Patton had completed their assignment and submitted a 900-page draft Code for section-by-section examination and enrollment. The demands of the legislative session, however, prevented the Joint Committee from bringing forward any of the bills necessary to enroll the Code. The committee met in conference with Robinson and Patton, on occasion, in order to query certain points and to discuss proposed amendments

[10] *Report of the Revisors* (February 1847), x, xii, vii. They submitted their first report to the legislature on February 6, 1847 and followed with subsequent reports on March 22, 1848, January 8, 1849, and May 31, 1849. Story, "Codification," 725.

[11] *Code of Virginia (1849)*, viii–ix. The seven delegates all represented counties east of the Blue Ridge Mountains: Moncure (Stafford), Scott (Fauquier), Harrison (Loudoun), Conway (Spotsylvania), Whittle (Mecklenberg), Smith (Alexandria), and Booth (Nottoway). The senators exhibited a little more geographic diversity: Thompson (Albemarle/Nelson/Amherst), Witcher (Patrick/Henry/Pittsylvania), Sloan (Berkeley/Morgan/Hampshire), Kinney (Augusta/Rockbridge), and Ambler (Fluvanna/Goochland/Louisa/Hanover).

to the revisor's reports. But it had accomplished very little by the time of the scheduled recess, in part, perhaps, because the assembly had devoted a month of its time debating the Wilmot Proviso and slavery in the District of Columbia. With the august task of enrolling the Code still before them, the legislators decided to hold a special session dedicated exclusively to completing the codification project.[12]

The legislature reconvened in the Special Session at the end of May 1849. Yet before discussion of enrollment could begin in earnest, some of the delegates called for an immediate adjournment because of a cholera threat in Richmond. Not everyone was convinced of the threat. A group of assemblymen led by Northampton delegate George Yerby believed that it was being exaggerated as a ploy to remove discussions of the Code from the public spotlight in Richmond. Consequently, the Special Session spent a good bit of its first days listening to testimony from a parade of doctors who offered varying assessments of whether or not the cholera was actually present in the city as well as debating alternate locations for the assembly. After a few days, anxiety or perhaps just the muggy summer air prevailed and the delegates voted to adjourn and to reconvene the following week at Fauquier White Sulphur Springs, a popular resort complex outside of Warrenton. There, throughout the remainder of the summer, the legislature gathered daily in the resort's grand ballroom to discuss, amend, approve, or reject each of the proposed revisions.[13]

Some contemporary observers expressed apprehension about the potential consequences of the Special Session. The editors at the *Richmond Whig* felt compelled to call attention to popular concerns about the "grave and important task" of enrolling the Code. They noted that the enrollment process was not simply an act of rubber-stamping a "simple revision and codification of existing laws"; rather, it entailed the scrutiny and potential "alteration of every law." They believed that the current assembly of elected delegates possessed above-average ability, but they worried that the people had not been "sufficiently impressed" with the gravity of the task at hand eighteen month previous when these representatives had been elected. Recognizing that the task of enrollment was "scarcely inferior to the formation of a Constitution" itself, they opined for a "more distinguished and able" body of statesmen, who would guard against the potential chaos of rampant innovations, which might "subvert the whole structure of society." Lacking such a distinguished assembly, they urged extreme caution given that the delegates were, in point of fact, "putting the Constitution in harness."[14]

The delegates themselves appeared much more at ease with the nature of the task but expressed concern about its magnitude. The 900 pages of laws

[12] *Journal of the Senate of Virginia*, December 8, 1848, 31.

[13] *Richmond Whig*, June 1 and 5, 1849; *Virginia: A Guide to the Old Dominion*, Compiled by Workers of the Writers' Program of the Work Projects Administration (Richmond: Virginia State Library and Archives, 1992), 613.

[14] *Richmond Whig*, July 16, 1849.

needed to be presented to both the House and the Senate as individual bills, debated, amended if desired, and voted on. Any incongruities between the Senate and House versions would require reconciliation. Many of the revisions that addressed technical points of law were enrolled with limited discussion, particularly when a revision sought to conform the law to existing practice. Other sections of the code had implicit political ends, however, and generated contentious debates, which undoubtedly sparked the fears of the editors at the *Whig*. Sections of the Code pertaining to the governor's power to pardon slaves, the taxation authority of the county courts, and the process of appointing inspectors generated debate over core political issues such as the expansion of executive power, taxation policies, protections afforded from creditors, the legal limits of slave ownership, and the nature of an independent judiciary. In addressing these issues, the process of enrollment thus anticipated and even shaped many of the more familiar constitutional debates that took place the following year.

Alignment in these debates strictly followed political party, not regional, allegiances. The Democratic majority embraced codification as a way to make the laws seem less capricious, more uniform, and more universal. Politically, they generally sought to concentrate power around the governor's executive authority, particularly at the expense of the county courts, which they considered institutional vestiges of the freeholder aristocracy. On the other side, opposition Whigs found themselves in a less tenable position: They desired a modernization of the law, but they chafed at the political consequences that might stem from it and argued to preserve traditional institutions. Codification represented an efficient means to remove those archaic aspects of the common law that impeded commercial transactions, but it also represented the necessary dismantling of freehold status on which political power in Virginia had been constituted. They thus decried the Democratic tendency to embrace the tenets of "Red Republicanism" – a reference to the European Revolutions of the previous summer – and its "monarchical platform" of a strong, centralized executive power. Whig delegate Robert E. Scott championed the "beautiful feature" of the Commonwealth's constitution that did not confer any "more power on the executive than was absolutely necessary," a principle that he proclaimed to be the essence of republicanism. He also noted that during the enrollment debates, Democrats seemed more prone to act on the principle of Louis Napoleon, who he quoted as saying "that Democracy was the Government of the people, in the hands of one man."[15]

The argument over the appointment process for inspectors, which threatened to derail the entire codification project, revealed the extent to which these partisan ideologies influenced the enrollment process. During the process of revision, Conway Robinson and John Mercer Patton sought to consolidate these sundry laws and standardize the appointment process. They explained

[15] *Richmond Whig*, August 10, 1849.

that they hoped "to remedy the incongruities and defects" of the existing inspection laws "by making a uniform rule" that would "put all inspectors on the same footing." That said, perhaps because of the disproportionate volume of laws dealing with tobacco inspection, they recommended retaining the traditional two-step process of nominating and appointing tobacco inspectors but insisted on a single process for appointing all other inspectors. They proposed that, with the exception of tobacco inspectors, all other commodity inspectors should be appointed annually by the county courts during the September or October term. They also suggested that the courts be given the explicit authority to remove these appointees in cases of negligence or misconduct.[16]

When the House of Delegates first took up discussion of these revised inspection laws during the Special Session, the topic of appointment authority did not arise. The issue garnered considerably more attention in the Democratic-controlled Senate, however. The revisors' recommendations were amended and the appointment power of flour and commodity inspectors was placed exclusively in the hands of the governor. George Deneale, a Democratic senator representing the grain-growing Valley counties of Rockingham and Pendleton, explained that the amendment was necessary because the county courts had become corrupted by the undue influence of merchants. Francis Rives, a Democrat from Petersburg, and Vincent Witcher, a leading Whig from Pittsylvania, balked at the change, initially noting that the section had already passed the House and the amendment would require sending it back for another vote. Acknowledging that the House had already given way on almost every other point, they thought it magnanimous, and in the best interest of completing the revision, if the Senate yielded on this particular issue of little note. Yet Deneale and other Democrats refused to budge. Rives responded by pointing out the obvious – the county courts had exercised this power for at least a century with no apparent problems. He argued for the advantages of local authority and believed that the courts were in a better position to assess "the qualities and fitness" of a particular man than "a distant Governor." But most importantly, he noted that the change "would make these offices political offices," subject to the patronage of the governor. Partisan politics would be introduced into an area where it had not formerly intruded, and Rives exclaimed that "he had not come here for the purpose of making a *party Code*." Witcher and other Whigs gladly affirmed Rives's views and repeatedly

[16] *Reports of the Revisors*, 458–459, 476–477. They also explained that although the previous Code of 1819 and subsequent acts had specifically identified "the different places of inspection," as was the case with tobacco inspection points, they had decided to omit such a lengthy listing in the new Code. In the case of tobacco, which commanded an entire chapter unto itself, they decided to refer to it exclusively as a crop because it had ceased possessing transferable value as a medium of exchange. The extended footnote on page 455 documenting the numerous preexisting exceptions to the established norms clearly demonstrates that the motives surrounding Robinson and Patton's recommendations concerning appointment were purely organizational and designed to promote efficiency, familiarity, and uniformity in the manner of appointing inspectors.

lamented the attempt to turn these offices into positions of patronage. Two votes were called on the amendment, both ending in a fourteen-to-fourteen tie that prevented the amendment from passing. But late in the afternoon, John S. Carlisle, a Democrat from the northwestern district surrounding Grafton, changed his mind in favor of the amendment. He explained that he originally thought the issue inconsequential but now he wanted to rebut the charges of making "this matter into a party question." He argued that because the governor was the one representative who served all the people of the state, all of whom benefited from the process of inspections, he should possess the power of appointment. A third vote thus sustained the amendment giving the governor the power of appointment, and the Senate sent it back to the House for approval.[17]

The House debated the amended section the following day along the same general lines of argument. The controversy was picked up by the newspapers and, once it has aroused popular sentiment, debate surrounding the appointment of inspectors dragged on for the better part of the month. Resolution was made necessary when the Senate threatened to adjourn from the Special Session without completing the enrollment of the Code. In the end, the General Assembly approved Robinson and Patton's recommendations as they pertained to the appointment of tobacco inspectors, but they gave the power to appoint all other inspectors to the governor. The reforms proved particularly advantageous for the governor's patronage power because those appointed as flour and commodity inspectors were entitled to select salaried deputies as well. The governor was also given the singular authority to remove any inspector or deputy inspector at any time, for the intentionally ambiguous charges of "neglect of duty, incapacity, or misconduct." Two years later, following the ratification of the Reform Constitution in May 1852, the legislature revisited the inspection laws and further amended them so that tobacco inspectors were appointed exclusively by the governor as well.[18]

The inspector controversy thus provided the clearest example of the intrusion of politics into the codification process. Yet other law reforms, which were less overtly political in discussion, reflected some nuanced but substantial changes to the constitutional structure of the Commonwealth. Such was especially the case with the reform of Virginia's land laws. Most notably, the writ of right was conflated with the action of ejectment to bring the authority for all real property causes under a "simple and comprehensive statute." The writ of right represented one of the oldest of the ancient writs. It principally commanded freeholders to resolve their disputes under the jurisdiction of the king. Ejectment, on the other hand, originally was founded as a remedial action that enabled leaseholders to recover damages in the event that they were removed

[17] *Richmond Enquirer*, August 10, 1849.

[18] *Richmond Enquirer*, August 10, 14, 24, 1849; *Richmond Whig*, August 10, 28, 1849; *Code of Virginia* (1849), 402–403, 414; George W. Munford, ed., *The Code of Virginia* (2nd edition, Richmond: Ritchie, Dunvant, & Co., 1860), 451.

from an estate prior to the end of their term. Eventually, ejectment became the preferred method for determining title to lands and tenements for freeholders as well as leaseholders, although, because it was not a comprehensive action, many of the other actions, including the writ of right, persisted for exceptional use. Robinson and Patton thus considered the reduction of all real actions into a comprehensive action of ejectment a logical extension of historical trends as well as of previous statutory reforms. They noted that revisions accomplished in 1818 had, for all practical purposes, made all the other traditional possessory and droitural actions – the writs of entry, assize, formedon in descender, reverter, and remainder – obsolete, and that both England and Massachusetts had pursued similar courses in regards to ejectment.[19]

The recommended procedural reforms to the action of ejectment represented a significant change aimed to make land more easily transferable. So did changes to the laws of conveyances. Drawing heavily from the British reforms, Virginia's revisors sought to reduce the complexity of transferring landed estates by bringing all transactions within a standardized form. To do so, any exceptional qualities traditionally associated with the freehold needed to be removed from the law. Accordingly, Robinson and Patton had proposed a statute that collapsed the common-law distinction between a grant and a livery of seisin for the purposes of transferring land by deed. They also formalized the practice that had arisen of conveying rights through deeds and wills to lands that were not actually possessed but that might be claimed as an abstract future right in the form of a remainder or a reversion.[20] In general, both Whig and Democratic legislators endorsed these reforms with very little discussion or amendment. Yet occasionally, as in the instance of the effort to reform married women's property rights, debate erupted and accordingly offered significant insight into the aspirations of those engaged in the implicit reordering of Virginia's property relations and, by extension, her constitution.

A MOST HUMANE PROVISION OF THE COMMON LAW

Significant debate occurred during the Special Session, rather unexpectedly, concerning the proposed reforms to dower – the right of a widow to one-third of an estate for life. An examination of these reforms perhaps best illustrates the complex challenges encountered as Virginians sought to reconcile their traditional values and practices with a commercial conception of land. For many, dower represented the affirmation of contemporary gender roles as well as the legal confirmation of obligation that informed the paternalist matrix of all domestic relations – including slavery. Judge John Allen explained that

[19] *Report of the Revisors*, 691–692 (see editorial footnote); Simpson, *Land Law*, 37–40, 144–150.

[20] *Reports of the Revisors*, 602–603. In so doing, they followed the latest English statute. J. Stuart Anderson, *Lawyers and the Making of English Land Law, 1832–1940* (Oxford: Clarendon Press, 1992).

because the widow's right to dower was "frequently the only resource left for her own support and the sustenance of her children," it had always been much respected as "a most humane provision of the common law." Legal treatise writers placed the origins of dower even further back in history, prefiguring the common law, in the covenant bond of Christian matrimony. This ancient form of dower, dower *ad ostium ecclesia* (literally translated as dower at the door of the Church), customarily occurred when "a man of full age...came to the church door to be married," and, following the betrothal ceremony, endowed his wife with "a certain portion of his land" in the presence of priest, family, and community. Dower was thus intimately connected to the establishment of the patrilineal, Christian household. By the eighteenth century, however, it was complicated by the fact that much of the value of land was derived not simply from its agricultural produce, but from rents, perpetuities, appreciation, and improvements. Within the context of the dynamic relations of a modern commercial society, dower appeared to some as the most visible vestige of an archaic system of property laws that contradicted the dogmas of economic progress. Reform was needed, but reformers recognized that adapting dower to a commercial-friendly legal order potentially could undermine the orthodoxy of domestic relations. It is perhaps not so surprising then that married women's property emerged as a central issue of law reform not only in nineteenth-century Virginia, but throughout the common-law diaspora.[21]

The challenges faced by the delegates in the Special Session had been anticipated by Virginia's judges' and legislators' long engagement with the complex issues surrounding the assignment of a widow's share. As in other instances, Virginia's lawyers considered dower to have once been a plan of original simplicity that had become complicated and confused over time. Many of these complications arose from previous efforts at reform, which had been intended to remedy particular inequities but often had unintended consequences of their own. The doctrine of jointure, established by the Statute of Uses during the reign of Henry VIII, stands as the most notable example in this regard. Jointure permitted the creation of a joint estate between husband and wife under the principles of equity, effectively nullifying the doctrine of coverture and obviating

[21] *Wilson v. Davisson*, 2 Robinson 398 (1843). That Allen wrote this as part of his dissenting opinion suggests the extent to which the custom was being threatened. Lomax, *Digest of the Laws of Real Property*, 1: 74. Lee Holcombe, *Wives & Property: Reform of the Married Women's Property Law in Nineteenth-Century England* (Toronto: University of Toronto Press, 1983); Norma Basch, *In the Eyes of the Law: Women, Marriage, and Property in Nineteenth Century New York* (Ithaca, NY: Cornell University Press, 1982); Sandra Moncrief, "The Mississippi Married Women's Property Act of 1839," *Journal of Mississippi History*, 47 (1985): 110–125; Phillip Girard, "Married Women's Property, Chancery Abolition, and Insolvency Law: Law Reform in Nova Scotia, 1820–1867," in Girard and Jim Phillips, eds., *Essays in the History of Canadian Law, Volume 3: Nova Scotia* (Toronto: Osgoode Society for Canadian Legal History, 1990), 106–113; Nancy E. Wright, "'The Lady Vanishes'; Women and Property Rights in Nineteenth-Century New South Wales," in John McLaren, A. R. Buck, and Nancy Wright, eds., *Despotic Dominion: Property Rights in British Settler Societies* (Vancouver: UBC Press, 2005).

the requirement for dower. In cases where jointure had been established, upon the death of the husband, the widow would simply maintain the estate for life. Yet the statute did not specifically abolish dower. Accordingly, in instances were jointure did not apply, or in instances where it acted disadvantageously to the widow, the right of dower continued to function. Thus, from the sixteenth century onward, these two practices developed together in the courts of law and of equity, making the jurisprudence of widow's property rights even more complex.[22]

Colonial Virginians inherited both concepts and all of their complexities. Compounding the issue in the colony, however, was the particular difficulty of determining whether or not slaves and indentured servants were attached to the land and thus necessarily included as part of the dowable estate. Customarily, widows in the Chesapeake settlements were entitled to a dower share in personal property as well as real property. This divergence from English law might be attributed to the importance placed on slaves and indentures, or it may just as well have reflected the practices of a disproportionately male society where widows, through remarriage, played a significant role in determining economic outcomes. In 1664, as part of the reconstruction following the Restoration, the Virginia assembly confirmed local practice by passing a statute defining dower as part of a general effort to institutionalize the colony's legal practices. The act, "concerning widows thirds," clarified confusion over the assignment of dower by specifying that in cases of a husband dying intestate, or in instances where the legitimacy of the will was in question, the estate should be "divided equally into thirds in terms of quality, as well as quantity" from which the widow would chose a lot that would comprise her dower. This initial statute specifically defined dowable estates in terms of real and personal property, stipulating that personal property, including slaves and indentures, be divided in thirds as well.[23]

Further statutory clarifications were deemed necessary, however. Nearly a decade later, the legislature revisited the process of assignment and limited the widows' share of the personal estate to an equal division in instances when there were more than two surviving children. This revised statute also established the mandatory standard of the third as the minimum share of real property for a widow irrespective of whether it was awarded by an existing will or in an intestate case. The most significant piece of legislation, however,

22 Susan Staves, *Married Women's Separate Property in England, 1660–1833* (Cambridge, MA: Harvard University Press, 1990).

23 Marylynn Salmon, *Women and the Law of Property in Early America* (Chapel Hill: University of North Carolina Press, 1986), 149–156; Lois Green Carr and Lorena S. Walsh, "The Planter's Wife: The Experience of White Women in Seventeenth-Century Maryland," *WMQ*, 3rd series, 34 (1977): 542–571. On the significance of widows and social mobility in the Chesapeake settlements, see Edmund Morgan, *American Slavery, American Freedom: The Ordeal of Colonial Virginia* (New York: W. W. Norton & Co., 1975), 164–170; See Hening's comments about the inclusion of the word "or" in the statute and its ramifications; *SAL*, 2:212. I am borrowing generously from Salmon's interpretation here.

was passed as part of an effort to elucidate and institutionalize common-law practices in 1705. The statute, which explicitly committed itself to "the more equal distribution of estates," addressed a host of issues surrounding potential adversarial claims between widows, heirs, children, and the recognized claims of creditors. Still, the law took pains to protect the privileged rights of widows. Virginia widows continued to receive dower in personal as well as real property, and, most significantly, it determined the widow's quarantine right of *capital messauge* – the right to remain in the "mansion house" – for an unlimited amount of time until her dower was assigned. This provision marked a substantial departure from English law, where a widow was entitled to only forty days of residence. Owing to the 1705 statute's comprehensive nature, it served as the foundation for Virginia's legal proceedings in cases of intestacy for the next century and a half.[24]

At the same time, with slavery developing into the principle form of labor in the colony, the legislature directly examined the question of whether or not slaves should constitute part of a widow's dower. It was an important question given the need for the dowable land to be productive in the absence of the system of rents that had developed in England. Prior to 1705, despite the custom of allowing personal property to comprise part of the dower, slaves often tended to be treated as exceptional cases and, when necessary, were partitioned between the widow and the heirs by the county courts. As part of the 1705 revisions, however, the House of Burgesses also passed a law declaring slaves were to be considered a form of real estate. Virginia's statute was modeled after a 1688 Barbadian law that had addressed the thorny legal question of whether, in the instances of intestacy, slaves should descend immediately to the heirs, or whether they should be considered assets to pay off the debts on the estate. Following the practice in Barbados, the Virginia law declared slaves to be considered real estate for purposes of descent, but they retained certain exemptions and were still treated as personal property in cases involving slave-traders, merchants, recovery procedures, and seizure for debts. The law also stipulated that the political rights of a freehold would not extend to slaveholders, despite the fact that they might now possess considerable real property. Neither did it require those who sold or transferred slaves to register the transaction as was required in transferring of land. In respect to dower rights, however, the Virginia law ensured that widows would not only be assigned land, but, by first setting apart the dowable slaves, they would also receive the necessary labor to maintain the productivity of the estate.[25]

[24] *SAL*, 2: 303, and 3: 371–373. Salmon, *Women and the Law*, 152.

[25] *SAL*, 3: 333–334. After 1671, the House of Burgesses charged the county courts with partitioning slaves because they believed the issue too complex to be addressed adequately by statute. For a detailed analysis of the statute and the subsequent consideration of slaves as real property, see Thomas D. Morris, *Southern Slavery and the Law, 1619–1860* (Chapel Hill: University of North Carolina Press, 1996), 66–71, 82–83. *Cf.* Salmon, 152–153. My interpretation differs from Salmon on this point. She argued that the law marked "a decline in widows' rights" because it only granted widows a life interest in slaves and demonstrated that "the assembly

This effort to treat slaves as real property failed. Within two decades, Virginians found it necessary to clarify the law to address the "many mischiefs" that had arisen from annexing slaves to the land. A 1727 law encouraged the disposition of slaves through wills by giving slaveholders the authority to grant slaves in either fee simple or fee tail. Legislators hoped that the presence of a legitimate will would remove some of the contests between the widow and the heirs from the courts. The revised statute also made some significant changes in the process of assigning dower by allowing widows and creditors to bring suit in a court of equity to determine adversarial claims against slaves. Furthermore, it granted a widow the right of election, noting that when she was not "satisfied with the provision made for her by her husband's will," she might reject it in favor of her dower rights, including her dower in slaves. These intended clarifications did little to improve the situation. By 1748, the Burgesses decided to abandon the scheme altogether. They repealed the previous acts and declared all slaves to be defined as chattels personal. The legislators explained that annexing slaves to the land, although originally well intended, had, in effect, caused some plantations to be overstocked with slaves and had created confusion on certain estates between which slaves were annexed to it and which slaves were held in fee simple. Beyond these practical problems, the legal fictions of considering slaves as real estate in some instances but retaining the qualities of personal estate for others had a deleterious effect on the clarity and consistency of property laws. Still, the Burgesses explicitly safeguarded dower rights in slaves by providing that widows would "have one full and equal third part of all ... slaves" to hold, along with their increase, "during her natural life," in a separate statute. These revisions were repealed by the king's prerogative, however, and Virginia's slaves remained annexed to the land for purposes of dower until after the Revolution.[26]

In 1792, as part of the larger republican revision of the laws, the General Assembly sought to address these historical complexities by consolidating all the previous acts or parts of acts dealing with dower into a universal and comprehensive statute of conveyances. This statute limited dower to real property only. It specifically prescribed that a widow was to be awarded "one full and equal third part of all lands, tenements, and any other real estate, whereof her husband, or any other to his use, was seized of an estate of inheritance, at any time during her coverture" and over which she had not relinquished her dower rights. It reaffirmed the traditional right of Virginia's widows to

still was unwilling to allow women absolute control over valuable slave property." Given that women did not have such authority prior to the 1705 statute, it is difficult to classify the legal change as a decline. Salmon does not address the need for labor to maintain the productivity of dower lands.

[26] *SAL*, 4: 222–228 and 5: 432–444. See the note protesting the repeal of certain laws. For commentary and analysis, see Morris, *Southern Slavery*, 69–71.The law abolishing entail ended the practice of annexing slaves to the land and thereby set the stage for their subsequent consideration as personality in instances of manumission and inheritance. It made no provision, however, for classifying or assigning slaves as a part of dower. *SAL*, 11: 39–40; *SAL*, 9: 226–227.

continued occupancy in the mansion house without rent until the time that her dower was assigned, and provided for equivalent protections under jointure as well. Jointure represented a bar to dower, but if the conveyance was made after the marriage or during the "infancy of the feme," than the widow retained a right of election to decide between the two. Furthermore, if her jointure failed because of either a legal defect or a lawful action, then she would still be entitled to dower from the residue of her husband's lands. The new law also explicitly incorporated the provision from the English Statute of Merton that provided damages for any widows who were wrongfully deforced from their dower. Thus, despite limiting the definition of dower in terms of real estate only, the statute was worded strongly in favor of supporting widow's rights over and above any rival claims of heirs, purchasers, tenants, and creditors. Adversarial claimants who wrongfully withheld dowable property were subject to pay damages to the widow in addition to restoring the property. In cases where the husband had defaulted on lands, it was the responsibility of the occupant to establish his claim against the widow, and indeed, even a judgment of default against the widow herself was not sufficient to bar her dower. Slaves, however, were deemed to be personal property and no longer subject to the law of dower.[27]

Nevertheless, the statutory redefinition did not immediately alleviate the problem of dealing with slaves in the assigning dower. In 1811, the Supreme Court of Appeals addressed the issue in the case of *McCargo v. Callicott*. The case raised the question of whether a widow who remarried, but who held slaves by dower from her first marriage, retained them in her own life estate, or whether, by coverture, they were vested in her second husband. When Susanna Callicott's second husband died, she refused to turn over her slaves to the executor, Littlejohn McCargo, so that they could be divided among the second husband's heirs. Mrs. Callicott had brought an undetermined number of slaves, representing one-third of the slaves from her first marriage, with her into this second marriage in addition to her dower lands. James Callicott, her second husband, had provided by will that she would inherit six slaves (listed by name and different from the slaves she was contesting to hold in dower) and other items of personal property for the rest of her life upon his death. Upon her death, the slaves and the other items were to be equally divided among his daughters. The Court ruled in favor of the heirs and denied Susanna Calllicott the slaves on the basis that they, along with the rest of her personal property, had been subject to coverture upon remarriage. Accordingly, her second husband could manage them as he saw fit. In this ruling, the Court sought to follow the 1792 Statute of Conveyances and to confine matters of dower to real property despite the fact that the original slaves had been assigned prior to that statute. In doing so, the Court implicitly encouraged any future questions about the transmission of slaves through dower to settlement in the

[27] *Statutes at Large of Virginia, 1792–1806*, 1: 128; Leigh, ed., *Revised Code of Virginia (1819)* (Richmond: Thomas Ritchie, 1819), 1: 403.

equity courts instead of in the courts of law. Indeed, irrespective of the legal limitation on dower in real property only, an untold number of slaves were assigned to widows by rulings in equity on the principles of justice.[28]

The proliferation of other forms of personal property caused confusion in determining the widow's share as well. Judges and commentators often disagreed over definitions and interpretations in matters of personal estate, creating greater ambiguity within the legal community. The question of whether or not jointure in the form of personal property acted as a bar to dower perplexed some of the most learned members of the Virginia bar. Henry St. George Tucker, in his *Commentaries*, noted the disparity between English and Virginia law in this instance, given that the 1792 statute of conveyances stipulated that "*if any estate*" was established as a jointure, it would bar the dower. Tucker understood this "generality of expression" to mean that it applied to jointure in personal estate as well as real estate. He offered as an example a woman who agreed to a jointure of "$10,000 in stock" in lieu of her dower. He did not doubt that her agreement barred dower "under the broad terms of the act," although he acknowledged that she retained the right of election and, once she became a widow, could renounce the bequest in preference for her dower. Tucker's contemporary and fellow law professor Judge John Tayloe Lomax disagreed. In his *Digest*, he explained that jointure had been created by the Statute of Uses and had always been understood to pertain to real estate only. Accordingly, Lomax contended that only settlements in real estate could "be a legal bar to dower," and any form of personal estate would simply supplement the dower.[29]

Confusion also arose from trying to determine the appropriate value of dower in commercially transferred land. Judges often faced substantial difficulties in determining the value of the third because of the increasing transfer and fluctuating market value of lands. The particular case of *Tod v. Baylor*, decided by the Virginia Supreme Court in May 1833, revealed many of these contemporary challenges. In November 1801, John Baylor had sold a 300-acre parcel of land in Caroline County to George Tod for the sum of $2,550. In compliance with the 1792 Statute of Conveyances, a deed was drawn up and sealed in two places, one seal requiring the signature of John Baylor and the second for the signature of his wife Anne. Her explicit endorsement conveying her future rights to the estate was required, or else the purchaser, Tod, would continue to bear the responsibility of relinquishing a third of these lands to her as a life estate in the event that she ever became a widow. Virginia's laws also demanded that Anne Baylor be examined separately from her husband, in a process called a privy examination, to ensure that she had not been coerced or deceived into relinquishing her title to dower in the conveyed land.[30]

[28] *McCargo v. Callicott*, 2 Munford 501 (1811).

[29] Henry St. George Tucker, *Commentaries on the Laws of Virginia*, 2: 72–73. See *Ambler v. Norton*, 2 Henning and Munford 23 (1809) and *Wiseley v. Findlay*, 3 Rand 361 (1825) for two cases bearing on the issue. Lomax's perspective is found in his *Digest of the Laws of Real Property*, 1: 119–120.

[30] *Tod v. Baylor*, 4 Leigh 498 (1833).

For some reason, the exact procedures were not followed in this instance. Anne Baylor never signed the actual deed of conveyance. At that time of the transaction, she "could not conveniently travel to the county court" to make the appropriate acknowledgment, so the court appointed two justices of the peace to ride out and conduct the necessary privy examination to ascertain that she understood all the ramifications of the conveyance and had willingly agreed to the transaction. The two justices accomplished their mission in August 1802 and, upon their return to the court, recorded a certificate stating that they had conducted the privy examination and that Anne Baylor had given "her acknowledgement of the conveyance of [the] 300 acres of land...freely and voluntarily, [and] without the threats or persuasions of her husband." Two years later, the Baylors sold an additional 320 acres to George Tod for $2,624. This time, both John and Anne signed and sealed the deed, and once again appointed commissioners conducted a privy examination and filed a certificate confirming Anne's willing participation in the transaction.[31]

In 1827, three years after John Baylor had died, Anne Baylor filed a bill in the Fredericksburg Superior Court of Chancery alleging "that neither of the deeds" of sale had been executed according to the provisions of the 1792 statute "and praying, therefore, that dower might be assigned her of both parcels of land." She also asked that the court provide an account of the rents and profits arising from these lands that should rightfully be due to her from the time of the death of her husband. George Tod responded to the charges by admitting to the facts of the case, but he insisted that the deeds had been "duly executed by Mrs. Baylor" according to the laws of Virginia and contended that she had thus "relinquished her right of dower in the lands."[32]

The chancellor disagreed with Tod and appointed a commission of freeholders who, with the assistance of a surveyor, were assigned "to lay off...one equal third part of both the parcels of land in question" for Mrs. Baylor's dower, taking into account the quality as well as the quantity of land. The chancellor also directed the commission to make an account of the profits arising from the land since the time of John Baylor's death, as well as an assessment of the improvements that Tod had made to the estate since his purchase. Upon completing the survey and accounting, the commissioners identified 140 acres of land from the first parcel and 110 acres from the subsequent parcel as dower, determined the annual value of the lands to be $280, and assessed the aggregate profits from the estate from the time of the death of John Baylor to be $1,068. Accordingly, the chancellor assigned both parcels to Anne Baylor and ordered Tod to pay her $356, which represented a third of the profits derived from the two parcels of land since he had purchased them two decades earlier.[33]

[31] *Ibid.*

[32] *Ibid.*

[33] 4 Leigh 497, 500. By the time the case came before the Supreme Court of Appeals in May 1833, it was unclear as to whether the value assessed to the land by the commissioner included the $1,270 worth of improvements that Tod had made since his purchase.

George Tod appealed the ruling, and his case was heard by the four members of the Supreme Court in May 1833. The opposing lines of argument advanced by Robert Stanard, the attorney for Tod, and Benjamin Watkins Leigh, representing Anne Baylor, revealed many of the contemporary questions concerning the administration of dower. Questions of appropriate jurisdiction between law and equity, the expected standards of technical procedures, and the issue of how to determine the value of the estate in question all stood at the focal point of contemporary debate about the efficacy of the common law in a commercial society. Leigh championed the customary practice of determining dower in a court of equity, which, despite being juxtaposed against the procedure in England, fully expressed a preference for the traditional common-law understanding of local justice. Similarly, he argued for a meticulous enforcement of the provisions enacted to protect the *feme covert* as provided for in the Statute of Conveyances. Finally, he maintained that although a widow could not be advantaged by an increase in value to the land attributed to improvements made to the property, she certainly was entitled to any "increased value of the land produced by general causes, unconnected with the improvements of the purchaser." He emphasized that the common law mandated that a widow was to be endowed based on the value of the land at the time of the assignment, not at the time of the transfer. Leigh thus characterized dower as a remedy whose ends was justice and whose fair resolution necessarily superseded the order established by the law. Conversely, Stanard advanced arguments that sought to reduce dower to a mere doctrine of the law, one which could be regularly and predictably adjudicated. He emphasized the inefficiency wrought by the dualistic jurisprudence of law and equity and portrayed Anne Baylor's petition for dower as an effort to unsettle the certainty of all the titles to land in Virginia.[34]

Upon hearing these two arguments, the Supreme Court of Appeals unanimously reversed the decree of the chancery court and remanded the case back to that court for further proceedings. Their ruling stipulated that dower should be assigned to Anne Baylor only from the land conveyed in the initial deed, the one that she did not sign, and that the value of that land should be determined from the transaction date of the deed. The justices clearly recognized the authority of the 1792 Statute of Conveyances in spelling out the procedure by which dower should be determined and assigned, but they all recognized that the limitations of that law in this particular case. Despite consensus pertaining to the case's final disposition, significant interpretative disagreement existed among the justices about how they arrived at the decision. Three of the four judges – Dabney Carr, Francis Taliaferro Brooke, and Henry St. George Tucker – wrote separate opinions explaining their understanding of the case. In these opinions, each of the justices sought to answer three basic considerations of the case. First, they contemplated whether or not the certification process, as it was carried out by the privy examiners, was correctly accomplished. Second,

[34] The rival arguments are detailed in 4 Leigh 499–507.

they asked if the deeds were valid. And third, they pondered what, if anything, should Anne Baylor be assigned as her dower and, if so, how should the value of that dower be determined.

Henry St. George Tucker grappled with this last question in particular, and pondered how a community best determined the value of a piece of land when the principle of value itself was defined by a market mechanism that championed fluctuations in value. In the initial opinion, Judge Carr had noted that the common law clearly stipulated that the value of the dower should be determined from the time of alienation, and that the widow was not entitled "to dower according to the improved value of the land." Tucker, however, distinguished between the physical improvements made to the property by the purchaser (such as a new barn) and "the accession of value arising merely from the progress of society and the general progressive increase in the value of lands consequent upon increasing wealth and population." He explained that, in equity, it was established practice to assign the widow value based on "improvement in the productive character of the soil which arises from the course of husbandry" when that improvement was made by the heir. He inferred that a similar claim could be made against the purchaser because the law of dower did not distinguish sharply between transfers made to the heir and transfers made to an outside party. Yet the question remained an open one. Tucker acknowledged that his "brethren differ[ed]" from him in this regard; indeed, Brooke went so far as to posit that, in the instance of Anne Baylor, the value of the land had actually depreciated since its alienation. More than a decade later, in 1846, Tucker returned to the question in his new edition of his *Commentaries*. He admitted that although the question had been "much argued and considered" during the case and a ruling given, for all practical purposes, it remained unresolved and ambiguous.[35]

FOR THE FURTHER PROTECTION OF MARRIED WOMEN'S PROPERTY

Ideas for reforming dower were therefore abundant by the time of the Special Session. In reporting on the Code, Conway Robinson and John Mercer Patton opposed simply replacing the common-law doctrine with a married women's property statute – as was the fashionable course of reform in other jurisdictions. They also explicitly rejected most of the tenets of the dower reforms implemented by Great Britain in 1833. In general, the British reforms had limited the definition of dowable lands to enhance the transferability of land. Robinson and Patton acknowledged that the British statute had "made very great innovations," and they praised the extension of a dower right to all lands to which the husband had a right of entry, as was the case in Virginia. Overall,

[35] 4 Leigh 509. Carr cited *Stout v. Jackson* (2 Rand. 132) and *Threkheld v. Fitzhugh* (2 Leigh 451) as analogous cases. Tucker opinion: 4 Leigh 511, 516–517 and *Commentaries on the Laws of Virginia*, 1: 61.

however, they believed that the reforms disadvantaged the widow and thus were contrary to the desires of "the people of Virginia." Accordingly, the British plan, or at least the more controversial sections of it, stood as the antithesis of the program of dower reform they proposed for Virginia.[36]

In this instance, then, instead of adapting a compatible plan of reform from another jurisdiction, Robinson and Patton sought to devise their own. In particular, they attempted to address the specific points of controversy that had been identified by the courts as well as to bring consistency to Virginia's existing practices, which had been confused by contradictory judicial decisions and legal opinions. To do so, they basically rewrote the laws concerning dower to establish it as a standard form of land transfer. The principal issues they addressed included providing an adequate definition of what types of property were subject to dower, determining when jointure acted as a bar to dower, deciding how to determine the value of land in adjudicating dower, and specifying the appropriate procedures – law or equity – by which dower should be recovered. Two fundamental assertions shaped their responses to these questions: first, they maintained that dower should be confined to real property; and second, dower should be settled in courts of law, not equity. In general, their recommendations tended to favor the rights of the widow over any adversarial rights of the heirs or creditors. They repudiated Lord Coke's maxim that the wife could not "enter into her dower by the common law but [was] driven to her writ of dower to recover the same" by replacing the writ of dower with the action of ejectment. Principally, however, they were motivated by an effort to impose procedural standards and regularity on the process.[37]

Yet despite these learned recommendations, the legislators who enrolled the Code had their own ideas pertaining to dower reform. During the first week of July 1849, James M. Laidley, a delegate from Kanawha, moved to have the Joint Committee on the Revision investigate the question of married women's property distinct from the recommendations made by the revisors. Laidley's motion was endorsed but amended by James Ferguson, the representative of the southwestern districts of Logan and Boone, who proposed creating a select committee exclusively to "enquire into the expediency of providing more effectually for the protection of the property of married women." An effort to postpone consideration of the issue was defeated narrowly, and a thirteen-member select committee was established to devise recommendations on the subject for consideration by the House of Delegates, and, if desirable, to draft an appropriate statute protecting married women's property.[38]

[36] *Reports of the Revisors*, 564–565. Staves, *Married Women's Separate Property in England*; Holcombe, *Wives & Property*.

[37] *Reports of the Revisors*, 564–567. See the exchange between Lomax, *Digest*, 1: 119 and Henry St. George Tucker, *Commentaries*, 2: 72 for insight into the controversy.

[38] *House Journal (1848–1849)*, 557–559. Laidley's original motion was made on July 3. Benjamin Hiner (Pendleton and Highland) moved to postpone the consideration of the resolution, but this motion was narrowly defeated. The delegates then approved Laidley's resolution with Ferguson's

Married women's property statutes generally allowed wives to own property, both real and personal, as a separate estate from that of their husbands. In 1839, in the wake of the British reforms, Mississippi became the first state in the Union to adopt a statute allowing for the existence of a separate estate. Maine, Michigan, Massachusetts, Texas, California, and New York followed in passing similar laws during the next decade. These laws were intended to protect the wife's property from her husband's creditors and to hold her liable for her own debts, irrespective of any claims of dower. By design, married women's property statutes divided the property of the household and legally attached it to each individual person. The creation of separate estates thus essentially abolished dower by obviating the legal fiction of coverture and the corresponding reciprocal principle of curtesy, whereby, upon the death of the wife, the husband was entitled to any lands that she possessed under coverture. [39]

In Virginia, too, efforts to enact a married women's property statute had been made even before the Special Session. A year earlier, two similar motions had been proposed in the House of Delegates to explore the expediency of a married women's property statute In January 1848, Jonathan B. Stovall of Halifax introduced a motion designed to "secure the property" that a wife brought to a marriage "from the debts, liabilities or engagements of the husband." He also proposed that married women should be allowed to hold as separate property any property that might be bequeathed or donated to them during their coverture. The provision was less an argument for equal property rights between the sexes than it was advantageous for fathers who might want to grant or leave property to their daughters, but who had concerns about it becoming lost to their son-in-law's creditors. Property transfers to women had become an everyday aspect of life in Virginia, and Stovall's motion represented an effort to secure those transfers through the law.[40]

Although the transfer of land naturally remained an important component of such exchanges, perhaps more significantly, Stovall's proposal facilitated the secure transfer of slaves through marriage as well. It was not uncommon for a bride to bring her "domestic servants" with her into the new household. As

amendment. The select committee consisted of Ferguson, Charles J. Faulkner (Berkeley), Hugh Sheffey (Augusta), Joseph Harvey (Westmoreland), Richmond Lacy (Charles City and New Kent), William M. Burwell (Bedford), James R. Strother (Rappahannock), William C. Worthington (Jefferson), John R. Kilby (Nansemond), Egbert Watson (Albemarle), Henry Irving (Cumberland), James Irvine (Campbell), and Algernon Wood (Frederick). The composition of the committee seemingly suggests a bias toward some form of statutory protection. Harvey and Strother were early advocates for a married women's property act and Ferguson, Burwell, Worthington, and Kilby voted to defeat the Hiner motion designed to quash the committee (as did Speaker Hopkins, who appointed the committee). Faulkner, Irvine, Irving, Wood, Lacy, and Watson voted in favor of the Hiner motion, but Faulkner became the spokesmen for the committee's recommendation. Sheffey did not vote on the Hiner motion and I cannot discern his initial attitude toward a statute.

[39] Basch, *In the Eyes of the Law*, 27–28, 136–161; Moncrief, "The Mississippi Married Women's Property Act of 1839."

[40] *House Journal (1847–1848)*, 211–212; *House Journal (1848–1849)*, 50.

it stood, any slaves transferred with their mistress following marriage found themselves, because of the doctrine of coverture, in the precarious situation of being legally owned by the new husband. Certainly, for those enslaved, the situation was precarious for a host of reasons, but relative to the transmission of property, transfer through marriage was analogous to being sold. Transferred slaves faced the potential threat of being claimed or sold to any of the husband's outstanding creditors, irrespective of the wishes of the wife or her father. In this manner, the centuries-old legal fiction of coverture actually undermined the intent to protect women's property from creditors and, indeed, even facilitated their claims.

Stovall's motion was tabled by the judiciary committee with very little discussion and was not taken up again during the session. In December 1848, however, during the following legislative session, Joseph F. Harvey of Westmoreland offered a similar resolution that advocated protecting married women's property "from the payment of the debts of their husbands, whether contracted before or after marriage." Harvey's resolution met with somewhat more success than did Stovall's. Garnering a host of coauthors from across the state, his resolution emerged from committee on February 13, 1849 and was designated as House Bill 386 – "A Bill to Protect the Property of Married Women."[41] A month later, Harvey offered an amendment to the bill, but because it represented exactly the type of substantial legislation that Robinson and Patton had implored the delegates to refrain from during the revision process, Samuel Price of Greenbrier referred it to the Joint Committee on the Revision for consideration as part of the new code. The motion on the issue made by James Laidley during the Special Session represented an effort to revisit the Harvey Bill.

On July 11, following a week of discussion, Charles Faulkner, the chairman of the Select Committee, presented the committee's report to the House of Delegates. At the time of the Special Session, Faulkner was one of the leading Whigs in Virginia. Like Conway Robinson, he embraced the principle of law reform but sought a conservative means to achieve that ends. Accordingly, Faulkner appeared as the leading advocate for the select committee's compromise proposal on married women's property. The committee recommended making three rather significant changes to customary practices to better secure the property of married women in a dynamic, commercial society. Tellingly, it focused primarily on protecting slaves belonging to married women – especially from their husband's creditors – and did not explicitly address the issue of real property. Foremost, the committee recommended vesting married women with ownership rights to any slaves that they either brought to the marriage or subsequently acquired while simultaneously recognizing that the husband had a life

[41] *House Journal (1848–1849)*, 50, 277, 280. The bill's coauthors were James Strother (Rappahanock), Robert E. Scott (Fauquier), Henry W. Thomas (Fairfax), Egbert Watson, William Worthington (Jefferson), John W. Syme (Petersburg), William Burwell (Bedford), and Algernon Wood (Frederick).

estate in such property. Second, they proposed protecting any property acquired by marriage from any debts that the husband had contracted prior to the marriage. Third, they also sought to remove the husband's responsibility for the debts contracted by the wife, which were payable by her personal estate.[42]

In presenting these recommendations, Faulkner attempted to assuage conservative delegates' concerns about the potential ramifications of the proposed amendments. He explained that the committee had "approached the subject...with extreme caution" and with the appropriate recognition that "no department of the law" contained more potential social consequences than "the law regulating relations between husband and wife." He pointed out that the committee had declined to pursue the fashionable course of drafting a married women's property statute, which would create a "total separation" of the property interest between husband and wife. It also had rejected adopting the community or partnership system that existed in Louisiana and other civil-law jurisdictions. Instead, by providing the husband with a life estate in his wife's slaves, the committee believed that they had preserved the unity of property within the household, and thus the material and spiritual unity of marriage. Faulkner praised the customs of coverture, curtesy, and dower as being "in accordance with the purposes of nature," and he cited as evidence the "more elevated" social condition of women in England and other countries where these common-law principles prevailed. He emphasized to the assembly that the committee had sought to adhere to those "long-cherished principles," and he did not consider the proposed amendments a "violent departure" in their efforts to better secure the property of married women.[43]

To ensure that these reforms did not replace dower, Faulkner proposed that the committee recommendations should be added as a separate clause to the section of the code dealing with marriage – not to the section addressing dower. Dower would thus remain a distinct category of law while the reforms to protect the property of married women would take the form of a state-sponsored prenuptial agreement. Indeed, in many respects, the proposal represented a desire to remove any financial impediments to marriage far more than it sought to protect property rights for married women. Not inconsequently, it also offered a way to isolate slavery from the vicissitudes of the commercial marketplace.

Yet, despite these assurances, many recognized the radical consequences of the proposals, particularly those imbedded in the tenets of the first amendment

[42] *Richmond Whig*, July 17, 1849. Faulkner defected to the Democratic Party in 1852 in reaction to the nomination of Winfield Scott as the Whig presidential candidate. By 1856, Faulkner was serving as the chairman of the National Democratic Committee and organizing James Buchanan's presidential campaign. Ample biographical information on this unheralded but remarkable statesman can be found Faulkner Family papers, *VHS* Mss1 F2725a FA2. An extended narrative of the family history and the personal highlights of his career can be found in the collection guide. For an unflattering physical description, see the *Fredericksburg News*, January 23, 1851.

[43] *Richmond Whig*, July 17, 1849.

dealing with the ownership of slaves. That amendment not only assigned wives ownership rights to any slaves they brought with them to the marriage; it also proposed treating such slaves in the same manner as real estate when transferring ownership. Accordingly, it demanded that husbands, who henceforth would possess a life interest, would necessarily be afforded a privy examination to ensure that they understood that they were relinquishing any future claims to their wife's property. The proposal thus sought to avoid the creation of separate estates between man and wife, but, in so doing, turned contemporary gender roles and ideals of mastery on their head; married women would possess a separate estate in their slaves, and their husbands would have legal protections for their future rights to these slaves. Robert Rives, a delegate from Prince George County, undoubtedly captured the sentiments of some of the other delegates when he responded to the committee's recommendations by mockingly suggesting that wives be given "full control of the person and the property of the husband during coverture in all instances." His jest was met with "much laughter" in the hall.[44]

The editors of the *Richmond Whig* also expressed dismay over the radical implications of the proposal. They applauded Faulkner for his intent to maintain the unity of the household estate, but they considered the amendments an "invasion of the family circle" designed to annihilate the "salutary subordination" of women, which they credited with making them the "purest specimens of humanity." The editorial comments represented an effort to employ the language of domesticity and separate spheres to preserve the traditional relations of a male-dominated, but unified, household. The editors pilloried the women who, they believed, would benefit from the proposed legislation by referring to them as Becky Sharps – a reference to the roguish heroine in Thackery's, *Vanity Fair*. They characterized such women as "keen enough to make their own way" and neither needing nor meriting "the aid of the law." The legislation itself, according to the *Whig*, reflected a "touch of Red Republicanism" and sought to introduce by subversion "French morals" and the "mercenary and libidinous spirit" of continental society onto the Virginia landscape of gender relations.[45]

Others protested the assignment of a life interest in slaves to husbands on far different grounds. Samuel Price, one of the Democratic leaders in the House, called for an amendment striking out the clause. Price argued that granting a husband a life interest in his wife's slaves would not protect them from his creditors. It would actually have the opposite effect. In the absence of other property, a creditor "might seize on" the life interest and thereby deprive both the wife and her children "the benefit of her slaves." He contended that the only true way to secure a married women's property was to create a separate estate for her. Price's substitute amendment generated a debate between those delegates who desired effective reform and those who balked at creating a division within the household estate. After a compromise effort failed, a majority

[44] *Richmond Whig*, July 17, 1849; *Richmond Enquirer*, July 24, 1849.
[45] *Richmond Whig*, July 17, 1849.

voted in favor of Price's amendment and struck out the husband's life interest from the proposed reforms.[46]

The preliminary vote in favor of the Price amendment unraveled any chance at compromise with conservative delegates on the subject. Indeed, in the end, even Charles Faulkner voted against the proposal because he believed that, without a life interest, the bill created a separate estate for married women. But the vote also caused a reorientation of the issues and opened up the debate to those delegates who wanted to expand the forms of property protected by the law. George Yerby proclaimed his ardent support for protecting the rights of married women, but he questioned why a wife with three slaves was protected in her possession of them, but "if she had $100,000 in money, it went into the husband's pocket" where he could squander it at will. George Townes proposed amending the bill to include public stocks in addition to property in slaves in the first section. He argued that the fundamental "objection to the present bill" was that it would implement an "unequal operation on the people of the Commonwealth." He echoed Yerby's complaints, noting that the section only secured property for women from slave-owning families and "utterly excluded" all others from protection.[47]

John A. Thompson addressed the issue within the framework of class; the proposed bill protected only the rich while leaving unprotected "that large and meritorious class" of poor families. As the representative of Jefferson County, he appropriately argued that it would effectively "undo Jefferson's partible inheritance" by fostering the preservation of large estates, "upon which an aristocracy will live in luxury and idleness." After Townes withdrew his amendment, Stephen Whittle moved to strike out the word "slaves" from the bill and replace it with the words "personal property." His amendment would thus protect any personal property a woman brought with her to the marriage from the debts of her husband. The motion failed, however, and in the end, the entire bill to further protect married women's property was divided into its separate sections and defeated in three votes. A similar proposal was discussed in the Senate but was defeated as well.[48]

Unable to agree on a suitable method to better protect married women's property, the legislators revisited the dower reforms recommended by Robinson and Patton. They embraced most of their recommendations but made some significant changes to the language of the section that generally favored widows at the expense of the procedural integrity sought by the revisors. Specifically, the legislators reversed the revisors and an opinion from the Supreme Court of Appeals and extended a dower entitlement to any surplus from lands sold to meet a lien or encumbrance. They also rejected the revisors' recommendations

[46] *Richmond Whig*, July 24, 1849.

[47] It warrants mentioning that both Yerby and Townes represented "eastern" districts typically identified with Virginia's slave-owning interest. Yerby was from Northampton County on the Eastern Shore and Townes represented Pittsylvania County in the Piedmont, although his district also included the city of Danville.

[48] *Richmond Whig*, July 24, 1849; *Senate Journal*, 319–320.

as to what forms of property could be conveyed or devised as jointure. As part of the effort to confine dower proceedings to real property only, Robinson and Patton had intended that jointure in real estate only would act as a bar to dower. The enrollers came down on the other side of the debate. They decided that jointure in both real estate and personal estate acted to bar dower. In so doing, they embraced the interpretation offered by Henry St. George Tucker that distinguished between the English common law and the law of Virginia. More significantly, they demonstrated their propensity to conflate real and personal property and erase the historical distinction between the two types of property.[49]

The inability of reformers to coalesce around a common platform stymied their potential for success. Charles Faulkner, in presenting the bill from the committee, believed that a majority would support a proposal focused on protecting property in slaves from debt. But his reluctance to create a separate estate for married women, and the desires of other reformers to expand the definition of protected property, subverted the effort. Faulkner's fellow Whig, Robert E. Scott, eulogized the committee's proposal by noting that, in the end, the only admirable quality of the bill was "the protection it afford[ed] husbands from creditors."[50] Nonetheless, the debate revealed much about attitudes toward the sundry species of property in Virginia. In trying to preserve property from the claims of creditors, and thus the vicissitudes of market relations, slaves emerged as the primary point over which it was believed consensus could be attained. Slaves, not land, represented the chief concern for legislators. Certainly, the question of slavery had informed discussions of dower and married women's property throughout the colonial period. The problem was not new in Virginia, but, unlike in earlier discussions, the debate during the Special Session did not revolve around whether or not slaves were attached to the land. Instead, slaves were characterized as a separate and distinguishable form of personal property. Indeed, in being afforded special attention in the effort to protect them from debt, they were treated as a privileged form of property.

A JURISPRUDENCE OF SLAVERY

The special attention directed at slaves in the debates over married women's property was hardly exceptional during the Special Session. Law reforms pertaining to slavery and free blacks garnered significant discussion, and tangential issues crept into the debates on other sections of the Code as well. Such attention should hardly come as a surprise given that fierce national debates

[49] *Code of Virginia (1849)*, 474–475; *Reports of the Revisors*, 565; *Wilson v. Davisson*, 2 Rob. 396. See discussion of the issue of jointure *supra* and in Lomax, *Digest*, 1: 119–120, Tucker, *Commentaries*, 2: 72, and *Wisely v. Findlay*, 3 Rand. 372. The legislature also omitted a section that enabled widows to claim dower from a second marriage even if they had received a dower from their first marriage. The omission meant that such cases would continue to be decided in Chancery.

[50] *Richmond Whig*, July 24, 1849.

over the admission of California to statehood and the question of slavery in the territories were ongoing. Closer to home, a recent antislavery effort, orchestrated by Henry Ruffner, had again raised the issue in state politics. Ruffner's plan offered an equivalent to the Wilmot Proviso for Virginia. He called for the abolition of slavery from the western districts of the state in order to confine the institution thereafter to the Piedmont and Tidewater regions. Despite its relative impotence, the plan reflected the obvious centrality of slavery to any discussion over reforming the essential constitution of the state.[51]

Similarly, the legislative attempt to use the codification process as an opportunity to construct further protections for property in slaves not only reflected the historical context in which the reforms occurred, but also revealed much about the reformers intentions in regards to the legal construction of slavery. Most notably, it showed an increasing concern about the potential volatility of private property rights to destabilize the institutional structures of a slave society. Problems arose from the allodial ownership rights of the master over a slave. This form of ownership had been sanctified during the postrevolutionary law reforms with the passage of the 1782 Manumission act, which confirmed allodial property rights of slave owners by granting them the right to manumit by deed or will without petitioning the legislature. Although these rights of ownership were never fully absolute – taxes had to be paid and, after 1806, manumitted slaves removed – the authority of the owner of his slaves was unquestioned. By the 1830s, Thomas Roderick Dew had repositioned slave ownership as the political basis for independence and civic virtue in order to replace the failed freehold ideal. But the prevalent commercial attitudes of capitalism subverted the slave owning ideal too. By the time of the codification project, Virginians had recognized that the same commercial pressures that had transformed land ownership threatened slave ownership as well. As the defense of slavery became more shrill, spokesmen encountered the incongruity of championing the paternalist attributes of the master-slave relation in opposition to the contract ideology of the wage labor system, while simultaneously recognizing that allodial ownership represented the foundational source of those contractual relations. The historical commitment to allodial property had become a source of ideological tension and ambivalence in Virginia's slaveholding republic.

The case of *Governor for Cockrell v. Williams* (1842) offers a clear example of how the rights of allodial ownership created tensions and confusion over the concept of mastery in the dynamic property relations of a commercial society. Cockrell was an insolvent debtor who, by law, surrendered his possessions to the sheriff for sale and payment to his creditors. Among his possessions was an equity of redemption in some slaves that he had conveyed by deed of trust to a man named Kennedy as a security for a debt owed to W. & J. Lane. The sheriff

[51] Henry Ruffner, *An Address to the People of West Virginia* (1847); for background on Ruffner's role in reform, see Alison Goodyear Freehling, *Drift Toward Dissolution: The Virginia Slavery Debate of 1831–32* (Baton Rouge: Louisiana State University Press, 1982), 229–235.

sold the equity of redemption as part of the schedule of the sale. Cockrell filed an action against the sheriff for "misconduct and malpractice" because he had not first paid off the deed of trust and sold the slaves at auction, exposing "the property to the view of the bidders." Cockrell asserted that the market value of the slaves was "far greater" than the amount for which they had been mortgaged. Accordingly, because the sheriff had not followed the latter course, they "were sold at a price far less than their real value." In delivering the unanimous opinion for the Court, Judge Briscoe Baldwin exonerated the sheriff by noting that he had no legal authority to sell the slaves "inasmuch as he could not transfer to the purchaser the title vested in the trustee." He could only sell the equity in redemption. Furthermore, because the sheriff had "neither the possession nor the right of possession," he did not have the means to bring the slaves to auction. Even if he attempted to auction them, the group of bidders would be knowledgeable in the fact that he could not actually give them possession. It was an easy decision by the Court, but the arrangement reflected some of the complexity and the ambiguity of allodial slave ownership in a commercial society.[52]

Legislators sought to resolve some of this ambiguity during the codification process. The proposal to allow married women to own slaves was designed, in part, to protect both women and slaves from the encroachment of marketplace relations, embodied in the persona of the creditor. Accordingly, it represented an effort to impose by legislative decree the standards of paternalist stewardship on the master-slave relation and then to isolate that relationship outside the laws of the marketplace. In that particular instance the effort failed, but in others areas the construction of a formal jurisprudence grounded in a prescribed legal standard of conduct for those who dealt with slaves achieved some success.

Robinson and Patton had made a significant change by removing the word "mulatto" from the Code. They suggested that any person with "one-fourth of negro blood" or with a "full negro" grandparent should be "deemed a negro" and thereby "render unnecessary the endless repetition" in the statutes. The enrollers revised the clause so that anyone meeting the one-fourth standard would still be considered a mulatto but then allowed that the word "negro" would henceforth be "construed to mean mulatto as well as negro." The introduction of the biological categorization of race – a concept that directed Southern law during the second half of the century – reflected the growing unsuitability of traditional forms of status in an emergent democratic legal order. The reconceptualizaton of rights as something vested in personhood required such new definitions (however inadequate they ultimately proved to be), to articulate the language and convey meaning in this new system of jurisprudence. Certainly much more has been and can be gleaned from the historical construction of race in the law, but for the purposes here, it is important to emphasize that the revisors sought to reduce the multiple descriptions of

[52] *Governor for Cockrell v. Williams*, 12 Leigh 508 (1842).

race to a common term and to provide meaning to that term through biological definition. They did so, in part, because traditional common-law categories for those who only possessed extraordinary rights were incongruous to the matrix of social relations in a democratic republic defined by racial slavery. Black Virginians, whether enslaved or free, could not merely be considered at law as servants, apprentices, denizens, or aliens. Nor could dictums such as *partus sequitur ventrum* prove efficacious in a society of mobile property. Rather, a new category of law needed to be created to determine which persons could be awarded and which persons could be denied rights.[53]

The practices associated with slave hiring also attracted the attention of the enrollers because they not only brought the customs of the marketplace directly into the realm of domestic slavery, but also divorced the practice of mastery from ownership. One section of the Code specifically addressed the laws necessary for "dealing with slaves and suffering them to go at large." Laws preventing the sale of alcohol to slaves and the purchase of goods from slaves without the permission of the master were refined. The traditional penalty levied against a master who permitted "a slave to go at large…or to hire himself out" as though he "were a free man" was extended to encompass any person so culpable, especially those who hired slaves for a term. Similarly, legislators clarified the expectations of those who did not own slaves but held them as "tenants for life." Most notably, they strengthened the restriction prohibiting tenants for life from removing slaves from the state without the consent of those individuals who possessed a remainder or reversion interest in the property, and the law was broadened to include any slaves brought by the wife to a marriage.[54]

Emancipation was another issue that brought the rights of ownership under the scrutiny of the need for formal public policies. Legislators debated the process and the consequences of allowing nonresident slave owners to manumit their slaves in Virginia. Some called for establishing a legal procedure to address the potential challenges posed by such an action, particularly in light of restrictions to manumission being made in other states. Others, however, expressed reservations. John Kilby, a delegate from Nansemond, noted that if such a law were enacted, a slave owner living in Maryland, where it was illegal to manumit slaves, might move his slaves to Virginia for the sole purpose of manumission and effectively "turn them loose on us." Despite admitting to the exceptional nature of the scenario, most legislators agreed and were unwilling to extend the rights of allodial ownership to nonresident slave owners.

53 *Reports of the Revisors*, 542; *Virginia Code (1849)*, 456–459. Barbara J. Fields, "Ideology and Race in American History," in J. Morgan Kousser and James M. McPherson, eds., *Region, Race, and Reconstruction: Essays in Honor of C. Vann Woodward* (New York: Oxford University Press, 1982), 143–177.

54 *Virginia Code (1849)*, 458–460; *Reports of the Revisors*, 542–543; *Richmond Whig*, July 10, 1849. By 1858, the legislature had decreed it a felony, punishable by imprisonment, for someone to remove a slave from the state without the legal consent of all vested parties. See the *Virginia Code (1860)*, 511, note.

Robert Rives wanted to go even farther; he proposed following the examples of Maryland and Georgia and prohibit all private manumissions. In the end, it was decided to leave the law in its current form rather than hastily craft new statutes to address these issues. Laws requiring that adequate provisions be provided for freedmen were made stronger by giving the county overseers of the poor permission to charge the former owner, or his estate, for any freedmen who became dependent on government relief. Furthermore, those persons manumitted were made liable to be incarcerated and hired out if they were not appropriately registered in the county of residence.[55]

Further changes to emancipation laws were made, arising from the revisors' explicit renunciation of the Virginia Supreme Court's 1824 decision in *Maria v. Surbaugh*. As discussed previously, the *Maria* case dealt with the complex matters of slaves emancipated by an owner's will at a future date; in this case, did the children of a woman emancipated in the future become free as well. The Court had ruled that manumission did not represent a transfer of property rights and, accordingly, condemned Maria, the child, to bondage despite her mother's manumission. This harsh opinion stood as the law of the land and was upheld on several occasions for the next twenty-five years until Robinson and Patton addressed the issue in the Code. They noted that even though the decision had been consistently "adhered to," they did not believe that "any court since would have made the same decision." They further suggested that if the policy of emancipation was considered "sound," then consistency required that "children born during the temporary slavery of their mother should become free when she becomes so." Accordingly, they inserted a clause into the Code that prescribed such. The statute was intended to mitigate some of the harshness of slavery as well as inhibit the sale of conditionally manumitted female slaves. Most significantly, however, the reform removed decisive authority from individual slave owners and established an enforceable standard of public policy in its place. The legislature endorsed it without any recorded debate.[56]

Conversely, laws regulating the conveyance of slaves generated sustained discussion during the enrollment process. Of specific concern was a revision inserted by the Joint Committee stipulating that a deed or a will was required to legitimate the conveyance of a gift even among members of the same household. Arguably, such a requirement would better secure the property for subsequent conveyances and would prevent fraud against creditors. Not everyone agreed. George Townes led the dissent, speaking out against this "radical change" to the established rules of evidence that was intended "to disturb our social relations." He called for adherence to "the sound principles of the Common Law," which allowed for the bona fide transfer of possession and which had been recommended by the revisors. Debate over the issue had erupted when Egbert Watson, a delegate from Albemarle, had proposed amending the committee's language

[55] *Richmond Whig*, July 10, 1849; *Virginia Code (1849)*, 465–468.

[56] *Maria and Others v. Surbaugh* (1824) 2 Randolph 228; *Report of the Revisors*, 542–543; *Virginia Code (1849)*, 458–459.

so as to require a written deed only in instances of gifts of slaves. Richard C. L. Moncure of Stafford, chair of the Joint Committee on the Revision, endorsed Watson's amendment. Moncure acknowledged that the rules of the common law were more than adequate in all other cases, but he believed that "propriety" demanded that the conveyance of slaves be subject to the same restrictions as those placed on the transfer of land.[57]

As was the case with the married woman's property amendment, some delegates protested the special treatment given to property in slaves. James Ferguson supported the new rule of evidence but did not understand why it was "not applicable to every species of personal property." Watson responded to him by explaining that gifts in other forms of personal property did not require a "principle of public policy" to protect them. He maintained that other forms of personal property "were rarely the pretext of frauds or the source of litigation." Gifts of slaves, on the other hand, represented the most "fruitful source of legislation," because actual possession within a shared household was "almost impossible to prove," and the sheer value of the gift of a slave was sufficient to prompt litigation.[58]

Watson's amendment, requiring the gifts of slaves to be recorded by deed, was defeated by a floor vote. The eventual language crafted for the section, however, established that practice by stipulating that if the "donor and the donee reside together at the time of the gift," then mere possession at the residence would not be sufficient to confer legal ownership. Gifts of slaves from fathers to sons who reside in the same household would not meet the legal standard of ownership in the absence of a deed. The traditional common-law expressions of bona fide possession – a witnessed public exchange, the paying of taxes, the provision of clothes and food – were nullified by the necessity of the written deed. Virginia required that the actual ownership of slaves be documented.[59]

The changes made to the laws of slavery during the codification process, as well as those reforms that failed, reflected the increasing tension between the social values attached to private ownership and those attached to slavery. Admittedly, the state had exercised its police powers to regulate slavery and manumission before, most notably in the wake of Gabriel Prosser's and Nat Turner slave rebellions. And the courts had consistently recognized such regulations as a legitimate and necessary power of the government. Yet, a fundamental shift in the regulatory focus was manifested during the Special Session. Previous regulations generally prescribed the dictates of lawful behavior for those enslaved or those who had been manumitted; now, the focus of legislation was increasingly directed at the actions of slave owners and possessors. This new focus represented a growing awareness that the paternalistic ideals

[57] *Richmond Whig*, July 10, 1849; *House Journal* (1848–1849), 563; *Report of the Revisors*, 601; See James Irvine's characterization of Moncure's position for the desired legal equivalency between land and personal property.

[58] *Richmond Whig*, July 10, 1849.

[59] *Virginia Code (1849)*, 500.

of mastery being articulated in proslavery apologies needed to be enforced by the system of jurisprudence. If an individual slave owner did not behave in an appropriate manner, than the state needed to intervene and reestablish the paternalist ethos. The evolution to this point had been a long time in coming, but the enrollment of the *1849 Code* signaled that slavery had emerged as the primary focus of Virginia's public policy.[60]

This trend continued during the Reform Convention the following year. There, slavery was legally recognized as a special interest that the state government needed to protect. The diminishment of landed property and the centrality of slavery in the debates over taxation proved most revealing in this respect. With the property qualifications for the franchise already abandoned in favor of personhood suffrage, and the irresolvable question of apportionment basis quelled by an uneasy compromise, the question of taxation loomed large. A consensus existed among the delegates for an *ad valorem* system of taxation, which would determine taxes based on a uniform assessment of all types of property, both real and personal. Similar uniformity clauses had been included in the state constitutions of Maryland, Tennessee, Arkansas, and some other southern states as a means to bind assessments on slaves to real property assessments in order to inhibit the respective legislatures from levying high taxes on slaves. In July, a committee report recommended a provision requiring uniformity and equality in taxing property "in proportion to its value."[61]

Henry Wise promptly proposed an amendment that would tax slaves on a per capita basis, not according to their value, but according to the rate of a poll tax that would be charged on a free white males over the age of twenty-one and under the age of forty-five. Slaves under the age of twelve and over the age of sixty would be exempted from the tax. Wise believed that a uniform tax on persons, more so than uniformity between land and personal property, would better guard against excessive taxation on slaves by a democratically elected legislature. He also submitted a number of property items pertaining to the mechanic arts and fine arts that were to be exempted from the *ad valorem* rate as well. In many respects it appeared as an odd and contradictory proposal; still, it was the one that represented an effort to reconcile a number of factional interests in the state.[62]

[60] Peter W. Bardaglio, *Reconstructing the Household: Families, Sex, and the Law in the Nineteenth-Century South* (Chapel Hill: University of North Carolina Press, 1995) traces this movement from household authority to an authority emanating from a paternalist state in significant detail.

[61] Robin Einhorn, *American Taxation, American Slavery* (Chicago: University of Chicago Press, 2008), 231–234. Maryland had adopted uniform assessment in 1776, whereas other slave states embraced the mechanism significantly later: Missouri in 1820, Tennessee in 1834, Arkansas in 1836, Florida in 1838, and Texas and Louisiana in 1845; Howard, *Commentaries*, 2: 1022–1026.

[62] Craig M. Simpson, *A Good Southerner: The Life of Henry A. Wise of Virginia* (Chapel Hill: University of North Carolina Press, 1985); Barton H. Wise, *The Life of Henry A. Wise of Virginia, 1806–1876* (New York: Macmillan Company, 1899).

Charles Faulkner protested against the idea of a per capita tax, which would assess slaves on the basis of their personhood instead of on their value as property. The one-time emancipationist now defended the historical consideration of slaves as property for the purposes of taxation. He invoked the "universally recognized" principle that "the revenue to meet the expenses of government must come from PROPERTY." And he posited that the only "sound and just" rule of taxation stipulated that "every citizen should contribute to the support of the government in proportion to the property which he enjoys under the protection of the state." Faulkner offered an amendment that called for an *ad valorem* property tax on all property except for those slaves under twelve years of age. His amendment also empowered the legislature to except other forms of property in the future. At first glance, it would appear that Faulkner's comments were incongruous with his emancipationist position during the 1832 slavery debate. Yet, his positivist ideas about the origin and nature of property rights remained prevalent. Faulkner did not characterize property as something pre-political, which men brought with them from a state of nature; rather, he argued that property should serve as the basis of taxation because it acquired "all of its value from the security which the power of government gives to it." Property would not exist in the absence of government; instead, he contended, the "rights of property would be a senseless and unmeaning jargon." In the two decades since the slavery debate, Faulkner's understanding of property had changed far less than the way in which it was basically understood throughout Virginia.[63]

Both positions, those of Faulkner and of Wise, reflected the substantial ideological changes that had occurred in Virginia and that were being made manifest in the processes of law and constitutional reform. The common-law characterization of land as a distinct form of property was discarded by an *ad valorem* system of taxation dedicated to uniformity in property. Indeed, hardly a murmur of dissent was made to defend the historical position of real estate. Instead, the most significant debate occurred over whether to base the tax exemption for slaves on their status as persons or property. In the end, a revised version of Henry Wise's proposal prevailed. A general system of *ad valorem* taxation was adopted, which provided for a uniform assessment on land and livestock but created an exception on slave property. Slave owners were guaranteed protection from any future tax increases by exempting slaves under twelve from taxation and by limiting the amount of the slave tax to a maximum rate of $300 per capita, irrespective of changes in market value. A poll tax was implemented on free white males, with half of the proceeds dedicated to the support of public schools – a cause particularly identified with the interest of western Virginians.[64]

[63] *Speech of C.J. Faulkner on the Subject of Taxation, July 7 and 8, 1851*, 5–6, Faulkner Family Papers, *VHS*.

[64] *Richmond Enquirer*, July 22, 1851 (Supplement); Link, *Roots of Secession*, 25; Green, *Constitutional Development*, 295.

Beyond, the subject of taxation, the relationship between slave owners and the legislature fundamentally changed with the adoption of the Reform Constitution. The document included a clause granting to the legislature the power to "impose such restrictions and conditions as they shall deem proper on the power of slave owners to emancipate their slaves."[65] Immediately, this legislative power was restricted to prohibit the General Assembly from emancipating slaves itself. Nonetheless, with this important qualification written into the fundamental law, the people of Virginia removed considerable authority from the individual slave owner and placed it in the hands of their elected representatives. Increasingly, the circumstances of the master-slave relation were situated within the realm of the public good and, accordingly, slavery was deemed a constitutional issue. Slavery was too important to be trusted to the responsibility of the individual slaveholder.

The ratification of the 1851 Constitution completed Virginia's legal and political reformation. This reformation had been decades in the making. As early as 1813, Thomas Jefferson had abandoned his commitment to allodial land tenure as the basis for republican self-government and called for reform. Substantial changes to republican citizenship had been initiated by the 1830 Constitution with the abandonment of the freehold qualification for the franchise. In the process, the traditional common-law conception of real property was redefined and the political attributes historically associated with landed status were marginalized by its inability to provide the essential stability in a society where land was transacted commercially. Ownership of a freehold became conflated with other forms of property ownership. Simultaneously, in Virginia, as elsewhere in the industrializing world, labor emerged as a species of property that, owing to its economic power, could make claims for possessing certain political characteristics of its own. In Virginia, however, slave labor remained the dominant form of labor in terms of productivity and any political characteristics assigned to it were attached to the owners of slaves. In the wake of the 1832 slavery debate, Thomas Roderick Dew reconciled the political attributes now associated with slavery with a republican political ideology grounded in allodial ownership. During the next decade, the increasing commercialization of the culture and the growing acceptance of the antislavery position in national politics furthered the appeal of Dew's republican model and fostered the tendency to identify slave ownership as a special property relation – the source of true individual liberty. Still, slavery fit uncomfortably within the common law, especially as a privileged form of property. By the 1840s, many reasons existed for reform but the most compelling was the need to create a new system of jurisprudence that could make real property transactions conform to the standard procedures and conditions of the personal property contract exchanges, and, simultaneously, establish slavery as an exceptional form of property. The

[65] *Code of Virginia* (2nd edition, 1860), 46. Kentucky had included a similar clause in its constitution as early as 1792.

codification project and the Reform Constitution represented the legal and political process of bringing the form of law, the juridical structure, and the constitution in line with the practices and principles of a slave state.

Democracy thus came to the Old Dominion, but it was a peculiar form of democracy, grounded as it was on the paradoxical foundations of personhood citizenship and the sanctified ownership of some persons by others. Slavery required legal sanctification because the economic value it provided to the state was precious, but also because the master-slave relationship was considered a repository of republican virtue and social stability in a world increasingly characterized by the self-interest of market relations. Yet, even in the midst of Virginia's reformation, some more astute commentators were expressing serious doubts about attaching any political value to any form of allodial ownership. They recognized that the individual rights extended by allodial ownership, far from providing a foundation for social stability, represented the principal source of social corruption. Individual ownership, whether in land or slaves, created an unsuitable base on which to build a stable political structure because, in the end, it was dependent on the capacity of private owners to transcend human frailty. Steeped in the Christian doctrine of original sin, and finding themselves in a world where the power of the market exchange was ubiquitous, commentators of a more conservative ilk reevaluated the Jeffersonian theory of allodial ownership and found it wanting. Accordingly, these conservative Virginians not only joined in the growing southern critique of the atomistic tendencies of the capitalist marketplace and democratic politics, but they formed the vanguard of rejecting the idea of private ownership as well.

Conclusion

The Reaction against Allodial Ownership

Simeon Souther owned his slave, Sam. As an allodial property owner, the law entitled Souther to punish Sam or any of his slaves with relative impunity. On the morning of September 1, 1849, Souther decided to exercise this right in order to reprimand Sam for getting drunk. Accordingly, Souther administered a "slight whipping" to Sam with switches from either an apple or a peach tree until a number witnesses, including some of Souther's other slaves and two white neighbors, could assemble. At that point, Souther tied Sam to a tree with ropes around his "wrists, neck, body, legs, and ankles" and continued to whip him with switches. After a time, Souther exchanged the switch for a shingle and cobbed his slave until he grew too tired to continue. He commanded two other slaves to continue the cobbing and, once he had recovered from his initial exertions, began to hit and kick Sam's face and body. Fatiguing himself yet again, Souther arrested the beating and, instead, applied fire to Sam's "back, sides, belly, groins, and privy parts." To "relieve" the burns, Souther and the two assisting slaves washed Sam with a warm-water solution containing steeped red-pepper pods that were designed to exacerbate the burning sensation. After a few more hours, Souther untied Sam, threw him to the ground and began to stamp on his head and temples. Still under the impression that Sam had merely feigned suffering during the beating, Souther had him carried to a nearby shed. There, Sam's feet were secured to a large piece of timber while a noose was put around his neck and tied to a bed post. The position caused him to experience a persistent sense of strangling and choking. Souther then resumed his beating and compelled two of his slaves to continue to apply fire to parts of Sam's body. At some point during the evening, Sam died.[1]

Simeon Souther was indicted for the murder of Sam by the Hanover County Circuit Court a year later. The indictment was delivered irrespective of legal precedent and a general understanding that afforded slave owners a free hand in meting punishment to their human property. Seven months later, in April 1851, a jury of Simon Souther's peers found him guilty of fifteen criminal counts,

[1] *Souther v. Commonwealth*, 7 Grattan 679–680 (1851).

including the "cruel and excessive whipping and torture" of a slave. They convicted him of murder and sentenced him to five years in prison. Souther appealed the verdict on the grounds that Sam was his personal property. He contended that Sam's death occurred inadvertently during the course of his lawful right to punish his slaves and, accordingly, by the precepts of the common law, he could only be charged with manslaughter. He also challenged the ruling on procedural grounds with the hopes of having the verdict thrown out on a legal technicality. The General Court heard his appeal during its penultimate term, in June 1851, and unanimously upheld the verdict and the sentence of the circuit court. In delivering the opinion, Judge Richard Field remarked on the case by noting that he believed "that the records of criminal jurisprudence [did] not contain a case of more atrocious and wicked cruelty." He acknowledged, however, that in principle, the law respected the authority of the owner over the slave and protected "the master from prosecution," even in cases of malicious punishment. Still, Field explained that because Sam had died from the punishment, "the principles of the common law in relation to homicide apply...without qualification or exception." The General Court decreed that the peculiar relation between a master and his slave afforded "no ground of excuse or palliation."[2]

It is tempting to dismiss the ruling by the General Court in *Souther* as exceptional because of the extent of the atrocities. Certainly, historians of the laws of slavery have noted the efforts of the southern courts to balance the conflict of humanity and interest in cases concerning slaves and have documented the considerable ambiguity that existed over the question of the homicide of slaves.[3] The ruling in *Souther* certainly confirms these interpretations, but it also reveals the full consequences of the reorientation of property law in Virginia and the growing public anxiety about the social consequences arising from the rights conveyed by allodial ownership. Significantly in this regard, the conviction of Simeon Souther overturned the General Court's prior ruling in the case of *Commonwealth v. Richard Turner* (1827), which had held that a master could not be indicted for the "malicious, cruel, and excessive beating of his own slave." Although the circumstances of the two cases were very similar, the majority of the court had refused to impinge on the rights of ownership in the *Turner* case. In issuing the majority opinion, Judge William Dade acknowledged that the colonial statute protecting masters from prosecution had been repealed during the postcolonial revisions, but he believed

[2] *Souther v. Commonwealth*, 7 Grattan 679–680 (1851).

[3] Mark Tushnet, *The American Law of Slavery, 1810–1860: Considerations of Humanity and Interest* (Princeton, NJ: Princeton University Press, 1981); Thomas D. Morris, *Southern Slavery and the Law, 1619–1860* (Chapel Hill: University of North Carolina Press, 1996), esp. 161–181; William E. Wiethoff, *A Peculiar Humanism: The Judicial Advocacy of Slavery in High Courts of the Old South, 1820–1850* (Athens: University of Georgia Press, 1996); and Judith Kelleher Schafer, "'Details are of a Most Revolting Character': Cruelty to Slaves as Seen in Appeals to the Supreme Court of Louisiana," in Paul Finkelman, ed., *Slavery & the Law* (Madison, WI: Madison House, 1997): 241–268.

that any determination of such a significant social question as was posed in *Turner* was the exclusive purview of the legislature. Yet, the legislature never tackled the question of legal impunity for slave owners – not even as part of the codification project. Judge Field's opinion in *Souther*, then, represented a new willingness to engage the subject of slave ownership from a perspective that, two decades earlier, had been considered beyond reproach.[4]

The General Court's ruling in *Souther* represented only one manifestation of the critique of allodial ownership. Increasingly, over the course of the decade leading up to secession, conservative Virginians challenged the liberal theory of individual property that had been born of Jefferson's allodial scheme. This critique emerged in different guises and at various instances, which were neither coordinated nor systematic, during the decade leading up to secession. Nevertheless some consistent themes prevailed. Foremost among them was the unsuitability of ownership, as it was then configured, to serve as an effective foundation for social relations. Virginians recognized that the dynamic transfer of property, made possible by its allodial characteristics, created too much fluidity and uncertainty for any meaningful measure of social or political value. Correspondingly, the competence of property owners was also brought into question. Whether revealed in the form of Simon Souther's cruelty or in one of the abundant examples of farmers living in squalor and debt, the essential capacity of individuals to govern themselves in day-to-day matters was considered an idyllic fantasy by a growing number of conservative Virginians, who called into question the social and political consequences of the ownership ideal. Occurring in the immediate context of the sectional crisis over slavery in the territories, this critique often focused its attention northward and portrayed its industrial capitalist society as a consequence of individual ownership run amuck.

The writings of George Fitzhugh stand as the most prominent example of this critique. His writings have been well documented and need little elaboration here except to emphasize his disdain for agrarianism and his proposal to reintroduce primogeniture and entail. Indeed, his plan for agricultural reform appeared distinctly *contra* Jefferson. Fitzhugh lamented the overreliance on agriculture in Virginia and called for a more diversified economy centered on communal and regional markets. Indeed, he anguished about the consequences of improved transportation networks on the sustainability of regional markets, which, he contended, would be unable to compete against the abundant and cheap commercial goods of the Atlantic trade. Fitzhugh blamed an "excess of trade," which he attributed directly to the lack of "fixedness and permanency of property," as the fundamental cause "of the frequent panics and revulsions" that afflicted "modern society." He maintained that irrespective of the form of

[4] *Commonwealth v. Richard Turner*, 5 Randolph 678 (1827). *SAL*, 12: 681; this statute repealed the 1669 law granting masters impunity. William Brockenbrough offered the lone dissent in Turner and grounded his opinion in the common-law strictures about homicide and manslaughter between master and servant.

government, in places where property was "not fixed, settled, or entailed," frequent "reverses of fortunes and many bankruptcies" resulted. He suggested that "trading would cease if there were nothing to trade for," and he sought to limit the sphere of commercial activity by entailing "lands and horse, and slaves, and all fixed capital" in order to remove it from "the reach of speculation." He contended that the revival of entail would "not only render the owners secure in their possessions," but would create substantial employment opportunities for the mass of "dependants, laborers, and tenants." Fitzhugh did not reject the idea of ownership outright but sought to remove the nefarious influences of trade and laissez-faire economic doctrines that subverted its stability. Accordingly, he appealed to the necessity of government to regulate the anarchical tendencies of capitalism, which, cloaked in the banner of liberty, were subverting the very essence of property. Property needed to be secured from the marketplace. This effort to restore property into a tangible and governmentally regulated entity stood at the heart of Fitzhugh's social philosophy. In this manner, his criticism of allodial ownership and call for the restoration of property anticipated the subsequent arguments advanced by Hilaire Belloc, G. K. Chesterton and the Distributist League of twentieth-century Britain. Closer to home, Fitzhugh's emphasis on the corrosive tendencies of capitalism on traditional household relations foreshadowed the social commentaries of the Southern Agrarians in their 1930 essays, *I'll Take My Stand.*[5]

Yet Fitzhugh was not simply a man ahead of (or behind) his times. Others, too, joined in repudiating the consequences of allodial ownership. George Frederick Holmes, in his damning review of Harriet Beecher Stowe's *Uncle Tom's Cabin*, criticized her social vision of individual freedom and equality as utopian and her advocacy of it as nefarious to government and the social order. He acknowledged the reality of the miseries and brutalities depicted by Stowe, but, Holmes maintained, these atrocities were not unique to slavery. Rather, they were acts of "constant recurrence" not attributable to any particular social institution but to the "innate frailties of humanity…the native wickedness of…individuals, and the inability of human wisdom of legislation to repress crime without incidentally ministering to occasional vices." Albert Taylor Bledsoe, Holmes's colleague on the faculty at the University of Virginia,

[5] George Fitzhugh, "Entails and Primogeniture," *De Bow's Review* (August 1859): 172–178. See his indictment of Adam Smith as a "dunce and a charlatan" in "Reaction and the Administration," *De Bow's Review* (October 1858): 414–416. Fitzhugh's ideas were articulated in numerous articles and essays in addition to his two principle works: *A Sociology for the South* (1854) and *Cannibals All!* (1857). On Fitzhugh's worldview see, Eugene Genovese, *The World the Slaveholders Made: Two Essays in Interpretation* (Wesleyan edition, Hanover, NH: Wesleyan University Press, 1988), and C. Vann Woodward, "George Fitzhugh, *Sui Generis*," published as an introduction to the Harvard republication of Fitzhugh, *Cannibals All!* (Cambridge, MA: Belknap Press, 1960). The Distributist argument is articulated in Hilaire Belloc, *An Essay on the Restoration of Property* (London: 1936; republished by IHS Press, 2002). Twelve Southerners, *I'll Take My Stand: The South and the Agrarian Tradition*, with an introduction by Louis D. Rubin, Jr., and biographical essays by Virginia Rock (Baton Rouge: Louisiana State University Press, 1977).

also offered a qualified view of ownership in his concurrent proslavery treatise, *An Essay on Liberty and Slavery*. Bledsoe too took issue with the abolitionists' characterization of the master-slave relation, most notably the idea that slaves were "divested" of their "human character." He dismissed the charge as hyperbole and appealed to the laws of the southern states as evidence that recognized and adjudicated "the rights of the slaves...as well as those of the masters."[6]

More directly, Jefferson's allodial ideal was accused of subverting the practice of agriculture itself. In October 1858, Congressman Charles Faulkner delivered a speech at an agricultural fair in his home district in the Shenandoah Valley. The speech was more than a political grandstanding event. In it, he offered a detailed analysis of the declining productivity of the Valley's agricultural sector and laid out his vision for renewal. Lacking much in the way of personal experience as a farmer, he confined most of his analysis to the structural and legal impediments that he saw stymieing the Valley's agricultural practices. In so doing, Faulkner too articulated a new vision of the agrarian ideal, one far removed from the Jeffersonian vision of allodial freeholders.[7]

His comments focused on the agricultural declension caused by the vast quantity of Valley lands owned by absentee owners and possessed by short-term tenants who had no permanent interest in the land. He approached the problem from an economic perspective, noting that "if the sole object of the farmer...was to raise bread and meat enough to keep...his family from starving," then he conceded that the "present system and the present yield" were sufficient. He believed, however, that "the object of the farmer should be, higher, nobler, and more consonant to the dignity of his occupation." Faulkner conceived the farmer's relation to the land as a means "of accumulating wealth, of imparting a liberal education to your children, and of surrounding your homesteads with all the comforts, enjoyments, and elegancies of life." Yet this ideal was not being realized in the Valley. He dismissed excuses that attributed declining productivity to the natural process of soil exhaustion and explained that there was "no natural tendency in the soil to deterioration. On the contrary, he maintained, the land exhibited "a continued tendency, through the action of the atmosphere, rain, and sun, to recover its exhausted fertility." Instead, Faulkner laid the blame on the people themselves. He suggested that they had proven themselves incapable to be effective stewards of this valuable resource. He noted that owner and tenant alike exhibited their strong "desire to produce for and profit from the marketplace," but they consistently proved unwilling "to adequately re-invest those profits back into the land."[8]

Faulkner believed that the secret to sustainable agriculture in the Shenandoah Valley lay in the methods of agricultural reclamation and improvement that

[6] George Frederick Holmes, "Uncle Tom's Cabin," *SLM* (December 1852): 721–731. Albert Taylor Bledsoe, *An Essay on Liberty and Slavery* (Philadelphia: J. P. Lippincott, 1856), 97–102.

[7] Charles Faulkner, *Address Delivered by Hon. Charles J, Faulkner, Before the Valley Agricultural Society of Virginia* (Washington, 1858).

[8] Faulkner, *Address*, 5, 16, 10.

had been adopted as part of the enclosure movement in England. He contended that it could "be very safely asserted that no people, now living, or whoever did live, [had] brought so much intelligence, enterprise, capital, and labor, to secure the highest possible production from the soil" as did the people of England. Citing the 1853 agricultural census, he noted that less than a century before, the "entire production of wheat in England fell short of sixteen million bushels," but now, national production topped 90 million bushels. That equated to an average of thirty bushels per acre cultivated. In contrast, the entire territorial extent of Virginia had produced only 11 million bushels in 1849. He ascribed this grave disparity to four principle causes: the English work ethic, which is "found in their systematic attention to all the requirements of good farming"; the "extraordinary liberality" with which they invest in the best fertilizers to restore their soil; their advanced system of drainage, which had profited from substantial governmental subsidies; and lastly, their advanced system of alternate rotation between "white and green crops," especially their cultivation of the turnip as a restorative root.[9]

He concluded by summarizing what he considered were, in addition to the absence of crop rotation, the three "principal obstacles to the successful cultivation of the lands of this valley." First, he blamed the temptation of western migration and the lure of "greener pastures" that encouraged farmers to migrate rather than improve their lands. He lamented the propensity of those who, "at a moment's warning" would "abandon the scenes of the birth and boyhood, and sell their lands whenever a fair price is offered for them. He explained that, consequently, farmers adopted agricultural practices dedicated "to a temporary occupation of the land and to the realization of immediate profits" over the more favorable orientation toward "a permanent investment of capital and labor for the benefit of themselves and their children." Second, Faulkner criticized the large size of the farms in the Valley. He acknowledged that a large farm could be profitably cultivated where "labor was cheap and capital abundant," as was the case in the tenant-labor farms of England and Scotland, but this model did not work in the Valley where "capital is so deficient and agricultural labor so high." Yet Faulkner also identified the widespread existence of tenants on "short and illiberal leases" as the third of the obstacles to agricultural improvement. He referred to a recent map made of Berkeley County that marked those tenements occupied by proprietors and those occupied by tenants. He admitted his surprise at the amount of land under lease, noting that in the most fertile and choicest portion of the county – the area between the Potomac River and the Baltimore and Ohio Railroad – more than one-third of the land was "under lease and in the hands of tenants." He suggested that this percentage was generally indicative of the Valley as a whole.[10]

Faulkner acknowledged that "almost the whole of the arable land in England" was held by tenant farmers and he affirmed the maxim, confirmed by

[9] Faulkner, *Address*, 10–11, 14–17.

[10] Faulkner, *Address*, 18.

the experience in England, which maintained that "a larger produce is obtained when it is occupied by a tenant than when it is cultivated by its proprietor." But, he continued, to accomplish such a result, land owners "must secure to the tenant a more permanent interest in the land than is usual in our present leases...of two, three, or even five years." He believed that no tenant could, on such a short lease, "feel any inducement to commence a system of improvement which can only look to the future for the fruits of well-directed labor." He proposed, therefore, implementing a practice of extended leases that would attach tenants to a specific spot of land and vest them with the motivation to improve on it. And he hinted that if such extended leases could not be accomplished through custom and practice, then Virginia should pursue it as a matter of public policy and enact laws requiring long leases. Accordingly, he advocated a policy of reform that would create a perpetual class of tenants who would be vested in the soil even if they did not actually own it.[11]

Faulkner's proposals, like those of George Fitzhugh, Holmes, and Bledsoe reflected just how much the commitment to allodial ownership and self-government had waned. The individual independence once promised by allodial ownership was no longer considered as a given. Accordingly, the wealth-creating ability of anyone – tenant or proprietor – who was permanently attached to the soil replaced the ownership imperative in significance. Indeed, for Faulkner, it had been the failure of individual owners to act responsibly that had created the deterioration of agriculture in the Valley. Undoubtedly, his call for reform was facilitated by the legal and political reformation that had divorced political rights from land ownership and vested them in individual personhood. In such a democratic political structure, it mattered little whether or not a man was a tenant or an owner of the land. What mattered was creating a permanent attachment to a particular piece of land, which, having been liberated of its traditional political attributes, could now be reconstructed on a purely economic basis.

Abandoning the commitment to the ownership ideal reflected the recognition that it did not necessarily foster the desirable qualities of self-reliance and individual responsibility. Collective recognition of this failure was manifested in the overwhelming rejection of the initial Homestead Bill by Virginia's congressional delegation. In December 1851, Tennessee Congressman Andrew Johnson introduced the bill out of committee that would grant "to any man who is the head of a family and a citizen of the United States, a homestead of one hundred and sixty acres of land out of the public domain, upon the condition of occupancy and cultivation of the same" for a specified period. The Virginia delegation set aside party and sectional differences to staunchly oppose the bill; out of fifteen delegates, only one spoke in favor of it and his support was qualified by amendments. Most of the arguments against it concerned the constitutionality of the provision, yet an underlying disbelief that the scheme

[11] Faulkner, *Address*, 18. See, as well, *Address on the Land Policy of the United States* (Washington, 1857).

would actually "encourage agriculture, manufacture, and commerce" infected the opposition arguments. Southside Congressman Thomas Averett proved the most vociferous opponent. He criticized the bill as a government charity program and saw no reason to believe that by giving the poor access to land it would somehow make them good farmers or good citizens.[12]

Throughout the decade of the 1850s, then, many Virginians sought alternate intellectual traditions on which to restore the stability of property. Some, like the Reverend Thomas Vernon Moore, looked to the Old Testament and the customs of Israelites as the fundamental basis of Christian society. In delivering a eulogy for Richmond attorney Richard Flournoy, Moore praised his life as a model of a Christian lawyer. He noted that Flournoy's life-well-lived disproved the popular belief that it was impossible for someone to be a good Christian and be engaged in the practice of the law. Quite to the contrary, he contended that the law did not repudiate Christian principles but manifested them. From this perspective, he sought to make a claim for Christianity on the legal profession and did so by emphasizing the steady influence of Mosaic laws on the English common law and, by extension, on the laws of Virginia. Notably, Moore identified the origins of the trial by jury and the law of inheritance, including primogeniture and entail, as originating in Hebraic practices.[13] George Fitzhugh, too, had looked to the Mosaic laws in portraying the practice of entail as a "system ordained by God." He praised the practice of "Jubilee" years that restored lands "in the hands of the descendants of the original proprietors." Fitzhugh believed that society was longing to return to these fundamental institutions. He noted that in the South, the practices of entailing slaves had already been largely reconstructed by laws "exempting part of them from execution for debt," and that this policy proved very popular among slaveholders. Rejecting the characterization of his proposals as reforms, he professed that "we propose nothing new, but only to return to institutions ordained by God, and tested and approved by human experience."[14]

Even more explicit in the rejection of allodial ownership, however, were the professions of those who sought to reconstruct elements of feudal law on Virginia's landscape. Fitzhugh drew from these sources, as did others. One of the more significant commentaries, however, emerged from the writings of Henry Augustine Washington. Washington was the son-in-law of Nathanial Beverley Tucker and had assumed Thomas Roderick Dew's faculty chair as the professor of History, Political Economy, and International Law at the

[12] *Congressional Globe*, House of Representatives, 32nd Congress, 1st Session, April 1, 1852 (Washington, 1852), 1018–1021. Jonathan H. Earle, *Jacksonian Antislavery and the Politics of Free Soil, 1824–1854* (Chapel Hill: University of North Carolina Press, 2004); Henry Nash Smith, *Virgin Land: The American West as Symbol and Myth* (Cambridge, MA: Harvard University Press, 1950).

[13] Thomas Vernon Moore, *The Christian Lawyer, or the Claims of Christianity on the Legal Profession: A Discourse Delivered at the Funeral of Richard W. Flournoy, Esq., in the First Presbyterian Church* (Richmond, 1857).

[14] George Fitzhugh, "Entails and Primogeniture," *DeBow's Review* (August 1859): 172–178.

College of William & Mary. In 1848, Washington achieved recognition for his historical essay, "The Social System of Virginia," which was published in the *Southern Literary Messenger* and which offered a sociological explanation for the significant contributions made by Virginia's colonial "landed aristocracy" on the American Founding. Michael O'Brien has analyzed Washington's original contributions and identified this essay as a seminal contribution to the development of the "Cavalier Myth" that pervaded southern letters well into the twentieth century. By 1852, Washington was also engaged in preparing a nine-volume edited collection of Jefferson's papers, which represented the first comprehensive effort to catalog these writings. His editorial efforts fostered an element of disdain for Jefferson's political viewpoints.[15]

Telling in this respect was the lecture Washington delivered to the Virginia Historical Society in January 1852, addressing the ideological origin of the state's 1776 Constitution. He emphasized the novelty of the Virginia Constitution as the "first written social compact ever reduced to practice, and made the foundation of an actual government," and, therefore, an epoch-making event "in the progress of human liberty." He acknowledged George Mason's role in the drafting but refused to credit the document to the ideas of any one man or even reflecting a commitment to a particular political theory. Instead, he characterized its design as an articulation of "the ancient and immemorial rights, franchises, and privileges" that Virginia's colonists had inherited "from England." Washington attached significance to the document as the fundamental instrument in "drawing a line between the powers of the government and the rights of the governed," which he believed was the distinguishing historical feature that allowed for human freedom to exist. He contrasted these circumscribed and limited powers with the tyranny of unregulated dominion, whether it appeared in the political forms of monarchy, aristocracy, or democracy. Like his fellow conservatives, Washington appealed to the necessity of government and emphasized the importance of it being both organic and circumscribed. He traced the recognition of such limited government to the Magna Carta, which he applauded as a glorious achievement. But he emphasized the organic quality of the charter as well, contending that it did not create a new system of government but simply declared and articulated "the immemorial common law of feuds." It was the feudal relation, grounded in the reciprocity of tenure, to which Washington attributed the origins of limited government. Accordingly, he asserted that the essential foundation of Virginia's democratic liberties had been "transmitted from the bosom of a proud and haughty [feudal] aristocracy."

[15] H. A. Washington, "The Social System of Virginia," *SLM*, 14 (1848): 65–81. Michael O'Brien, ed., *All Clever Men, Who Make Their Way: Critical Discourse in the Old South* (Athens: University of Georgia Press, 1992), 228–262 and *Conjectures of Order: Intellectual Life and the American South, 1810–1860* (Chapel Hill: University of North Carolina Press, 2004) 1: 315–319; Elizabeth Fox-Genovese and Eugene D. Genovese, *The Mind of the Master Class: History and Faith in the Southern Slaveholders' Worldview* (Cambridge: Cambridge University Press, 2005). H. A. Washington, ed., *The Writings of Thomas Jefferson*, 9 vols. (Washington, 1853–1854).

Without making any direct reference to Thomas Jefferson, he acknowledged that, "in our times," he and his fellow Virginians routinely heard praises "of the free spirit of the Saxon laws," and admitted that there was "much justice in these eulogies." For Henry Washington, however, it was an "indisputable fact" that all the constitutional "limitations and restrictions" that impaired the "the omnipotence of...governments" and provided for the basis of human freedom were "of *Norman* descent."[16]

[16] H. A. Washington, *The Virginia Constitution of 1776: A Discourse Delivered before the Virginia Historical Society at their Annual Meeting, January 17, 1852* (Richmond, 1852).

Bibliography of Primary Sources

Manuscript Collections

Alderman Library, University of Virginia, Charlottesville
Aylett Family Papers
  Barbour Family Papers
  Bouldin Family Papers
  Bryan, Elizabeth Coalter (Diary)
  Cabell Family Papers
  Cooke, John Rogers (Diary)
  Daniel Family Papers
  Faulkner Family Papers
  Grinnan Family Papers
  Massie Family Papers
  Montague, Thomas B. Notebook
  Preston Family Papers
  Rives Family Papers
  Ruffin, Thomas (Diary)
Cocke Family Papers
Edgehill-Randolph Family Papers
  McDowell, James Papers
  Stuart, Archibald and Briscoe G. Baldwin
Library of Congress, Washington, DC
  Thomas Jefferson Papers
Library of Virginia, Richmond
  Floyd, John B. Executive Papers
  Floyd, John B. Executive Letter Box
  Leigh, William Papers
  Legislative Petitions, 1831–1832
  Tazewell Family Papers
Virginia Historical Society, Richmond
  Allen Family Papers

Published Manuscript Papers

The Letter and Papers of Edmund Pendleton, 1734–1803. 2 volumes. Edited by David John Mays, Charlottesville: University Press of Virginia for the Virginia Historical Society, 1967.

The Official Papers of Francis Fauquier, Lieutenant Governor of Virginia, 1758–1768. 3 volumes. Edited by George Reese, Charlottesville: University Press of Virginia for the Virginia Historical Society, 1981.

The Papers of George Mason, 1725–1792. 3 volumes. Edited by Robert A. Rutland, Chapel Hill: University of North Carolina Press for the Omohundro Institute of Early American History and Culture, 1970.

The Papers of George Washington, Colonial Series. 10 volumes. Edited by W. W. Abbot, et al, Charlottesville: University of Virginia, 1983–1995.

The Papers of Thomas Jefferson. 36 volumes. Edited by Julian Boyd, et al., Princeton, NJ: Princeton University Press, 1950–2009.

The Writings of James Madison. 9 volumes. Edited by Gaillard Hunt. New York: G. P. Putnam's Sons, 1900–1910.

The Writings of Thomas Jefferson. 9 volumes. Edited by Henry A. Washington. Washington: 1853–1854.

The Writings of Thomas Jefferson. 10 volumes. Edited by Paul Leicester Ford. New York: G. P. Putnam and Sons, 1892–1899.

The Writings of Thomas Jefferson. 20 volumes. Edited by Andrew A. Lipscomb. Washington, DC: 1903–1907.

Virginia Court Cases Cited

Ambler v. Norton, 2 Hening and Munford 23 (1809)
Bass v. Scott, 2 Leigh 356 (1834)
Burnsides v. Reid, 2 Washington 43 (1794)
Cadwallader v. Mason, Wythe 188 (1793)
Clayborn v. Hill, 1 Washington 177 (1793)
Commonwealth v. Burcher, 2 Robinson 826 (1843)
Commonwealth v. Carter, 2 Virginia Cases 319 (1822)
Commonwealth v. Cherry, 2 Virginia Cases 20 (1815)
Commonwealth v. Long, 2 Virginia Cases 318 (1822)
Commonwealth v. Reynolds, 4 Leigh 663 (1833)
Commonwealth v. Turner, 5 Randolph 678 (1827)
Commonwealth v. Willson, 2 Leigh 739 (1830)
Crenshaw and Crenshaw v. Slate River Company, 6 Randolph 245 (1828)
Ford v. Gardner, 1 Hening & Munford, 72 (1806)
French v. Successors of Loyal Company, 5 Leigh 627 (1834)
Godwin v. Lunan, Jefferson 96 (1771)
Governor for Cockrell v. Williams, 12 Leigh 508 (1842)
Hamilton v. Maze, 4 Call 196 (1791)
Hite v. Fairfax, 4 Call 42 (1786)
Kerby v. Commonwealth, 7 Leigh 749 (1836)
The Case of the Loyal and Greenbrier Companies, 4 Call 21 (1783)
Maria and Others v. Surbaugh, 2 Randolph 228 (1824)
McCargo v. Callicott, 2 Munford 501 (1811)
Maze v. Hamilton, 4 Call 33 (1782)

Maze v. Hamilton, 2 Wythe 51 (1789)
Moran v. Commonwealth, 9 Leigh 651 (1839)
Paul v. Paul, 2 Hening & Munford, 525 (1808)
Ross v. Keewood, 2 Munford 141 (1811)
Stout v. Jackson, 2 Randolph 132 (1823)
Souther v. Commonwealth, 7 Grattan 679 (1851)
Threlkeld v. Fitzhugh, 2 Leigh 451 (1830)
Tod v. Baylor, 4 Leigh 498 (1833)
Turpin v. Locket, 6 Call 113 (1804)
Wilson v. Davisson, 2 Robinson 398 (1843)
Wiseley v. Findlay, 3 Randolph 361 (1825)

Published Codes and Statutes

Hening, William Waller, ed. *The Statutes at Large; Being a Collection of all the Laws of Virginia, 1619–1792*. 13 volumes. Richmond, 1823.
The Code of Virginia. Richmond: William F. Ritchie, 1849.
The Code of Virginia. 2nd edition. G. W. Munford, comp. Richmond: Ritchie, Dunnavant & Co., 1860.
The Code of Virginia. 3rd edition. G. W. Munford, comp. Richmond: James E. Goode, 1873.
The Revised Code of the Laws of Virginia: Being a Collection of all such Acts of the General Assembly being of a Public and Permanent Nature, as are now in force. 2 volumes. B. W. Leigh, comp. Richmond: T. Ritchie, 1819.
Supplement to the Revised Code of the Laws of Virginia: Being a Collection of all the Acts of the General Assembly being of a Public and Permanent Nature, Passed since 1819. Richmond: S. Shepherd, 1833.
Wythe, George W., ed. *The Revised Code of 1792*. Richmond, 1794.

Other Government Documents

Congressional Globe. House of Representatives, 32nd Congress. Washington, DC, 1852–1853.
Documents Containing Statistics of Virginia Ordered to be Printed by the State Convention Sitting in the City of Richmond, 1850–51. Richmond, 1851.
Journals of the House of Delegates of the Commonwealth of Virginia. Richmond, Annually. *Journals of the Senate of the Commonwealth of Virginia*. Richmond, Annually. *Proceedings and Debates of the Virginia State Convention, 1829–1830*. Richmond, 1830.
Register of the Debates and Proceedings of the Virginia Reform Convention. Richmond, 1851.
The General Assembly of Virginia, 1619–1978: A Bicentennial Register of Members. Cynthia Miller Leonard, comp. Richmond: Virginia State Library published for the General Assembly of Virginia, 1978.

Journals and Newspapers

American Jurist
De Bow's Review
Fredericksburg News

Lynchburg Virginian
National Law Intelligencer
Quarterly Law Journal
Richmond Enquirer
Richmond Whig
Southern Literary Messenger
Southern Planter

Published Sources

Allmendinger, Jr., David F., ed. *Incidents of My Life: Edmund Ruffin's Autobiographical Essays*. Charlottesville: University Press of Virginia, 1990.

Ambler, Charles, ed. *The Life and Diary of John Floyd*. Richmond: Richmond Press, 1918.

Appleby, Joyce and Terence Ball, eds. *Jefferson: Political Writings*. Cambridge: Cambridge University Press, 1999.

Barbour, James. *Speech in the Virginia Reform Convention, February 27, 1851*. Richmond, 1851.

Bentham, Jeremy. *A Fragment on Government: Being an Examination of what is delivered, on the Subject of Government, in General in the Introduction to Sir William Blackstone's Commentaries: with a Preface in which is given a Critique of the Work At Large* (London: 1776) in John Bowring, ed. *The Works of Jeremy Bentham*, Volume I. Edinburgh, 1843.

Bland, Richard. *An Inquiry into the Rights of the British Colonies* (Williamsburg: Alexander Purdie, 1766) republished in Robert L. Scribner, ed. *Revolutionary Virginia: The Road to Independence*, volume I, William J. Van Schreeven, comp. Charlottesville: University Press of Virginia, 1973.

"A Fragment on the Pistole Fee, claimed by the Governor of Virginia, 1753," Worthington Chauncey Ford, ed. Brooklyn, 1891.

Bledsoe, Albert Taylor. *An Essay on Liberty and Slavery*. Philadelphia: J. B. Lippincott, 1857.

Bolling, Philip A. *The Speech of Philip A. Bolling (of Buckingham) in the House of Delegates of Virginia with respect to Its Coloured Population*. Richmond: T. W. White, 1832.

Brockenbrough, William. *Brief Sketch of the Courts of this Commonwealth*. Preface to 2 Virginia Cases. Richmond, 1826.

Brodnax, William. *The Speech of William H. Brodnax (of Dinwiddie) in the House of Delegates of Virginia on the Policy of the State with respect to its Colored Population*. Richmond: T. W. White, 1832.

Brooke, Francis Taliaferro. *A Narrative of My life; for My Family*. Richmond: Macfarlane & Fergusson, 1849.

Brown, John Thompson. *The Speech of John Thompson Brown, in the House of Delegates, on the Abolition of Slavery*. Richmond: T. W. White, 1832.

Bryson, W. Hamilton, ed. *Essays on Legal Education in Nineteenth Century Virginia*. Buffalo: William S. Hein & Co., 1998.

Carter, Landon. *A Letter from a Gentleman in Virginia to the Merchants of Great Britain*. London, 1754.

Catterall, Helen, ed. *Judicial Cases Concerning American Slavery and the Negro*. Washington, DC: Carnegie Institute, 1926.

Chinard, Gilbert, ed. *The Commonplace Book of Thomas Jefferson: A Repertory of His Ideas on Government*. Baltimore: Johns Hopkins University Press, 1926.

The Correspondence of Jefferson and Du Pont De Nemours, with an Introduction on Jefferson and the Physiocrats. Baltimore: Johns Hopkins University Press, 1931.

Dew, Thomas Roderick. *Lectures on the Restrictive System*. Philadelphia, 1829.

A Review of the Debate in the 1831–1832 Virginia Legislature. Richmond, 1832.

A Digest of the Laws Customs, Manners and Institutions of the Ancient and Modern Nations. New York, 1852.

Faulkner, Charles J. *The Speech of Charles Jas. Faulkner (of Berkeley) in the House of Delegates of Virginia, on the Policy of the State with Respect to Her Slave Population*. Richmond: T. W. White, 1832.

Speech of C.J. Faulkner on the Subject of Taxation, July 7 and 8, 1851, 5–6, Faulkner Family Papers, *VHS*.

Address on the Land Policy of the United States. Washington, DC, 1857.

Address Delivered by Hon. Charles J, Faulkner, Before the Valley Agricultural Society of Virginia. Washington, DC, 1858.

Fitzhugh, George. *A Sociology for the South, or, the Failure of a Free Society*. Richmond: A. Morris, 1854.

Cannibals All! or, Slaves without Masters. Richmond: A. Morris, 1857. Reprint edited by C. Vann Woodward. Cambridge, MA: Belknap Press of Harvard University Press, 1960 and 1988.

"Reaction and the Administration," *De Bow's Review* (October 1858): 414–416.

"Entails and Primogeniture," *De Bow's Review* (August 1859): 172–178.

Floyd, John. *Speech in Convention on Taxation*. Richmond, 1851.

Garnett, James Mercer. *A Reply to Freeholders of King and Queen, King William, Essex, Caroline, Middlesex*. Richmond, 1829.

Gilmer, Francis Walker. *A Vindication of the Laws, Limiting the Rate of Interest on Loans; from the Objections of Jeremy Bentham, and the Edinburgh Reviewers*. Richmond: Franklin Press, 1820.

Sketches, Essays, and Translations. Baltimore: Fielding Lucas, 1828.

Grigsby, Hugh Blair. *Discourses on the Life and Character of Littleton W. Tazewell*. Richmond: 1860.

"Sketches of Members of the Constitutional Convention of 1829–30," *VMHB* 61 (1953), 219–332.

The Virginia Convention of 1776. Richmond, 1855.

The Virginia Convention of 1829–1830. Richmond, 1856.

Harrington, James. *The Commonwealth of Oceana and a System of Politics*, edited by J. G. A. Pocock. Cambridge: Cambridge University Press, 1992.

Harrison, Fairfax, ed. *Aris Sonis Focisque. The Harrisons of Skimino*. N.p. 1910.

Harrison, Jesse Burton. "Review of the Slave Question, extracted from the *American Quarterly Review* December 1832" (Richmond: T. W. White, 1833).

Hening, William Waller. *The New Virginia Justice*. 3rd Edition. Richmond: Cochran, 1820.

Holcombe, James P. *An Introduction to Equity Jurisprudence, on the Basis of Story's Commentaries*. Cincinnati: Derby, Bradley, & Co., 1846.

An Address delivered before the Society of Alumni; of the University of Virginia at Its Annual Meeting ... June 29, 1853. Richmond: Macfarlane & Fergusson, 1853.

Sketches of the Political Issues and Controversies of the Revolution: A Discourse delivered before the Virginia Historical Society at their Ninth Annual Meeting, January 17, 1856. Richmond, 1856.

"Is Slavery Consistent with Natural Law? An Address delivered before the Virginia State Agricultural Society" in *Southern Literary Messenger* (December 1858), 401–421.

The Election of a Black Republican President an Overt Act of Aggression on the Right of Property in Slaves: The South Urged to Adopt Concerted Action for Future Safety; A Speech before the People of Albemarle on the 2d Day of January, 1860. Richmond, 1860.

Howison, Robert R. *A History of Virginia, From Its Discovery and Settlement by Europeans to the Present Time*. Richmond: Drinker and Morris, 1848.

Humphreys, James. *Observations on the Actual State of the English Laws of Real Property with the Outlines of a Code*. London: John Murray, 1826.

Jacob, Giles. *The General Laws of Estates: or, Freeholder's Companion: containing the laws, statutes, and customs relating to the freehold and other estates, in which is comprised the whole law of tenures of lands*. London, 1740.

Jacobs, Wilbur R., ed. *The Appalachian Frontier: The Edmond Atkin Report and Plan of 1755* (Lincoln: University of Nebraska Press, 1967).

Jefferson, Thomas. *Notes on the State of Virginia*, edited and with an introduction and notes by William Peden. Chapel Hill: University of North Carolina Press, 1992.

Kennedy, John Pendleton. *Swallow Barn; or A Sojourn in the Old Dominion*. Originally published in 1832; reprinted with an introduction by Lucinda H. MacKethan. Baton Rouge: Louisiana State University Press, 1986.

Kercheval, Samuel A. *A History of the Valley of Virginia*. Winchester, Va.: Samuel H. Davis, 1833.

Leigh, Benjamin Watkins. *A Letter from Appomattox to the People of Virginia*.Richmond: 1832.

Lomax, John Taylor. *A Digest of the Laws Respecting Real Property Generally Adopted and in Use in the United States; Embracing more Especially the Law of Real Property in Virginia*. Philadelphia, 1839.

Marshall, John. *A History of the Colonies Planted by the English on the Continent of North America from their Settlement, to the Commencement of that war which Terminated in their Independence*. Philadelphia, 1824.

Marshall, Thomas. *The Speech of Thomas Marshall, in the House of Delegates of Virginia, on the Abolition of Slavery*. Richmond: T. W. White, 1832.

McDowell, Jr., James. *The Speech of James McDowell, Jr. (of Rockbridge) in the House of Delegates of Virginia on the Slave Question*. Richmond: T. W. White, 1832.

Moore, Thomas Vernon. *The Christian Lawyer, or the Claims of Christianity on the Legal Profession: A Discourse Delivered at the Funeral of Richard W. Flournoy, Esq., in the First Presbyterian Church*. Richmond, 1857.

Munford, George W. "Abstract from the Reports of the Clerks of the Court of Appeals and of the Circuit Superior Courts of Law and Chancery, for the Year ending 30th August, 1845." Richmond, 1845.

Paine, Thomas. "Public Good: Being an Examination into the Claim of Virginia to the Vacant Territory, and the Right of the United States to the Same: to Which is Added Proposals for Laying off a New State, to be Applied as a Fund for Carrying on the War, or Redeeming the National Debt." Reprinted in *The Writings of Thomas Paine*, edited by Moncure Daniel Conway. New York: G. P. Putnam's Sons, 1906.

Peterson, Merrill, ed. *The Portable Thomas Jefferson*. New York: Penguin Books, 1975.

Randolph, Edmund. *History of Virginia*, edited with introduction by Arthur H. Schaffer. Charlottesville: University Press of Virginia, 1970.

Randolph, Thomas Jefferson. *The Speech of Thomas Jefferson Randolph, in the House of Delegates of Virginia, on the Abolition of Slavery*. Richmond: T. W. White, 1832.

Address of Thomas J. Randolph to the Voters of Albemarle, Nelson, and Amherst. N.p.: 1850).

Revolutionary Virginia: The Road to Independence. 7 volumes. William J. Van Schreeven, comp., Robert L. Scribner and Brent Tarter, eds. Charlottesville: University Press of Virginia, published for the Virginia Independence Bicentennial Commission, 1973–1983.

Robinson, Conway. *Practice in the Courts of Law and Equity in Virginia*. 3 volumes. Richmond: Samuel Shepherd, 1832–1839.

An Essay upon the Constitutional Rights as to Slave Property, 1840.

Views of the Constitution of Virginia, 1850.

Practice in the Courts of Justice in England and the United States, 7 vols., 1854–1874.

Robinson, Conway and James M. Patton. *Reports of the Revisors*. 4 reports. Richmond: Samuel Shepard, 1847–1849.

Robinson, Mason. *Views of the Constitution of Virginia, Contained in the Essay of One of the People*. Richmond, 1850.

Ruffner, Henry. *Address to the People of West Virginia. Delivered at Lexington, Virginia, in September, 1847*. Wheeling, 1862.

Slaughter, Philip. *The Virginian History of African Colonization*. Richmond: Macfarlane and Fergusson, 1855.

Somner, William. *A Treatise of Gavelkind, both Name and Thing*,2nd Edition. London, 1676.

Story, Joseph. *Commentaries on the Constitution of the United States; with a Preliminary Review of the Constitutional History of the Colonies and the States, before the adoption of the Constitution*. 3 volumes. Boston, 1833.

Commentaries on Equity Jurisprudence as Administered in England and America. 3 volumes. Boston, 1836.

"Codification of the Common Law," in William W. Story, ed. *Miscellaneous Writings of Joseph Story*. Boston, 1852.

Southerners, Twelve. *I'll Take My Stand: The South and the Agrarian Tradition*, with and Introduction by Louis D. Rubin, Jr., and biographical essays by Virginia Rock. Baton Rouge: Louisiana State University Press, 1977.

Taylor, John. *Arator: Being a Series of Agricultural Essays, Practical and Political*, M. E. Bradford, ed. Reprinted by the Liberty Fund, 1977.

Construction Construed and Constitutions Vindicated. Richmond, 1820.

Tyranny Unmasked, F. Thornton Miller, ed. Reprinted by the Liberty Fund, 1992.

Tucker, George. *The Valley of the Shenandoah, or Memoirs of the Graysons*. 1824 edition; republished with an Introduction by Donald R. Noble, Jr., Chapel Hill: University of North Carolina Press, 1970.

The Life of Jefferson, with Parts of His Correspondence. Philadelphia, 1837.

Tucker, Henry St. George. *Notes on Blackstone's Commentaries: For Use of Students*. Winchester, 1826.

Commentaries on the Laws of Virginia, Comprising the Substance of a course of lectures delivered to the Winchester Law School, 2 vols. 3rd Edition. Richmond: 1846; reprinted by the Lawbook Exchange, 1998.

The Opinion of Chancellor Tucker: Delivered at the April term of the Winchester chancery court, in the case of the vestry of St. James' Parish; against the overseers of Shelbourne Parish, in the County of Loudoun. Leesburg, 1830.

Address to the students of the University of Virginia, on the 11th day of the session, 1842. Charlottesville, 1842.

Lectures on Constitutional Law: for the use of the law class at the University of Virginia. Richmond, 1843.

Introductory lecture: delivered by the professor of law in the University of Virginia at the opening of the Law School in September, 1841 (Charlottesville: Magruder & Noel, 1841).

A Few Lectures on Natural Law. Charlottesville, 1844.

Tucker, Nathaniel Beverley. "*A Lecture on the Study of Law; Being an Introduction to a Course of Lectures on That Subject in the College of William and Mary*. Richmond, 1834.

"A Note on Blackstone's Commentaries," *Southern Literary Messenger* (January 1835), 227–231.

A Discourse on the Genius of the Federative System of the United States. Richmond, 1839.

A Discourse on the Importance of the Study of Political Science, as a Branch of Academic Education in the United States. Richmond, 1840.

A Series of Lectures on the Science of Government, Intended to Prepare the Student for the Study of the Constitution of the United States. Philadelphia, 1845.

The Principles of Pleading. Boston, 1846.

Tucker, St. George, ed. *Blackstone's Commentaries: With Notes of Reference, to the Constitution and Laws, of the Federal Government of the United States; And of the Commonwealth of Virginia*. 5 volumes. Philadelphia: 1803, reprinted by The Lawbook Exchange, Ltd., 1996.

A Dissertation on Slavery with a Proposal for the Gradual Abolition of It, in the State of Virginia. Philadelphia, 1796.

Washington, H. A. "The Social System of Virginia," *Southern Literary Messenger* 14 (1848): 65–81.

The Virginia Constitution of 1776: A Discourse Delivered before the Virginia Historical Society at Their Annual Meeting, January 17, 1852. Richmond, 1852.

Willey, Waitman T. *Speeches before the State Convention of Virginia on the Basis of Representation: on the County Courts and County Organization and on the Election of Judges by the People*. Richmond, 1851.

Wirt, William. *The Letters of the British Spy*, edited and an introduction by Richard Beale Davis. Chapel Hill: University of North Carolina Press, 1970.

Sketches of the Life and Character of Patrick Henry. 15th edition, corrected by the author. Hartford, CT: Silas Andrus & Son, 1852.

Index